THE NIETZSCHE
LEGACY
IN GERMANY
1890 - 1990

Weimar and Now: German Cultural Criticism
Martin Jay and Anton Kaes, General Editors

THE NIETZSCHE LEGACY IN GERMANY 1890-1990

STEVEN E. ASCHHEIM

UNIVERSITY OF CALIFORNIA PRESS
Berkeley • *Los Angeles* • *London*

We wish to thank the following publishers for permission to reprint from articles upon which chapters in this book are based:

"Zarathustra in the Trenches: The Nietzsche Myth and World War I." In *Religion Ideology and Nationalism in Europe and America: Essays Presented in Honor of Yehoshua Arieli.* Jerusalem: The Historical Society of Israel and The Zalman Shazar Center for Jewish History, 1986.

"Nietzschean Socialism—Left and Right, 1890–1933," *Journal of Contemporary History* (April 1988).

"After the Death of God: Varieties of Nietzschean Religion," *Nietzsche-Studien,* vol. 17 (1989).

We also wish to thank *Der Spiegel: Das Deutsche Nachrichten-Magazin* for permission to reprint its cover illustration of issue number 24, 1981.

University of California Press
Berkeley and Los Angeles, California

University of California Press
London, England

First Paperback Printing 1994

Library of Congress Cataloging-in-Publication-Data

Aschheim, Steven E., 1942–
    The Nietzsche Legacy in Germany, 1890–1990 / Steven E. Aschheim.
        p.   cm. — (Weimar and now : German cultural criticism ; 2)
    Includes bibliographical references and index.
    ISBN 0-520-08555-8
    1. Nietzsche, Friedrich Wilhelm, 1844–1900—Influence.
    2. Germany—History—20th century.   I. Title.   II. Series: Weimar
    and now ; 2.
    B3317.A769   1992   91-30867
    193—dc20   CIP

Printed in the United States of America

2   3   4   5   6   7   8   9

The paper used in this publication meets the minimum requirements of American National Standard for Information Sciences—Permanence of Paper for Printed Library Materials, ANSI Z39.48-1984 ∞

To George Mosse
teacher and—above all—friend

Contents

Illustrations

Following page 200

Acknowledgments

This study could never have been undertaken, let alone completed, without the support and assistance of many friends and colleagues. I cannot possibly name all those who over the years have taken the time to discuss the project with me. Nevertheless I must make special mention of Jeffrey Herf and Jerry Muller who read the manuscript in its entirety and offered judicious, constructive criticism. As always, George Mosse has been a source of personal and scholarly inspiration and it is to him that this book is dedicated. My friend John Landau has throughout endured my bleatings, tried to clarify my thinking, and prodded me on. Robert Alter, Yehoshua Arielli, Klaus Berghahn, David Biale, Menachem Brinker, Michael Heyd, Martin Jay, James Joll, Leo Lowenthal, Paul Mendes-Flohr, Rudolf Vierhaus, and Robert Wistrich gave unfailingly informed and helpful advice.

Edward Dimendberg and Michelle Nordon of the University of California Press were constantly encouraging. The extent to which this book is readable is due, in no small measure, to the mighty editing efforts of Edith Johnson. Frank Moser did the photographic work with his customary gentleness and good humor. The Historische Kommission zu Berlin and the Max Planck Institut für Geschichte in Göttingen awarded me generous research grants. Ze'ev Rosenkrantz and Michael Toch provided much-needed technical assistance.

While many libraries were consulted during the course of this work, I must single out the National and University Library in Jerusalem. Its endless treasures and friendly and competent staff make scholarship a pleasure.

I would like to thank Richard Frank Krummel for pointing out various spelling and technical errors that crept into the first edition and which I have tried to correct here.

I have left my most pleasurable debt for last. Without the humanizing influence of my wife Hannah and our children Ariella, Yoni, and Daniel, this book would have been unthinkable. They know how grateful I am.

CHAPTER I

The Historian and the Legacy of Nietzsche

Interpretation

Leg' ich mich aus, so leg' ich mich hinein:
Ich kann nicht selbst mein Interprete sein
Doch wer nur steigt auf seiner eignen Bahn
Trägt auch mein Bild zu hellerm Licht hinan.

Interpreting myself, I read myself in and enter:
I cannot be my own interpreter.
But all who climb on their own way
Carry my image, too, into the breaking day.

Nietzsche, *The Gay Science*

"Great men are inevitably our creation, just as we are theirs."

Ernst Bertram, *Nietzsche*

Friedrich Nietzsche's impact upon the cultural and political sensibilities of the twentieth century has been altogether extraordinary. Since the 1890s his shaping presence has been felt continuously throughout Europe, the United States, and as far as Japan.[1] This study is an attempt

---

1. The documentation of Nietzsche's influence began early. See Gèneviève Bianquis, *Nietzsche en France* (Paris: F. Alcan, 1929); Guy De Pourtales, *Nietzsche en Italie* (Paris: Grasset, 1929). More recent studies of his impact upon national cultures include Patrick Bridgwater, *Nietzsche in Anglosaxony: A Study of Nietzsche's Impact on English and American Literature* (Leicester: University of Leicester Press, 1972); Bernice Glatzer Rosenthal, ed., *Nietzsche in Russia* (Princeton, N.J.: Princeton University Press, 1986); Gonzalo Sobejano, *Nietzsche en Espana* (Madrid: Gredos, 1967); David S. Thatcher, *Nietzsche in England 1890–1914: The Growth of a Reputation* (Toronto: Toronto University Press, 1970). Nietzsche's impact throughout the Hapsburg Empire is clearly evident in Laszlo Peter and Robert B. Pynsent, eds., *Intellectuals and the Future in the Hapsburg Monarchy 1890–1914* (London: Macmillan, 1988). This influence was not limited to Western spheres. In Japan as early as the 1890s, Nietzsche functioned as a modernizing force, the most influential articulator of an individualism foreign to traditional Japanese culture (Hans Joachim Becker, *Die Frühe Nietzsche-Rezeption in Japan [1893–1903]: Ein Beitrag zur Individualismusproblematik im Modernisierungsprozess* [Wiesbaden: Otto Harassowitz, 1983]).

to chronicle and analyze the nature and dynamics of that influence in Germany where it was most dense, sustained, and fateful. Forty years ago Walter Kaufmann observed that Nietzsche was so much a part of German life that a serious study of the relationship would grow into nothing less than "a cultural history of twentieth-century Germany, seen in a single, but particularly revealing, perspective."[2]

What follows is an attempt to furnish such a history. It will not, however, yield any single perspective. For the challenge and significance of the Nietzschean impulse resides precisely in its pervasiveness, in its manifold and often contradictory penetration of crucial political and cultural arenas. It would, indeed, be more accurate to speak not of one but many "Nietzschean impulses" that both influenced and reflected their changing times. Through these Nietzschean refractions we hope moreover to light up some of the more important patterns and directions of an emerging, volatile political consciousness, acutely aware of crisis and searching for novel ways to overcome it.

Nietzsche's historical legacy must be understood as a product of the dynamic interaction between the peculiar, multifaceted qualities of his thought and its appropriators. This was always a relatively open-ended, reciprocal, and creative process[3] that entailed selective filtering and constant reshaping of Nietzschean thematics according to divergent perceived needs.[4] It was a fluid heritage that both affected, and was affected by, different circles of men and women responding to the concrete and changing circumstances of the Wilhelmine Kaiserreich, World War I, the Weimar Republic, national socialism, and beyond. Through these politically interested mediations Nietzsche was turned into a persistent and vital part of the fabric of national life.

This complex process can only be grasped by examining both its

2. Walter Kaufmann, *Nietzsche: Philosopher, Psychologist, Antichrist,* 4th ed. (Princeton N.J.: Princeton University Press, [1950] 1974), 9. Nietzsche's influence on modern thought and his role within the various academic disciplines will be discussed only inasmuch as they affected his broader impact upon German politics, culture, and identity.

3. For a statement on the general nature of reception processes see Hans Robert Jauss, *Toward an Aesthetic of Reception,* trans. Timothy Bahti, intro. Paul de Man (Minneapolis: University of Minnesota Press, 1986).

4. On the dynamic nature of Nietzsche's reception see the comments in Massimo Ferrari Zumbini, "Untergänge und Morgenröten: Über Spengler und Nietzsche," *Nietzsche-Studien* 5 (1976), 219. Commentators have long been aware that the representation of Nietzsche's philosophy was intimately related to the evolving history of Nietzschean interpretation itself. See the comments on this and Nietzsche's timeliness in Gerhard Lehmann, *Die deutsche Philosophie der Gegenwart* (Stuttgart: Alfred Kroner, 1943), 184.

thematic and chronological dimensions. In order to give shape and structure to that larger picture we have concentrated on group patterns and organized clusters of influence. The focus shall be on institutions, movements, and broad ideational currents. Individual attitudes and relationships to Nietzsche will be discussed only insofar as they illuminate more general dimensions of the Nietzsche legacy. We have had to sacrifice some of the complexity and creative intensity characteristic of so many of these individual encounters in order to retain a synoptic perspective.[5] Clearly, any attempt to draw a composite portrait of these multiple appropriations within their unfolding ideological and historical contexts will entail selection. Given the density of the subject and the almost overwhelming wealth of available documentation, exhaustive treatment would be impossible, even undesirable;[6] encyclopaedic comprehensiveness would amount to little more than a cataloging exercise that would obscure rather than highlight the key connections. In this work we hope to provide the kind of suggestive analysis that touches on and illuminates the range of pertinent and representative sources.

This book is animated by the conviction that, to understand the many influences, Nietzsche's work cannot be reduced to an essence nor can it be said to possess a single and clear authoritative meaning. The cultural historian cannot claim access to a privileged grasp of the unadulterated text by which all subsequent uses should be judged.[7] There should be no set portrait of the "authentic" Nietzsche, nor dogmatic certainty as to his original intent. Only a *Rezeptionsgeschichte* sensitive

5. Numerous encounters mentioned in this book—Thomas Mann and Nietzsche, Oswald Spengler and Nietzsche, Gottfried Benn and Nietzsche, Carl Jung and Nietzsche, etc.—have received detailed analysis elsewhere. Here we have had to console ourselves with Nietzsche's admonitions concerning the limitations of such "infamous 'and'" studies. See his "Expeditions of an Untimely Man" in *Twilight of the Idols & The Anti-Christ*, trans. R. J. Hollingdale (Harmondsworth, Eng.: Penguin, 1968), 76–77. Naturally, the scope and depth of Nietzsche's impact on individuals varied enormously. For some his influence was passing, others received him rhapsodically and enduringly, still others accepted him in a more tentative, fragmentary fashion. (Throughout this book I cite readily available translations of Nietzsche's works.)
6. For a measure of the size and scope of Nietzsche's reception within Germany only up to 1918 see the indispensable bibliographic guide by Richard Frank Krummel, *Nietzsche und der deutsche Geist*, 2 vols. (Berlin, New York: Walter de Gruyter, 1974/1983). For a multilingual but far less comprehensive listing that goes beyond 1918 see the compilation by Herbert W. Reichert and Karl Schlechta, *International Nietzsche Bibliography* (Chapel Hill: University of North Carolina Press, 1960).
7. "The effects or structure of a text are not reducible to its 'truth,' to the intended meaning of its author, or even its supposedly unique and identifiable signatory" (Jacques Derrida, "Otobiographies: The Teaching of Nietzsche and the Politics of the Proper Name," in *The Ear of the Other: Otobiography Transference Translation*, ed. Christie V. McDonald, trans. Peggy Kamuf and Avital Ronell [New York: Schocken Books, 1985]), 29.

to the open-ended, transformational nature of the Nietzsche legacy will be able to appreciate its rich complexity.

To date, rather surprisingly, no such study has appeared. Instead the major post–World War II analyses have typically adopted essentialist approaches in which the history of the Nietzsche legacy is rendered either as a record of deviations from, or as faithful representations of, a prior interpretive construction of the "real" Nietzsche. These inevitably turn out to be moralistic, static histories in the apologetic or condemnatory mode, less interested in the actual processes of influence and dissemination than in judging the various appropriations.[8]

Walter Kaufmann's extremely influential interpretation of Nietzsche and the Nietzsche heritage is an obvious example. He begins, for instance, with what he calls the "Nietzsche legend," constructed by those authors he holds responsible for a pernicious "misconstruction": the belief that Nietzsche was hopelessly ambiguous, lacked a coherent philosophy, and was subject to divergent interpretations. The makers of this legend—important Nietzscheans such as Elisabeth Förster-Nietzsche, Stefan George and his circle, Ernst Bertram, and Karl Jaspers—are analyzed not in terms of their political intentions, institutional settings, and historical contexts but only insofar as they contributed to what Kaufmann holds to be dangerous misuses and unequivocal misinterpretations. It should come as no surprise that the Nazi–Nietzsche relationship is discussed entirely in these terms, as one of out-and-out distortion and radical abuse of the master's essentially antipolitical project.[9] Georg Lukacs's definitive Marxist reading is characterized by a diametrically opposed, but similarly essentialist, point of view. He portrays Nietzsche exclusively as the irrationalist spokesman of the post-1870 reactionary bourgeoisie and as an inherently proto-Fascist thinker, father to a nazism which, given the logic and dictates of historical developments, was inexorably bound to faithfully reflect his ideas.[10]

The philosopher is not only free to judge and evaluate—he is obliged to do so. Cultural historians, however, must be exceedingly wary of such exercises. It is the dynamic nature of Nietzsche's influence, the

---

8. To be sure, the historian must be alert to overt invention, expurgation, selective editing, and outright falsification of Nietzsche's texts; the notorious tampering activities of Elisabeth Förster-Nietzsche are well known.

9. See Kaufmann, *Nietzsche*, 4. Chapter 10 exemplifies his treatment of the Nazi question.

10. Georg Lukacs, *The Destruction of Reason*, trans. Peter Palmer (Atlantic Highlands, N.J.: Humanities Press, 1981).

complex diffusion and uses of his ideas, not their inherent truth, falsity, or even plausibility that must lie at the center of historical analysis.) Essentialized approaches tend to obscure rather than illuminate the historical record by pressing the relevant material into a preconceived mold. Whether or not they were justified, different interests and readers *did* come up with different interpretations. The task is to map their agendae, contexts, and consequences. Nietzscheanism, in one version or another, permeated many of the more important political and cultural strains of the twentieth century. No simple rendering of such influence does justice to this story. The cultural landscape and historical texture is simply too rich, open, and differentiated to bear the weight of these essentialist and unidirectional arguments.

Historians have been similarly culpable in reducing the Nietzsche legacy to either a reactionary or progressive impulse, even in the most recent studies. Restricted constructions of Nietzsche and Nietzscheanism have been pressed into the service of interested historical theses. In his work on the persistence of the old European order through 1914, Arno J. Mayer, for instance, has claimed that the primary function of Nietzsche's thought was to act as a rhetorical and ideological prop for late nineteenth-century aristocratic interests. This view presents Nietzscheanism as "ideally suited to help the refractory elements of the ruling and governing classes" articulate their antidemocratic, illiberal, and reactionary ideas.

Mayer blithely ignores the fact that those conservative forces embodying the ancien régime were almost inevitably anti-Nietzschean, instinctively opposed to Nietzsche's anti-Christian immoralist posture, and shocked and frightened by his radical questioning of authority and tradition. These circles were aware that Nietzsche spoke of a *new* "self-creating nobility" and that he intended an aristocratic ethos quite different from that of the hereditary classes and the landed gentry.[11] On the few occasions that such an alliance was attempted during Nietzsche's own lifetime he registered his disapproval in no uncertain terms:

> In one particular case I once did get to see all the sins that had been committed against one of my books—it was *Beyond Good and Evil*—and I could

---

11. Arno J. Mayer, *The Persistence of the Old Regime: Europe to the Great War* (New York: Pantheon, 1981), 290; see also 275–329. Mayer does not provide notes or documentary evidence to back up such assertions. For more discussion of the relationship between Nietzscheanism and ruling elites see chapter 4. On Nietzsche's reference to the "new nobility" see "Thus Spoke Zarathustra," in *The Portable Nietzsche*, trans. and ed. Walter Kaufmann (New York: Viking, [1954] 1968), 315.

make a pretty report about that. Would you believe it? The *Nationalzei-tung*—a Prussian newspaper . . . —I myself read, if I may say so, only the *Journal des Debats*—actually managed to understand the book as "a sign of the times," as the real and genuine Junker philosophy for which the *Kreuzzeitung* merely lacked the courage.[12]

A suitable rendering of Nietzsche's thought could, no doubt, have performed such an upper-class function. The empirical record demonstrates, however, that in the case of the ruling classes (with only a few notable exceptions) this simply did not pertain. By and large, traditional elites continued to regard the philosopher as a dangerous and insane subversive. When the right did seriously adopt Nietzsche it was *after* World War I during the Weimar Republic, and then it was the work of mainly radical–revolutionary elements.

In his 1983 study, R. Hinton Thomas comes rather closer to the mark when he argues that Nietzscheans were typically dissidents and radicals estranged from the established social order.[13] Far from representing the reactionary (or even the conservative) sectors of society they were characteristically emancipationist, progressive, and moved by humanistic concerns. Socialism, anarchism, feminism, the generational revolt of the young—these were all touched by the libertarian magic of Nietzsche.

While Thomas tells an important part of the story, his one-sided focus ultimately also skews the total picture.[14] Only by means of significant omissions and special pleading can the pre-1918 Nietzscheans be regarded as wholly within the emancipatory camp. In any case, the crucial point is that it was never possible to subsume the Nietzsche legacy under either a simplistic "reactionary" or "progressive" heading. This is so not only because Nietzsche himself would have scoffed at such teleological labelings which, indeed, he helped to undermine. From the beginning Nietzschean thematics appealed to a remarkably wide range of political and cultural interests. Most were radical in nature, pursuing eclectic visions of cultural transvaluation and political re-

12. Friedrich Nietzsche, "Why I Write Such Good Books," in *On the Genealogy of Morals and Ecce Homo*, trans. and ed. Walter Kaufmann (New York: Vintage, 1969), 262.

13. R. Hinton Thomas, *Nietzsche in German Politics and Society 1890–1918* (Manchester: Manchester University Press, 1983).

14. Many parts of Thomas's *Nietzsche in German Politics* are indeed valuable and have been incorporated here. Nevertheless, his focus on progressive and "liberational" elements is too partial and insufficiently nuanced to capture the complexity of the reception process. Just to cite one important example, Thomas does not even mention Elisabeth Foerster-Nietzsche and her crucial activities as head of the Nietzsche Archives at Weimar. Only ideological blinkers can account for this omission.

demption. But, as we shall see, while this quest included progressive circles it also characterized more unclassifiable interests: sectors of the avant-garde, diverse wings of the life-reform movement, and most importantly those who created the twentieth-century, German, postconservative, "revolutionary right."

It is a central contention of this book that Nietzsche and the Nietzscheans were both makers and beneficiaries of a broader iconoclastic process that cut across and obscured such predictable left and right, progressive and reactionary distinctions.[15] They also challenged simple dichotomies between modern and premodern, rational and irrational. In numerous and unexpected ways the Nietzscheans combined archaic with futuristic elements.

Because previous scholarship has generally assumed that Nietzscheanism possessed a kind of inherent political personality, it has bypassed the multiple motivations and complex processes according to which divergent interests actively adopted and re-clothed Nietzsche's ideas. Nietzscheanism, like its master, was never monochromic. Critical scavenging of Nietzsche's works and themes led divergent European-wide audiences to fuse him with a broad range of cultural and political postures: anarchist, expressionist, feminist, futurist, nationalist, nazi, religious, sexual-libertarian, socialist, *völkisch*, and Zionist. It was, indeed, through these fusions, that both Nietzsche and Nietzscheanism became a significant force. What follows therefore is a study in the dynamics of historical mediation which analyzes the diffusion, popularization, assimilation, rejection, and prismatic transfiguration of Nietzsche within changing historical and ideological contexts.

Why in the first place did Nietzsche exert such a unique protean fascination? Why was he able to attract so many generations of appropriators? Why was he regarded as so vital a force by so many groups? While much of the fascination lies in the particular interactions and scavengings, in the specific whims and dictates of selection, and in the concrete reworkings and diverse applications, the beginnings of an answer must surely be found in aspects of the Nietzschean corpus itself. Without its vast storehouse of suggestive themes, ideas, and categories or its scintillating language and rhetoric, no subsequent "Nietzscheanisms" would have been possible.

Nietzsche's congeniality to so many contrary tendencies and interests

15. For a different viewpoint, on the erosion of these distinctions, see Zeev Sternhell, *Neither Right nor Left* (Berkeley: University of California Press, 1986).

and capacity to elicit open-ended responses reflected a central property of his post-Hegelian thought and method: his rejection of systematizers and systems and his determination to attack problems from a plurality of perspectives. "I mistrust all systematizers and avoid them," wrote Nietzsche. "The will to a system," he added, "is a lack of integrity."[16] His aphoristic style reflected his rejection of fixed systems. Indeed, Nietzsche regarded style as a barometer of inner complexity. "Considering that the multiplicity of inward states is exceptionally large in my case," he wrote, "I have many stylistic possibilities—the most multifarious art of style that has ever been at the disposal of one man."[17] Nietzsche's determinedly shifting narrative point of view clearly facilitated varied appropriations.

Equally important for the understanding of the history of Nietzsche's reception is what Walter Kaufmann has described as the philosopher's "sustained celebration of creativity," his call for the "creation of new values and norms."[18] This influenced the nature and modes of appropriation because here was an openness in principle, an invitation to stake one's own path; the self-determining creative act was to provide the content and fill in the contours of the vision. Kurt Rudolf Fischer's remarks about the Übermensch are applicable to most other Nietzschean themes and categories:

> We undercut Nietzsche if we wish to determine what the "Übermensch" is. Because I think it is part of the determination of the "Übermensch" not to be determined—that we shall have to experiment, that we shall have to create. Nietzsche puts emphasis on the creativity of man and therefore we should accentuate that the conception of the "Übermensch" is *necessarily not* determined. We cannot ask whether an author has confused the issue, or has presented us with a dangerous alternative.[19]

This openness constituted a crucial part of the attraction and Nietzscheans of every stripe responded to the call for dynamic self-realization, for completion of the vision.[20]

Nietzsche's most widely read text, *Thus Spoke Zarathustra*, did, after all, demand this in an intoxicating manner.

16. "Maxims and Arrows," in *Twilight of the Idols*, 25.
17. Nietzsche, "Why I Write Such Good Books," in *Ecce Homo*, 265.
18. Kaufmann, *Nietzsche*, 414; see also p. 250.
19. See Kurt Rudolf Fischer's comments in the discussion of Robert E. McGinn's "Verwandlungen von Nietzsches Übermenschen in der Literatur des Mittelmeerraumes: d'Annunzio, Marinetti, und Kazantzakis," *Nietzsche-Studien* 10/11 (1981–1982), 611.
20. Exactly this spirit is evident in Martin Buber, "Ein Wort über Nietzsche und die Lebensworte," *Die Kunst im Leben* (December 1900), 13.

What is good and evil, *no one knows yet,* unless it be he who creates. He, however, creates man's goal and gives the earth its meaning and its future. That anything at all is good and evil—that is his creation.[21]

The rhetoric may have been scintillating but most Nietzscheans after all were human, all too human. Quite unable to perform acts of this lonely, creative kind they rushed into the consoling arms of protective political and ideological frameworks. Only thus could Nietzsche be made palatable, a fact that also could be rationalized in Nietzschean terms. As one devotee put it, the master demanded some kind of interpretation and completion if one was not to stand helpless before his creative chaos.[22]

Nietzsche was thus subjected to diverse forms of hermeneutic institutionalization, a process in which projection rather than creation seemed to dominate. The detailed content of generalized notions such as the *will to power, Dionysianism, transvaluation of all values, eternal recurrence,* and *immoralism* could and were fitted into preexisting ideological preferences.

For all that, Nietzsche's capacity to act as a projective foil also inspired a number of independently important works. These typically transformed Nietzsche into a kind of mirror image, an affirmation of the appropriator's own conceptual and political predilections. Carl Gustav Jung's fascinating marathon *Zarathustra* seminar (1934–1939) is an excellent, but by no means a lone, example.[23] Jung simultaneously fashions Nietzsche into a prescient forerunner of the notion of the collective unconscious as well as a living example of its inner workings, a confirmation of Jung's own system of analysis. Such works are compelling documents in their own right. They too must be fitted into the dynamic history of Nietzsche reception.

Nietzsche's appropriators wore selective blinders; they did not have to buy the whole Nietzsche or nothing. Readers could and did pick critically from the extraordinarily rich variety of positions and perspectives contained in his work. Some emphasized while others totally disregarded the distinctions between the early, middle, and later writings. The texts thus varied in their salience and perceived value. Nietzsche the scathing critic, the relentless unmasker of truth and custodian of culture, could be distinguished from or combined with the great defender

---

21. Nietzsche, "On Old and New Tablets," in *Portable Nietzsche,* 308.
22. Heinrich Berl, "Nietzsche und das Judentum," *Menorah* 10 (1932), 59–69.
23. C. G. Jung, *Nietzsche's* Zarathustra: *Notes of the Seminar Given in 1934–1939,* 2 vols., ed. James L. Jarrett (Princeton, N.J.: Princeton University Press, 1988).

of life against the depredations of deadening intellect. The great stylist,
lyricist, and poet was variously severed from or fused with his persona
as immoralist, ironist, and nihilist and his work as transvaluator and
ruthless grand legislator, prophet of the future.

Admirers, opponents, and critics alike agreed that one did not simply
read Nietzsche; rather, as Thomas Mann put it in 1918, one "experienced" him.[24] In a uniquely intense and immediate manner, Nietzsche
touched upon what contemporaries regarded as the key experiential
dimensions of their individual and collective identity. From the beginning, canonizers and condemners alike tended to regard him as critic and
maker of a new kind of European modernity characterized by the predicament of nihilism and its transvaluative, liberating, and cataclysmic
potential. Although many of his opponents portrayed him as reactionary
and antimodern, the dominant perception was that Nietzsche pointed
dramatically forward, embodying a force that strived to go beyond the
conventions of the eighteenth and nineteenth centuries. More than any
other thinker, Nietzsche was the prism through which such existential
issues could be addressed and a resource through which to express its
changing meanings and forms. Upon reading the philosopher, the keen
observer Gerhard Hilbert wrote in 1911 that Nietzsche was a seismometer of modern Europe's spiritual and intellectual life, a stamping ground
(*Tummelplatz*) and battlefield (*Schlachtfeld*) upon which its tensions,
conflicts, and possibilities were played out.[25] Consciously or not, wrote
another devotee, "we all carry part of him within us."[26]

This still-prevalent symbolic load inevitably entailed political mobilization. Even those who argued that any political appropriation constituted misuse and distortion of his thought understood that the sheer

24. Thomas Mann, *Reflections of a Nonpolitical Man,* trans. Walter D. Morris (New
York: Frederick Ungar, 1983), 13.
25. Gerhard Hilbert, *Moderne Willensziele* (Leipzig: A. Deichert, 1911), 19. This was
a very common theme adjusted to suit the proclivities of the particular commentator.
Thus, as one Christian critic interested in reinvigorating a tired Church put it, Nietzsche's
struggle against his own era and its Christianity was "the anticipation of our own struggle; Nietzsche's inner tension, from which his spirit sprang, is our tension" (Theodor
Odenwald, *Friedrich Nietzsche und das heutige Christentum* [Giessen: Alfred Toepel-
mann, 1926], 17, 23). Nietzsche was a kind of incarnation, "a personality of phenomenal
cultural plenitude and complexity, summing up all that is essentially European" (Thomas
Mann, "Nietzsche's Philosophy in the Light of Contemporary Events" in *Thomas Mann's
Addresses: Delivered at the Library of Congress 1942–1949* [Washington, D.C.: Library
of Congress, 1963], 69). Most recently Ernst Nolte has revived this notion of Nietzsche
as a personalized battleground in his *Nietzsche und der Nietzscheanismus* (Frankfurt am
Main and Berlin: Propylaen, 1990).
26. Albert Kalthoff, *Zarathustrapredigten: Reden über die sittliche Lebensauffassung
Friedrich Nietzsches* (Leipzig: Eugen Diederichs, 1904), 4.

expressivist power of the texts made the temptation well-nigh irresistible. As Georges Bataille—that most "pure" of all Nietzscheans—declared, Nietzsche's thought constituted *"without any hope of appeal, a labyrinth,* in other words, the very opposite of the *directives* that current political systems demand from their sources of inspiration." Yet, he regretfully conceded, the master's teachings

> represent an incomparable seductive force, and consequently quite simply a "force," that politicians are tempted to enslave, or at the very least to agree with, in order to benefit their enterprises. The teachings of Nietzsche "mobilize" the will and the aggressive instincts; it was inevitable that existing activities would try to draw into their movement these now mobile and still *unemployed* wills and instincts.[27]

Despite Nietzsche's own repeated warnings—"I *want* no 'believers'; I think I am too malicious to believe in myself; I never speak to masses.—I have a terrible fear that one day I will be pronounced *holy*"[28]—the mythicisation and political appropriation of Nietzsche was inevitable. In the real world few would be able to pay heed to Zarathustra's admonition that "only when you have all denied me will I return to you."[29]

All this, however, does not on its own explain why Nietzsche became a compelling force after 1890. For this we need a more focused historical perspective. Nietzsche's newly achieved magnetism was at first linked to his perceived relevance as a critic of Wilhelmine society and as a prophet for its overcoming. Nietzsche articulated a growing disaffection for the pieties and conventions of Wilhelmine Germany. As the century drew to a close, the Kaiserreich provided fertile ground upon which Nietzscheanism could flourish, for it generated a welter of modern protest and reform movements.[30]

This was closely related to a broader shift in thought and disposition which marked significant areas of European life from the late nineteenth century on. Nietzsche was an important contributor to, and a major beneficiary of, this shift. The broad diffusion of his work throughout Europe was inextricably bound up with it. Indeed, the very emergence

27. Georges Bataille, "Nietzsche and the Fascists" (1937), in *Visions of Excess: Selected Writings,* ed. Allan Stoekl, trans. Allan Stoekl et al. (Manchester: Manchester University Press, 1985), 185, 187.
28. Nietzsche, "Why I Am a Destiny" in *Ecce Homo,* 326.
29. Nietzsche, "On the Gift-giving Virtue" in *Portable Nietzsche,* 190.
30. Thomas Nipperdey, "War die wilhelminische Gesellschaft eine Untertanen-Gesellschaft?" in *Nachdenken über die deutsche Geschichte* (Munich: C. H. Beck, 1986), 178–179.

of Nietzscheanism—of multiple Nietzschean tendencies—at the turn of the century cannot be understood outside of this broader context. Nietzsche's heritage was integral to its critique of civilization and on-going quest for personal, political, and cultural recovery. His tensions, categories, and sensibility both prefigured and mirrored central elements of this postliberal mood.

This late nineteenth-century development has long been recognized as a cultural and political watershed. Historians have variously labeled this "change in the public spirit of Europe,"[31] as the revolt against positivism and materialism, as a generational rebellion against the liberal bourgeoisie, as the era of the discovery of the unconscious, and as the age of irrationalism and neo-Romanticism. Underlying and often accompanying these tendencies was the emergence of a full-blown modernism.[32] This self-conscious, though painful, rupture with the past; its fundamental questioning of established limits, authority, and tradition; and its insistence on self-creation and the subjective dimension of meaning was similarly informed by obvious Nietzschean characteristics.

In its antipositivist, antiliberal, and antibourgeois zeal, many proponents of this mood increasingly emphasized youthful dynamism and movement for its own sake and regenerative expressivism rather than fixed and reasoned content. It was a sensibility that closely replicated what Nietzsche had written in 1882 about "the explosive ones" in *The Gay Science:*

> When one considers how much the energy of young men needs to explode, one is not surprised that they decide for this cause or that without being subtle or choosy. What attracts them is the sight of the zeal that surrounds a cause—as it were, the sight of the burning fuse, and not the cause itself. Subtle seducers therefore know the art of arousing expectations of an ex-

31. This is the chapter title of George Mosse's excellent analysis of that change in his *The Culture of Western Europe: The Nineteenth and Twentieth Centuries,* 3d ed. (Boulder and London: Westview Press, 1988).

32. Amongst many studies investigating these tendencies see H. Stuart Hughes, *Consciousness and Society: The Reorientation of European Social Thought 1890–1930* (New York: Random House, 1958). Chapter 2 is entitled "The Decade of the 1890's: The Revolt against Positivism" and chapter 4, "The Recovery of the Unconscious"; see too Gerhard Masur, *Prophets of Yesterday: Studies in European Culture 1890–1914* (New York: Harper Colphon, 1966). For the most systematic view of this period as the age of irrationalism see Lukacs, *Destruction of Reason.* Lukacs viewed irrationalism and modernism as virtually identical, and was quite unwilling to grant the least productive and creative role to the latter. For a far more sympathetic view of modernism and its relations to the overall trends of the time, see Carl E. Schorske, *Fin-de-Siècle Vienna: Politics and Culture* (New York: Alfred A. Knopf, 1980); Nipperdey, "War die wilhelminische Gesellschaft," 179.

plosion while making no effort to furnish reasons for their cause: reasons are not what wins over such powder kegs.[33]

Zeev Sternhell has argued that the themes and styles of this intellectual revolution paved "the way for the [Fascist] mass politics of our own century."[34] The proto-Fascist sensibility was certainly an outgrowth of the larger revolt. Yet what Sternhell calls this "vast movement of thought" cannot be simply reduced to its Fascist moment. Like Nietzsche too, its potential for emancipation and positive creativity was as marked as and as interconnected with its more destructive and irrational moments.

It would, no doubt, be an exaggeration to equate this political–cultural revolution solely with Nietzsche. There were always other forces and influences at work. Nevertheless, he was its central inspiration. For contemporaries and later historians alike, this dissenting, rebellious disposition and its search for heightened experiences transcending the banalities of everyday life seemed inconceivable without Nietzsche.

No one had more acutely articulated belief in the fructifying power of myth. The words of the prescient twenty-seven-year-old as they appeared in 1872 in *The Birth of Tragedy* were emblematic of this later generation:

> Without myth every culture loses the healthy natural power of its creativity; only a horizon defined by myths completes and unifies a whole cultural movement. Myth alone saves all the powers of the imagination and of the Apollonian dream from their aimless wanderings.[35]

Elastic Nietzschean categories, concerns and emphases were easily integrated into the diverse interests invested in the shift.

Nietzsche's vitalism was moreover a seminal influence on the post-1890 *Lebensphilosophie* fad and its claims for the primacy of intuition and life over stultifying reason.[36] Nietzsche too had dwelled on what was to become a central and continuing fin-de-siècle European preoc-

33. Nietzsche, "The explosive ones," in *Gay Science*, 106.
34. Zeev Sternhell, "Fascist Ideology" in Walter Laqueur, *Fascism: A Reader's Guide* (Harmondsworth: Penguin, 1976), 333–334.
35. *The Birth of Tragedy*, trans. Walter Kaufmann (New York: Vintage, 1967), 135.
36. Georg Simmel was the most famous representative of this trend. See chapter 4 in Lukacs's *Destruction of Reason* for a particular, critical view of both *Lebensphilosophie* and Simmel. See too Max Scheler, "Versuche einer Philosophie des Lebens," *Die Weissen Blätter* 1 (1913/14), 203–233; Heinrich Rickert, *Die Philosophie des Lebens: Darstellung und Kritik der philosophischen Modeströmungen unserer Zeit*, 2d ed. (Tübingen: J. C. B. Mohr, 1922), 17ff.

cupation: the perception of pervasive decadence and degeneration and the accompanying search for new sources of physical and mental health. In an age increasingly interested in eugenics, his masculine and militant prescriptions for regeneration fell upon receptive ears. The notions of a higher, rejuvenated humanity and a more authentic, living culture partly shaped the period's obsessive interest in the new man and new society.

Carl Schorske has described the aftereffects of this new consciousness as nothing less than "post-Nietzschean culture." After Nietzsche, Schorske writes:

> European high culture entered a whirl of infinite innovation. . . . Into the ruthless centrifuge of change were drawn the very concepts by which cultural phenomena might be fixed in thought. . . . The many categories devised to define or govern any one of the trends in post-Nietzschean culture—irrationalism, subjectivism, abstractionism, anxiety, technologism—neither possessed the surface virtue of lending themselves to generalization nor allowed any convincing dialectical integration into the historical process as previously understood. Every search for a plausible equivalent for the twentieth century to such sweeping but heuristically indispensable categories as "the Enlightenment" seemed doomed to founder on the heterogeneity of the cultural substance it was supposed to cover.[37]

Their considerable variety notwithstanding, we need to make an initial generalization about Nietzscheans and the nature of their Nietzscheanism. For our purposes Nietzscheans were simply those who regarded themselves as significantly influenced by Nietzsche and sought to give this influence some concrete or institutional expression. Nietzscheanism never constituted one movement reducible to a single constituency or political ideology; it was rather a loose congeries of people attached to different social milieux, political movements, and cultural–ideological agendae.

The inchoate character of Nietzscheanism was not necessarily a weakness. Its penetrative strength lay precisely in the fact that it was not a clearly demarcated ideology backed by a central political apparatus. The Nietzschean impulse became a potent protean force precisely because it was diffuse and not organized. It required no formal commitment and possessed no authorized dogma. Its capacity to selectively influence and be reconstructed by various ideological and political constructs facilitated entry into an astonishing range of institutions. In practice it did not operate as an independent entity or as a fixed ideol-

37. Schorske, *Fin-de-Siècle Vienna*, xix.

ogy but rather as an infiltrative sensibility, a system of selective representations which could be grafted on to other systems.

To be sure, there was an attempt to provide Nietzscheanism with an official home: the Nietzsche Archives under the direction of Nietzsche's sister, Elisabeth Foerster-Nietzsche. While this controversial and internally disputatious place did, as we shall see, play a part in the creation and perpetuation of the Nietzsche heritage, it never became a normative or authoritative center. Nietzscheanism became a social and political force through annexations that took place outside of its purportedly official address.

Nietzscheanism thrived in eclectic and syncretistic contexts. Because it functioned by virtue of its implantation into other preexistent structures it was not constitutive or autonomous. It thus could perform a number of crucial functions: it acted variously as an inspirational solvent, leavener, catalyst, and gadfly.

Nietzscheanism was thus publicly effective to the degree that it was structured and mediated by other forces and ideologies. There was no naked nihilism here, no pure Nietzschean dynamic but always framing processes and casuistic exercises of accommodation. Nietzschean thematics required tendentious anchoring and domestication. Suitably nationalized (or socialized or Protestantized), its dynamic was placed at the service of goals which tended either to tame its radical drive, or to selectively deploy and unleash it.

How did such casuistry work? Although there were always gleanings and references in Nietzsche's texts that could lend these annexations a semblance of plausibility, it was clear that Nietzsche was not identical with any of the political appropriations made in his name. All his appropriators were obliged to explain how Nietzsche, despite obvious contradictions or even hostility, was in effect compatible with their favored position, perhaps even its most enthusiastic representative. Placing Nietzsche within any framework entailed a filtering system in which desired elements were highlighted and embarrassing ones deleted or downplayed. More significant were the exercises that sought to distinguish the real or the deep (German, Christian, socialist) Nietzsche from the merely apparent one. Nietzsche was constantly decoded and recoded; "correct" readings made to yield the desired underlying and "authentic" meanings and messages.

This work then is about the dense and changing relations between Nietzsche and German politics and culture. It is also about the complex and interconnected modalities of irrationalism and modernism and

Nietzsche's definitive complicity in both. I shall argue that these two dispositions, so central to twentieth-century consciousness, were never simply destructive and reactionary nor emancipatory and progressive. The dangers and positive possibilities could never be neatly severed. Germany's leading irrationalist and modernist, the inveterate Nietzschean Gottfried Benn, captured this in his 1933 remark that the "*irrational* means close to creation, and capable of creation."[38]

Nietzsche was foundational to this specific consciousness of creation as radical and experimental secular freedom; in later discourse he became the central symbol of the post-Christian, postrationalist, nihilist predicament and its correlated, profoundly destructive, and liberating possibilities. This capacity for symbolically incarnating fundamental issues marked Nietzsche's reception throughout its history. It certainly characterized those stormy pre–World War I years in which the battle over Nietzsche's entry into German life took place. It was then that the attempt to either incorporate or banish the Nietzschean presence from German culture became acute. These struggles set the stage for his fateful entrance into German history.

38. Gottfried Benn, "Answer to the Literary Emigrants," in *Primal Vision*, ed. E. B. Ashton (New York: New Directions, 1971), 48.

CHAPTER II

Germany and the Battle over Nietzsche, 1890–1914

The name Nietzsche is the highest idea of the German name,
the holy shrine of the German spirit and the sin and bad
conscience of all German people.

Rudolf Pannwitz

Nietzsche has become the means of raising a mental
pestilence, and the only hope of checking its propagation
lies in placing Nietzsche's insanity in the clearest light, and
in branding his disciples with the marks most suited to
them, viz., as hysterical and imbecile.

Max Nordau

Friedrich Nietzsche's explosion upon the German political and cultural
scene occurred ironically during the years of his insanity. Only in the
1890s did he first begin to reach and preoccupy significantly large audiences. This does not mean that prior to this period Nietzsche was
entirely without influence. William McGrath has demonstrated, for instance, how members of the Austrian Pernerstorfer circle—which included such future luminaries as Gustav Mahler and Viktor Adler—
were inspired by Nietzsche as early as 1875–1878. Their critique of
contemporary society, their dissatisfaction with liberalism, and their
search for an alternative, Dionysian politics and total culture was
driven by an essentially Nietzschean impulse.[1] But this was an Austrian
movement. Georg Brandes's famous 1888 lectures on Nietzsche's "aristocratic radicalism" were similarly given not in Germany but in

1. William J. McGrath, *Dionysian Art and Populist Politics in Austria* (New Haven,
Conn., and London: Yale University Press, 1974).

Copenhagen.[2] Nietzsche wrote as late as 1888: "In Vienna, in St. Petersburg, in Stockholm, in Copenhagen, in Paris, in New York—everywhere I have been discovered; but not in the shadows of Europe, Germany."[3]

This was not entirely accurate. Prior to 1890 he did exert a kind of subterranean influence in Germany, appealing to individual readers or specialized obscure societies such as the Leipzig Genius Club[4] founded in 1886 or a medley of radical fringe groups. Nietzsche remarked in 1887:

> A strange fact, which comes more and more to my attention. I have gradually come to have some "influence"—all underground of course. Among all the radical parties (Socialists, Nihilists, Anti-Semitists, Christian-Orthodox, Wagnerians) I enjoy an amazing and almost mysterious esteem.[5]

It was only after that date, however, that Nietzsche emerged as a significant national presence.[6] From that time on the Nietzschean thematic permeated vital areas of German thought and action, shaping in manifold and contradictory ways its political attitudes and imagination.

Nietzsche's influence never failed to evince vociferous opposition. Indeed, even those favorably inclined hotly contested the meaning of the Nietzschean message and the direction it should take. Yet all this simply underlines the fact that for the post-1890 literate public some sort of confrontation with Nietzsche—the man, the image and his works—was becoming virtually obligatory. One way or another Nietzsche entered into the mainstream of German life.

The initial appeal of Nietzscheanism was clearly international. It spoke to any number of fin-de-siècle concerns and fulfilled functions that cut across geographical boundaries. Yet in Germany the legacy was most fully elaborated; there the myriad faces of the Nietzschean heri-

---

2. Brandes's "Aristokratischer Radikalismus: Eine Abhandlung über Friedrich Nietzsche" appeared for the first time in Germany in 1890 in *Deutsche Rundschau* 63, no. 7 (April 1900), 52–89.

3. Nietzsche, "Why I Write Such Good Books," in *Ecce Homo,* 262.

4. Amongst its members were people who would participate in various streams of the Nietzschean story, including Bruno Wille and Arno Holz. Holz wrote a satirical comedy, *Sozialaristokraten,* parodying Wille's brand of individualist, elitist Nietzscheanism. Gerhart Hauptmann and Wilhelm Boelsche also participated (Robert Weber, *Geschichte des klassisch-philologischen Vereines zu Leipzig von 1865–1890* [Leipzig: G. Kreysing, 1890]). See Krummel, *Nietzsche und der deutsche Geist* 1, 91.

5. Friedrich Nietzsche to F. Overbeck, 24 March 1887, quoted in Karl Löwith, *From Hegel to Nietzsche: The Revolution in Nineteenth-Century Thought* (New York: Holt, Rinehart and Winston, 1965), 423, n. 59.

6. In Krummel's *Nietzsche und der deutsche Geist* the entries for the twenty-two-year period up to 1889 cover only 79 pages. Those of the 1890s cover 192 pages!

tage were most systematically and continuously played out. Whether positively or negatively conceived, Nietzsche occupied a strategic place in individual and collective German self-definition and national debate. Both as hero and heretic he became a central national preoccupation, at times even an obsession.

A glance at Krummel's *Nietzsche und der deutsche Geiste,* an encyclopaedic compilation of the German reception of Nietzsche up to 1918, demonstrates that during these years an encounter with Nietzsche—at least for the intelligentsia—was virtually mandatory. As the twenty-five-year-old socialist Kurt Eisner wrote in 1892:

> The "Nietzsche Problem" is becoming an inner experience (*Erlebnis*) for all those called to it. Only when everyone attempts to represent their own personal relationship to Nietzsche, his thoughts and feelings, the suppositions and notions which make up the "Nietzsche Problem," will one be able to master it.[7]

Excepting the intelligentsia, Nietzsche's reading public was concentrated in the literate middle classes. The commemorative meetings and Nietzsche evenings—social gatherings accompanied by musical and spoken texts—followed the classic pattern of bourgeois salon culture and *Verein* life dating back to the late eighteenth century.[8]

But exposure to Nietzsche was by no means restricted to this sector. Occasionally bewildered aristocrats and patricians pondered—while mostly rejecting—him and the more educated members of the German working class had at least some familiarity with the man and the outlines of his thought.[9]

Although it was not just in Germany that people read Nietzsche existentially, obvious forces facilitated the specific passion in his reception there. A great deal of the magic lay in the lyricism, beauty, and power of Nietzsche's language. The philosopher was a German thinker with German roots addressing what were thought to be largely German problems. Nietzsche's opponents considered this unfortunate and went out of their way to minimize his Germanness (*Deutschtum*). They emphasized his "Slavic" way of thinking, and his Polish and even "Mon-

---

7. Kurt Eisner, *Psychopathia Spiritualis: Friedrich Nietzsche und die Apostel der Zukunft* (Leipzig: Wilhelm Friedrich, 1892), 9.
   8. Hubert A. Cancik, "Der Nietzsche-Kult in Weimar (II)," in *Die Religion von Oberschichten: Religion, Profession, Intellektualismus,* ed. Peter Antes and Donate Pahnke (Marburg : Diagonal, 1989), 89, 110–111. I thank Guy Strumsa for this reference.
   9. Adolf Levenstein, *Friedrich Nietzsche im Urteil der Arbeiterklasse* (Leipzig: F. Meiner, 1914).

golian" roots as a means of banishing him from German respectability and the German pantheon.[10]

Nevertheless, during the 1890s and thereafter various groups began to translate Nietzsche's Germanness and the Nietzsche–German relationship into something of an ideology. It is striking how many enthusiastic readers simply converted their Nietzsche experience into a unique intellectual experience, a *Sondererlebnis* predicated upon peculiarly German characteristics of thought and sensibility. They held that Germanness was an ontological precondition for truly grasping the philosopher. Nietzsche's works were experienced and portrayed as comprehensible only in the German idiom. *Zarathustra,* Heinrich Rickert commented, was a virtually untranslatable document.[11] Nietzsche was seen as both symptom and critical articulator of national being and becoming: his personal odyssey and Germany's fate were held to be inextricably linked. Spengler expressed this special sense of symbiosis thus:

> Goethe's life was a full life, and that means that it brought something to completion. Countless Germans will honor Goethe, live with him, and seek his support; but he can never transform them. Nietzsche's effect is a transformation, for the melody of his vision did not end with his death. . . . Nietzsche's type of vision will pass on to new friends and enemies, and these in turn will hand it down to other followers and adversaries. Even if someday no one reads his works any longer, his vision will endure and be creative.
>
> His work is not a part of our past to be enjoyed; it is a task that makes servants of us all. As a task it is independent of his books and their subject matter, and thus a problem of German destiny. In an age that does not tolerate otherworldly ideals . . . when the only thing of recognizable value is the kind of ruthless action that Nietzsche baptized with the name of Cesare Borgia—in such an age, unless we learn to act as real history wants us to act, we will cease to exist as a people. We cannot live without a form that does not merely console in difficult situations, but helps one get out of them. This kind of hard wisdom made its first appearance in German thought with Nietzsche. . . . To the people most famished for history in all the world, he

10. Theodor Fritsch, "Nietzsche und die Jugend," *Hammer: Blätter für deutschen Sinn* 10, no. 29 (March 1911), 115. For a continuing emphasis in the Weimar period on Nietzsche's Polish origins see Karl Kynast, "Der Fall Nietzsche im Lichte rassenkundlicher Betrachtung," *Die Sonne* 2 (1925), 533–540, 722–728. This tendency continued through the Third Reich and was stressed especially by Christian opponents trying to discredit Nietzsche (Hans Goebel, *Nietzsche heute: Lebensfragen des deutschen Volkstums und der evangelischen Kirche* [Berlin: Kranz, 1935], 19).

11. Heinrich Rickert, *Die Philosophie des Lebens.* Quoted in Krummel, *Nietzsche,* vol. 1, 414.

showed history as it really is. His heritage is to live history in the same way.[12]

Spengler's 1924 remarks were made in the context of the polarized politics of the Weimar Republic where a suitably nationalized Nietzsche had already been fashioned in the radical-right image.[13] But the perception of Nietzsche's Germanness was by no means limited to such circles. There were many others with different political opinions who continued to regard the philosopher's Germanness as central but interpreted its meaning in terms far removed from the politics of a brutalized will to power.[14] What they all had in common was the belief that Nietzsche was in some important way an essentially German phenomenon, a belief which, as we shall see, became integrated into an assortment of political postures.

Given Nietzsche's many, extreme anti-German statements, such a creed required special casuistic explanation. The rather eccentric Rudolf Pannwitz, a follower of Stefan George, put it in typically paradoxical fashion. Nietzsche in essence was no German but what he lived and created was possible only as a German experience.[15] Countless commentators stressed that it was precisely in his criticisms of Germans and Germanness and in his European perspective that Nietzsche was most quintessentially German! As Thomas Mann wrote in 1918: Nietzsche's "immortal European drama of self-conquest, self-discipline and self-crucifixion with the intellectual sacrificial death as a heart-and-brain-rending conclusion" was unthinkable outside of "the Protestantism of the Naumberg's preacher's son" and the "Nordic-German, burgerly-moral sphere."[16]

12. Oswald Spengler, "Nietzsche and His Century," in *Selected Essays,* trans. Donald O. White (Chicago: Gateway, 1967), 196–197.
13. As one example of this annexation see Franz Haiser, *Die Judenfrage vom Standpunkt der Herrenmoral: Rechtsvölkische und linksvölkische Weltanschauung* (Leipzig: T. Weicher, 1926). He states that while only Germans were capable of grasping Nietzsche in full, they first had to overcome philistinism in themselves (92).
14. The cultivated Nietzschean Count Harry Kessler, for instance, was appalled by Spengler's ruminations in that lecture:

> For an hour a fat person with a fleshy chin and brutal mouth . . . spouted the most trite and trivial rubbish. Any young worker in a Worker's Educational Association who tried to inform his fellows about Nietzsche's philosophy would have done better. Not *one* original idea. Not even *false* glitter. Everything uniformly shallow, dull, insipid and tedious (*The Diaries of a Cosmopolitan: Count Harry Kessler 1918–1937,* trans. and ed. Charles Kessler [London: Weidenfeld and Nicolson, 1971], 333–334).

15. Rudolf Pannwitz, *Einführung in Nietzsche* (München-Feldafing: Hans Carl, 1920), 1.
16. Mann, *Reflections,* 104.

Karl Löwith, a keen participant in the German encounter with Nietzsche, claimed that non-Germans could not really grasp the bond. Only this affinity, he argued, explained Nietzsche's almost unlimited influence within German borders. "Without this last German philosopher German development cannot be understood. . . . Like Luther he is a specific German event (ereignis,) radical and fateful."[17]

The Protestant connection and its secularizing consequences were clearly relevant. The notion that the Nietzschean frame and its overall problematic was essentially a post-Protestant affair, a function of collective crisis and rupture, was widespread amongst those centrally involved in Nietzschean discourse. Jung (like Nietzsche, the son of a pastor) argued in 1936 that Nietzsche could not touch

> people who are singing the community song, because they don't need to bother with it—they remain a remnant of the Catholic church. They did not develop as Protestants, but remained historical derelicts of the original Christian church. But if they develop further as Protestants they will necessarily come to the tremendous problem to which Nietzsche came, namely, to the idea of the Superman, to the idea of the thing in man that takes the place of the God that has been hitherto valid.[18]

Nietzsche's whole point of view, Jung insisted, was a direct outgrowth of the Protestant conception of radical responsibility, the extravagant belief in one's ability and in the moral task of higher self-creation.[19]

Regardless of how one explained the peculiar intensity of the relationship, by the 1890s Nietzsche's significance was recognized by opponents and proponents alike. It was then that the battle over Nietzsche and the struggle over his legacy were joined. This decade saw the emergence of what was dubbed "the Nietzsche cult" and which, in reality, were a series of Nietzsche cults. This only fueled the stridency of the polemics.

Nietzsche's first obvious followers were the youth and avant-garde of the 1890s. His galvanizing effect was clearly related to the circum-

17. Karl Löwith, *Mein Leben in Deutschland vor und nach 1933: Ein Bericht* (Stuttgart: J. B. Metzlersche, 1986), 6.
18. Jung, *Nietzsche's Zarathustra*, vol. 2, 909–910. Nietzsche's influence on Jung was early and profound:

> You see, I was a boy when he was a professor at the university. I never saw him, but I saw his friend Jakob Burckhardt very often, and also Bachofen, so we were not separated by cosmic distances. Nietzsche's mind was one of the first spiritual influences I experienced. It was all brand new then, and it was the closest thing to me (vol. 1, 301).

19. Ibid., 920ff.

stances of the Kaiserreich and to its perceived spiritual and political mediocrity. Nietzsche, wrote one observer, both exposed and was the victim of the inauthenticity of bourgeois society.[20] In early works like *The Birth of Tragedy* and *Untimely Meditations*,[21] he provided biting and presciently relevant tools for a critical indictment of that society as well as guidelines for overcoming its decadent condition. The patrician Count Harry Kessler summed up his generation's perception of Nietzsche from this time thus:

> There grew within us a secret Messianism. The desert, to which every Messiah belongs, was in our hearts; and suddenly, like a meteor, Nietzsche appeared. . . . The way in which Nietzsche influenced, or more precisely possessed, us cannot be compared with the effect of any other contemporary thinker or poet. He did not merely speak to reason and fantasy. His impact was more encompassing, deeper, and more mysterious. His ever-growing echo signified the eruption of *Mystik* into a rationalized and mechanized time. He bridged the abyss (*Abgrund*) between us and reality with the veil of heroism. Through him we were transported out of this ice age, reenchanted and enraptured (*entrueckt*).[22]

Regardless of their differences most early participants in Nietzsche's reception of the philosopher sensed he was a pivotal turn-of-the-century figure. Nietzsche's furnishing of new criteria for modern ethics, wrote Georg Simmel in 1896, was nothing less than "a Copernican deed."[23] Upon Nietzsche's death in 1900 the rhetoric became even more adulatory. In his eulogy the historian Kurt Breysig put it thus: Nietzsche was the guide to a new human future, a man whose stature was comparable only to Buddha, Zarathustra, and Jesus Christ. These were men whose visions encompassed whole nations and whose effects could be measured only in aeons.[24]

There was a growing conviction amongst friend and foe alike that

20. Kurt Hildebrandt, "Nietzsche als Richter: Sein Schicksal" in *Nietzsche als Richter unsrer Zeit*, E. Gundolf and K. Hildebrandt, 65–104. (Breslau: Ferdinand Hirt, 1923), 97.

21. The essays in *Untimely Meditations* (published only in 1893) had all appeared long before: "David Strauss, the Confessor and Writer" and "On the Use and Disadvantage of History for Life" in 1873, "Schopenhauer as Educator" in 1874, and "Richard Wagner in Bayreuth" in 1876 (Friedrich Nietzsche, *Untimely Meditations*, trans. R. J. Hollingdale, intro. J. P. Stern (Cambridge: Cambridge University Press, 1983).

22. Harry Graf Kessler, *Gesichter und Zeiten: Erinnerungen* (Berlin: S. Fischer, 1962), 229, 243.

23. Georg Simmel, "Friedrich Nietzsche: Eine moralphilosophische Silhouette," *Zeitschrift für Philosophie und philosophische Kritik* 2 (1896), 202–215.

24. Kurt Breysig, "Gedenkrede an Friedrich Nietzsches Bahre," *Die Zukunft* 32 (8 September 1900), 413–414. We shall later see to what extent the positive myth of Nietzsche was promoted by his death.

Nietzsche had outlined a critical and prophetic vision that broke pre-
viously invisible and impassable barriers. The publication in 1901 of
The Will to Power only reinforced this perception. "What I relate,"
Nietzsche wrote in the preface,

> is the history of the next two centuries [written] as a spirit of daring and
> experiment that has already lost its way once in every labyrinth of the future;
> as a soothsayer bird-spirit who *looks back* when relating what will come; as
> the first perfect nihilist of Europe who, however, has even now lived through
> the whole of nihilism, to the end, leaving it behind, outside himself.[25]

The tone of his writings spoke to previously tabooed and unexplored
levels of experience.[26] Even those who regarded Nietzsche as a notorious reactionary had to deal with the fact that the philosopher couched
his thought in exceedingly modern and experimental terms.[27]

Like the works themselves the tone of much of Nietzschean discourse
was extreme. Acolytes as well as opponents of Nietzsche discerned the
subversive quality of his thought and the challenge that he posed to the
fabric of respectable social order. What else did the critique of Christianity, indeed, of morality itself, the transvaluation of values, and the
clash between convention and creative freedom imply? It was this perceived extremity that drove makers of the Nietzsche image to employ
mythic language, typically in the heroic–prophetic or demonic–pathological mode. Contemporaries were quite aware of this tendency. As
early as 1905 one critic complained that Nietzsche's venerators and
despisers alike described the philosopher in what amounted to transhu-
man terms, as if he were simply either a radiant, heavenly meteor or a
bloodthirsty wolf who had emerged from the forests.[28]

Almost from its beginnings Nietzschean discourse assumed wider
symbolic functions, mirroring both the hopes and anxieties of the
changing times. Nietzsche, wrote one observer, was the *Modephilosoph*
of the period because of his extraordinary affinity to modern sensibil-

25. Friedrich Nietzsche, *The Will to Power*, trans. Walter Kaufmann and R. J.
Hollingdale, ed. Walter Kaufmann (New York: Vintage, 1968), 3.
26. See R. A. Nicholls, "Beginning of the Nietzsche Vogue in Germany," *Modern
Philology* 56 (1958), 25, 37, for some similar thoughts. I do not accept the conception
that the Nietzsche cult divides into two periods and that prior to 1900 the critical works
were stressed while thereafter the prophetic ones were emphasized. In the Pernerstorfer
circle the critical and the constructive were combined (indeed they saw in totality a
Nietzschean ideal). Kessler similarly fused the two.
27. For some reflections on Nietzsche and modern political and social life see Arthur
Ruppin, "Moderne Weltanschauung und Nietzsche'sche Philosophie," *Die Gegenwart* 10
(1903), 147ff.
28. Karl Joel, *Nietzsche und die Romantik* (Jena and Leipzig: Eugen Diederichs,
1905), 68.

ity. His sensitive soul reflected "the good and evil spirits of our time . . . he expressed in glittering language what others only darkly intuited."[29]

Endowing Nietzsche's thought and personage with the aura of supernatural potency has been a distinguishing and enduring characteristic of Nietzsche reception from the 1890s through to the present.[30] Nietzsche's effect was also often described in epidemiological terms, as if his thought were contagious, infectious. It was this purported, transformative power that gave Nietzsche his special continuing notoriety. "The view," Sander Gilman has written in an incisive analysis, "that Nietzsche was a 'dangerous thinker'—not merely that he espoused dangerous thoughts, but that he caused dangerous acts—is a leitmotiv of Nietzsche reception from the fin-de-siècle to Georg Lukacs."[31] As we shall see later, this power extended to his being uniquely indicted as the cause of two world wars.

This image was already present in popular literature by 1902. In Wilhelm von Polenz's *Wurzellocker,* for instance, Nietzsche is portrayed as a bewitching wizard, an ideological sorcerer.[32] Nietzsche's sickness, wrote the rabid anti-Semite Theodor Fritsch, dwelled in his work and thus infected weak, unformed minds and, no doubt, influenced the wave of youthful suicides of the time.[33] Shocked upholders of public order blamed the philosopher's influence on vulnerable youth in matters not only suicidal but also murderous,[34] and not only in Germany. In America Clarence Darrow even employed this as a defense in the famous Leopold–Loeb case. Nathan Leopold, Jr., argued Darrow, committed murder because he believed in the amoral Nietzschean superman: "he thought it applied to him, and he could not have believed

29. Hilbert, *Moderne Willensziele,* 19. It is worth noting that these comments came from somebody who in many ways was quite critical of Nietzsche.

30. That this was both an ongoing predisposition and sometimes literally intended can be seen in the study by the American psychologist Samuel J. Warner in which Nietzsche and satanism are collapsed into identical embodiments of the drive to personal and mass destruction (*The Urge to Mass Destruction* [New York and London: Grune and Stratton, 1957]).

31. Sander Gilman, "The Nietzsche Murder Case; or, What Makes Dangerous Philosophies Dangerous" in *Difference and Pathology: Stereotypes of Sexuality, Race, and Madness* (Ithaca, N.Y.: Cornell University Press, 1985), 59.

32. Wilhelm von Polenz, *Wurzellocker* (Berlin: F. Fontane, 1902), 7ff. See Krummel, *Nietzsche,* vol. 2, 63–65.

33. Fritsch, "Nietzsche und die Jugend," 113.

34. For some examples see Wilhelm Carl Becker, *Der Nietzschekultus: Ein Kapitel aus der Geschichte der Verirrungen des menschlichen Geistes* (Leipzig: Richard Lipinski, 1908), 35ff.

it excepting that it either caused a diseased mind or was the result of a diseased mind."[35] During these early years the struggle for the Nietzschean banner revolved around alternative strategies for his banishment or legitimization. Nietzsche's ideas were always integrally linked to the myth of the man and his subsequent fate. Critics and celebrators agreed that the philosopher's thought, being, and life were an important unity; they simply interpreted and evaluated that fact differently.

Opponents of Nietzsche had a certain advantage: mercilessly and with some delight they exploited his madness. It was all too easy to link the clinical pathology with the ideas and thus dismiss the work as well as the man. Nietzsche, as the title of a well-known work of the period had it, was a case of *psychopathia spiritualis*.[36] This insanity demonstrated not only the palpably dangerous nature of Nietzschean notions but also the diseased nature of his devotees.

The fact of derangement was regularly incorporated into the philosophical critique to explain its perverted contents. Nietzsche's inherited pathology, Dr. Hermann Türck wrote in 1891, was translated into his moral and philosophical system.

> Thus, it may happen that an intellectual and highly gifted man, born with perverted instincts, and feeling as torment . . . the nonsatisfaction of instinct, will hit upon the idea of justifying the passion for murder, the extremest egoism . . . as something good, beautiful, and according to Nature, and to characterize as morbid aberration the better opposing moral instincts.[37]

Works such as Paul Moebius's 1902 study dedicated to analyzing Nietzsche's madness and the consequent ideational distortions provided the necessary stamp of professional, medical, and psychological authority.[38]

35. Gilman, *Difference and Pathology*, 73. Gilman provides examples of German court cases and suicides. Even in the 1980s in Israel the mass media went out of their way to stress that Mordecai Vananu, convicted for leaking photographs of Israel's atomic reactor installation at Dimona, had read and was influenced by Nietzsche (Nahum Barnea, "A Look Inside the Diary" (in Hebrew), *Koteret Rashit* (19 November 1986), 11–15.

36. Eisner, *Psychopathia Spiritualis*. (The work was originally published in *Die Gesellschaft* in 1891.) Its title was a play on Baron Richard von Krafft-Ebing's *Psychopathia Sexualis*.

37. Hermann Türck, *Friedrich Nietzsche und seine philosophischen Irrwege* (Dresden: Gloess, 1891), 7.

38. Paul Julius Moebius, *Über das Pathologische bei Nietzsche* (Wiesbaden: J. F. Bergmann, 1902). The work concludes with the warning: "Be mistrustful, for this man has a brain disorder." Moebius's work was highly praised in respected standard psychiatric handbooks like Emil Kraepelin's *Psychiatrie* in both the 1903 and 1909 editions. See Krummel, *Nietzsche*, vol. 2, 77–78, n. 63.

Pro-Nietzscheans, of course, viewed things quite differently. As one critic put it, no modern psychiatric auto-da-fé would be able to repress Nietzsche's lasting contribution.[39] They sought instead to endow Nietzsche's madness with a positively spiritual quality. The prophet had been driven crazy by the clarity of his vision and the incomprehension of a society not yet able to understand it (replicating Nietzsche's own theme in the famous "God is Dead" passage).[40] Upon meeting the ill philosopher, Rudolf Steiner proclaimed that the reality of the spiritual realm was revealed to him: "In inner perception I saw Nietzsche's soul as if hovering over his head, infinitely beautiful in its spirit-light, surrendered to the spiritual worlds it had longed for so much."[41] The German Expressionist fascination with the liberating possibilities of madness found in Nietzsche both a spokesman and an exemplar.[42] With Nietzsche's madness, wrote August Horneffer a little more conventionally, came a radiant inner peace, an end to the unrelenting struggle of his earlier years. It was precisely in this condition that the magic and majesty of his personality was most manifest.[43]

This clearly was an ongoing theme not limited to Germany. Nietzscheans everywhere argued in similar vein. "How do we know," wrote Isadora Duncan in 1917, "that what seems to us insanity was not a vision of transcendental truth?"[44] For Bataille, the movement towards wholeness began with madness and Nietzsche's madness was redolent with Christlike associations. He reminded his readers of William Blake's

> proverb that *had others not gone mad, we should be so.* Madness cannot be cast out of the human generality, for its completion requires the madman. Nietzsche's going mad—in our stead—thus rendered that generality possible; and those who had previously lost their reason had not done it as brilliantly.[45]

39. Joel, *Nietzsche und die Romantik,* 327.
40. For this immensely influential text see Nietzsche, *Gay Science,* 181–182.
41. Quoted in Colin Wilson, *Rudolf Steiner, The Man and His Vision: An Introduction to the Life and Ideas of the Founder of Anthroposophy* (Wellingborough, Eng.: Aquarian Press, 1985), 87–88.
42. Wieland Herzfelde, "Die Ethik der Geisteskranken," *Die Aktion* 4 (1914). See also Augustinus P. Dierick, *German Expressionist Prose: Theory and Practice* (Toronto: University of Toronto Press, 1987), 206–207.
43. August Horneffer, "Nietzsches Todestag," *Die Tat* 2 (1910–1911), 356–360.
44. Isadora Duncan, *Isadora Speaks,* ed. Franklin Rosemont (San Francisco: City Light Books, 1983), 121.
45. Georges Bataille, "Nietzsche's Madness," 3 January 1939 in *October* 36 (Spring 1986), 44. See too in the same source "On Nietzsche: The Will to Chance," 55.

We must, however, return to the anti-Nietzscheans. Their project of
defamation was, of course, never simply limited to the fact of madness.
Their attack was typically integrated into a larger critique of the civilization which had produced Nietzsche and which he supposedly reflected. The most significant—and symptomatic—example of this genre
was Max Nordau's famous *Degeneration* which appeared in German in
1892 and was quickly translated into numerous languages.[46]

Nordau's representation of the trends of his time was not so much
analysis as an expression of outrage, the incomprehension of bourgeois
positivism as it confronted the incipient modernist revolution intent on
questioning, even destroying, all its revered postulates. However one
chooses to regard the fin-de-siècle cultural and intellectual revolution, it
clearly challenged the liberal worldview and its assumptions of respectability, rationality, and discipline; its conventional middle-class morality; and its belief in order, science, and progress.

Nordau conceived of the fin-de-siècle as as much a moral problem as
a temporal phase. He wrote that it represents

> a practical emancipation from traditional discipline. . . . To the voluptuary
> this means unbridled lewdness, the unchaining of the beast in man; to the
> withered heart of the egoist, disdain of all consideration for his fellow-men,
> the trampling under foot of all barriers which enclose brutal greed of lucre
> and lust of pleasure; to the contemner of the world it means the shameless
> ascendancy of base impulses and motives. . . . And to all, it means the end
> of an established order, which for thousands of years has satisfied logic,
> fettered depravity, and in every art matured something of beauty.[47]

The unifying thread in all of Nordau's ruminations was the concept
of degeneration, a slogan central to the political vocabulary of an age of
rapid urbanization, industrialization and mass society. Here was a concept that cut across the ideological spectrum. If it was mainly conservative in provenance, it was also employed by bewildered liberals (like
Nordau), discontented socialists, and the incipient radical right.[48]

Committed as he was to the mid-nineteenth-century conception of
liberal modernity, Nordau was intent on denying progressive credentials to the modernists he criticized. As a physician he could do this by
attributing to these artists and philosophers and their works the clear

46. For a useful history of the book see George Mosse's introduction in Max Nordau,
Degeneration (New York: Howard Fertig, 1968). See too P. M. Baldwin, "Liberalism,
Nationalism, and Degeneration: The Case of Max Nordau," *Central European History*
13, no. 2 (June 1980).
47. Nordau, *Degeneration*, 5.
48. J. Edward Chamberlin and Sander L. Gilman, eds., *Degeneration: The Dark Side
of Progress* (New York: Columbia University Press, 1985).

attributes of physical and mental degeneration. They, he proclaimed, are no

> heralds of a new era. They do not direct us to the future, but point backwards to times past. Their word is no ecstatic prophecy, but the senseless stammering and babbling of deranged minds, and what the ignorant hold to be the outbursts of gushing, youthful vigour and turbulent constructive impulses are really nothing but the convulsions and spasms of exhaustion.[49]

This was the framework into which Nordau located Nietzsche. The philosopher was no forward-looking prophet but an insane throwback, symptom of and spokesman for the prevailing degeneration. Insofar as any meaning could be extracted from the delirious ideas of this wild madman it derived from "illusions of sense and diseased organic processes." Nietzsche's strictures on conscience, morality, and sensuality, for instance, were all functions of his sadism. No "image of wickedness and crime can arise without arousing him sexually, and he is unable to experience any sexual stimulation without the appearance in his consciousness of an image of some deed of violence and blood."[50]

There is no small irony in the fact that Nordau's central categories in many ways mirrored the Nietzschean universe of discourse. "Tell me, my brothers," Zarathustra asked, "what do we consider bad and worst of all? Is it not *degeneration?*"[51] Both regarded civilization to be threatened; both were concerned with the sources of decadence and the loss of vitality, with regeneration. There was even something quite Nietzschean in Nordau's eugenic suggestions: "Those degenerates, whose mental derangement is too deep-seated, must be abandoned to their inexorable fate. They are past cure or amelioration. They will rave for a season, and then perish."[52]

Anti-Nietzschean tracts grew in volume and vehemence in response to Nietzsche's rapid popularization. Nietzsche became a familiar part of the German cultural and political landscape not only by means of learned philosophical tomes but through more popular media. Numerous novels and plays served to more widely diffuse various versions of the man and his thought.[53] Even more important was the role of the

---

49. Nordau, *Degeneration,* 15–33.
50. Ibid., 416, 451.
51. Nietzsche, "Thus Spoke Zarathustra," 187.
52. Nordau, *Degeneration,* 551. See too the language on p. 556.
53. There were plays of all kinds—critical, satiric and tragic. See J. V. Widmann, *Jenseits von Gut und Boese: Schauspiel in drei Aufzügen* (Stuttgart: J. G. Cotta, 1893). By 1886 Widmann had labeled Nietzsche's works dangerous. He was not conservative but progressive, concerned by Nietzsche's antidemocratic, elitist, and antifeminist views (J. V.

popular press which made the name of Nietzsche a household word and familiarized basic aspects of his life and work to large national audiences. Journals and magazines did the same for particular institutions and special interests.[54]

Nietzscheana—its slogans, thematics, aesthetics—began to penetrate the prosaic as well as the profound. At least for the literary classes, Nietzsche became a commonplace, domesticated into the trivia of everyday life. Thus Maximilian Harden, editor of *Die Zukunft*, could write to a friend concerning an afternoon tennis game: "*Also spielte Zarathustra!*" (Thus played Zarathustra!)[55] On innumerable occasions appropriate proverbial Nietzschean expressions and aphorisms were invoked, transformed into a kind of folk wisdom, and applied to circumstances ranging from the merely trivial to the profoundly sinister ("what does not destroy me, makes me strong;" "that which is falling should be pushed").

Many of these responses took place at the immediate, existential level. The popular writer Emil Ludwig (1881–1948) found that Nietzsche was the inevitably effective "magical" remedy against depression and hypochondria.[56] People from numerous walks of life—and countries—started to have intoxicating Zarathustra experiences. The poet Richard Dehmel had an eight-day-long possession enraptured by the bellicosity (*Kampflust*) of its rhythms.[57] Le Corbusier had a *Zarathustra-Erlebnis* in 1908.[58]

The spread of Nietzscheana was apparent too in the fact that

Widmann, "Nietzsches gefährliches Buch," *Der Bund* 37, no. 326 [1886]). There was also Arno Holz's satirical *Sozialaristokraten*. The comedy was written in 1896 and staged in Berlin in June 1897. A later example, staged by the Wagner Society in Berlin in 1912, was Paul Friedrich's *Das Dritte Reich: Die Tragödie des Individualismus* (Leipzig: Xenien, 1910). Here Nietzsche's life history was recounted as a "tragedy for which indirectly we are all guilty."

54. For a description of the explosion of magazines, journals, and the press in Germany and the diffusion of Nietzsche see Joelle Phillipi, "Das Nietzsche-Bild in der deutschen Zeitschriftenpresse der Jahrhundertwende" (Inaugural diss., Universität des Saarlandes, Saarbruecken, 1970).

55. Harden was an influential mediator of an aggressive, positive Nietzscheana. His important *Die Zukunft* not only provided a forum for many articles by Elisabeth Foerster-Nietzsche but encouraged Nietzscheanism in general. See amongst its many germane articles the anonymous "Neues von Friedrich Nietzsche" (1 April 1893); Alexander Tille, "Nietzsche als Ethiker der Entwicklung" (10 November 1894); Max Marschalk, "Frei nach Nietzsche" (26 December 1896); Josef Hofmiller, "Nietzsche und Wagner" (10 April 1897); Michael Georg Conrad, "Zarathustra" (18 March 1898); Hans von Müller, "Nietzsche's Vorfahren" (28 May 1898).

56. Emil Ludwig, *Geschenke des Lebens: Ein Rückblick* (Berlin: E. Rowohlt, 1931), 159ff.

57. Emil Ludwig, *Richard Dehmel* (Berlin: S. Fischer, 1913), 118ff.

58. Paul Venable Turner, *The Education of Le Corbusier* (New York, 1978), 56ff.

Nietzschean concepts became increasingly incorporated into German and European political vocabulary, part of the available stockpile of slogans and catchwords.[59] Graphic and elastically employable terms like *will to power*, *Übermensch* and *beyond good and evil* and concepts such as master-and-slave morality, the transvaluation of values, and ressentiment were integrated into the language.

One indication of their growing familiarity is the fact that Nietzschean terminology was itself used to subvert Nietzschean values. In liberal and socialist circles notions such as *the blonde beast, master morality*, and *beyond good and evil* were applied to political enemies. In M. G. Conrad's 1895 study, "The *Übermensch* in Politics,"[60] for instance, that concept was employed in a totally negative way, as a critical tool to capture and criticize the self-image of two "Nietzschean" elites—the power politicians and the self-glorifying intellectuals and artists of the undemocratic Kaiserreich. Already Conrad used the Übermensch motif almost without reference to Nietzsche, unmooring the term from the works in which it was originally embedded. As is so often the case, the influence was most effective when its origins remained blurry or irrelevant. Nietzsche's ideas were determining a whole mode of life, Raoul Richter commented in 1906, without people even being aware of the source.[61]

The popularization of Nietzsche and his work was never limited to abstract ideas and the printed word. This was done through more concrete, tangible forms of expression, such as music. Nietzsche not only profoundly influenced self-consciously modern music[62] but it was also through this medium that the Nietzschean world and its atmospherics were emotively conveyed. Richard Strauss's tone poem "Also Sprach

59. One index of this is the multiple inclusion of Nietzsche-related notions contained in Otto Ladendorf, *Historiches Schlagwörterbuch: Ein Versuch* (Stuttgart and Berlin: Trübner, 1906). See Krummel, *Nietzsche*, vol. 2, 223.

60. M. G. Conrad, *Der Übermensch in der Politik: Betrachtungen über die Reichzustände am Ende des Jahrhunderts* (Stuttgart: Robert Lutz, 1895). Although this book was unrelentingly critical it was also true that, as editor of *Die Gesellschaft*, Conrad was a tireless promoter of Nietzsche and the "new" literature.

61. Raoul Richter, "Friedrich Nietzsche und die Kultur unserer Zeit," rep. in *Essays*, ed. Lina Richter (Leipzig: F. Meiner, 1913), 112.

62. Nietzsche was routinely described as a thinker with an essentially musical (hence German) sensibility (Bernard Scharlitt, "Das Musikalische Element in Friedrich Nietzsche," *Die Musik* 4 [1904], 108–112). By 1901 Nietzsche's role in German modern music was already quite apparent. Arthur Seidl documented that role and listed the many compositions inspired by his work and poems (*Moderner Geist in der deutschen Tonkunst* [Berlin, 1901] 24–43, 89–117, 139ff). For Nietzsche's influence on modern music, see Paul Riesenfeld, "Nietzsches Bedeutung für die moderne Musik," *Allgemeine Musik-Zeitung* 32 (16, 23, 30.6. 1905), 427ff, 441f, 457ff.

Zarathustra," premiered in Frankfurt am Main in November 1896, was perhaps the most famous but by no means the only example.[63] Mahler's *Third Symphony* was heavily indebted to Nietzschean thematics and was originally entitled *The Gay Science*.[64]

These creations, however, reached limited audiences in concert halls. In a visual age of mass communication the diffusion could reach far more people through the creation of an iconography of Nietzsche and his ideational world—the subject of a superb full-length study by Jürgen Krause.[65] The history of Nietzsche's reception is replete with examples of the search for suitable visual ways in which to represent the man and the message. In its first few issues, for instance, the glossy, illustrated *Pan* not only featured Nietzschean poems in his honor but numerous drawings and sculptures of the philosopher as well. Most impressive was Ernst Moritz Geyger's illustration for Nietzsche's parable "The Giant." There the giant—presumably a version of the Übermensch, perhaps even Nietzsche himself—was represented in the shape of a monumental Greek sculpture, replete with angel wings. Beneath, contemptible dwarfs in academic dress scurry about doing their utmost to prevent the giant from performing a giant's work (illus. 1).[66]

While *Pan* was particularly interested in disseminating the myth of the man and his ideas, it was by no means an isolated example. Between 1890 and 1914 an array of magazines, newspapers, and journals published portraits, paintings, sketches, and sculptures of Nietzsche. This was a popular genre designed to idealize and palpably transmit the myth of the man, his prophecy, and martyrdom.[67] At any rate, it was thus received and interpreted.

It was around this time, too, that Nietzsche's moustache became his defining visual symbol (illus. 2). The face became as famous as the slogans and the image, a desired commodity. From the mid-1890s,

63. Self-conscious musical modernists like Alban Berg were enthusiastic Nietzscheans (*Briefe an seine Frau* [Munich and Vienna: Längen-Müller, 1965], 16, 31, 88, 123ff).
64. See Krummel, *Nietzsche*, vol. 2, 167 and n. 186.
65. Jürgen Krause, *"Märtyrer" und "Prophet": Studien zum Nietzsche-Kult in der bildenden Kunst der Jahrhundertwende* (Berlin and New York: Walter de Gruyter, 1984). As Krause has already covered the topic in full I merely concentrate on some major points which relate to the present work. See too Dietrich Schubart, "Nietzsche konkretionsformen in der bildenden Kunst 1890–1933," *Nietzsche-Studien* 10/11 (1981/1982).
66. "Der Riese: Friedrich Nietzsche," *Pan* 1, no. 2 (1895), opposite 94. The very first issue opened with a Nietzsche fragment, "Zarathustra vor dem Könige," (p. 1) and "Das Königslied," a poem by Paul Scheerbart, pp. 2–3. Max Klinger's famous bust of "Der Philosoph" was also reproduced.
67. Krause, *"Märtyrer" und "Prophet,"* has an extensive listing of these attempts and some of the considerations behind them.

encouraged by the Nietzsche Archives, there were sales of what Krause has called "Nietzsche-cult products"—replicas in *Kleinplastik* of Nietzsche statuettes, paintings, and the like.[68] For those who could not afford these, there were always cheap photographic reproductions to be found in illustrated magazines and newspapers. Thus for Hermann Hesse, during his 1895–1898 period in Tübingen, Nietzsche became a kind of cultural pin-up: two images hung on Hesse's wall.[69] Like Goethe, Nietzsche began to take on an aura, an assumed authority. His face, together with a suitable quote, adorned postcards advocating exotic causes such as vegetarianism.[70] His appearance on private bookplates became increasingly common. One, for instance, pictured Nietzsche as a latter-day Christ, bedecked with a crown of thorns (illus. 3). Working-class journals began to use his famous face for satirizing the capitalist commercialization of culture. In January 1914, for instance, the *Arbeiter-Zeitung* featured a facetious advertisement of Nietzsche writing a testimonial for Bersons (the trademark of a company, Beer & Sohn) (illus. 4).[71]

The consumer side of Nietzscheanism admittedly never reached the mass proportions of the cult surrounding Otto von Bismarck of the same era with its Bismarckian roses, Bismarckian *Erdbier,* and Bismarckian clothes. Nevertheless, various circles—especially of architects and craftsmen—sought to give practical expression to his inspiration through the creation of real and imagined Nietzschean "life styles." The most famous and striking example was the work of Peter Behrens. Behrens designed his own Zarathustrian villa as a centerpiece of the experimental Darmstadt artists' colony. The house was adorned with symbols such as the eagle, Zarathustra's diamond, and the *Edelstein* that radiated "the virtues of a world which is not yet here" (illus. 5).[72]

Behrens sought to realize Nietzsche's prophecy of the "great style" (*Stil*)—a synthesis in which the vision of the unity of art and life would

68. Krause, *"Märtyrer" und "Prophet,"* 131, 119–120.

69. Bernhard Zeller, *Hermann Hesse in Selbstzeugnissen und Bilddokumenten* (Hamburg: Reinbeck, 1963), 32ff.

70. See Krause, *"Märtyrer" und "Prophet,"* illus. 10. The quote is rather dubious. See also chap. 4, n. 110.

71. This history is told in Edward Timms, *Karl Kraus Apocalyptic Satirist: Culture and Catastrophe in Hapsburg Vienna* (New Haven and London: Yale University Press, 1986), 309.

72. Tilmann Buddensieg, "Das Wohnhaus als Kultbau: Zum Darmstädter Haus von Behrens," in *Peter Behrens und Nürnberg* (Munich: Prestel, 1980). My thanks to Christiane Schütz for drawing my attention to Behrens's Nietzschean connections.

be fulfilled. He was aware of the tension endemic to most "social applications" of Nietzscheanism. Was it possible to overcome the contradiction of creating a residence in the elitist spirit of the artist as superman, on the one hand, and designing a habitable house of the future for everyman on the other?[73] The monumental side was less problematic for Behrens who, like his colleague, the theatre reformer Georg Fuchs, sought to fuse beauty with power and individual will with state authority. Here Nietzsche moreover symbolized not revolutionary transvaluation but Germany's contemporary economic and political power.[74] This was evident in the German pavilion Behrens designed for the Turin 1902 Exposition. In a surreal cavern "light flooded the interior in which the industrial might of the Second Reich was on display. Zarathustra, cited explicitly, progresses towards the light. The society of German high capital affirmed its presence, identifying itself as new spirituality."[75]

This was hardly architecture in the Dionysian or Zarathustrian mode. Rather, as the acute architectural historians Manfredo Tafuri and Francesco Dal Co have observed, it was a new synthesis increasingly intended to take place "under the Apollonian sign of industrial organization." Behrens's designs, especially for the *Allgemeine Elektrizitäts Gesellschaft* (AEG), represented

> his own rather shrunken interpretation of Nietzsche: not the liberating rejoicing of Zarathustra, but a somewhat mournful quest for a New Order. Not, therefore the desacralization called for by the avant-garde, but an aspiration toward synthesis. The city and the industrial universe were not considered as effects or causes of the destruction of values or of the advent of an anguished chaos but as premises for a new totality, for the conservation of culture brought about by absorbing its antithesis, civilization.[76]

Other Nietzsche-influenced architecture was not, of course, designed to prop up the state and the emerging industrial order but expressed Zarathustrian solitude, emphasizing Nietzsche's contrast of the "flatlands of the contemptible mob" with the majesty of icy peaks. The expressionist architect Bruno Taut (1880–1938) was the most promi-

---

73. Ibid., 44; see too Alan Windsor, *Peter Behrens: Architect and Designer* (London: Architectural Press, 1981).

74. See Georg Fuchs's enthusiastic description of Kaiser Wilhelm as the realization of the Nietzschean will to power in his *Der Kaiser und die Zukunft des deutschen Volkes* (Munich and Leipzig: Müller, 1906), 72ff; quoted in Krummel, *Nietzsche,* vol. 2, 155.

75. Manfredo Tafuri, Francesco Dal Co, *Modern Architecture,* trans. Robert Erich Wolf (New York: Harry N. Abrams, 1979), 96.

76. Ibid., 96–97.

nent exemplar of a wider cult of mountains closely associated with Nietzsche and Nietzschean imagery. "Life," declared Zarathustra, "wants to build itself up into the heights with pillars and steps; it wants to look into vast distances and out toward stirring beauties: therefore it requires height."[77] Taut's "Alpine Architecture" was perhaps the most radical attempt to translate this vision into graphic form. Its strikingly Zarathustrian imagery envisioned the transformation of whole chains of mountains into "landscapes of Grail-shrines and crystal-lined caves" and the later covering of whole continents with "glass and precious stones in the form of 'ray-domes' and 'sparkling palaces.' "[78] (illus. 6) In honor of the post–World War I German revolution he envisaged a towerlike "Monument to the New Law" adorned with numerous quotations on the vast and illuminated hoardings of the crystal pyramids. His expressionist eclecticism was characteristic: Zarathustra's speech "On the New Idol" was combined with quotations from Luther and Karl Liebknecht.[79]

There were some delicious ironies in the process of popularization. Zarathustra, the man and the setting, fitted in perfectly with anti-industrial naturalist imagery, with the cult of *Bergeinsamkeit*, the longing to escape the crowded cities and to feel the pristine mountain air.[80] The painter Giovanni Segantini, an enthusiastic Nietzschean,[81] painted scenes of the Engadine, the mountain area that inspired the writing of *Thus Spoke Zarathustra*. Soon flocks of pilgrims and tourists made their way to these mountains. The *Einsamkeitserlebnis*—the experience of being alone—was transformed into a mass business! Segantini was quite aware of the need to address the masses with a kind of Nietzschean gimmickry. For the Paris 1900 World Exhibition he had originally planned a massive Engadin total work of art (*Gesamtkunstwerk*) replete with technical effects to create a total experience (*Totalerlebnis*).[82]

77. Nietzsche, "Thus Spoke Zarathustra," 213. From beginning to end "Zarathustra" is permeated with images and metaphors of heights and mountains. For another instance, see *Zarathustra*, "The Wanderer," Third Part, 264–266.
78. Wolfgang Pehnt, *Expressionist Architecture* (New York and Washington, D.C.: Praeger, 1973), chap. 5. On Alpine architecture see pp. 82–83 and for Nietzsche's general influence, pp. 41–43. For all Taut's emphasis on majestic solitude, he also envisaged mass tours of edification for workers who would observe his works from the air (p. 208).
79. Ibid., 208.
80. Walter Hammer, "Nietzsche im Hochgebirge," *Davoser Blätter* 37, no. 34 (19 September 1908). See too Ernst Bertram, "Nietzsche und die Berge," *Deutsche Alpenzeitung* 11 (1911–1912), 279–282.
81. "Giovanni Segantini," *Pan* 1, no. 3 (1895), 193–195.
82. Krause, *"Märtyrer" und "Prophet,"* 77, especially n. 344.

The emergence of a Nietzschean kitsch industry testifies to a penetration beyond the merely literary and philosophical. Its gaudy quality
was precisely what Nietzsche had condemned as symptomatic of the
philistinism of the mass age. Paul Friedrich's play *The Third Reich,* for
instance, had Zarathustra appear on stage dressed in a silver and gold
costume and a purple coat with a golden ribbon in his blonde hair and
a leopard skin draped over his shoulder.[83]
  For hostile critics during these years, the cult of Nietzsche was becoming more worrisome than Nietzsche himself. The cult became the
subject of an inordinately large and anxious literature.[84] Already in
1892 Nordau could write of the various Nietzsche Jünger as if they
were an obviously identifiable group with clear characteristics:

> His disciples believe in this brag, and with upturned eyes, bleat it after him
> in sheep-like chorus. The profound ignorance of this flock of ruminants
> permits them, forsooth, to believe in Nietzsche's originality. As they have
> never learnt, read, or thought about anything, all that they pick up in bars,
> or in their loafings, is naturally new and hitherto non-existent.[85]

Even earlier Hermann Türck had expressed this in more sociological
terms. Nietzscheans, he proclaimed, were the "intellectual proletariat"
of the Great Cities. They were jubilant at their discovery of Nietzsche.
It was his essential modernity as "the prophet of the devil and the father
of the lie" which attracted "free spirits" without constructive engagement or employment in urban centers like Copenhagen, Munich, and
Berlin.[86]
  Inasmuch as the early academic reception of Nietzsche was both
hostile and slow,[87] there may have been an initial grain of truth to the
observation that Nietzsche tended to attract more marginal and
"bohemian" elements.[88] In 1900 Karl Kraus called such modish
Nietzscheans "the super-apes of the coffee-house" (*Überaffen des*

83. Friedrich, *Das Dritte Reich.*
84. For an example of this genre see Becker, *Der Nietzschekultus.* For a Christian
critique see Dr. Adelbert Düringer, "Der Nietzschekultus," *Beweis des Glaubens im
Geistesleben der Gegenwart 5* (1908), 238–242.
85. Nordau, *Degeneration,* 442, 454–457.
86. Türck, *Friedrich Nietzsche,* quoted in Krummel, *Nietzsche,* vol. 1, 98.
87. Walter Eckstein, "Friedrich Nietzsche in the Judgement of Posterity," *Journal of
the History of Ideas 6* (1945).
88. Hubert Treiber, "Nietzsches 'Kloster für freiere Geister': Nietzsche und Weber als
Erzieher," in *Die Religion von Oberschichten,* ed. Peter Antes and Donate Pahnke (Marburg: Diagonal-Verlag, 1989).

Kaffeehauses).[89] But as his appeal widened to encompass almost every current of cultural life, an almost endless number of first-rate intellects were attracted to Nietzsche. As time went on it became increasingly clear that no simplistic sociology of ideas could encompass the range, complexity, and nuances of his appeal. By 1910 Mann—hardly a bohemian—recognized not only the protean dimensions of Nietzsche's appeal but also the differentiated fascination he held for different generations:

> We who were born around 1870 are too close to Nietzsche, we participate too directly in his tragedy, his personal fate (perhaps the most terrible, most awe-inspiring fate in intellectual history). Our Nietzsche is Nietzsche militant. Nietzsche triumphant belongs to those born fifteen years after us. We have from him our psychological sensitivity, our lyrical criticism, the experience of Wagner, the experience of Christianity, the experience of "modernity"—experiences from which we shall never completely break free, any more than Nietzsche himself ever did. They are too precious for that, too profound, too fruitful. But the twenty-year-olds have from him what will remain in the future, his purified aftereffect. For them he is a prophet one does not know very exactly, whom one hardly needs to have read, and yet whose purified results one has instinctively in one. They have from him the affirmation of the earth, the affirmation of the body, the anti-Christian and anti-intellectual conception of nobility, which comprises health and serenity and beauty.[90]

Critics of the Nietzsche cult were perhaps closer to the mark when they sought to account for its popularity by focusing on the vulnerabilities and deficiencies of the Kaiserreich. Youth were so attracted to Nietzsche, according to the famous conservative educator Friedrich Paulsen, because the fin-de-siècle signified the general breakdown of traditional patterns of authority and respect. In an essentially transitional age, the discovery of Nietzsche seemed almost predestined. No one, after all, had greater contempt for the past and the present.[91]

As perplexed conservatives pondered Nietzsche's growing and pernicious influence, the only antidote they could offer was precisely the kind of traditionalism Nietzsche and the Nietzscheans were intent on destroying. Nietzsche, one anonymous Lutheran wrote in 1897, was

89. *Die Fackel*, 2, 51 (August 1900), 21–22. Quoted in Vivetta Vivarelli, "Das Nietzsche-Bild in der Presse der deutschen Sozialdemokratie um die Jahrhundertwende," *Nietzsche-Studien* 13 (1984), 531.

90. From Mann's notes, "The new generation" as quoted in T. J. Reed's superb study *Thomas Mann: The Uses of Tradition* (Oxford: Oxford University Press, 1974), 136–138.

91. Friedrich Paulsen, "Väter und Söhne: Eine sozialpädogogische Studie aus der deutschen Gegenwart," *Deutsche Rundschau* (May 1907), 229–230.

too un-German, paradoxical, and sick for German society. Only traditional national and religious characteristics could oppose these qualities: "We trust that our German Volk, under the power of Christian
faith, will have the strength to overcome the sickness of the Nietzsche
cult without difficulty."[92]

Nietzsche was typically regarded as a new, unexpected challenge to
the traditional, godless enemies of conservatism. He was paradoxically
represented as akin to the forces of socialism, a modern "seducer,"
whose message worked even more insidiously than the "odious equal-
izing of social democracy."[93] However unlikely it may have appeared,
wrote the philosopher and publicist Ludwig Stein, these apparent enemies had coalesced and Nietzscheanism had penetrated various circles
of socialism itself. The key to his following was Nietzsche's "neo-
cynicism."[94] It was simple to find substantiating Nietzschean texts; the
philosopher had written in *Beyond Good and Evil:* "Cynicism is the
only form in which base souls approach honesty; and the higher man
must listen closely to every coarse or subtle cynicism."[95] "Perhaps," he
wrote in *Untimely Meditations,* "no philosopher is more justified than
the Cynic; for the happiness of the animal, as the perfect Cynic, is the
living proof of the rightness of Cynicism."[96]

Nietzsche's intellectual bombs, Stein maintained, were capable of
blowing up "all our religious, moral, and political ideas" and his metaphysical joy in the act of destroying all cultural goods was a faithful
reflection of the cynicism of the times. The intoxicated response to
Nietzsche was another symptom of the fin-de-siècle's cynical reaction to
the oversatiation of culture.[97] That unholy army of Nietzschean neo-

92. "Moderne Sophistik: Ein Wort über den Nietzsche-Kultus," *Allgemeine Evange-
lisch-Lutherische Kirchenzeitung* 30 (1897). Quoted in Krummel, *Nietzsche,* vol. 1, 183.
93. A. Baumeister, "Friedrich Nietzsche, ein gefährlicher Verführer der heran-
wachsenden Jugend," *Lehrproben und Lehrgänge* 1 (1902), 2. Baumeister compared this
odious social democracy with the saving graces of Friedrich Naumann's "humanitarian
national socialism." See too the comparative, pro-Naumann work by Georg Biedekapp,
Friedrich Nietzsche und Friedrich Naumann als Politiker (Göttingen: Fritz Wunder,
1901).
94. Ludwig Stein, "Friedrich Nietzsche's Weltanschauung und ihre Gefahren,"
Deutsche Rundschau nos. 6, 8 (March, May 1893), especially no. 6, pp. 376, 380. By
locating him within the age-old tradition of cynicism Stein tried to take the sting out of
Nietzsche's originality.
95. Friedrich Nietzsche, *Beyond Good and Evil: Prelude to a Philosophy of the
Future,* trans. Walter Kaufmann (New York: Vintage, 1966), 38.
96. Nietzsche, "On the uses and disadvantages of history for life," in *Untimely Meditations,* 61.
97. For a late twentieth-century version of this theme, see Peter Sloterdijk, *Critique of
Cynical Reason,* trans. Michael Eldred (Minneapolis: University of Minnesota Press,

cynics (out to shock and subvert for its own sake) was particularly attracted to Nietzsche's use of the aphorism, that weakest of philosophical argumentations. Neither a consequential nor a logical mode of thinking, it was, Stein insisted, ideally suited to a confused mass age of newspaper production, socialist libraries, salons, and boudoirs.[98] Liberals and conservatives were not the only ones to be alarmed by the Nietzsche cults. Democrats and socialists of various hues similarly expressed their concern and sought in their polemics (often booklength!) to account for them and provide the necessary therapy consonant with their own ideological premises. Nietzscheanism, Georg Tantzscher argued as early as 1900, neatly fitted the needs of its acolytes, who all belonged to the free-floating intelligentsia. Nietzsche's indeterminate thought perfectly reflected the social condition of its articulators, caught as they were between isolation and a sense of mission, the drive to withdraw from society and the longing to lead it.[99] In Kurt Eisner's eyes Nietzscheans did not really require special explanation: they were simply modish radicals mindlessly attracted to fashions that appeared more modern and more extreme than the radicalisms of yesterday.[100] In his 1897 book on the Nietzsche cult, the sociologist Ferdinand Tönnies[101] went further than this and described Nietzscheanism as pseudoliberational. Those converted to the doctrine, he wrote, were captivated by the promise of the release of creative powers, the appeal to overcome narrow-minded authority and conventional opinions, and free self-expression.[102] It was important, there-

1987). Nietzsche is central in this work and discussed in terms of his own "decisive self-characterization," as

that of a "cynic" (*Cyniker*). . . . Nietzsche's "cynicism" (*Cynismus*) offers a modified approach to "saying the truth": It is one of strategy and tactics, suspicion and disinhibition, pragmatics and instrumentalism—all this in the hands of a political ego that thinks first and foremost about itself, an ego that is inwardly adroit and outwardly armored. (p. xxix)

98. Stein, "Nietzsche's Weltanschauung," 383.
99. Georg Tantzscher, *Friedrich Nietzsche und die Neuromantik: Eine Zeitstudie* (Jurjew [Dorpat]: J. G. Krueger, 1900), 5.
100. Eisner was referring to such literary Nietzscheans as Ola Hansson, Hermann Conradi, and O. J. Bierbaum; the philosophical excursions of Albert Kniepf; and Julius Langbehn's *völkisch* political tract, "Rembrandt als Erzieher," a title modeled after Nietzsche's "Schopenhauer as Educator."
101. For an excellent portrait of Tönnies and his intellectual and political development see Arthur Mitzman, *Sociology and Estrangement: Three Sociologists of Imperial Germany* (New York: Knopf, 1973).
102. Ferdinand Tönnies, *Der Nietzsche-Kultus: Eine Kritik* (Leipzig: O. R. Reisland, 1897), 10.

fore, to demonstrate that the modern, forward-looking feel and tone of Nietzsche was superficial. In an age of sharpened class differences, these apparently liberational impulses served elitist, conservative, and laissez-faire functions. For those who were not prepared to give up their inherited social position and were previously unable to justify it in moral or national terms, Nietzsche's immoralist notions of mastery and ruthlessness provided the necessary doctrine.[103] These and other followers were, as Tönnies entitled another publication, "Nietzsche nitwits."[104]

Other "democratic" opponents of the Nietzsche cult took issue with Tönnies. One such critic argued that while Junkers and industrialists might have used Nietzsche as a philosophical justification for their interests, very few did so because there was no way to translate his "comic and gruesome" ideas into reality. The ruling circles were too realistic to try. Moreover, Tönnies was mistaken to reduce Nietzscheanism to the Sturm-und-Drang impulses of the young. There was nothing political about Nietzsche and his appeal. The "psychology of the Nietzsche cult," was rather a form of sick decay, premature cynicism, and tired renunciation. This was the basis of Nietzsche's appeal to a youth that had been infected by the sickness of their times.[105] A little later, in 1908, in his book *The Nietzsche Cult: A Chapter in the History of Aberrations of the Human Spirit,* W. Becker argued for a multipurpose role for the various Nietzschean cults, although he too seem puzzled that so many cultured and intellectual circles were so attracted to the Nietzschean message.[106] Nietzsche appealed to youth because he seemed to provide a new and modish "depth." They did not, however, pick up on the brutalizing thematic as much as did a "whole row of German colonial officials in Africa" who employed Nietzsche's *herrenmoral* ideal as one suited perfectly to the colonial mode of rule, sanctioning the ruthless domination of "higher people" over those of lower rank. The Übermensch was rendered possible only by virtue of ruthless treatment of nonmembers of the elite.[107]

It is interesting to note that, unlike most of the conservative critics,

103. Ibid., 109–110.

104. Ferdinand Tönnies, *Ethische Kultur und ihr Geleite: [in der "Zukunft" und in der "Gegenwart"],* vol. 1, *Nietzsche-Narren,* vol. 2, *Wölfe in Fuchspelzen* (Berlin: F. Dümmler, 1893).

105. See Erich Schlaikjer, "Der Nietzsche-Kultus" and "Zur Psychologie des Nietzsche-Kultus" in *Die Hilfe 5,* nos. 10, 13 (5 March, 26 March 1899).

106. Becker, *Der Nietzschekultus,* 99.

107. Ibid., 6–7, 97.

many of the reform-minded opponents of the Nietzsche cult had a more complex relationship to Nietzsche. Dismissal of the cults did not necessarily entail outright dismissal of the philosopher himself. This certainly applies to Tönnies. Nietzsche's pivotal influence on turn-of-the-century German sociology has been analyzed in excellent recent scholarship.[108] What is relevant here, however, is that a major impulse behind Tönnies's famous and politically ambiguous dichotomy between *Gemeinschaft* and *Gesellschaft* was Nietzsche's early, communitarian *Birth of Tragedy*.[109] The organic nature of Dionysian, pre-Socratic, prerationalist community informed not only Tönnies's descriptive account of Gemeinschaft but also, following Nietzsche's critique of post-unification German political and cultural life, his hopes for its regeneration and rebirth.

In 1873 when he discovered *Birth of Tragedy*, Tönnies read it "almost with the feeling of a revelation" and thereafter wrote imaginary letters to the philosopher, visited his mother in Naumburg, and even traveled to Sils Maria where he saw his hero but was unable to summon the courage to speak to him![110] Tönnies's anti-Nietzscheanism was thus directed only at the later "immoralist" Nietzsche, his antisocial and radically individualized aestheticism, his elitism, and his contempt for the masses. The early Nietzsche, Tönnies proclaimed, was "a kind of democrat who still believed in the secret depths of the German popular spirit." As late as 1893, Tönnies could recommend to youth the *Birth of Tragedy* for there it was not isolated Übermenschen but a Dionysian Gemeinschaft that could serve as the inspirational basis for a revival of German culture.[111]

Interestingly, the great tragic ironist, Lebensphilosophie sociologist, and Nietzsche enthusiast Georg Simmel (1858–1918) constructed a diametrically opposed sociology—also inspired by Nietzsche. Simmel's career represented the translation of the modernist idiom into sociolog-

108. On the influence of Nietzsche's antiscientific bent on the special character of German sociology see Wolf Lepenies, *Between Literature and Science: The Rise of Sociology* (Cambridge: Cambridge University Press, 1988). I thank Jerry Muller for the latter reference. For the emphasis on the tragic in German sociology, see Harry Liebersohn, *Fate and Utopia in German Sociology, 1870–1923* (Cambridge, Mass., and London: MIT Press, 1988). See too Treiber, "Nietzsches 'Kloster,'" 141ff.
109. See Jürgen Zander, "Ferdinand Tönnies und Friedrich Nietzsche," in *Ankunft bei Toennies: Soziologische Beiträge zum 125. Geburtstag von Ferdinand Toennies*, ed. Lars Clausen and Franz Urban Pappi (Kiel: W. Mühlau, 1981), 185–227.
110. Liebersohn, *Fate and Utopia*, 23–24.
111. Tönnies, *Ethische Cultur*, 13–24. Quoted in Liebersohn, *Fate and Utopia*, 37–38.

ical language.[112] Like Nietzsche, Simmel dissolved all certainties into a
constantly shifting flux.[113] His most prized value, *Vornehmheit*, the
ideal of distinction, derived from Nietzsche.[114] As distinct from Tönnies's preoccupation with Gemeinschaft, Simmel regarded Vornehmheit
as the crucial mode by which individuals could be *separated* from the
crowd and endowed with "nobility." Here was an entirely new ideal
created by the challenge to maintain or create personal values in a
money economy. What was important here was the emphasis on difference and what Nietzsche had called "the pathos of distance."[115]
Distance—crucial to Simmel's very choice of topics such as the mediating links between domination and subordination, outsiders and
insiders[116]—was a function of growing complexity and also the social
precondition for this kind of Nietzschean Vornehmheit. It was small
wonder then that in 1897 Simmel critically reviewed Tönnies's
Nietzsche Cult. He angrily repudiated the accusation that Nietzsche
was simply an immoralist. Nietzsche had criticized traditional morality,
he argued, only in order to make way for a superior morality. Nietzsche
did urge for the pursuance of specific values—Vornehmheit, beauty,

112. This was apparent already in Simmel's *Über soziale Differenzierung* (Amsterdam: Liberae, [1890] 1966). See too K. Peter Etzkorn, ed., *Georg Simmel: The Conflict
in Modern Culture and Other Essays* (New York: Teachers College Press, 1968).
113. Georg Simmel, *Schopenhauer und Nietzsche: Ein Vortragszyklus* (Leipzig:
Duncker and Humblot, 1907). Simmel told Ernst Tröltsch that he considered this his most
important book (Tröltsch, *Gesammelte Schriften*, vol. 3 [Tübingen: J. C. B. Mohr,
1922]), 121. Quoted in Krummel, *Nietzsche*, vol. 2, 273, n. 234. On Simmel generally see
Liebersohn, *Fate and Utopia*, chap. 5, and Kurt H. Wolff's "Introduction" in *The Sociology of Georg Simmel* (New York: Free Press, 1950). For
a very critical antimodernist critique see Lukacs, *Destruction of Reason*, 442–458.
114. Simmel, *Schopenhauer und Nietzsche*, 170–192; see too Simmel's "Zum Verständnis Nietzsches," *Das freie Wort* 2 (1902–1903), 9ff.
115. Every enhancement of the type "man" has so far been the work of an
    aristocratic society—and it will be so again and again—a society that believes
    in the long ladder of an order of rank and differences in value between man
    and man, and that needs slavery in some sense or other. Without the *pathos
    of distance* which grows out of the ingrained difference between strata—
    when the ruling caste constantly looks afar and looks down upon subjects
    and instruments and just as constantly practices obedience and command,
    keeping down and keeping at a distance—that other, more mysterious pa-
    thos could not have grown up either—the craving for an ever-widening of
    distances within the soul itself, the development of ever higher, rarer, more
    remote, further-stretching, more comprehensive states—in brief, simply the
    enhancement of the type "man," the continual "self-overcoming of man," to
    use a moral formula in a supra-moral sense. From Nietzsche, *Beyond Good
    and Evil*, 201.
116. Klaus Lichtblau, "Das 'Pathos der Distanz': Präliminarien zur Nietzsche-
Rezeption bei Georg Simmel," in *Georg Simmel und die Moderne*, ed. Heinz-Jürgen
Dahme and Ottheim Rammstedt (Frankfurt am Main: Suhrkamp, 1984), 231–281.

strength—that enhanced life and which, far from encouraging egoism, demanded great self-control.[117]

The centrality and selective deployment of Nietzsche for the sociologies of Tönnies and Simmel has been well summarized by Harry Liebersohn:

> *Vornehmheit* could not have been further removed from *The Birth of Tragedy's* merging of wills in a homogeneous unity. It represented the later Nietzsche whose repudiation of feeling for others Tönnies could not abide. . . . Their conflicting moralities vied for the inheritance of the great immoralist: Tönnies's notion of the rational welfare of the whole versus Simmel's devotion to impersonal individual discipline. The early and late Nietzsche served as advocate for their conflicting ideals of *Gemeinschaft* and *Gesellschaft.*[118]

Although Tönnies's critique was animated by a socialist impulse, his analysis was not really Marxist. It was the playwright Paul Ernst in 1890 who probably penned the first critical Marxist analysis of both Nietzsche and his cultic public. Ernst (whose Marxism was not long-lived thereafter) wrote as a "dialectician" who saw Nietzsche as the "philosopher of decadence" and "brutality," a thinker who belonged "to that class of bourgeois decadents which stood in opposition to the achieved goals of bourgeois thought." His readership was similarly composed of these middle-class decadent elements—only to them were the disconnected essays and aphorisms intelligible. Nietzsche was "*Geistreich,* trivial, sloganizing in the worst sense."[119]

Later Marxist criticism tended to view Nietzscheanism as it served capitalism, imperialism, and afterwards, fascism. The leading theoretician of the Socialist Democratic Party (SPD), Franz Mehring, who pioneered much of this thinking, provided a simple materialist explanation for the cult and its motivations:

> Nietzscheanism is a healthy guzzle (*Fressen*) for the *literatus vulgaris,* one which tickles their ego-mania . . . provides a thrill and allows one to play a

---

117. Georg Simmel, "Der Nietzsche-Kultus," *Deutsche Literaturzeitung* 42 (23 October 1897), 1645–1651.

118. Liebersohn, *Fate and Utopia,* 142.

119. Paul Ernst, "Friedrich Nietzsche: Seine historische Stellung, seine Philosophie," *Freie Bühne* 1, nos. 18, 19 (4 June, 11 June 1890), 489ff, 516–520. With a change in politics came a change in Ernst's evaluation of Nietzsche as well. By 1900 he could describe Nietzsche as a "psychologist" whose importance resided not in his external historical position but in his capacity to provide the individual with joy and energy. With his questions concerning the nature and goal of life, Nietzsche had brought honor once again to philosophy (*Friedrich Nietzsche,* 2d ed. [Berlin: Gose and Tetzlaff, 1904]). See too Krummel, *Nietzsche,* vol. 2, 65.

little *Sturm und Drang,* but with all this—and this above all!—enables them under every circumstance to feast from the fleshpots of capitalism.[120]

Nietzscheans—and this was to be the authorized Marxist line throughout—were the ultimate in bourgeois pseudoradicalism, never touching the real bases of exploitation and always keeping the socio-economic structure and class distinctions firmly intact.

What was striking in many of the hostile assessments of the Nietzsche cult was the assertion that Nietzsche's legacy was certain to be short-lived. The cult of Nietzsche, it was generally thought, was explicable in terms of one aspect or another of the sociology or psychology of the Kaiserreich. Nietzscheanism itself possessed no lasting or paradigmatic qualities. It was merely symptomatic and ephemeral. Predictions of its imminent demise began in Nietzsche's own lifetime. Both the language and the content of Jürgen Habermas's remarkably unprescient 1968 declaration that Nietzsche was no "longer contagious" thus fitted into a long tradition.[121] The Catholic journal *Der Türmer* noted in 1910 that the fumes (*Dunstmasse*) of Nietzsche were detectable in the multitude of new *Weltanschauungen* that had mushroomed since his cometlike appearance. But the man who had proclaimed the death of God was now himself irrecoverably sunk in the grave. He was, indeed, a victim of his own followers:

> All Nietzsche disciples die separately; no two share the same opinion; everyone goes his own way. . . . Nietzsche is dead, totally dead, not because of his enemies but most of all through his own celebrators who slowly, but thoroughly, have made him cold.[122]

These chronic burials were always premature. As Nietzsche's relative Richard Öhler, a leading figure at the Nietzsche Archives and a later Nietzsche–Nazi publicist, wrote in his 1911 reply to *Der Türmer,* Nietzsche's influence was only beginning to take effect.[123] One had to

120. Franz Mehring, review of *Psychopathia Spiritualis* by Kurt Eisner, *Die Neue Zeit* 10 (1892), 668.

121. Jürgen Habermas, "Zur Nietzsches Erkenntnistheorie," in Friedrich Nietzsche, *Erkenntnistheoretische Schriften* (Frankfurt, 1968). Rep. in *Kultur und Kritik: Verstreute Aufsätze,* Jürgen Habermas (Frankfurt, 1973), 239–263. See too "Conservative Politics, Work, Socialism and Utopia Today," in *Autonomy and Solidarity: Interviews with Jürgen Habermas,* ed. Peter Dews, 131–147 (London: Verso, 1986). Habermas admits this prognosis was a mistake and addresses himself to Nietzsche's contemporary "virulent influence" (132–133).

122. F. Hermann, "Weltanschauungen und Nietzsche," *Der Türmer* 13, no. 2 (November 1910), 228.

123. Richard Öhler, "Ist Nietzsche wirklich tot?" *Der Türmer* 13, no. 4 (January 1911).

differentiate the deeper currents of the master, wrote the Nietzsche scholar Raoul Richter, from the superficial, ephemeral trivialization of the day. There was a world of difference between the philosopher and the raw, self-indulgent circles who had momentarily adopted him as hero for the day. (Richter himself exemplified the Nietzscheans in his tendency to dismiss competing interpretations and to argue for the depth and representativeness of his particular version.)

The pro-Nietzscheans were closer to the mark in arguing that Nietzsche was simply "unburiable." It was a grand misunderstanding, wrote the progressive critic Franz Serväs in 1895, to believe that one could "refute" and thereby "surpass" Nietzsche. Nietzsche was not a piece of learning but a part of life, a cry against individual and cultural inauthenticity. Nietzsche was "the reddest blood of our time" and although he was supposed to have died already a thousand times, it was not he who had died. "Oh, we shall still all have to drink from his blood! Not one of us will be spared that."[124]

This kind of existential–mythical language typified the discourse of Nietzsche worshipers. In this there was a kind of symmetry between the cult and the anticult. While discreditors employed the demonic–pathological mode, proponents typically indulged in the heroic–prophetic mode. Max Zerbst's 1892 vision of a "new God, a fresh, joyful earth God, a Siegfried in the realm of the spirit, a powerful super-courageous dragon-killer"[125] represented a counterversion in reply to Türck's mentally and morally insane Nietzsche.

Those who predicted a quick disappearance did not realize that it was precisely the fact that there was no uniformity of opinion or binding authoritative organization that ensured Nietzscheanism's long and varied life. Its elasticity and selective interpretive possibilities constituted its staying power and facilitated its infusion into so many areas of cultural and political life.

The Nietzsche Archives under the directorship of Nietzsche's sister, Elisabeth Förster-Nietzsche, was equally a collection of diverse personalities and interests, seemingly always beset by conflicts; its influence

124. Franz Serväs, "Kritik und Kunst," *Neue deutsche Rundschau* (1895), 165:

Nietzsche ist das röteste Blut unserer Zeit, und dieser ist dampfend vergossen worden auf dem Götzenalter der Zeit. Und da soll Nietzsche tot sein, selbst wenn er tausendmal gestorben wäre? Oh, wir werden noch alle trinkem muessen von seinem Blut! Keinem Einzigen von uns wird erspart bleiben.

125. Max Zerbst, *Nein und Ja! Antwort auf Dr. Hermann Türck's Broschüre Friedrich Nietzsche und seine philosophischen Irrwege* (Leipzig: C. G. Naumann, 1892). See too Krummel, *Nietzsche,* vol. 1, 110.

was never constitutive nor singular. Nevertheless, it did attempt to act as Nietzsche's official repositor, editor, and disseminator of his works and to institutionalize the cult, to build its monuments, to compose its liturgy and to organize its rituals and ceremonies. The choice of Weimar as its site was designed in part to enable it to compete with the self-styled protector of German spirituality at Bayreuth. Unlike Cosima Wagner's Bayreuth shrine to Richard, however, the identification of Nietzsche with Weimar and his sister was at best problematic. Nothing comparable to the unifying *Bayreuther Blätter* appeared. Moreover, Nietzsche admirers were often put off by Förster-Nietzsche's activities and what they considered to be the highly un-Nietzschean—provincial, conformist, sanitizing and petit bourgeois—atmosphere of the archives.[126] It would be a grave mistake, therefore, to confuse the history of Nietzscheanism in Germany with the history of the archives.[127]

Nevertheless, Förster-Nietzsche and her coworkers did play an important role in the popularization and monumentalization of the philosopher. The makers of the Nietzsche myth at the archives were always intensely aware of its cultic import. As one activist put it, this was no mere "archive" but a "house of creative powers." Visiting the Nietzsche house was not merely an activity but itself an *Erlebnis!* It was one thing to read Nietzsche in a dining car or a café and quite another to encounter him in Sils Maria or the archive.[128]

From its beginnings through the Nazi period the archives attempted to orchestrate the myth and liturgy around Nietzsche. Apart from its regular editorial and publishing activities, special meetings and memorial ceremonies relating to Nietzsche's life and death facilitated the mythologization.[129] Indeed, similar occasions were arranged to honor his sister's birthday (eliciting the scorn of liberal intellectuals, one of whom satirized her as an "Übermenschenkaffeekränzchen").[130]

126. This included some who also worked at the archives such as Rudolf Steiner and the Horneffer Brothers.
127. Equally distortive would be the total omission of its activities, which R. Hinton Thomas nevertheless manages (*Nietzsche in German Politics and Society*).
128. Richard Öhler, *Die Zukunft der Nietzsche-Bewegung* (Leipzig: Armanen, 1938), 12.
129. See, for instance, the varied and often heady contributions in *Zur Erinnerung an Friedrich Nietzsche* (Leipzig: Druck and C. G. Naumann, 1900). See too Spengler's speech, "Nietzsche and His Century."
130. For her sixtieth-birthday celebration see the report in the *Berliner Tageblatt* (25 July 1906), quoted in Krummel, *Nietzsche*, vol. 2, 252; Alfred Kerr's "Die Übermenschin" (*Tag* [27 July 1906]) is a poetic satire on these celebrations. See too the

Förster-Nietzsche's infamous role at the archives are by now quite familiar.[131] Here we need only mention the attempts to create an authorized Nietzsche, and the ways in which Förster-Nietzsche and her quick succession of associates attempted to construct definitive counterversions of Nietzsche and Nietzscheanism. Elisabeth's later notoriety should not blind us to her considerable early successes and the respect in which she was held. Despite the scandals and criticisms that her idealizations of her brother elicited,[132] for a considerable time large sections of the press regarded her version as trustworthy and portrayed her as the legitimate protector of the Nietzschean treasure, selflessly sacrificing herself on behalf of this holy mission.[133]

In her biography of Nietzsche and in countless articles[134] she sought both to depathologize the philosopher and to take the sting of subversion out of his ideas. She desired, above all, to make Nietzsche respectable. Here was a healthy and patriotic man, a selfless and loving brother, son, and friend. Friedrich Nietzsche was a saintlike figure, a man of both outward and inner beauty, sociable and convivial yet destined to loneliness by an incomprehending public, a staunchly patriotic Prussian who, in time of war, had rushed to his country's colors and had been wounded in the process.

Förster-Nietzsche tirelessly countered allegations that Nietzsche's collapse was the result of a sexual infection acquired when he was a student or of an inherited disease. On all sides the family was of fine stock, strong, and healthy. Nietzsche himself had been a robust child. His illness was the result of a riding accident exacerbated by his war experience when he contracted diphtheria. In previous years there had been no warning of mental illness. His great sensitivity was the result of the indifference and hostility around him. The mental collapse was due

proceedings honoring Förster-Nietzsche on her seventy-fifth birthday, *Den Manen Friedrich Nietzsches* (Munich: Musarion, 1921).

131. H. F. Peters, *Zarathustra's Sister: The Case of Elisabeth and Friedrich Nietzsche* (New York: Markus Wiener, 1985). Kaufmann's *Nietzsche* also contains an incisive analysis of her activities and notorious editorial practices.

132. Peters, *Zarathustra's Sister,* provides numerous examples of the conflicts, court cases, and scandals in which Förster-Nietzsche became involved. The accounts of her inability to take any criticism, editorial or otherwise—especially to accept even a hint that she was myth-making—as well as her tendency to believe that she was the victim of blaspheming conspiracies are legion. For just one instance of a public challenge to her rendering of Nietzsche and her role at the archives see Erdmann, "Vom Monopol auf Nietzsche," *Der Kunstwart* 20 (June 1907).

133. For a useful account of Förster-Nietzsche's role in the diffusion of the heroic myth of Nietzsche see Phillipi, "Das Nietzsche-Bild," the section entitled "Elisabeths Nietzsche-Mythos: Nietzsche als Halbgott."

134. For a full list see Krummel, *Nietzsche.*

to poisoning from an overdose of a dangerous sleeping medicine: chloral hydrate. This, she authoritatively maintained, was the only correct version of Nietzsche's illness.

These written works were only part of the story. In the drive to monumentalize Nietzsche into a towering national hero, the more accessible, publicly visible texture of the Nietzsche cult becomes apparent. The archives played an exclusive role for only there were there resources, space, and will to realize at least some of the many projects that were envisaged.

Nietzsche iconographers were faced with a problem endemic to all political appropriation of Nietzsche: reconciling his elitist components with mass functions, canalizing the individualism into some form of palatable community. Nietzscheanism, almost by definition, was a matter of transmuting—or dissolving—these tensions.

While Nietzschean preachers of power and beauty, like Georg Fuchs, Kurt Breysig, and Anthony Mario Ludovici,[135] sought to reconcile individual will and state authority, they also sought to externalize the Nietzschean unions of life and art, power and spirit. The various grand plans to construct Nietzsche stadiums, monuments, and temples, as Krause has convincingly shown, vividly demonstrates these tensions and attempted resolutions.

Many of these projects remained on the drawing board, including Fritz Schumacher's 1898 design of a round temple situated on lonely heights. On top of the temple Schumacher envisaged a figure with arms aloft, while beneath stood bowed dark giants in chains, symbolizing the ascent from *Sklavenmenschen* to *Höhermenschen* (illus. 7).

There were other striking reminders of the philosopher within the archives. A statue of the ill Nietzsche sat beneath a heroic representation of the philosopher with the Zarathustrian symbols of snake and eagle (illus. 8). Henry van de Velde, the famous Belgian architect, redesigned the archives (a project completed in 1903) representing the Nietzschean aesthetic in architectural terms by way of an optimistic, harmonious classicism. This reflected the earlier, more cosmopolitan group of Nietzscheans. Van de Velde's Nietzsche was essentially European, a champion of the higher redeeming values and of the regenerating powers of art and the spirit.

The post-Nazi imagination tends to confuse political architecture

135. Krause, *"Märtyrer" und "Prophet,"* 155. Ludovici's *Nietzsche and Art* (London: Constable, 1911) was a unique attempt to write a Nietzschean history of art in terms of rising aristocratic and decadent–democratic epochs.

and ceremonies with the Fascist bent. Yet in the case of Nietzscheanism the most monumental and grandiose of all plans came from the enlightened, cosmopolitan adherents. In 1911 van de Velde's associate, the patrician Count Kessler, envisaged the construction of a gigantic festival area, a memorial to Nietzsche consisting of a temple, a large stadium and a huge statue of Apollo. Thousands were intended to pour into this public space where art, dance, theater, and sports competition would be combined into a Nietzschean totality. For Kessler this was the literal translation of Nietzsche into mass activity.[136]

Many of the most cultivated "Europeans" regarded the idea as an inspired one. Kessler secured the agreement of Aristide Maillol to construct the statue of Apollo using Vaslav Nijinsky as the model. For his organizing and fund-raising committee Kessler was able to enlist international luminaries like Henri Lichtenberger, André Gide, Anatole France, Walther Rathenau, Gabriele d'Annunzio, Gilbert Murray and H. G. Wells, amongst others.[137] The project never got off the ground. At least one reason was Förster-Nietzsche's attitude. For a surprisingly long time she had supported the cosmopolitan activities of Kessler and van de Velde, even initially supporting this project. But the period of agreement had been coming to an end for some time. Although she only officially withdrew her support in 1913 she had expressed her reservations almost as the project was conceived: "The aping of Greekdom through this rich, idle mob from the whole of Europe is horror to me."[138]

This shift was indicative of the future of Nietzscheanism in Germany. Prior to 1914 it encompassed and fused—indeed, confused—a variety of political outlooks. It was constantly coined in a fluid and ambiguous liberational idiom that blurred conventional categories and defied easy judgments as to their political direction. With the Great War, as we shall see in chapter 5, the orientation became increasingly (though never exclusively) nationalist and later merged with a radical-right perspective.

All that, however, was still in the future. Prior to World War I the texture of Nietzscheanism appeared variegated. Individuals, groups,

---

136. See the description in Krause, *"Martyrer" und "Prophet,"* 199ff.

137. See Hartmut Pogge von Strandmann, ed., *Walther Rathenau: Industrialist, Banker, Intellectual, and Politician: Notes and Diaries 1907–1922,* trans. Caroline Pinder-Cracraft et al. (Oxford: Clarendon, 1985), 113, n. 107.

138. Harry Kessler to Hugo von Hoffmansthal, 16 April 1911, in *Hugo von Hofmannsthal–Harry Graf Kessler Briefwechsel 1898–1929,* ed. Hilde Burger (Frankfurt am Main: Insel, 1968), 323ff.

and movements attached themselves to one or another of these visions and sought in selective ways to make them an integral part of their lives. Many of these versions—ranging from the profound to the hopelessly prosaic—were at first to be found in the activities of the avant-garde. We therefore begin our analysis with an examination of Nietzschean impulses within that sector of German society.

CHAPTER III

The Not-So-Discrete Nietzscheanism of the Avant-garde

All ordered society puts the passions to sleep.
Nietzsche, *The Gay Science*

Over the years Nietzsche would influence many segments of German society. His initial and most explosive and enduring impact, however, was upon diverse circles of the intellectual, artistic, and literary avant-garde. This was well-nigh inevitable given their fin-de-siècle sense of foreboding crisis and transformational possibilities: their temperamental resonances and ideational affinities with the Nietzschean sensibility were palpable.

Nietzsche played a definitive role in the agenda of the avant-garde. He provided the basic epistemological tools of its modernist revolution and inspired its elitist, prophetic élan. His exhortation "to *be* something new, to *signify* something new, to *represent* new values"[1] was, as Count Kessler perceptively noted, emblematic of this Nietzschean generation.[2] The avant-garde found in Nietzsche sustenance for their alienation from the establishment's high culture and their desire to overcome the nineteenth century. He was a central force in the impulse to radical critique and the revolt against positivism and materialism. He was the major force behind its proclivity for Lebensphilosophie and its celebration of post-Enlightenment, irrationalist modalities.

As a rule these circles appropriated two elements that at best stood in tension with each other and at worst were flatly contradictory: the dynamic project of radical, secular self-creation and the Dionysian im-

---

1. Nietzsche, *Beyond Good and Evil*, 191.
2. Harry Kessler, *Gesichter und Zeiten: Erinnerungen* (Frankfurt am Main: Fischer, [1921] 1988), 210.

pulse of self-submersion. Almost all manifestations of the Nietzschean avant-garde reflected this tension, a tension of which many contemporary participants were quite aware. People like Ludwig Klages, for instance, explicitly insisted upon the negation of Nietzschean self-creation and the adoption of what he took to be the philosopher's Dionysian absorption of self. The most common response was, however, to either mute the tension or to seek in some way to fuse the individualistic and even antisocial impulse within the search for new forms of "total" community.

This salvationist Nietzschean impulse may strike a foreign note to those attuned to the poststructuralist Nietzsche of the late twentieth century who loudly heralds the illusory nature of all systems of truth and totality. Today's Nietzschean message is deconstructive, its canonic text the posthumously published 1873 fragment "On Truth and Lie in an Extra-Moral Sense":

> What then is truth? A mobile army of metaphors, metonyms, and anthropomorphisms—in short, a sum of human relations, which have been enhanced, transposed, and embellished poetically and rhetorically, and which after long use seem firm, canonical, and obligatory to a people: truths are illusions about which one has forgotten that this is what they are; metaphors which are worn out and without sensuous power.[3]

But a hundred years ago Nietzsche's modernist appropriators—while aware of the nihilist predicament they had inherited—concentrated on creative, positive reconstruction, enlisting Nietzsche as champion of sweeping visions of cultural and political redemption.[4] Notwithstanding the epistemological crisis, like Nietzsche himself, they stressed the expansive rather than self-subverting possibilities of new interpretations and drew up transvaluative programs of "regeneration"

3. Friedrich Nietzsche, "On Truth and Lie in an Extra-Moral Sense," in *Portable Nietzsche*, 46–47; 42–47.

. 4. Ernst Behler has pointed out that the deconstructionist Nietzsche leaves out the (more difficult) "positive reconstructive" tendencies of his work. "In fact, the deconstructive Nietzsche is a Nietzsche without *Zarathustra*" ("Nietzsche jenseits der Dekonstruktion," in *Nietzsche und die philosophische Tradition,* ed. Josef Simon, 88–107 [Würzburg: Königshausen and Neumann, 1985], 104). This point may, however, need qualification. Recent postmodernist Nietzsche scholarship, as Robert C. Solomon incisively points out, has turned to the problematic fourth book of Zarathustra which, unlike the earlier parts, does not discuss the conditions for the creation of new values but amounts to "an explosion of that very ambition" ("Nietzsche, Postmodernism, and Resentment: A Genealogical Hypothesis" in *Nietzsche as Postmodernist: Essays Pro and Contra,* ed. Clayton Koelb, 267–293 [Albany: State University of New York Press, 1990], 271; Daniel W. Conway, "Nietzsche contra Nietzsche: The Deconstruction of *Zarathustra*," in *Nietzsche as Postmodernist;* Kathleen Higgins, *Nietzsche's Zarathustra* [Philadelphia: Temple University Press, 1987] chap. 7).

designed to overcome this nihilism.[5] They advocated the formation of a new Übermenschlich type and pictured him in ways consonant with what they took to be the desiderata of a transformed future civilization. The details and content of such visions differed from Nietzschean to Nietzschean and it will be part of our task to delineate some of these major projects. These avant-garde projects tended to challenge and create alternatives to standard left–right, progressive–reactionary categories. In their various guises they eroded older certainties and created new eclectic combinations and possibilities of cultural, political, literary, and even sensual exploration.

Like Nietzsche himself, many of the aesthetic circles described in this chapter claimed to be nonpolitical, even antipolitical. Nietzsche's attraction for those interested in making life a work of art was self-evident. But their rejection of the banality of contemporary society and political life was itself political. All formulated some kind of critique of the status quo (even if it was limited to generalized indictments of the philistine mediocrity, the materialism and leveling forces of the day) and posited counterideals of power and culture, of individual and social life.

In the 1890s Nietzsche's writings began to appear regularly in literary and experimental journals such as *Die Gesellschaft*[6] and became a prominent part of the German avant-garde's conceptual armory. The eclectic excitement, the search for authenticity, and the feelings of superiority and momentous discovery still impressed these countercultural participants many years later: "What I was engaged in," recalled Ernst Blass of café life in imperial Berlin,

---

5. Nietzscheans liked to stress the liberational aspects contained in the will to power rather than the epistemological dangers of perspectivism. Both were present in *The Will to Power*:

That the value of the world lies in our interpretation; . . . that previous interpretations have been perspective valuations by virtue of which we can survive in life, i.e., in the will to power, for the growth of power; that every elevation of man brings with it the overcoming of narrower interpretations; that every strengthening and increase of power opens up new perspectives and means believing in new horizons—this idea permeates my writings. The world with which we are concerned is false; . . . it is 'in flux,' as something in a state of becoming, as a falsehood always changing but never getting near the truth: for—there is no 'truth' (p. 330).

6. Founded in 1885, *Die Gesellschaft*'s editor, Michael Georg Conrad (1846–1927), was a convinced although discriminating Nietzschean. His journal was often similarly nuanced. Discussions and reviews of Nietzsche—as well as poems and songs dedicated to him—by Leo Berg, G. Ludwigs, A. Sommerfeld, Joseph Steinmayer, Martha Asmus, and Robert Klein were featured. It also originally published Eisner's "Friedrich Nietzsche und die Apostel der Zukunft: Beiträge zur modernen Psychopathia spiritualis" (vol. 7 [November, December 1891], 1505–1536, 1600–1664).

... was ... a war on the gigantic philistine of those days. ... Yes, it was a spirited battle against the soullessness, the deadness, laziness, and meanness of the philistine world. ... Soul was still worth something. ... Even the timid and the silent learned how to talk and express themselves, learned to recognize what it was they really felt deeply about it. ... What was in the air? Above all Van Gogh, Nietzsche, Freud too, and Wedekind. What was wanted was a post-rational Dionysos.[7]

Like psychoanalysis (itself still an avant-garde phenomenon) Nietzscheans explored the irrational depths; they too were fascinated with the murky areas of the unconscious. Freud's complex, highly ambivalent personal relationship to the philosopher is well known. He denied in any way being influenced by Nietzsche—indeed, purposely avoided reading him in order to keep his mind free from such influence. Yet this great explorer of the unconscious stated several times that Nietzsche "had a more penetrating knowledge of himself than any other man who had ever lived or was likely to live."[8] There were thematic affinities between Freud and Nietzsche. Both sought to banish teleological and metaphysical explanation and engaged in unmasking activities; both stressed "self-creation" (even if they understood the process differently). Both, as Jung noted, formulated profound critiques of their times, both were answers "to the sickness of the nineteenth century."[9]

For purposes of our study, however, the differences are as important as the similarities. Various commentators have pointed out that with Freud the unconscious was democratized: the "self-making" project was not limited, as in Nietzsche, to an elect few.[10] Moreover, unlike Nietzsche and his followers, Freud insisted on conducting his explora-

7. Ernst Blass, "The old Cafe des Westens," in *The Era of German Expressionism*, ed. Paul Raabe, trans. J. M. Ritchie (London: Calder & Boyars), 29.

8. Ernest Jones, *The Life and Work of Sigmund Freud*, vol. 2, *Years of Maturity 1901–1919* (New York: Basic, 1955), 343ff. For a detailed examination of Freud's relationship to Nietzsche see Henri F. Ellenberger, *The Discovery of the Unconscious: The History and Evolution of Dynamic Psychiatry* (New York: Basic, 1970), 271ff and the excellent article by Lorin Anderson, "Freud, Nietzsche" in *Salmagundi* 47–48 (Winter-Spring 1980).

9. C. G. Jung, *Nietzsche's "Zarathustra,"* vol. 2, 1354, n. 8. See also "The Contingency of Selfhood," chapter 3 in Richard Rorty's *Contingency, Irony and Solidarity* (Cambridge: Cambridge University Press, 1989).

10. Phillip Rieff, *Freud: The Mind of the Moralist* (New York: Harper & Row, 1961), 36.

For Freud, nobody is dull through and through, for there is no such thing as a dull unconscious. What makes Freud more useful and plausible than Nietzsche is that he does not relegate the vast majority of humanity to the status of dying animals. For Freud's account of unconscious fantasy shows us how to see every human life as a poem, . . . as an attempt to clothe itself in its own metaphors. (Rorty, *Contingency*, 35–36)

tions within a "scientific" frame (despite the clear indications that he went far beyond the normal conventions of nineteenth-century positivism). For Jung, of course, it was precisely Freud's individualist–rationalist bent that made Nietzsche the more incisive thinker, more attuned to the deeper realities:[11]

> It is a great discovery that below or aside from one's psyche, or consciousness, or mind, is another intelligence of which one is not the maker, and upon which one depends. You see, Freud's great fear is that there may be something outside which is not "I"; to say there is a greater intelligence outside of one's own mind means that one must be crazy. Like Nietzsche. Unfortunately for Freud, Nietzsche was not the only one who had such thoughts; it was the conviction of all the thousands of years before Nietzsche, that man's intelligence was not the last word, that even his mind was the result of something behind the screen—that we are not the makers, but we are made. Your mind is not the creative god that makes a whole world jump into existence out of nothing. There is a preparation. There is, prior to consciousness, an unconscious out of which consciousness once arose, and that is an intelligence which surely exceeds our intelligence in an indefinite way.[12]

For Freudians like Arnold Zweig, however, it was just this desire to harness and treat the unconscious as much as to comprehend it which gave Freud the clear edge over Nietzsche—and presumably Jung! Zweig pointedly named his 1936 essay on Freud's life and achievements "Apollo Masters Dionysos."[13] Even earlier he had penned a comparative analysis in a letter to Freud:

> To me it seems that you have achieved everything that Nietzsche intuitively felt to be his task, without his being really able to achieve it with his poetic idealism and brilliant inspirations. He tried to explain the birth of tragedy; you have done it in *Totem and Taboo*. He longed for a world beyond Good and Evil; by means of analysis you have discovered a world to which this phrase actually applies. Analysis has reversed all values, it has conquered

---

11. Nietzsche was, however, at times accused of being too "materialist," especially in his belief that humans invented values capable of transcending the instinctual realm. In that sense both Freud and Nietzsche were deemed guilty:

> It was that old euhemeristic hypothesis that man has invented the gods. So [Nietzsche] followed on in the idea that man has invented morality. That was the materialistic view of his age. And you see, that is Freud's chief prejudice. He thinks man has invented something which can repress an instinct. Of course nothing can repress an instinct except another instinct; it is a conflict of instincts.

Jung, *Nietzsche's "Zarathustra,"* vol. 1, 649–650.
12. Ibid., 370–371.
13. A. Zweig, "Apollon bewältigt Dionysos," *Das Neue Tagebuch*, 18 (1936).

Christianity, disclosed the true Antichrist, and liberated the spirit of resurgent life from the ascetic ideal.

Analysis has reduced the will to power to what lies at its basis. . . . And thanks to the fact that you are a scientist, and furthermore a psychologist who advances step by step, you have attained what Nietzsche would so gladly have achieved himself: the scientific description and explanation of the human soul—and, more than that, since you are a physician, you have taught and created the possibility of influencing and curing it.[14]

While psychoanalysis strained to attain respectability, Nietzscheanism reveled in notoriety, much to the consternation of its more level-headed followers.[15] Nietzschean immoralism, the attacks on conscience and praise of criminal "health of soul,"[16] provided deliciously subversive intimations for an overt attack on middle-class respectability and the possibilities of lawless liberation. As one enthusiast put it: "Today, I believe, one sends the best and the strongest to the jails." It was there that the selection of tomorrow's Übermensch should begin.[17]

With their stridently antiscientific, antirationalist bent and their wild Dionysian rhetoric the novels, poems, and polemics of the literary Nietzscheans sought to unleash the immoralist possibilities of the unconscious.[18] In Italy, Gabriele d'Annunzio (1863–1938), future leader of the first Fascist republic at Fiume, wrote novels (*The Triumph of Death* [1894]; *The Virgin of the Rocks* [1895]) in which the Mediterranean Übermensch discovers his hidden self through the experience of the perverse, the exotic, and an exquisite lust for death. By 1899 d'Annunzio had been translated into German, but well before then Germany had produced a literature with similar themes.[19] The hero of

14. Ernst Freud, ed., *The Letters of Sigmund Freud and Arnold Zweig* (New York: Harcourt Brace, 1970), 23–24.

15. Of these turn-of-the-century circles a dismayed Mann wrote in 1918: "They innocently believed him [Nietzsche] to be the 'immoralist' he called himself; they did not see that this descendant of Protestant ministers had been the most sensitive moralist who ever lived, a morally possessed man" (*Reflections*, 398).

16. *Will to Power*, 223; see too Friedrich Nietzsche, *Daybreak: Thoughts on the Prejudices of Morality*, trans. R. J. Hollingdale, intro. Michael Tanner (Cambridge: Cambridge University Press, 1982), 18, 100–101, 164.

17. Leo Berg, *Der Übermensch in der modernen Literatur* (Paris, Leipzig, Munich: Albert Langen, 1897), 269ff. Quoted in Treiber, "Nietzsche's 'Kloster,'" 149, n. 39.

18. The catalogue of writers who introduced Nietzschean themes into their work is large. Amongst the better-known ones were Hermann Bahr, Richard Dehmel, Albert Kniepf and Karl Henckell.

19. *Der Triumph des Todes* appeared in 1899 (Berlin: S. Fischer). His "In Memoriam Friedrich Nietzsche" was also translated (Leipzig: Insel, 1906); it stressed Nietzsche as "a son of the Greeks" and the "barbarian" element. See too Robert E. McGinn, "Verwandlungen von Nietzsches Übermenschen in der Literatur des Mittelmeerraumes: D'Annunzio, Marinetti und Kazantzakis," *Nietzsche-Studien* 10/11 (1981/1982), 599.

Hermann Conradi's 1887 novel *Phrasen,* for instance, is a self-conscious Nietzschean who believes that the innocence he longs for will arise from his great passion for a prostitute.[20] At the same time there appeared a slew of feminist novels—such as Mathieu Schwann's *Liebe* (1901)—preaching a Zarathustrian poetics of love and a longing for sexual liberation.[21]

This radical Nietzschean libertarianism and emancipating eroticism was not limited to literary fiction. For some it was actualized into a determined alternative lifestyle conducted outside and against the mainstream. The story of the infamous Otto Gross (1877–1920) encapsulates some of its more extreme tendencies. Gross was himself an early brilliant psychoanalyst who hardly fit into the conventional framework of analysis and quickly dissented from some of its hardening orthodoxies. A drug addict, bohemian, sexual and cultural revolutionary, anarchist, and paranoiac, he was the sworn enemy of what he regarded as the repressive, authoritarian, patriarchal order of his day.[22] That order was embodied in his father, a renowned positivist criminologist. The two stood for diametrically and generationally opposed visions of the world. Their conflict created a public sensation when the newspapers announced that the father had incarcerated the son in an insane asylum!

Like many emergent Nietzscheans, Gross's ideas could not be fitted into any conventional framework. His prescription for emancipation blended Nietzsche with an idiosyncratic rendering of psychoanalysis and Johann Bachofen's matriarchy.[23] For Gross the task of the unconscious was to act as the ferment of revolt within the psyche. "The psychology of the unconscious," Gross proclaimed,

> is the philosophy of revolution . . . the incomparable transvaluation of all values, with which the coming time will be filled, begins in the present with the thought of Nietzsche on the background of the soul [*über die Hinter-*

20. See the incisive comments by R. A. Nicholls, "Beginning of the Nietzsche Vogue in Germany," *Modern Philology* 56 (1958).

21. See too Grete Meisel-Hess's 1911 novel, *Die Intellektuellen.*

22. For a more complete exposition of Gross's life and thinking see chapter 1 of Martin Green's fascinating *Mountain of Truth: The Counterculture Begins: Ascona, 1900–1920* (Hanover and London: University Press of New England, 1986). The following account also borrows from Russell Jacoby's *The Repression of Psychoanalysis: Otto Fenichel and the Political Freudians* (Chicago and London: University of Chicago Press, 1986), 40–45. Jacoby's demonstration of the repressed radical and Marxist roots of psychoanalysis also indicates some of its Nietzschean connections.

23. For Bachofen's views on matriarchy, see Uwe Wesel, *Der Mythos vom Matriarchat* (Frankfurt am Main: Suhrkamp, 1980).

gründe der Seele] and with the discovery of the so-called psychoanalytic technique through Freud.[24]

Jung, Gross's analyst, described to Freud his patient's outlook thus: "The truly healthy state for the neurotic is sexual immorality. Hence he associates you with Nietzsche."[25]

Like Nietzsche, Gross was especially concerned with the strong, exceptional individual. The status quo, he argued, clearly allowed such strong personalities no possibility of self-fulfillment. Capitalist society rendered them pathological because it allowed them no scope for what amounted to extravagant forms of self-realization. Nietzsche had recognized this conflict between the individual and society and thus founded "the discipline of biological sociology."[26] Nietzsche, Gross declared, understood that such contradictions led "to the elimination of precisely the healthiest and strongest individuals—those gifted with the greatest tendencies towards expansion—by reprisals on the part of the general public, to a negative selection, and hence to a decline of the race, to a progressive growth of hereditary degeneration."[27]

Gross is still described today as a Nietzschean.[28] Yet his case makes clear that more often than not Nietzscheanism became a force precisely because it did not operate as a discrete, defined system. It could be easily integrated into broader theories and dissenting moods, where it was only one element in a melange of influences. Nietzscheanism operated well in syncretistic political and ideological contexts. Gross joyfully mated Marx, Bachofen, Freud, and Nietzsche, oblivious to their differences, and selectively honed in upon their common antirepressive, life-affirming, and revolutionary thematics.[29]

Extreme and idiosyncratic though he may have been, Gross operated

24. Otto Gross, "Zur Überwindung der kulturellen Krise," *Die Aktion: Wochenschrift für Politik, Literatur und Kunst* 3 (6 December 1913), 384ff.

25. Jung to Freud (25 September 1907), *The Freud/Jung Letters* (Princeton, N.J.: Princeton University Press, 1974), 90.

26. Wolfgang Schwentker, "Passion as a Mode of Life: Max Weber, the Otto Gross Circle and Eroticism," in *Max Weber and his Contemporaries,* ed. Wolfgang J. Mommsen and Jürgen Osterhammel, 483–498 (London: German Historical Institute, 1989), 484.

27. Otto Gross, "Die Einwirkung der Allgemeinheit auf das Individuum," in *Von geschlechtlicher Not zur sozialen Katastrophe,* ed. K. Krieler (Frankfurt, 1980), 17. Quoted in Schwentker, "Passion as a Mode of Life," 485.

28. Eric Hobsbawm, *The Age of Empire 1875–1914* (New York: Vintage, 1989), p. 214.

29. While Gross's Marxist ideas were not as noticeable as his anarchist, Freudian, and Nietzschean impulses, this did not prevent the journal *Sowjet* (May 1920) from eulogizing Gross as a spiritual proletarian: "Otto Gross had to starve in a bourgeois world, because the logic of his life, which diametrically opposed the logic of that world, would have it so" (quoted in Green, *Mountain of Truth,* 47–48).

within the context of a small but significant pre–World War I counter-culture. There was even an Otto Gross circle which, in the words of Marianne Weber, "questioned the validity of universally binding norms of action and either sought an 'individual law' or denied any 'law' so as to let only *feeling* influence the flow of life."[30]

Like much of pre–World War I libertarian Nietzscheanism, this had a decidedly international flavor, crossing borders as easily as it did political and intellectual orthodoxies. Martin Green has recently reminded us that perhaps the most noteworthy home for such counter-cultural projects was located in the small Swiss village of Ascona where Gross was a familiar figure. There some remarkable feminists, pacifists, literary figures, anarchists, modern dancers, and surrealists came together to develop their radical ideas and to conduct diverse "life-experiments." Ascona was part Tolstoyan and part anarchist with a decidedly naturalist, at times even occult, orientation.[31] Amongst the better-known luminaries involved were D. H. Lawrence, Franz Kafka, Jung, and Hermann Hesse.

Nietzscheanism commingled with all these tendencies without necessarily operating as a separate program. It played a more subtle role as an inspirational subtext, a pervasive atmospheric presence. Insofar as the nature of that presence can be identified it was certainly not the masculine and heroic Nietzsche that Asconans stressed. They were not will-to-power but Dionysian Nietzscheans who aspired to a kind of ecstatic dynamism. They sought to create beauty in motion and to affirm life-creating values—above all that of eros. The Asconan search for eros and beauty, for freeing the body and soul in motion, found its most dynamic physical expression in the idea and development of modern dance. Here the notions of self-creation and Dionysian community could fuse.

Dance was the area where Ascona contributed most enduringly to the development of European high culture. In this endeavor the Nietzschean impulse was crucial. Asconans did not envisage dance as a fragmented specialty but as part of a greater totality and as an essential element of revolt against the repressive physical and mental constraints of bourgeois society.

In *Zarathustra* Nietzsche wrote: "And we should consider every day

---

30. Quoted in Schwentker, "Passion as a Mode of Life," 485.
31. Occult circles in general approved of Nietzsche, citing his deeply religious nature. See the horoscope with detailed illustrations in Friedrich Schwab, "Hinter den Kulissen: Friedrich Wilhelm Nietzsche," *Zentralblatt für Okkultismus: Monattschrift zur Erforschung der Gesamten Geheimwissenschaften* 1 (1907/1908).

lost on which we have not danced at least once."[32] Long before this he had linked cultural and political regeneration with aesthetics. Both dance and the dancer figured centrally as sensuous incarnations of his liberational vision. *The Birth of Tragedy* conceived of the dancer as one in whom all productive power was contained, and included one godlike dancer who was himself transformed into a work of art. Rudolf Laban (1879–1958) was the moving force behind Asconan applications of this vision. His case illustrates the essential open-endedness of this Dionysian Nietzscheanism, a political ambiguity that could lead equally into right-wing as much as anarchist modes of redemption. Contemporaries regarded Laban as the incarnation of modern dance, a man who cast himself as the bearded Dionysian satyr. He thought of himself as apolitical, yet his utopian aim was the re-creation of communitarian collective ecstasy very close to the vision of *The Birth of Tragedy* with its rejection of human fragmentation into separate and alienated individuals. He posited life as a kind of perpetual festival, "at which [all] are participants in communal thinking, feeling, and doing."[33] His total commitment to dance, his notion that it would regenerate life as a whole, was a mode of putting the early Nietzsche into practice.

Precisely because the emphasis here was not on form but on expressiveness and on the generalized ideal of community without specifying its content, Laban's *Birth of Tragedy* collectivity could find expression in both the Asconan and the National Socialist context. Initially Laban was able to move with relative ease from one to the other. In 1934 he became director of the *Deutsche Tanzbühne* in Nazi Germany. The same dynamic notions that had given shape to his Asconan libertarianism were now simply nationalized. On 20 June 1936 twenty thousand people watched Laban's massive dance display for the Eleventh Olympic Games, entitled "Of the warm wind and the new joy," and based upon Nietzschean themes and a text from *Also Sprach Zarathustra*. The Nazis were suspicious of Laban's "free" creations and before the major performance of this display he was declared *Staatsfeindlich*.[34]

Asconan dance and a species of Nietzschean feminist radicalism also seemed to fit together. The Asconan dancer and close associate of Laban, Mary Wigman, was a keen reader of Nietzsche. Her ecstatically possessed (some said demonic) dancing—discharging tension through

32. Nietzsche, *Thus Spoke Zarathustra*, 322.
33. Rudolf Laban, *Ein Leben für den Tanz* (Leipzig, 1935), 172. Quoted in Green, *Mountain of Truth*, 102.
34. Ibid., 110–111.

whirling, jerking, and thrusting movements—was explicitly Dionysian, much of it done to the drumming and recitation of *Zarathustra*.[35] Associates regarded her as a feminist realization of the Nietzschean programme of autonomous self-creation. "Mary Wigman is creative. A woman who forms great art out of her own body. She is not accommodation to men. She is sovereign women."[36] She too moved with relative ease from one form of radicalism to another. Wigman's dancing, Laban wrote in 1934, was German precisely because it stressed expression and not form, and in 1935 both Wigman and Laban demanded an art that would be linked to German myth.

Avant-garde dance and feminist-erotic Nietzscheanism easily crossed frontiers. Isadora Duncan, who Karl Federn described as the incarnation of Nietzsche's intuition,[37] was also an Asconan devotee. Together with Federn, the dancer ecstatically first read Nietzsche in Berlin in 1902: "The seduction of Nietzsche's philosophy ravished my being."[38] Indeed, her memoirs spoke of Nietzsche as "the first dancing philosopher"[39] and opened with his motto: "If my virtue be a dancer's virtue, and if I have often sprung with both feet into golden-emerald rapture, and if it be my Alpha and Omega that everything heavy shall become light, everybody a dancer and every spirit a bird: verily that is my Alpha and Omega."[40] In her 1903 lecture, "The Dance of the Future," the Asconan devotee summed up her vision of a transvalued superwoman in clearly Nietzschean terms: "Oh, she is coming, the dancer of the future: more glorious than any woman who has yet been: more beautiful than the Egyptian, than the Greek, than the early Italian, than all women of past centuries—the highest intelligence in the freest body!"[41]

35. Of these experiments one observer noted disapprovingly the "drumming and dancing to Nietzsche. However, what mattered more to us than the primitive writhing of their beautiful souls was some form of dynamic action against the boring repetitiveness in art and disgust at deep-rooted senile tradition." Christian Schad, "Zurich/Geneva: Dada," in *The Era of German Expressionism*, 163.

36. Rudolf von Delius, *Mary Wigman* (Dresden, 1925), 32. Quoted in Green, *Mountain of Truth*, 193.

37. Karl Federn, "Introduction," in Isadora Duncan, *Der Tanz der Zukunft* (Leipzig: E. Diederichs, 1903), 7. Not surprisingly it was Eugen Diederichs who published this lecture. He was an ardent supporter of the dance movement which he regarded as part of the overall regenerative thrust away from the overurbanized, alienating elements of imperial Germany (Green, *Mountain of Truth*, 171–172).

38. Isadora Duncan, *My Life* (New York: Liveright, 1942), 141.

39. Ibid., 341.

40. Nietzsche, *Thus Spoke Zarathustra*, 6.

41. Duncan was combining Nietzsche with Wagner and his "music of the future." Quoted in Green, *Mountain of Truth*, 169.

Without doubt the most exotic example of such radicalism was Valentine de Saint Point (1875–1953), author of the outrageous 1913 "Futurist Manifesto of Lust." The great-granddaughter of Alphonse de Lamartine, she was a theorist and practitioner of dance, and presented her own creations at the Theatre du Champs-Elysees in 1913 and the Metropolitan Opera House in 1917. The manifesto that de Saint Point addressed in part "to those women who only think what I have dared to say," was almost a parody of eclectic, erotic–liberationist Nietzscheanism. In this vision women represent "the great galvanizing principle to which all is offered":

> Lust when viewed without moral preconceptions and as an essential part of life's dynamism, is a force.
> Lust is not, any more than pride, a mortal sin for the race that is strong. Lust, like pride, is a virtue that urges one on, a powerful source of energy.
> Lust is . . . the sensory and sensual synthesis that leads to the greatest liberation of spirit. . . .
> Lust is the act of creating, it is Creation. . . .
> Christian morality alone, following on from pagan morality, was fatally drawn to consider lust as a weakness. Out of the healthy joy which is the flowering of the flesh in all its power it has made something shameful and to be hidden, a vice to be denied. It has covered it with hypocrisy, and this has made a sin of it. . . .
> *We must make lust into a work of art.*[42]

Not even the most outspoken Nietzschean women working in the organized framework of German feminism would have dreamed of advocating what her manifesto proposed: "A strong man must realize his full carnal and spiritual potentiality. The satisfaction of their lust is the conquerors' due. After a battle in which men have died, *it is normal for the victors, to turn to rape in the conquered land, so that life may be re-created.*"[43]

In addition to being a dancer de Saint Point was a playwright, poet, and novelist whose subjects included war, death, instinct, and female desire. Her "Manifesto of the Futurist Woman" (1912) demonstrated clearly her Nietzschean bent.[44] There she translated the notion of the Übermensch into a new myth of the masculinized superwoman. It was absurd, she contended, to divide humanity into men and

42. Valentine de Saint Point, "Futurist Manifesto of Lust 1913," in *Futurist Manifestos,* ed. Umbro Apollonio (London: Thames and Hudson, 1973), 70–74.
43. Ibid., 71.
44. This manifesto is reprinted in *Futurism and Futurisms* (New York: Abbeville, 1986), 602–603.

women. In fact, the division was between masculinity and femininity. The complete being, the hero and the Übermensch, definitionally combined the two: "An exclusively male individual is nothing but a brute; an exclusively female is nothing but weakness." But, as de Saint Point's male futurist counterparts agreed, one was living in an essentially weak, feminine historical period: masculinity was lacking in both men and women. For both a new doctrine of energy had to be taught so that an epoch of superior humanity could be reached. For both it was "the brute who must become the model." Femininity was now certainly not desirable. Women had allowed themselves to be tamed: "But call out a new word to her, give her a war cry and with joy she will ride again on her instinct and lead you towards undreamed-of conquests. . . . *Let women rediscover her own cruelty and violence that make her turn on the beaten, just because they are vanquished,* and mutilate them."

This Nietzschean dynamic was, of course, rather difficult to sustain and, after leaving the futurist movement in early 1914, de Saint Point became attracted to esotericism, moved to Egypt, converted to Islam (where she took the name of Raouhya Nour el Dine), and became an Arab nationalist, launching the newspaper *Le Phoenix* in its support![45]

Futurism was, of course, an Italian modernist, nationalist movement that heavily harnessed Nietzsche.[46] Imperial Germany possessed no equivalent avant-garde and proto-Fascist celebration of speed and technology. Only during the Weimar Republic did such a machine-oriented, radical nationalism make itself apparent.[47] Of course, modernism did not necessarily entail any particular attitude toward industrial society. Its Nietzsche-influenced characteristics—the radical questioning of all received canons; its expressive rather than mimetic posture; its belief that truth, values and beauty were self-created rather than objectively discovered entities—could and did operate in both directions: as exhuberant celebration and as alienated condemnation of the modern technological world. Prior to 1914 German modernism expressed itself in the peculiar guise of expressionism, a movement whose relationship to

45. Ibid., 562.
46. For an encyclopaedic overview of futurism and its Nietzschean connections, see ibid.
47. Jeffrey Herf, *Reactionary Modernism: Technology, Culture, and Politics in Weimar and the Third Reich* (Cambridge: Cambridge University Press, 1984).

the industrial-technological order was significantly more ambivalent than that of Futurism.[48]

In virtually every one of its manifold guises—painting, sculpture, architecture, literature, drama, and politics—expressionism and Nietzsche were linked. While there were some exceptions, most expressionists were—in some way and degree—either acknowledged Nietzscheans or Nietzscheans by osmosis.[49] The most talented and problematic German expressionist, Gottfried Benn, retrospectively summed up the relationship thus:

> Actually, everything that my generation discussed, dissected in its deepest thoughts—one can say suffered through; one can say: enlarged upon—all of that had already been expressed and explored, had already found its definitive formulation in Nietzsche; everything thereafter was exegesis. His treacherous, tempestuous, lightning manner, his feverish diction, his rejection of all idylls and all general principles, his postulation of a psychology of instinctual behavior as a dialectic—"knowledge as affect," all of psychoanalysis and Existentialism. They were all his achievements. As is becoming increasingly clear, he is the great giant of the post-Goethean era.[50]

For expressionists, Nietzschean epistemology was liberating in that it rendered metaphysical truth and objective reality as little more than illusions. Kurt Pinthus, editor of the important expressionist anthology *Menschheitsdämmerung*, put it thus: "Reality is not outside us, but

---

48. The work by Walter H. Sokel, *The Writer in Extremis: Expressionism in Twentieth-Century German Literature* (Stanford: Stanford University Press, 1959) remains definitive.

49. For the movement's effect on architecture see Wolfgang Pehnt, *Expressionist Architecture*, 41–43, 80, 82. Expressionist artists often portrayed Nietzsche himself. Eduard Munch painted him and Otto Dix sculpted him (Krause, "*Martyrer*" *und* "*Prophet*," illus. 23, 31). For a discussion of some Nietzschean–expressionist links see Stephen Eric Bronner and Douglas Kellner, eds., *Passion and Rebellion: The Expressionist Heritage* (New York: J. F. Bergin, 1983). Nietzsche appears throughout but see especially chaps. 1, 8. Nietzsche's osmotic influence has been argued in Wolfgang Paulsen, *Georg Kaiser: Die Perspektiven seines Werkes* (Tübingen: M. Niemeyer, 1960), 104. Various monographs have been written on the relationship between individual expressionists and Nietzsche (G. C. Tuntall, "The Turning Point in Georg Kaiser's Attitude toward Friedrich Nietzsche," *Nietzsche-Studien* 14 [1985]; H. W. Reichert, "Nietzsche und Carl Sternheim," *Nietzsche-Studien* 1 [1972]). Surprisingly, Hinton Thomas includes virtually nothing of the expressionists even though he had written a book himself on the subject in which Nietzsche was a prominent feature (Richard Samuel and R. Hinton Thomas, *Expressionism in German Life, Literature and the Theatre (1910–1924)* [Cambridge: W. Heffer and Sons, 1939]).

50. Gottfried Benn, "Nietzsche: Nach fünfzig Jahren," in *Gesammelte Werke*, vol. 1, ed. Dieter Wellershoff (Stuttgart: Klett-Cotta, 1962), 482. Translated in Roy F. Allen, *Literary Life in German Expressionism and the Berlin Circles* (Ann Arbor, Mich.: University of Michigan Research Press, 1983), 26.

rather in us. . . . All the great ideas of mankind did not engender themselves through the force of the facts, not through the demands of reality, but rather immediately out of the self-creative, future-directed spirit of man."[51] Nevertheless, the crisis was there and no one comprehended its depth more acutely than did Benn. He recognized that the Nietzschean world was post-theist and nihilist, one in which no system or philosophy was possible—or even desirable. Indeed, early on he had outlined the themes that were to become the province of late twentieth-century Nietzscheans. Nietzsche, he wrote, had destroyed philosophy, theology, philology, biology, causality, politics, eros, truth, being, and identity. There was no transcendental, binding Archimedian point. Nietzsche had demonstrated the error of assuming that humans had an intrinsic or metaphysical content. There was, indeed, no such thing as the "person"—there were only symptoms. What was most basic in Nietzsche, Benn stressed, was the move from content to expression, the extinction of substance in favor of expression.[52]

Free and creative expression was above all the *métier* of the artist, and pre–World War I German expressionism celebrated Nietzsche's elitist vision of the sublime if painful role of the isolated artist-superman who in creating experienced what the herd would never know. Given their portrayal of the pressures of bourgeois conformity and the emerging mass society, the expressionist artist typically espoused an elitist, Nietzschean immoralism. In the metaphorical landscape of the lonely Zarathustrian heights, in the shadow of the death of God, stood the artist beyond conventional notions of good and evil: a Nietzschean law unto himself. In Paul Kornfeld's "The Seduction" (1913), for instance, the outcast-hero takes upon himself the right to kill a bourgeois merely because the hero is disgusted by him. When Georg Kaiser was sued for debts he had incurred, he proclaimed that the assumption "'All are equal before the law' is nonsense." For the genius the act of creativity, of producing meaning itself, was paramount "even if his wife and children should perish because of it."[53]

This kind of immoralism extended to a celebration of madness. For expressionism, madness could provide an illuminating perspective. The language of the insane expressed a freedom from everyday conventions

51. Kurt Pinthus, "Rede für die Zukunft," *Die Erhebung* 1 (1919), 410–412. Quoted in Tibor Kneif, "Ernst Bloch and Musical Expressionism," in Bronner and Kellner, *Passion and Rebellion*, 343.

52. "Nietzsche: Nach Fünfzig Jahren," 488–493.

53. Sokel, *Writer in Extremis*, 66.

and oppressive laws.[54] In a sense the ultimate expressionist Übermensch was the mad person conceived as the incarnation of a liberating lawlessness. Georg Heym in 1906 confided to his diary his longing to realize the Übermensch ideal in his own person,[55] and took this impulse to its limits in his story entitled "The Madman." There madness is depicted as a form of ultimate salvation. Because ordinary laws do not apply to those who are mad, insanity is equated with utter freedom, symbolized by the final image: the madman soaring like a bird high above reality.[56]

Nietzsche's remark that "ordered society puts the passions to sleep" typified the expressionist critique of the deadening bourgeois world. Like other segments of the avant-garde, expressionists typically combined this rejection of contemporary society with a variety of vitalist Dionysian solutions. Most explicitly rejected the restraining and ordering Apollonian dimension: "Even the statues of the Greeks," wrote Kurt Pinthus, "do not . . . aim at 'noble simplicity and serene greatness.'"[57]

Many expressionists closely echoed Nietzsche's Lebensphilosophie strictures. "Is life to dominate knowledge and science," Nietzsche asked, "or is knowledge to dominate life? Which of these two forces is the higher and more decisive? There can be no doubt: life is the higher, the dominating force, for knowledge which annihilated life would have annihilated itself with it."[58] This expressionist vitalism, as Walter Sokel has pointed out, differed from its French counterpart and preferred an antiintellectual interpretation of Nietzsche.[59] Henri Bergson's *elán vital* posited a distinction between the unconscious flow of life and ossifying intellect. Yet the partially rational faculty of memory was a tool for comprehending the irrational stream of life (a role that for Freud was

---

54. Wieland Herzfelde, "Die Ethik der Geisteskranken," *Die Aktion* 4 (1914). See also chapter 5 of Augustinius P. Dierick, *German Expressionist Prose: Theory and Practice* (Toronto: University of Toronto Press, 1987).

55. "*O dass es mir gelingen möchte, mein Leben nun umzugestalten, um ein Pfeil zum Übermenschen zu werden*" (Georg Heym, *Dichtungen und Schriften*, vol. 3, ed. K. L. Schneider [Hamburg: Ellermann, 1960], 44ff.). See Krummel, *Nietzsche und der deutsche Geist*, vol. 2, 232.

56. "Der Irre," in *Der Dieb: Ein Novellenbuch* (Leipzig: E. Rowohlt, 1913). See the perceptive analysis in Dierick, *German Expressionist Prose*, 204–208.

57. *Die Erhebung* 1 (1919), 415ff. Quoted in Samuel and Hinton Thomas, *Expressionism*, 70.

58. Friedrich Nietzsche, "On the uses and disadvantages of history for life," in *Untimely Meditations*, trans. R. J. Hollingdale (Cambridge: Cambridge University Press, 1983), 121.

59. See Sokel, *Writer in Extremis*, 87ff.

fulfilled by psychoanalysis). In German expressionism that mediating, controlling factor was largely absent. Dionysian anticerebralism was meant to proceed unchecked. The expressionists tended to lose the sense of tension between intellect and antiintellect which, according to Sokel, characterized the German tradition.

German expressionist vitalism typically voiced bitter critiques of the stultifying educational system and championed the discovery of the liberating powers of youth. Texts such as Nietzsche's *Untimely Meditations* (1874–1876), especially "The Use and Abuse of History for Life" (1874), provided important inspirations and legitimations for these impulses. There Nietzsche mercilessly pilloried the educational institutions of the time and mocked the kind of sterile rationalism which, he argued, was an impediment to life. Youth, he proclaimed, were the primary carriers of the regenerating powers of life and it was their primary mission to liberate it.

It was not surprising that the typical nemesis of the expressionist imagination turned out to be either the professor or the repressive father. In his drama *Ithaka*, Gottfried Benn's spokesman, Roenne, is moved to murder a professor who insists upon the supreme value of scientific knowledge. Roenne's harangue inciting fellow students to commit the deed is couched in terms immediately recognizable to those aware of the Nietzschean universe of discourse: "We are the youth. Our blood cries out for heaven and earth, and not for cells and worms. . . . We want to dream. We want ecstasy. We call on Dionysus and Ithaca!"[60]

It was, of course, Frank Wedekind who, through his pioneering and sensational play *Spring Awakening* (1895), became the model for later expressionist approaches.[61] Like Nietzsche he combined a searing indictment of the repressive educational system with a plea for life, but Wedekind sharpened the focus by equating life with the liberation of adolescent sexual instinct.

The initial expressionist impulse was concerned with the individual rather than society and was basically indifferent to concrete questions of politics and economics, being more concerned with the symptoms of bourgeois sickness than its causes.[62] Its ecstatic, unprogrammatic,

60. Quoted in ibid., 94.

61. Peter Jelavich, "Wedekind's *Spring Awakening:* The Path to Expressionist Drama," in Bronner and Kellner, *Passion and Rebellion.*

62. George L. Mosse, "Literature and Society in Germany," in *Masses and Man: Nationalist and Fascist Perceptions of Reality,* 21–51 (New York: Howard Fertig, 1980), 46–47.

Nietzschean, revolutionary sentiments were too unchanneled and vague to have much real political effect. The inchoate expressionist longing for deliverance—founded usually on emotion rather than concrete social analysis—could take on tangible form only when wed to larger political frameworks. For many of those expressionists who did become thus politicized, whether toward the right or left, their open-ended Nietzschean radicalism remained central to the ways in which they defined their affiliation.

In the imaginings of those like Arnolt Bronnen and Hans Johst, who later would become actively involved in national socialism, the Nietzschean imagery of a youthful and liberational life-affirming cruelty was central and took on an increasingly crude form.[63] Bronnen's plays illustrate the brutalization of the expressionist–Nietzsche nexus. In *Vatermord* (parricide) an adolescent kills his Social Democratic father, dismisses his mother, and goes out into the world. There is no motive for the deed other than the vitalist freedom the act itself endows. The emphasis on the deed as such, on the dynamic for its own sake, was a leitmotif of Nietzsche-influenced activism. In the even more extreme sequel, *Die Geburt der Jugend* (*The birth of youth*), the post-Nietzschean consequences of the death of God theme is even more graphically represented. Roving bands of youth on horseback trample over the aged and shout that they are God.[64]

More than any other expressionist, however, it was Gottfried Benn who grappled with the consequences of the death of God. His entire career, including his short but passionate attachment to nazism, was an attempt to deal with that Nietzschean predicament. He accepted Nietzsche's nihilism, Michael Hamburger commented, "as one accepts the weather."[65] Prior to 1933, Benn posited a theoretical nihilism that denied the possibility of any metaphysical truth.[66] At that stage his solution to nihilism pointed to a twentieth-century form of primitivism. The transcendence of nihilism meant ridding oneself of the torment of modern self-consciousness, induced by

63. Hans Johst was aware of this tendency and tried to neutralize it within his works. Upon listening to the hero of *The Young Man* (1916) proclaim his creed, his adversary Professor Moralclean responds: "You'd do better to study your grammar than declaim a misunderstood Nietzsche!" (in *Der junge Mensch: Ein ekstatisches Szenarium,* quoted in Sokel, *Writer in Extremis,* 94).

64. Ibid., 100.

65. Michael Hamburger, "Gottfried Benn," in *A Proliferation of Prophets,* 206–243 (Manchester: Carcanet, 1983), 207.

66. George L. Mosse, "Fascism and the Intellectuals," in *Germans and Jews,* 144–170 (London: Orbach and Chambers, 1971), 154–155.

humanity's rift with nature. This meant a return to the preconscious, prelogical, primal, and inert state.[67] Anchorage in this Dionysian-like transindividual (*Überindividuellen*) condition was, however, possible only in organic, animal form. As Benn put it in his April 1932 talk to the Prussian Academy of Art: "One of the classic perceptions of the post-Nietzschean epoch derives from Thomas Mann and reads: '*everything transcendent is animal, everything animal transcends.*'"[68]

Benn's denunciation of science and humanitarianism and his longing for primitivist forms, however, also allowed him to find (albeit temporarily) that principle of transcendence within a more tangible political home, in the kind of community that nazism heralded. For Benn national socialism seemed to embody the Nietzschean dynamic in both its primal and future-oriented senses. It satisfied the longing for the authentic symbolized by the modern barbarian, a rootedness in the Volk as well as the promise of the creation of the New Man—a new biological type—the Aryan, whose great task it was to do battle against decadence in all its guises.[69]

The expressionists, like many other Nietzscheans, wavered between an apolitical individual stance and a sense of redemptive social mission, a hunger for union with communities.[70] Even for those leftists who defined themselves in explicitly social and political terms—such as the pacifist and anarchist circles around Franz Pfemert's *Die Aktion* or Kurt Hiller—their analysis ignored specific social institutions; they posited their redemptive goal in subjective and highly abstract terms of individual "self-realization."

Kurt Hiller and his "new club," founded in March 1909, for instance, regarded Nietzsche as their chief inspiration.[71] Their "new pathos," stressing an "increased psychic temperature" and universal merriment (*Heiterkeit*), was informed by the familiar Dionysian

---

67. Dierick, *German Expressionist Prose*, 189.

68. Gottfried Benn, "Akademie-Rede," in *Gesammelte Werke* vol. 1, ed. Dieter Wellershoff, 431–439 (Stuttgart: Klett-Cotta, 1977), 436.

69. See Gottfried Benn's 1933 speech "Der neue Staat und die Intellektuellen," rep. in Benn's *Gesammelte Werke* vol. 1, 440–449. See also Mosse, "Fascism and the Intellectuals," 155.

70. Käthe Brodnitz, "Die futuristische Geistesrichtung in Deutschland, 1914," in *Expressionismus: Der Kampf um eine literarische Bewegung*, ed. Paul Raabe (Zürich: Arche, 1987), 46, 50.

71. This account is heavily drawn from Roy Allen, "Der Neue Club," chap. 4 in *Literary Life*.

dimension.[72] The new pathos, Hiller noted,[73] was informed by what Nietzsche had said in *Ecce Homo:* "I estimate the value of men, of races, according to the necessity by which they cannot conceive the god apart from the satyr."[74] Hiller pursued, as he described it, a radicalism that had little to do with "the mathematized old-morality."[75] What was needed was a new post-theist and neohellenic heroism (*Heldentum*) as Nietzsche had proclaimed it.[76]

Hiller nevertheless typified that wing of the expressionist movement that rejected an undifferentiated anticerebralism and insisted instead on using the shaping, moderating Apollonian dimension: perhaps his best-known slogan was "Let mind become master" (*Geist werde Herr*).[77] Walter Sokel has pointed out that Hiller's ideal, unlike other versions of the vitalist New Man that sought action for its own sake, emphasized "action guided by reason in the cause of love."[78]

Most expressionists were, however, attracted to the Nietzschean vision of the self-legislating, creative Übermenschlich artist working in splendid isolation from the masses. In this respect one measure of Nietzsche's influence is the fact that many early expressionists who came to reject this antisocial stance and to affirm anew the bonds of human solidarity found it necessary to indulge in an overt and passionate cutting of the Nietzschean umbilical chord.

This repudiation led in different directions. In 1896, for instance, Heinrich Mann had constructed a rather right-wing, nationalist Nietzsche: his Übermensch had to be understood as a positive "social and race symbol."[79] Later, with his turn from Romantic aestheticism to social democracy, Mann penned a democratic critique of the arrogant superman who was now cut off from the concerns and dignity of ordinary people.[80] (His brother Thomas made a similar shift but after

72. On universal merriment see Krummel, *Nietzsche,* vol. 2, 395.
73. Ibid., 82–83. Hiller's entire talk, "Das Cabaret und die Gehirne," appears in his *Die Weisheit der Langeweile! Eine Zeit und Streitschrift,* 2 vols. (Leipzig: K. Wolff, 1913), 236–239.
74. Nietzsche, *Ecce Homo,* 245.
75. Ibid., 391.
76. The depth of Nietzsche's impact on Hiller can be seen in his *Leben gegen die Zeit* (Hamburg: E. Rowohlt, 1969). See Krummel, *Nietzsche,* vol. 2, 102.
77. For more on this aspect of the new pathos see the remarks by Erwin Löwenson, another member of the club, in his *Georg Heym oder vom Geist des Schicksals* (Hamburg and Munich: H. Ellermann, 1962), 61, 57ff.
78. Sokel, *Writer in Extremis,* 173.
79. Heinrich Mann, "Zum Verständnis Nietzsches," *Das Zwanzigste Jahrhundert* 6 (1896), 246, 245–251.
80. Heinrich Mann, "Geist und Tat," in *Macht und Mensch* (Munich: Kurt Wolff, 1919).

World War I. In both cases dissociation from the the antidemocratic bias did not mean negating the philosopher: other more appropriate aspects were now emphasized.)

In the case of Reinhard Sorge (1892–1916), the turn from an initial enthusiasm for Nietzsche—his *Odysseus* was based upon the idea of the eternal recurrence and the later *Prometheus* depicted the earthly establishment of a race of supermen[81]—to a rejection of the myth of the Übermensch led to his conversion to Roman Catholicism and "a radicalism of brotherly love." In his accusatory *Gericht über Zarathustra: Vision* (1912; "Judgment upon Zarathustra: A vision") he bitterly chronicled his disillusion, in language which ironically betrayed Nietzsche's continuing, painful influence:

> Do you know who that boy is? Look, Zarathustra, he loved you, he was your disciple. Your ardor seized his, and he squandered all for your sake. Because his ardor was such that he loved you above everything . . . your spirit was turned earthward, my spirit allowed itself to be deceived. For the sake of your ardor it deceived itself.
>
> Then came the hour when it turned upward, do not ask how, the spirit is its own answer. . . . The command came from above to be a fighter against the brother-spirit (Zarathustra), to judge him by the authority of Heaven.[82]

If Nietzsche was a ubiquitous presence within expressionism the same could be said of his role within the avant-garde circle around Stefan George known as the *George Kreis*. The disaffection from establishment and bourgeois culture, the emphasis on the creative artist and spiritual elite as incarnation of the Übermensch, and the ambiguously conceived politics of regeneration similarly characterized this circle. There were also significant differences between the two, and the ways in which they harnessed Nietzsche to their own needs. Expressionist subjectivism and irrationalism provided its own self-justifying dynamic. For George, aestheticism was the justification: the intuitive and the irrational facilitated apprehension of the poetic and the beautiful. Expressionism was an inchoate manifestation of a mood and an impulse. In the case of George the poet-seer, everything flowed from his own patrician person. Like the characters of expressionist imagination, here was a self-proclaimed prophet who followed no rules, but instead created the laws and values. Once formulated, however, they took on an authority inconceivable to the more dynamic, indeed chaotic, expressionist sensibility.

81. On Sorge's early positive attitude and the division of his work into Nietzschean and post-Nietzschean phases, see Samuel and Hinton Thomas, *Expressionism*, 20, 23. On *Odysseus* and *Prometheus* see ibid., 75.
82. Quoted in Sokel, *Writer in Extremis*, 156.

The George Kreis was an initiate community of disciples, a sect with no formal or binding statutes yet utterly under the thrall of its master. The fluid inner circle, this "secret Germany," probably never exceeded more than forty members. Yet it succeeded far beyond its numbers in becoming a kind of elitist cultural model; its impact on antiestablishmentarian German poetry, criticism, and historiography was enormous.[83]

Nietzsche's legacy touched Stefan George and his Kreis in both latent and manifest ways. The conscious and unconscious functions that Nietzsche fulfilled for the master and his disciples, their dependence on the philosopher as well as their outright attempt to supersede him, to enlist his authority, and to distance themselves from him provide a good example of the complexity of Nietzsche appropriation.[84] That complexity should not, however, obscure the fact that the George project is virtually incomprehensible outside of its post-Nietzschean context.

In the preface to the 1886 edition of *The Birth of Tragedy* Nietzsche lamented that he had not dared to speak in the poetic language commensurate with his work: "It should have *sung,* this 'new soul'—and not spoken!"[85] In his 1900 eulogy to Nietzsche George made it clear that he would undertake that project.[86] His circle's journal (founded in 1892), the Blätter für die Kunst, was born, as the George disciple and poet Karl Wolfskehl wrote in 1910, "because one poet [Nietzsche] ignited a flame in another [George]."[87]

What, in the view of the George Kreis, did Nietzsche provide? He furnished the tools for their critique of the nineteenth century and voiced the heroic promise of a rediscovered German spirituality on a new creative basis. It was he who set the elitist tone for their patrician struggle against the age of mediocrity. The nature of the struggle was itself defined in dynamic Nietzschean terms: renewal was possible only through the innovative activity of the prophetic, law-creating poet who lived at a time when no return to a bygone age was possible. Because

83. Georg Peter Landmann, ed., *Stefan Georg und sein Kreis: Eine Bibliographie* (Hamburg: E. Hauswedell, 1976); Landmann, ed., *Der George-Kreis: Eine Auswahl aus seinen Schriften* (Stuttgart: Klett-Cotta, 1980).

84. Walter Kaufmann has argued that George lacked "sympathetic understanding of what mattered most to Nietzsche" and that "his picture of Nietzsche was highly personal and clearly determined by his own aspirations" (*Nietzsche,* 9–11). Again, the accuracy of George's perceptions is not as relevant here as the fact that his portrait of Nietzsche reveals much about himself.

85. Nietzsche, *Birth of Tragedy,* 20.

86. *Blätter für die Kunst* (May 1901), 5.

87. Karl Wolfskehl, "Die Blätter für die Kunst und die Neue Literatur," *Jahrbuch für die geistige Bewegung* 1 (1910), 1.

classical religious, mythical, and philosophic traditions had broken down, his daunting task was to create them anew. Renewal was defined through the ideal of beauty and aesthetic form. This too was fashioned after the Nietzschean conception of the will to power, not political power but the power of the seer who would transform the nation, especially with the help of beautiful and heroic youth.[88]

It was from Nietzsche, moreover, that they imbibed much of their antiscientific posture and vitalist aestheticism. They routinely employed Nietzschean conceptions of the heroic and the mythical—categories which they then applied to Nietzsche himself:

> With him the whole tremendous treasure of German spirituality, which since the extinction of the Roman world . . . had remained underground, came at last to light. With that began the real, great struggle under whose banner we stand today. The last irreconcilable battle of the powers that have shaped our lives became with Nietzsche a public matter.

In a wayward Europe he "perceived a way which lead out of this chaos into the cosmos."[89]

For George and his followers the cosmic and the really meaningful dimensions of life could not be apprehended rationally or through scientific means. Only aesthetic and the poetic sensibilities could achieve this. Such Romantic convictions, of course, were not novel to George. As Wolf Lepenies has recently demonstrated, these views had a long-standing pedigree.[90] Georgians, however, injected this Romantic critique with essentially Nietzschean ingredients. Their critique of science and academic scholarship, especially the inadmissibility of its self-referential validation, began with Nietzsche's dictum in *The Birth of Tragedy* that "the problem of science . . . cannot be recognized in the context of science."[91]

George juxtaposed communal scientific knowledge with the Nietzschean aristocratism of the solitary sage. "One knowledge the same for all," he wrote, "is fraud."[92] If amongst his circle there were differing assessments as to the possibilities of rationality, all agreed that the errors of artistic heroes were more important than the truths of the

88. George L. Mosse, "Caesarism, Circuses and Monuments" in *Masses and Man,* 104–118. See p. 116 on the politics of George's aestheticism.

89. Wolfskehl, "Die Blätter," 4–5.

90. Lepenies, *Between Literature and Science,* part 3. I follow Lepenies's account of George here.

91. Nietzsche, *Birth of Tragedy,* 18.

92. Stefan George, *Der Stern des Bundes,* vol. 2 of *Werke* (Munich: Deutscher Taschenbuch, 1983), 167.

mediocre. They read Nietzsche as the man who, in overcoming the nineteenth century, had taught that society had nothing to do with life and certainly could not claim the right to impose laws upon it.[93]

Science and scientists could not teach men how to live; poetry and the poet gifted with intuitive and prophetic powers could. "Inner experience" was both method and key to salvation—history was to be transfigured back into consciously forged myth. As vindication, Nietzsche's vision of "the poet as signpost to the future" was constantly invoked:

> That poetic power available to men of today which is not used up in the depiction of life ought to be dedicated, not so much to the representation of the contemporary world or to the reanimation and imaginative reconstruction of the past, but to signposting the future:—not, though, as if the poet could, like a fabulous economist, figuratively anticipate the kind of conditions nations and societies would prosper better under and how they could then be brought about. What he will do, rather, is emulate the artists of earlier times who imaginatively developed the existing images of the gods and *imaginatively develop* a fair image of man; he will scent out those cases in which, in the *midst* of our modern world and reality and without any artificial withdrawal from or warding off of this world, the great and beautiful soul is still possible, still able to embody itself in the harmonious and well-proportioned and thus acquire visibility, duration and the status of a model, and in so doing through the excitation of envy and emulation help to create the future.[94]

This poet and his poetry, in line with Nietzsche's ideal, would produce art in which life itself had penetrated.[95] George's disciple Friedrich Gundolf's analysis and dismissal of the masses was written in paraphrased Nietzschean terms: "Whoever has regarded this 'people' on a Sunday afternoon in cities great or small, and has done so with eyes open and not befogged by humanitarian, social, or progressive catch phrases, loses all desire to engage in any intelligent relationship with it."[96]

We should note here the public contours in which George wanted his relationship to Nietzsche to be seen. Admiring as his 1900 eulogy was, in the last analysis Nietzsche had to be regarded as a tragic figure:

93. In *Birth of Tragedy* Nietzsche wrote: "And science itself, our science—yes, what, regarded as a symptom of life, is the meaning of life at all? To what end, worse *from what cause*—all science?" Translated in Lepenies, *Between Literature and Science*, 206.

94. Nietzsche, *Human, All Too Human*, trans. R. J. Hollingdale (Cambridge: Cambridge University Press, 1986), 235–236.

95. Wolfskehl, "Die Blätter," 5.

96. Friedrich Gundolf, "Wesen und Beziehung," in *Beiträge zur Literatur und Geistesgeschichte* (1911), 173. Quoted in Lepenies, *Between Literature and Science*, 264.

Dull trots the crowd below, do not disturb it!
Why stab the jelly-fish or cut the weed?
For a while yet let pious silence reign
and let the vermin that stain him with praise
and are still fattening in the musty fumes
that helped to stifle him, first waste away!
But then, resplendent, thou wilt face the ages
like other leaders with the bloody crown.

Redeemer thou thyself the most unblessed— . . .
Didst thou create gods but to overthrow them,
never enjoying rest or what thou built?
Thou hast destroyed what in thyself was closest
to tremble after it with new desire
and to cry out in pain of solitude.

He came too late that said to thee imploring:
There is no way left over icy cliffs
and eyries of dread birds—now this is needed:
constraint within a circle closed by love.[97]

George's Nietzsche dies in heroic futility, unable to enter the new world he had prophesied. George himself is the fulfillment of this Nietzschean vision. This, indeed, was the official line of the Kreis: Nietzsche had paved the way for what was to come, the forerunner not the realization.[98] "Nietzsche," wrote Kurt Hildebrandt, "was a pathbreaker and a forerunner, not a fulfiller."[99] By ending this poem: "now this is needed / Constraint within a circle closed by love," George made his supersession of the philosopher clear. Nietzsche's vision had to be encircled. Only through such a community could the political and spiritual Reich be realized. What Nietzsche lacked, wrote George, was a "plastic God."[100]

97. Translated in Kaufman, *Nietzsche*, 10.
98. Heinz Raschel accuses George of distorting Nietzsche and argues that George's aestheticism was quite different from that of the late Nietzsche; if anything, Nietzsche interpreted the poet ironically in *Zarathustra*. But again what interests us are appropriated uses of Nietzsche, not the validity or invalidity of the interpretation (*Das Nietzsche-Bild im George Kreis: Ein Beitrag zur Geschichte der deutschen Mythologeme* [Berlin, New York: Walter de Gruyter, 1984], 23).
99. Hildebrandt, "Nietzsche als Richter," 100. His works include *Nietzsches Wettkampf mit Sokrates und Plato* (Dresden: Sybillen, 1922); *Wagner und Nietzsche: Ihr Kampf gegen das Neunzehnte Jahrhundert* (Breslau: Ferdinand Hirt, 1924); *Gesundheit und Krankheit in Nietzsches Leben und Werk* (Berlin: Karger, 1926). See especially his critique from the Nazi period of Karl Jaspers, "Über Deutung und Einordnung von Nietzsches System," *Kant-Studien* 41, nos. 3/4 (1936) and "Die Idee des Krieges bei Goethe Hölderlin Nietzsche," in *Das Bild des Krieges im Deutschen Denken* 1, ed. August Faust, 401–409 (Stuttgart, Berlin: W. Kohlhammer, 1941).
100. George to Gundolf, 11 June 1910, in *Stefan George–Friedrich Gundolf Briefwechsel*, ed. R. Böhringer and George Peter Landmann (Munich, Düsseldorf: Küpper,

Yet the structure of the George community itself had a decidedly Nietzschean texture. Self-consciously aristocratic, it was supposed to be held together by cultural affinities and not binding regulations. This mode of organization could apply only to special elites. Rudolf Pannwitz, another George circle member, put it best: Nietzsche was "not a prophet for the volk but rather a prophet for the prophets."[101]

Like other Nietzschean avant-garde circles, George's circle regarded itself as fundamentally apolitical and was quite indifferent, if not actively hostile, to political parties. Yet their aesthetic impulse towards transformation and national renewal was political in the broadest sense. Like other Nietzschean radicalisms it lacked a formal programme, leaving the nature of that renewal vague. The circle encompassed people ranging from a future leader of the German resistance to nazism, Count von Stauffenberg, to anti-Semites like Ludwig Klages; Jews like Ernst Kantorowicz, Gundolf and Wolfskehl; and those like Ernst Bertram who were attracted to nazism. The circle was, as Lepenies points out, "capable not only of political manoeuverability but also of political reversionism: . . . George was as right to emphasize his distance from Wilhelmine Germany as Rudolf Borchardt was to emphasize the acceptance of the George circle by the Prussian state."[102]

Whatever the internal differences, all adherents of the circle were overtly critical of the democratic system, especially the Americanized Weimar brand. They were patricians far removed from the vulgar Nazi sensibility. They contributed to an antiegalitarian, antidemocratic discourse that nevertheless aided the rise of a force they despised. They also called for the creation of a new German mythology. The related emphasis on intuition, inner experience, and vital as opposed to dead (*Lebensfeindlich*) scientific knowledge, the antiacademic conception of history was inspired directly by Nietzsche.[103]

The task of history writing was regarded as explicitly legend making,

---

1902). "*Nietzsche, der Sucher des neuen Gottes und Gesetzes, ward der Zerstörer des entseelten Glaubens, aber noch nicht der Erwecker des Lebendigen, weil er nur die Kräfte verehren lehrte, aber nicht die Bilder, weil er nur Dämonen anzubeten wusste aber keine Götter*" (Gundolf and Hildebrandt, *Nietzsche als Richter*, 42).

101. Pannwitz, *Einführung in Nietzsche*, 4; Pannwitz, "Was ich Nietzsche und George Danke," *Castrum Peregrini* 38, nos. 189/190 (1989).

102. Lepenies, *Between Science and Literature*, 268.

103. George's circle with all its antiacademic bias nevertheless deeply influenced academic trends, especially in the fields of criticism and historiography via two of its most distinguished academic members, Friedrich Gundolf and Ernst Kantorowicz.

as it described exemplary Übermenschen. Only the great figures were worth studying and only poets with similarly constituted souls could truly grasp and present their subjects. Neither objectivity nor a scientific spirit would do—the great figures had to be presented as contemporary models. Heroes, Gundolf commented, should not be humanized (*vermenschlicht werden.*)[104] Although Goethe and Hölderlin were invoked, Nietzsche above all was presented as inspiring these conceptions.

It was not merely as methodological inspiration, however, but as heroic subject of such myth making that Nietzsche figured in Ernst Bertram's 1918 enormously important *Nietzsche*.[105] That work, reissued seven times between 1918 and 1927, played a crucial role in the history of the *völkisch* appropriation of Nietzsche and his transfiguration into a Germanic right-wing prophet. We shall concern ourselves with the details and casuistic structure of that process in various parts of this book. Here we need only note Bertram's direct relationship to the George circle. Published under the imprimatur of the series "*Werke der Wissenschaft aus dem Kreise der Blätter für die Kunst*" George—as a disillusioned Bertram later made clear in his correspondence—attempted to dictate what this Nietzschean image should be.[106] Its Georgian subtitle, *Versuch einer Mythologie,* was self-explanatory. There was an open disinterest in examining Nietzsche's life according to the conventional methods of historical scholarship. Instead, Nietzsche was made into a Germanic legend, his life and thought transmuted into a nation-saving prophetic myth.

For other associates of George this mythical dimension pointed to religious–cosmic as well as national–political dimensions. "Nietzsche lived and created in this world of fulfilled and free myth which is also the logos and the psyche of the cosmos," wrote Pannwitz, a fringe figure around the Kreis and a sworn Nietzschean who, amongst other things, had published various works that attempted to give poetic expression to the master's philosophical vision. Pannwitz regarded Nietzsche's Übermensch as nothing less than "cosmic man . . . the synthesis of all human types . . . the crystalline individual representative of the cosmos." Viewed thus Nietzsche was the creator of a religion which had overcome transcendence and was "fully mythical, fully cosmic." For Pann-

104. Friedrich Gundolf, *Dichter und Helden* (Heidelberg: Weisssche Universitäts buchhandlung, 1921), 49.

105. Ernst Bertram, *Nietzsche: Versuch einer Mythologie* (Berlin: Bondi, 1918).

106. Raschel, *Nietzsche-Bild,* 134. Bertram's relationship and disillusion with George appears in the published correspondence between Bertram and Ernst Glöckner.

witz this led to a kind of mystic Oriental religion blending individualism with German regeneration.[107]

However idiosyncratic, Pannwitz was by no means the only Kreis figure drawn to such visions. George's early associates, Alfred Schuler (1865–1923) and Ludwig Klages (1872–1956), similarly enunciated a mythical outlook informed by an occult search for cosmic radiations (*Ausstrahlungen.*)[108]

This particular cosmic view accompanied a rabid anti-Semitism, notions of blood, and primal earthly visions. One historian has diagnosed these conceptions as part of "the mystical origins of National Socialism."[109] Like other radicalisms touched by the Nietzschean impulse, this spiritual aspect too combined progressive and reactionary elements in unpredictable ways.

From 1897 to 1904 George, Schuler, and Klages were members of an esoteric pagan–gnostic circle in Munich-Schwabing known as the Cosmics. Influenced by a variety of sources (especially Bachofen's *Mutterrecht*), it also appropriated a suitably Nietzschean side.[110] This was reflected in its critique of liberal rationalism and industrial modernity, its anti-Christian bias, and above all the quest for Dionysian community which, according to this group, could be practically achieved through the re-creation and celebration of heathen festivals.[111]

Nietzsche's influence on the eclectic Schuler, the charismatic leader of the group, was clear.[112] Schuler's Nietzsche was not the prophet of

107. Pannwitz, *Einführung in Nietzsche*, 5–8. Pannwitz created a number of *Mythen*. Five of his plays, written between 1904–1910, were published in 1913 under the title *Dionysische Tragödien*, and dedicated to "Nietzsche, the creator of our new life." As Samuel and Hinton Thomas note, unlike Hugo von Hofmannsthal, Pannwitz did not give his versions of classical themes a modern character. Rather they were Nietzschean reconstructions of Greek plays (*Expressionism*, 63, n. 3, 73). For his religious interpretations, see Pannwitz, *Aufruf zum Heiligen Kriege der Lebendigen* (Munich-Feldafing: H. Carl, 1920).

108. For a good treatment of this outlook see J. H. W. Rosteutscher, *Die Wiederkunft des Dionysos: Der naturmystische Irrationalismus in Deutschland* (Bern: A. Francke, 1947), 223ff.

109. George L. Mosse, "The Mystical Origins of National Socialism," in *Masses and Man*, 197–213.

110. The link between the two was also explored in 1929 by the leading Nazi Nietzschean, Alfred Bäumler ("Bachofen und Nietzsche," in *Studien zur deutschen Geistesgeschichte* [Berlin: Junker und Dünnhaupt, 1937]).

111. Roderich Huch, *Alfred Schuler, Ludwig Klages, Stefan George: Erinnerungen an Kreise und Krisen der Jahrhundertwende in München–Schwabing* (Amsterdam: Castrum Peregrini, 1973). See too the autobiographical novel by Franziska Gräfin zu Reventlow, *Herrn Dames Aufzeichnungen* (Munich: Biederstein, 1958).

112. On Schuler see Mosse, *The Crisis of German Ideology*, 75–77, 211–212; Gerald Plumpe, *Alfred Schuler: Chaos und Neubeginn, zur Funktion des Mythos in der Moderne* (Berlin: Agora, 1978). For Nietzsche's influence on Schuler see Schuler, *Fragmente und*

individualism. In Schuler's view the individual did not count; what was crucial were the deeper, unconscious layers and unifying powers of race, "soul," and blood. He valued Nietzsche's mythic regeneracy and vitalism, the apocalyptic texture and the belief that buried creative and instinctual powers could be released. Schuler's historical periodization, his dismissal of the Reformation and the French Revolution as Judaized and devitalized ressentiment phenomena were, he believed, fashioned after Nietzsche's characterization of these in *The Genealogy of Morals*.[113] His Nietzsche, moreover, taught the cycle of awesome destruction and new beginnings. "Nietzsche said," he lectured, "that with collapse new sources reveal themselves, and so is it also in life. Violent destructions must proceed first before the new sources out of which the future flows are brought to light."[114]

The philosopher was even the intended recipient of Schuler's occult therapy. For two years Schuler made preparations to cure Nietzsche's madness through the freely interpreted rite of an ancient Corybantic dance. It was never implemented, partly because of the difficulty of enlisting suitable youths for the cultic dance![115] The fact that both Klages and Wolfskehl approved of the plan indicates the atmosphere generated within such esoteric circles.[116]

Schuler's most influential disciple was Ludwig Klages (who bitterly broke with George in 1904). The virulently anti-Semitic Klages, a prolific publicist, renowned graphologist, and cult philosopher of the Weimar Republic, dedicated his career to the elaboration and articulation of the cosmic outlook which he acquired from those years in

Vorträge aus dem Nachlass, intro. Ludwig Klages (Leipzig: J. A. Barth, 1940), 27f, 33, 34.

113. For a comparative textual analysis see Plumpe, *Alfred Schuler*, 126–127.

But Judea immediately triumphed again, thanks to that thoroughly plebian (German and English) *ressentiment* movement called the Reformation. . . . With the French Revolution, Judea once again triumphed over the classical ideal, and this time in an even more profound and decisive sense: the last political noblesse in Europe, that of the *French* seventeenth and eighteenth century, collapsed beneath the popular instincts of *ressentiment*.

Nietzsche, *Genealogy of Morals*, 54.

114. Schuler, *Fragmente*, 170, 244, 275.

115. Ibid., 60ff. Julius Langbehn was another völkisch thinker to try to cure Nietzsche. After winning the confidence of Nietzsche's mother and his psychiatrist, Otto Binswanger, Langbehn started taking Nietzsche out for long walks. He hoped to obtain funds to set Nietzsche up as a royal child in a household run by Langbehn. Nietzsche's mother halted the project after learning Langbehn wanted to assume legal guardianship (Ronald Hayman, *Nietzsche: A Critical Life*, [London: Quartet, 1981], 340).

116. Huch, *Alfred Schuler*, 29–30. For the relationship of this plan to Schuler's cosmology see Plumpe, *Alfred Schuler*, chap. 5, especially p. 124.

Schwabing.[117] Klages was a post-Nietzschean in every sense of the term. Like Benn and the expressionists, his work can be understood as a critical exegetical dialogue with Nietzsche. Simultaneously expositor of his thought and elaborator of key insights, Klages's system selectively appropriated Nietzsche as well.[118]

The Klagesian Nietzsche was the great herald of the cosmic soul, clearly referring to the Dionysian Nietzsche of wild self-abandon. As with Schuler, Klages provided no room for Nietzsche's individualism. His great achievement consisted in understanding Greek tragedy as "breaking the chains of individual life by cosmic life." Indeed, the animating drive behind Klages's system was the search for this primal, cosmic "Dionysian intoxication." His programmatically irrationalist categories—"elemental ecstasy" and "erotic rapture," for instance—derived from *The Birth of Tragedy* which sought, as Klages put it, to penetrate "through the limits of 'individuation' into the life of the elements."[119]

For Klages the Dionysian realm was important because there life manifested itself. Klages was the most radical German exponent of irrationalist Lebensphilosophie, taking its Nietzschean premises to their most extreme conclusions.[120] In order to fashion that philosophy he made a basic distinction between life-affirming Seele (soul) and life-destroying Geist (mind), as the title of his most famous work, *The Mind as Opponent of the Soul,* made crystal clear. This distinction, Klages wrote, was basic, an *Urbegriff* similar to Nietzsche's juxtaposition of the Dionysian and the Socratic.[121] *Geist* on the one hand represented all those forces of modern, industrial, and intellectual rationalization which destroyed nature, peace, organicism, and the cosmic dimension. *Seele* on the other hand represented the possibility of an authentically

117. As Karl Löwith wrote in 1927, there was a veritable Klages cult during this period consisting of *Weltanschauungsdilettanten* who regarded him as a man of unsurpassed metaphysical depth ("Nietzsche im Lichte der Philosophie von Ludwig Klages," *Reichls philosophischer Almanach* 4 [1927], 285). In the foreword to his *Der Geist als Widersacher der Seele,* Klages claimed that he was "the most looted (*ausgeplünderte*) contemporary author" ([Leipzig: J. A. Barth, [1926] 1937], xviii).
118. Knowledge of the extent of Nietzsche's influence on Klages is commonplace as Löwith attests ("Nietzsche im Lichte"). The usually highly critical Kaufmann gives Klages's work on Nietzsche particularly respectful—if not concurring—treatment (*Nietzsche,* 187).
119. Ludwig Klages, *Vom Kosmogonischen Eros,* 6th ed. (Bonn: H. Bouvier, 1963), 82, 79. The above quotes also appear on pp. 55–58. See also the remarks on *The Birth of Tragedy,* 224.
120. Löwith, "Nietzsche im Lichte," 286.
121. Klages, *Geist als Widersacher,* xxii.

lived life—the overcoming of alienated intellectuality in favor of a new-found earthly rootedness.[122]

We should not forget that Klages was also a renowned graphologist. Consistent with his broader antiscientific, antipositivist outlook he described himself not as a psychologist but as a "researcher of the soul," and he proclaimed Nietzsche as the father of "soul research" (*Seelenforschung*). For Klages, Nietzsche's psychological achievement was the demarcation of the battleground between Yahweh's ascetic priests and the orgiasts of Dionysius; his psychological sensitivity provided extraordinary illumination pursued through his relentlessly honest self-knowledge and unmasking (*Enttäuschungstechnik*.)[123]

While the vitalistic, Dionysian researcher of the soul was celebrated, the Nietzsche of the will to power was radically dismissed. For Klages the aggressive and consumptive will to power was "de-eroticized sexuality."[124] Nietzsche's individualist insistence on self-overcoming was an act of Geist in disguise, derived from precisely the Socratism and Christianity which he was supposed to have abhorred.[125] The will to power was the agent of an abstracted and aggressive mind, of capitalism and socialism, that cut people off from their natural, earthly roots. As the agent of destruction the will to power was nothing but the "will to kill life."

Like so many other commentators Klages did not limit his analysis to Nietzsche's thought: through his Seelenforschung and graphology he

122. Klages and Jung inhabited a similar universe of discourse. Jung's comments on Klages in his seminar on *Zarathustra* are instructive.

> What Klages understood by *Geist* is the idea which developed toward the end of the 19th century; namely, intellect in the form of books, science, philosophy, and so on. But never before had *Geist* meant that; it was merely a degeneration of the original meaning of the word. To Nietzsche, *spirit* meant the original thing, an intensity, a volcanic outburst, while to the scientific or rationalistic spirit of the second half of the 19th century, it was an ice-cold space in which there were things, but it was no longer life. Naturally if you understand *Geist* in this way, it is the deadliest enemy of the soul you could think of.

"Nietzsche's *Zarathustra*," 1128.

123. Ludwig Klages, *Handschrift und Charakter* (Leipzig: J. A. Barth, 1921). By 1929 this had already been through thirteen editions. See too the collection that Klages edited, *Graphologisches Lesebuch*, 5th ed. (Munich: J. A. Barth, [1930] 1954); Ludwig Klages, *Die psychologischen Errungenschaften Nietzsches* (Leipzig: J. A. Barth, 1926), 9–16, 210. It may be that Klages's Nietzschean psychology was designed as an Aryan, irrationalist alternative to rationalist Jewish Freudianism.

124. Klages, *Vom kosmogonischen Eros*, 87.

125. This theme forms an important part of Klages's major work on Nietzsche, *Psychologischen Errungenschaften*.

also provided the requisite mythologization of Nietzsche's persona. Like other exceptional individuals he partook of primordial being and because of that was destined to cut a tragic figure. Nietzsche was one of the "martyrs of paganism: their souls struggled and died for the fervour of Life."[126] His epochal service had been to break open the church walls. This "greatest breaker of chains in the whole history of mankind"[127] broke through "oceans of errors before us . . . but also for us." But, and here Klages resumed the old George Kreis line, this was a Nietzsche who could intuit, but never himself enter, the new world towards which he had pointed.[128]

Nietzsche's tragedy was that he was torn apart by the incompatible Dionysian longing for self-abandon and the constant Übermenschlich striving to self-overcome. Attracted to rationalist Socratism as much as he was repelled by it, Nietzsche never transcended the inner tension between the orgiastic pagan and Christian self-overcoming elements of his character.[129]

Klages pointed to a dual impulse which had exerted equal fascination for different avant-garde circles in Germany. These two Nietzschean themes—the "masculine" imperative of dynamic and sovereign self-creation and the more "feminine" submersion into a transindividual Dionysian whole—were both woven, however inchoately, into its aspirations. Some stressed one aspect over the other. At times attempts were made to combine the two or the tension was simply allowed to stand unresolved. Either way, these thematics encouraged and reinforced the open-ended and eclectic radicalism characteristic of the Nietzschean avant-garde.

Klages exemplifies the classificatory difficulties of this postliberal Nietzschean radicalism.[130] His was an all-encompassing irrationalism, a vitalist politics of antimodern, cosmic Dionysianism fueled by anti-Semitism, anti-individualism, and the mystique of "blood." He is commonly identified with an ideological line that led directly to nazism. Marxist critics regarded his organic Dionysian epistemology as pro-

126. Ludwig Klages, *Rhythmen und Runen* (Leipzig: J. A. Barth, 1944), 332.
127. Quoted in R. Hinton Thomas, "Nietzsche in Weimar Germany and the Case of Ludwig Klages," in *The Weimar Dilemma: Intellectuals in the Weimar Republic*, ed. Anthony Phelan, 71–91 (Manchester: Manchester University Press, 1985), 82.
128. Klages, *Rhythmen*, 522.
129. Klages, *Psychologische Errungenschaften*, 179–207.
130. In another context Gerd Klaus Kaltenbrunner has noted the peculiar mix of progressive and regressive elements in such radicalisms ("Zwischen Rilke und Hitler— Alfred Schuler," *Zeitschrift für Religion und Geistesgeschichte* 19, no. 4 [1967], 342).

foundly reactionary, a device for denying all historical progress.[131] Klages, Ernst Bloch declared, banished the future as a possibility. He did this in part by attacking the dream-drenched utopian core of Nietzsche: he "halves Nietzsche's heroisms by removing the will to power; he 'halves' Nietzsche's teleology: man is not something that must be overcome, but merely something which must be archaically circumvented, deprived of goals." Moreover, Bloch added, he destroyed "the bridge to the future, on which precisely all of Nietzsche's dream abodes had been situated." The question of truth and falsity had always been bothersome to Fascists. Klages's archaic mythology extinguished the problem almost entirely.[132]

Yet with his attack on Nietzschean self-overcoming and the masculine will to power, as Hinton Thomas has pointed out, Klages also enunciated a critique of power which was the very antithesis of the Nazi celebration of it. According to this analysis, Klages offered a critique of power, repression, and aggression in which all the modern alternatives of liberalism, socialism, and capitalism seemed culpable.[133] From this point of view, Klages's ideas belonged to the anarchist–liberationist Asconan, not the authoritarian, tradition.[134]

This mix of elements always attracted the German and European avant-garde. Their radicalism was a response to real issues of liberal and industrial modernity. Almost definitionally hostile to bourgeois tastes and politics, Nietzsche provided them with a marvelous thematic reservoir with which they could proceed into a postliberal world. It is this perhaps which accounts for the ease with which certain Asconans, life-reformers, expressionists and George Kreis adherents could move from anarchist–liberationist to Fascist and Nazi positions.[135] These dissenting

131. Klages was "the first thinker since Nietzsche in whose works vitalism was overtly creating concrete myths" (Lukacs, *Destruction of Reason*, 526, 522ff). He was a direct forerunner of national socialism, Lukacs believed, but, given his reservations, destined more for the coffeehouses than the streets.

132. Ernst Bloch, "Romantik des Diluvium," in *Erbschaft dieser Zeit* (Zürich: Oprecht and Helbling, 1935), 246, 250–251. See too the new English version, *Heritage of Our Times*, translated by Neville Plaice and Stephen Plaice (Berkeley, Los Angeles, and Oxford: University of California Press, 1991), 306, 309–310.

133. Hinton Thomas, "Nietzsche in Weimar Germany," 84–87.

134. "Ludwig Klages can represent for us the Schwabingites who did *not* come to Ascona (those who *might*, who *should*, have been there, because of their ideas)" (Green, *Mountain of Truth*, 162). The relationship to Ascona may not only have been spiritual; rumors abounded that Klages was the lover of Ascona's highly influential, emancipating eroticist, Reventlow.

135. Fascism in many ways regarded itself as an avant-garde phenomenon. Certainly many of the intellectuals attracted to it did (George L. Mosse, "Fascism and the Avant Garde" in *Masses and Man*, 229–245).

impulses cut across and combined with all kinds of political and cultural postures. All were characterized by postrationalist propensities. One road from this could and did lead to fascism and nazism but this was not the only path taken.

The avant-garde was, however, limited coteries of creative artists and intellectuals. In order to document the process by which Nietzsche was more broadly diffused we must turn our attention to more popular areas, to those interest groups and movements, even whole communities, that sought somehow to weave a Nietzschean pattern into the fabric of their institutions.

CHAPTER IV

Nietzscheanism Institutionalized

Society's stomach is stronger than mine, it can digest me.
Nietzsche, *Human, All Too Human*

Nietzscheanism was not—nor could it have been—a separate politi-cal ideology backed by its own political party or movement. The Nietzschean impulse became a potent protean force precisely because it was not organized. Requiring no formal commitment, possessed of no set dogma, its very elasticity facilitated entry into multiple areas of German institutional and community life. It did so inevitably through processes of dynamic and contextual selection; it was shaped and fil-tered according to the perceived needs of the appropriating institution. With some the reception was wholehearted and rhapsodic, with others, more tentative and fragmentary. As a rule it assumed explicit, conscious form; occasionally it operated subliminally, insinuating itself into the thematics of those very groups that voiced anti-Nietzsche sentiments. Galvanized as a rule for radical purposes it often led to unintended conservative consequences. Because Nietzscheanism was seldom an in-dependent constitutive force, it was subject to institutional constraints and competing ideological imperatives. Nevertheless it performed a va-riety of crucial functions: it acted as solvent, leavener, catalyst, and gadfly, challenging established postures and categories, while being ab-sorbed or re-created by them.

The history of the Nietzschean moment within late nineteenth- and early twentieth-century German feminism is keenly illustrative of these characteristics. There was something typically ironic about this celebra-tory feminist appropriation. Nietzsche's emphasis on power, hardness, and masculinity; his assessment that "good nature is in a woman a form of degeneration";[1] his cutting comments on the emancipation of women;[2] and his famous admonition: "You are going to women? Do not forget the whip!"[3] hardly seemed conducive to his becoming a champion of the feminist cause. As one caustic male critic put it, the "modern woman" had an ambivalent relationship to Nietzsche's whip: in the name of "emancipation" she sought to liberate herself from it but at the same time an ancient drive impelled her back to it.[4]

For those women attracted to Nietzsche's ideas there were two broad strategies for confronting the problem: one could argue that despite his hostile views on women's issues, his general message was of fundamental importance[5] or that the perception of Nietzsche's hostility to women was superficial and incorrect: Nietzsche was, in fact, unusually perceptive and championed the feminist cause at the very highest level of self-realization.[6] Whatever the particular line of reasoning, Nietzsche held out the prospect of a new kind of female liberation in which historical and institutional repressions of the past could be overcome. Like many other turn-of-the-century contemporaries, these women harnessed Nietzsche both for critical diagnosis and as inspiration towards

1. Nietzsche, *Ecce Homo,* 266.
2. Emancipation of women—that is the instinctive hatred of the abortive woman, who is incapable of giving birth, against the woman who is turned out well— the fight against the "man" is always a mere means, pretext, tactic. By raising themselves higher, as "woman in herself," as the "higher woman," as a female "idealist," they want to lower the level of the general rank of woman; and there is no surer means for that than higher education, slacks and political voting-cattle rights. At bottom, the emancipated are anarchists in the world of the "eternally feminine," the underprivileged whose most fundamental instinct is revenge.

(Nietzsche, *Ecce Homo,* 267)
3. Nietzsche, *Zarathustra,* 179.
4. Oskar Ewald, "Nietzsche und die Frauen (Die Peitsche Zarathustras)," *Wage* 6, no. 50 (1903), 1324–1328. See Krummel, *Nietzsche,* vol. 2, 138.
5. Hedwig Dohm, "Nietzsche und die Frauen," *Die Zukunft* 25 (24 December 1898), 534–543.
6. Eva, "Nietzsche und die Frauen," *Wiener Sonn- und Montags-Zeitung* 40, no. 37 (15 September 1902), 2ff. Quoted in Krummel, *Nietzsche,* vol. 2, 90. Nietzsche did indeed present himself as a thinker who understood women, although the level at which he championed their self-realization was clearly a matter of interpretation:

May I here venture to surmise that I *know* women? That is part of my Dionysian dowry. Who knows? Perhaps I am the first psychologist of the eternally feminine. They all love me—an old story—not counting *abortive* females, the "emancipated" who lack the stuff for children.—Fortunately, I am not willing to be torn to pieces: the perfect woman tears to pieces when she loves. . . . Ah, what a dangerous, creeping, subterranean little beast of prey she is! And yet so agreeable! . . . Woman is indescribably more evil than man; also cleverer; good nature is in a woman a form of degeneration. (*Ecce Homo,* 266)

a newfound freedom going beyond all previously sanctioned social limits.

These sentiments were most accessibly reflected and expressed in the popular literature of the day. As early as 1894 Hedwig Dohm's story—with its explicitly Nietzschean title, *Werde, die du bist* (Become what you are)—explored the frustrations of a women whose life, lived according to her prescribed role of service to others, was reduced to an odyssey of self-denial and self-obliteration. Dohm made no secret of the culprit: conventional morality had decreed that women could have "no self," so its tablets "had to be destroyed." The heroine, not surprisingly, regards Nietzsche as "the greatest living philosopher," the source of her passion to "transcend things as they are and climb away to greater heights."[7] Typical, too, of the genre was Mathieu Schwann's novel, *Liebe* (1901). This was peppered with quotes from *Zarathustra,* its New Woman driven by the Nietzschean-inspired desire to "dip deep into full, whole, undivided life." The novel made clear that repressive morality was rendering genuine love impossible and that "life-destroying prudery" was encouraging prostitution.[8] In Käthe Schirrmacher's 1895 novel *Halb,* the New Woman had already proclaimed:

> We want to be modern! That means a break with misunderstood Greek and Roman ideas—a break with orthodox religion—freedom, use of our energy, nature—independence, experimentation rather than abstraction and stereotype—a triumphant ego! In such a transition the weak may succumb, those transitional types that are no longer very old and not yet very new—but we, we will make it![9]

But feminist Nietzscheanism was, of course, not limited to the literary realm: it also became integral to a new kind of radical feminist politics. German women's organizations, like so many other realms of Wilhelmine society, were separated into working-class and bourgeois components.[10] Until the mid-1890s both followed roughly conventional courses. Socialist women conformed to the broad party outlook and

---

7. Hedwig Dohm, *Wie Frauen Werden—Werde, die du bist* (Breslau: Schles, Buch dr., Kunst-v. Verl. Aust., 1894). Quoted in Hinton Thomas, *Nietzsche in German Politics and Society,* 89–90. Hinton Thomas's chapter on the feminist movement is perhaps the best in the whole book.

8. Ibid., 89. Hinton Thomas also discusses the Nietzschean feminism of the very popular writer Gabriele Reuter (ibid., 90–91).

9. Quoted in Alfred G. Meyer, *The Feminism and Socialism of Lily Braun* (Bloomington: Indiana University Press, 1985), 31–32; see too 197, nn. 8, 9.

10. For a systematic history and outline of the German feminist problematic see Richard J. Evans, *The Feminist Movement in Germany 1894–1933* (London and Beverly Hills: Sage, 1976).

integrated their feminism within a disciplined Marxist ideology. Bourgeois feminists, while critical of prevalent sexism and discriminatory
practices, sought on the whole to preserve such social institutions as the
political system, existent property relations, the monogamous family,
and the church. Their conservative temperament often went hand in
hand with a reluctance to confront embarrassing subjects like prostitution, sexuality, and venereal disease. Within such circles Nietzsche's
presence was clearly unwelcome.

Only with the apparent radicalization of the women's movement
around the mid-1890s did the Nietzschean impulse began to make itself
apparent. Within German feminism Nietzscheanism was a dissident
moment, an expression of internal ferment. The iconoclastic Social
Democrat Lily Braun (1865–1916) and the radicalized bourgeois feminist Helene Stöcker (1869–1943) typified this tendency. For Braun,
Nietzsche at first signified the intoxicating possibility of individual
emancipation and general human liberation rather than a specific feminist message. In her memoirs, reporting on her conversation with
George Bernard Shaw, she expressed this exhilaration:

> The will to power, the highest possible development of the personality as the
> goal for the individual, the superior human being as the goal of humanity:
> the tones that had met me in England this time suddenly united into one
> single full chord. My heart beat almost to bursting like that of a prisoner
> whose leg chains are being taken off, and whose prison door is opening so
> that he can roam freely. He sees nothing more than the old familiar world of
> his youth, and yet it appears to him miraculously new. I was still half a child
> when I heard the first call to personal liberation out of Nietzsche's *Fröhliche
> Wissenschaft:* "Life says: Do not follow me, but yourself! Your own self!"
> Was this not this same summons today addressed to all humanity?[11]

Braun's female liberationism was therefore envisaged as a heroic
Nietzschean act of self-creation culminating in the formation of a superwoman. As a socialist she also collectivized this Nietzschean act: for
both moral and political reasons the creation of the superwoman was to
be conducted in solidarity with others similarly oppressed. The end
result would be the release of women's creative powers in all spheres of
life, especially those traditionally blocked to them.[12]

This generalized call to women to live life to the full and to reject the
narrow roles ascribed by bourgeois society was also an essential part

11. Lily Braun, *Memoiren einer Sozialistin,* vol. 2, *Kampfjahre* (Munich: Albert Langen, 1911), 585; translation from Meyer, *Lily Braun,* 103.
12. Meyer, *Lily Braun,* 141ff.

of the message that Stöcker—the most prominent and effective Nietzschean feminist in Germany—imparted in her string of writings from as early as 1893 on.[13] Nietzsche had demanded of both sexes a "higher, brighter, more joyous culture." He had set forth the task of the future, the challenge to unite the apparently irreconcilable: "being at once a free person, a unique personality, and a loving woman."[14]

Until around 1900 Stöcker's feminist Nietzscheanism, however radical, did not go beyond the demands acceptable to the movement as a whole. Only then did she muster her Nietzscheanism to mount a head-on attack on conventional sexual practices and institutions.[15] The New Morality she championed went far beyond the conventional feminism of the women's organization, *Bund Deutscher Frauenvereine* (League of German Women's Associations).

The New Morality explicitly took its inspiration from Nietzsche who had "led the great search." It sought a "reform of sexual ethics,"[16] which would constitute an essential part of the joyous creation of "new forms and new feelings for new people."[17] The New Morality laid down a critique of both conventional marriage and sexual life-denying asceticism.[18] Sexuality, for women as well as for men, was a fundamental part of life, a legitimate and positive part of being human.

It was *one* artist in particular—one of the greatest of the past century—who gave us a religion of joy which spiritualizes, enhances, and idolizes every-

13. Helene Stöcker, "Frauengedanken," in her *Die Liebe und die Frauen* (Berlin, 1908), 24–29; Stöcker, "Friedrich Nietzsche und die Frauen," *Das Magazin für Litteratur* 67 (1898), 128–132, 153–158.
14. Helene Stöcker, "Nietzsches Frauenfeindschaft," *Die Zukunft* 34 (1901), 432.
15. Evans has suggested a relevant biographical reason for this turn. "Stöcker's views began to change because of an unhappy love affair with a married man" (*Feminist Movement*, 118). Whereas before she had not disapproved of marriage she now came to regard it as a serious constriction, a matter of property, and even of prostitution rather than the relationship of love that Nietzsche had advocated. Even more radically, she came to reject chastity as a womanly virtue and preached a Nietzschean form of active sexual liberation. Her love affair was with none other than the extremely right-wing, almost fanatically Nietzschean Alexander Tille, whom we shall discuss later in the chapter. It was precisely their common Nietzscheanism—especially its eugenic emphases—that drew them together. Stöcker also extracted a Zarathustrian lesson from her plight. As she put it to fellow feminist Anna Pappritz, she now sought strength not happiness (Amy Hackett, "Helene Stöcker: Left-Wing Intellectual and Sex Reformer," in *When Biology Became Destiny*, ed. Renate Bridenthal et al. [New York: Monthly Review Press, 1984], 111–112, 128, n. 6).
16. *Mutterschutz: Zeitschrift zur Reform der sexuellen Ethik*. See the intensely Nietzschean opening statement by Stöcker, "Zur Reform der sexuellen Ethik" 1, no. 1 (1905).
17. Stöcker, "Frauenfeindschaft," 432.
18. Nietzsche was again at the center of this antiascetic moment (Helene Stöcker, "Von neuer Ethik," *Mutterschutz* 2, no. 1 [1906], 3–4).

thing earthly. Friedrich Nietzsche taught us how to "overcome" the passions. For centuries the Church has known only one means to deal with them: castration. Nietzsche understood that with such a radical cure we destroy life itself, that we attack life itself at the roots. Thus he teaches the spiritualization of sensuality, "love" as the greatest triumph over sterile ascetism.[19]

As a biological and spiritual imperative, love was to be allowed beyond the restraints of marriage. The double standard that permitted only men sexual satisfaction outside matrimony had to be abolished. Proponents of the New Morality repeatedly argued that there was no necessary connection between love and the formal legal institution of marriage. Marriage, they insisted, too often rendered relations a matter of property. Lily Braun held that children who were born out of wedlock were potentially the elite of humanity, being the products of pure love, yet in Christian society and under capitalism these most valuable members of humanity were destined to perish.[20]

The institutional expression of the New Morality was the breakaway *Bund für Mutterschutz* (League for the Protection of Mothers) established in 1905. By 1912 it could claim about four thousand members. Apart from Stöcker and Braun, well-known figures such as Iwan Bloch, Hedwig Dohm, Ellen Key, Max Marcuse, Werner Sombart and Max Weber endorsed its activities.[21] The league advocated state recognition of unformalized marriages, established hostels for unmarried mothers, promoted free love, and provided easier access to contraception. It was in constant tension with the more conservative Bund Deutscher Frauenvereine which resisted their attempts to legalize abortion and after 1909 refused to grant them membership.

Liberals and the mainline women's organizations regarded the league, especially its Nietzsche connection, as an outrage to Wilhelmine respectability. Anton Erkelenz pointedly advised Stöcker "to pursue her Nietzscheanism *outside* the League."[22] Its critics, most notably Helen Lange, regarded erotic Nietzscheanism as a betrayal of the moderating, cultivating, Bildungs conception of personality and as an outright attack on the "honor of bourgeois morality." The source of this boundlessness, of this enslavement to the passions and the breakdown of

---

19. Helene Stöcker, "Nietzsches Frauenfeindschaft," in *Die Liebe und die Frauen* (Munich, 1905), 65ff, vii; translation from Schwentker, "Passion as a Mode of Life," 495–496, n. 16.
20. Meyer, *Lily Braun,* 118.
21. For a more comprehensive list see Evans, *Feminist Movement,* 121–122.
22. Ibid., 128.

sexual control was inevitably traced to Nietzsche.[23] Interestingly enough, there were also critics who admired Nietzsche, preferring to blame his "ultraradical feminist" acolytes, half-educated dilettantes who, unlike their master, had no sense of historical evolution and who mistakenly saw in him only the herald of immediate and limitless gratification.[24]

These outraged protests against anarchistic eroticism and immoralist boundlessness were rather misdirected. Stöcker and the women associated with the Bund für Mutterschutz were far more staid than the avant-garde Nietzschean feminists discussed in the last chapter. Indeed, in many ways their Nietzschean feminism revealed a conservative bias ironically undermining the empowerment they sought. While de Saint Point demanded the masculinization of women, they insisted upon the need to fully realize a separate, intrinsically feminine nature. Nietzsche's endlessly invoked injunction to "become what you are" was interpreted less as a call to individual self-creation than as an imperative to fulfill women's innate propensities. These feminists were thus inclined to quote Zarathustra's assertion that "everything about a woman has only one solution, namely pregnancy" and "the aim is always the child."[25] The league's founder, Ruth Bre, always emphasized love and motherhood.[26] Braun too constantly celebrated motherhood as the essential destiny of women and as the most noble form of self-actualization.[27] This generic notion of female self-realization increasingly became the focus of the New Morality. Very early on a perceptive critic allied to the mainstream women's movement noted that this emphasis on a pure female nature (*reine Weibnatur*) implicitly affirmed male supremacy. "In truth," she wrote, "Nietzscheanism in the female world signifies a renunciation of the demands of the 'radical egalitarians.' It establishes anew the [centrality of] the biological role and also, in transfigured form reaffirms male domination."[28]

Like other Nietzschean offshoots, this brand of feminism blurred

---

23. On Lange and the many other critics of the New Morality see Hinton Thomas, *Nietzsche*, 80–86.

24. Eva, "Nietzsche und die Frauen," 2ff.

25. See the analysis in Hinton Thomas, *Nietzsche*, 88.

26. For more on this völkisch social Darwinian feminist who sought the end of the "capitalist rule of man" and the restoration of matriarchy see Evans, *Feminist Movement*, 120–122, 159–160.

27. Meyer, *Lily Braun*, 125.

28. Marie Hecht, "Friedrich Nietzsches Einfluss auf die Frauen," *Die Frau* 6, no. 8 (1898/1899), 486–491; rep. in *Literarische Manifeste der Jahrhundertwende 1890–1910*, ed. Erich Rupert and Dieter Bänsch, 543–549 (Stuttgart: J. B. Metzlersche, 1970), 549, n. 16; 545.

conventional distinctions, rendering its political direction dangerously ambiguous.[29] Critics were similarly wary of the eugenics of the New Morality which, as one historian has remarked, "far from merely being a hedonistic call to shake off the shackles of old-fashioned repressive codes . . . was primarily a theory of practical evolutionism based on Darwinist and Nietzschean ideas."[30]

Well before the rise of nazism, eugenics was attractive to progressive as well as reactionary fin-de-siècle sources.[31] German feminist eugenics was closely tied to its Nietzschean Lebensphilosophie, which was glaringly apparent in the league's guidelines. It advocated a "joyous, life-affirming world-view" and sought "to protect life above all at its source, to let it emerge pure and strong."[32] From very early on Stöcker considered the Nietzschean eugenic vision valid.[33] Although this was clearly not a racist conception, and while her proposed measures were always educational and voluntary, she nevertheless advocated a species of Nietzschean "social hygiene" that today appears peculiarly suspect. Her New Ethic was biologically based and was aimed, after all, at nothing less than "the creation of a new human. One will have to find means of preventing the incurably ill or degenerate from reproducing."[34] Similar bio-eugenic guidelines characterized the league's activities and determined the women they helped.[35] Like so much else within political Nietzscheanism, the rejection of the present and the search for new worlds and a new humanity entailed peculiar combinations and socially and morally ambiguous results.

Feminist Nietzscheanism was an expression of a dissident impulse

---

29. Holding such Nietzschean views did not entail any inherently political position. Stöcker never joined the Socialist party, although she remained a left-wing intellectual, social reformer, and pacifist. Braun, like Stöcker, could never be dubbed orthodox; she maintained her feminism within an increasingly belligerent, war-affirming, and nationalistic frame.

30. Meyer, *Lily Braun*, 117.

31. Eugenically oriented social reform was often the work of "enlightened" people, including "Francis Galton (Darwin's cousin), Herbert Spencer, Cesare Lombroso, Ernst Häckel and Emma Goldmann" (Allan Janik, "The Jewish Self-hatred Hypothesis," in *Jews, Antisemitism and Culture in Vienna*, ed. I. Oxaal et al., 75–88 [London and New York: Routledge and Kegan Paul], 84).

32. Hackett, "Helene Stöcker," 115.

33. "Friedrich Nietzsche und die Frauen," *Bühne und Welt* 6, no. 20 (1904), 857–860. Of Nietzsche she concluded: "*Vielleicht auf keinem anderen Gebiet, wie auf dem einer höheren und ernsteren Auffassung von Liebe und Ehe, ihrer Bedeutsamkeit fuer die Zukunft der Rasse, für die Erhöhung des Typus Mensch lassen sich sein Wirkungen so sicher und segensreich spüren.*"

34. Helene Stöcker, "Zur Reform," 9. See too Hackett, "Helene Stöcker," 119, for more on the Nietzschean influence on Stöcker's eugenic thought.

35. Evans, *Feminist Movement*, 158ff.

within a single political movement. German Jewry provides a larger, community-wide canvas on which to portray the multileveled process of Nietzsche's reception. Here was an important minority group that assimilated Nietzsche into various aspects of its self-consciousness and its cultural and institutional life.

We must limit ourselves to examining organized streams of Jewish community life, omitting the considerable involvement of individual Jews with Nietzsche. We cannot consider the early and prominent role of people like Siegfried Lipiner, Georg Brandes and Georg Simmel[36] in interpreting and popularizing Nietzsche; these endeavors were done in the name of general, not Jewish, culture (and have been treated as such in this study). To be sure, they were not always perceived as such. After 1890, for instance, Nietzschean anti-Semites attributed what they took to be the prevalent distorted understanding of the philosopher—as libertarian and nihilist internationalist—to the Jewishness of his mediators,[37] whereas in the mid-1930s, when Nietzsche achieved something akin to official state recognition, Jewish commentators approvingly emphasized the ethnic background of his popularizers.[38] We must leave unresolved the recently made claim that precisely their marginality predisposed Jews to adopt a passionate interest in Nietzsche because his themes were so conducive to their post-traditional and assimilatory needs.[39] Here we must limit ourselves to the disparate functions Nietzsche fulfilled within explicitly Jewish contexts.

The differentiated but mainly positive response of even the most conservative and official organs of the German Jewish community reflected the complex centrality of Jews and Judaism to Nietzsche's work. In both his hostile and friendly deliberations, he insisted on the fateful role of Jews within European history. Whether one regards these views as a unified and coherent element of Nietzsche's larger systematic out-

---

36. Simmel was not strictly speaking a Jew. His Jewish father converted to Catholicism and his mother came from a Jewish family who baptized her as a Lutheran. Simmel himself was baptized and married a non-Jewish wife. The perception that Simmel was Jewish nevertheless persisted (Peter Gay, "Encounter with Modernism," in *Freud, Jews and Other Germans* [New York: Oxford University Press, 1978], 98).

37. For an Austrian example see "Friedrich Nietzsche und die Modernen," *Deutsche Zeitung*, no. 10294 (28 August 1900).

38. See for instance Leo Hirsch on Siegfried Lipiner, "'Beinahe Echt?': Nietzsche und der jüdische Prometheus," *Central Verein Zeitung* 14, no. 25 (20 June 1935).

39. Jacob Golomb, "Nietzsche and the Marginal Jews" (in Hebrew), *Jerusalem Studies in Jewish Thought* 4 (1985), 97–143. Since the present work examines the enormous range and intensity of Nietzsche's appeal to the general literate public, such claims to Jewish exceptionality are problematic.

look or as disparate and self-contradictory, from the Jewish point of view there was much in his oeuvre that required confrontation and could be usefully mined.[40] How could one avoid negotiating and interpreting ambiguous passages like the following one from *Morgenröte* with its simultaneously affirmative and ominous tone?:

> Among the spectacles to which the coming century invites us is the decision as to the destiny of the Jews of Europe. That their die is cast, that they have crossed their Rubicon, is now palpably obvious: all that is left for them is either to become the masters of Europe or to lose Europe. . . . They themselves know best that a conquest of Europe, or any kind of act of violence, on their part is not to be thought of: but they also know that at some future time Europe may fall into their hands like a ripe fruit if only they would just extend them. To bring that about they need, in the meantime, to distinguish themselves in every domain of European distinction and to stand everywhere in the first rank until they have reached the point at which they themselves determine what is distinguishing. . . . Then, when the Jews can exhibit as their work such jewels and golden vessels as the European nations of a briefer and less profound experience could not and cannot produce, when Israel will have transformed its eternal vengeance into an eternal blessing for Europe: then there will again arrive that seventh day on which the ancient Jewish God may *rejoice* in himself, his creation and his chosen people—and let us all, all of us, rejoice with him![41]

From early on Jewish analysts were aware that Nietzsche covered both negative and positive extremes. On the one hand he endowed the Jews with a world-historical stain. *On the Genealogy of Morals* held the "priestly people" responsible for nothing less than beginning "*the slave revolt in morality:* that revolt which has a history of two thousand years behind it and which we no longer see because it—has been victorious." The history of Israel, as depicted in *The Antichrist,* consisted of "the radical falsification of all nature, all naturalness, all reality, of the whole inner world as well as the outer." Yet at the same time, Jewish readers found in Nietzsche perhaps the most pronounced non-Jewish opponent of the racist and anti-Semitic "swindle," and the most outspoken ad-

---

40. For three recent attempts to examine Nietzsche's views on Jews and Judaism in relation to his whole philosophy, see Arnold M. Eisen, "Nietzsche and the Jews Reconsidered," *Jewish Social Studies* 48, no. 1 (Winter 1986); Willard Mittelman, "Nietzsche's Attitude toward the Jews," *Journal of the History of Ideas* 49, no. 2 (April–June 1988); Jacob Golomb, "Nietzsche's Judaism of Power," *Revue des études juives* 147 (July–December 1988).

41. Perhaps foreseeing what his Jewish commentators constantly referred to as a European "Jewish Renaissance" this passage is couched in extremely double-edged language (Nietzsche, *Daybreak*, 124–125).

mirer of the capacities of the European Jews of his time.[42] His views on the Bible too could not be bettered:

> The *Old* Testament—that is something else again: all honour to the Old Testament! I find in it great human beings, a heroic landscape, and something of the very rarest quality in the world, the incomparable naivete of the *strong heart;* what is more, I find a people. In the New one, on the other hand, I find nothing but petty sectarianism, mere rococo of the soul, mere involutions, nooks, queer things.[43]

Jewish appropriations of Nietzsche began to appear parallel to his general popularization. Despite his problematic side, the celebratory, apologetic, and defensive Jewish uses of Nietzsche very soon assumed prominence. After all, no other contemporary European thinker of similar stature had been more complimentary to the Jews and more scathing to their enemies. The overwhelmingly liberal, middle-class Jewish community was thus predisposed to look more favorably upon Nietzsche than were other—liberal or conservative—sectors of the bourgeoisie.

Overall, Nietzsche was converted into an asset for the Jewish community. Most of the appraisals published in its journals emphasized the positive elements. The more awkward, negative ingredients were not omitted but muted or explained away. As early as 1892 the organ for liberal German Jewry, the *Allgemeine Zeitung des Judentums,* carried a number of admiring and balanced expositions celebrating Nietzsche, his praise for Jewry, and hopes for a Jewish renaissance.[44] Similarly admiring pieces appeared throughout the community in better-known as well as comparatively obscure sources and in more scholarly works.[45] At the

42. Nietzsche, *On the Genealogy of Morals,* 33–34; "The Antichrist," in *The Portable Nietzsche,* 592. Nietzsche's pro-Jewish remarks are legion. A little-known, extreme version of this is to be found in a discarded draft for a passage from *Ecce Homo:*

> Whoever reads me in Germany today, has first de-Germanized himself thoroughly as I have done: my formula is known, "to be a good German means to de-Germanize oneself"; or he is—no small distinction among Germans—of Jewish descent.—Jews among Germans are always the higher race—more refined, spiritual, kind. *L'adorable* Heine, they say in Paris. (p. 262)

For a summary of these more positive views see Kaufmann, *Nietzsche,* chap. 10.
43. Nietzsche, *Genealogy of Morals,* 144.
44. Leo Berg, "Friedrich Nietzsche über das Judenthum," *Allgemeine Zeitung des Judentums* 56 (1892), 282–284; Maximilian Stein, "Friedrich Nietzsche und das Judentum," *Allgemeine Zeitung des Judentums,* 64 (1900), 451–453.
45. Auguste Steinberg's "Nietzsche und das Judentum" (*Ost und West* 3, no. 8 [1903], 547–556) was one of the better-known sources. This highly respectful piece was sympathetic to Zionism and takes Nietzsche to task for envisaging Jewish renaissance in terms of its absorption into Europe rather than taking into account the reawakening of a

same time Nietzsche was often employed as an authoritative crutch in the ongoing defense against anti-Semitism: indeed, anti-Semitism was itself sometimes diagnosed within the Nietzschean frame and classified as a classical form of ressentiment.[46] Under national socialism (in which Nietzsche had become an official, national prophet) entirely new forms of apologetics and accommodations were, of course, required. Jews highlighted their role in the antipositivist revolt and in the discovery of Nietzsche and made it into a virtue, inverting older anti-Semitic accusations: "Today one must hammer into the brain," wrote one Jewish commentator in 1934, "that it was Jews who almost alone took a stand for Nietzsche and against trite materialism: Georg Brandes in the north, Henri Bergson in the west, Berdyczewski in the east." It was a prevalent misconception that "at the beginning of the century there were only Kommerzienräte [councillors of commerce] and 'historical' materialists amongst our parents. The opposite is the case."[47]

These were not the only general functions Nietzsche fulfilled in Jewish life. Like elsewhere in Germany the Nietzschean idiom, its slogans and catchwords, soon became commonplace and were applied to a variety of Jewish situations. These had various applications. They helped, for instance, as tools in the formulation of a newly conceptualized sense of Jewish solidarity. Thus the popular German Jewish magazine Ost und West—a journal devoted to mediating the largely pre-

modern Jewish national self-consciousness. For an example of the more obscure, see the anonymous "Nitzsche und das Judenthum" (Dr. Adolf Bruell's Populär-wissenschaftliche Monatsblätter 21, no. 3 [1 March 1901], 49–52). (The incorrect spelling remained throughout.) This article stressed that while Nietzsche viewed Jews from without he was nevertheless the "great ethnological analyst of the Jewish problem" (p. 52). Also see the long section on Nietzsche in the scholarly work by Albert Lewkowitz, a teacher at the Jewish theological seminary in Breslau, in his Religiöse Denker der Gegenwart: Vom Wandel der modernen Lebensanschauung (Berlin: Philo, 1923).

46. For such a diagnosis, see Theodor Lessing, Deutschland und seine Juden (Prague: Neumann, 1933). See too "Nietzsche, ein Opfer des Antisemitismus," Mitteilungen des Vereins zur Abwehr des Antisemitismus, no. 15 (1901); "Nietzsche und der Antisemitismus," Mitteilungen des Vereins zur Abwehr des Antisemitismus, no. 14 (1904). For the later period see "Nietzsche und der Antisemitismus," Allgemeine Zeitung des Judentums 82 (1918), 89–90; "Friedrich Nietzsche als Wegbereiter völkischer und judenfeindlicher strömungen?" Bayerische isrealitische Gemeindezeitung 7, no. 1 (1 January 1931), 1–2; K. W. Goldschmidt, "Nietzsches Stellung zum Judentum," Berliner Gemeindeblatt (February 1931). Such activities were not confined to Jews. See the German Democratic party's Wider den Nationalsozialismus (Berlin, 1932), in particular August Weber's article, "Die Nationalsozialisten sind auf dem Wege des politischen Mordes vorangegangen!" 51–52. See too P. B. Wiener, "Die Parteien der Mitte," in Entscheidungsjahr 1932: Zur Judenfrage in der Endphase der Weimarer Republik, ed. Werner E. Mosse, 289–321. (Tübingen: J. C. B. Mohr, 1966), 297.

47. Leo Hirsch, "Friedrich Nietzsche und der jüdische Geist," Der Morgen 10 (1934), 187.

emancipated Jewish world of Eastern Europe to an acculturated German Jewish audience[48]—without mentioning Nietzsche's name portrayed the mutually antithetical yet complementary qualities of eastern and western Jewry in categories derived directly from *The Birth of Tragedy*. Eastern Jews were fundamentally Dionysian, western Jews, Apollonian, and their mutually fruitful synthesis would bring about the same kind of Jewish renaissance that Nietzsche had envisaged for Germany.[49] Nietzschean folk wisdom also consoled; in the attempt to provide a modicum of hope and meaning to the prevalent suffering under nazism, German Jewish leaders repeatedly turned to the famous aphorism: "Whatever does not destroy me makes me stronger."[50]

Of course, the Nietzschean idiom was as easily employed to undermine as to bolster Jewish solidarity. Thus in 1910 Friedrich Blach transmuted Jewish assimilation into a life-affirming Nietzschean act. Forcefully advocating collective Jewish self-immolation he wrote: "Well then, so be it, free and joyful suicide. For I no longer want to be the self that I was born. 'Die at the right time: thus spake Zarathustra.' We have endured too long."[51]

But these were all incidental uses. There were far more direct and substantive appropriations. It is an interesting measure of the popularity of Nietzsche-like slogans that a leading liberal rabbi—Cesar Selig-

48. On the general history and dynamics of this question see Steven E. Aschheim, *Brothers and Strangers: The East European Jew in German and German–Jewish Consciousness, 1800–1923* (Madison: University of Wisconsin Press, 1982).
49. Fabius Schach, "Ost und West," *Ost und West* 3, no. 8 (1903), 547–555. See too Gert Mattenklott, "Nietzscheanismus und Judentum," in *Jahrbuch*, vol. 1, *Probleme deutsch-jüdischer Identität*, ed. Norbert Altenhofer and Renate Heuer, 57–71. (Frankfurt am Main: Archiv Bibliographia Judaica, 1985), 60–61. I thank Itta Shidletzky for this reference.
50. Quoted in Jacob Boas, "Countering Nazi Defamation: German Jews and the Jewish Tradition, 1933–1938," *Leo Baeck Institute Yearbook* 34 (1989), 219. See also Fritz Goldschmidt, "Mehr Selbstvertrauen," *Centralverein-Zeitung* 12 (28 September 1933), "Rosch Haschana, 5696," *Centralverein-Zeitung* 14 (26 September 1935); Ernst Jacob, "Freiheit durch Bindung: Pessachbetrachtung," *Centralverein-Zeitung* 13 (29 March 1934). Ironically, if Jews looked to Nietzsche for consolation, the Nazis were invoking him for precisely opposite purposes. Commenting on a *Mischling* mother (a mother of mixed blood) a Nuremberg Nazi official proclaimed: "A mother who behaves in such a way is so strongly influenced by Jewish ideas that presumably all attempts to enlighten her will be in vain. . . . For the National Socialist *Weltanschauung* which is determined by blood can only be taught to those who have German blood in their veins. In this case, one ought to put into practice Nietzsche's dictum: 'That which is on the point of collapse should be given the final push'" (Jeremy Noakes, "The Development of Nazi Policy towards the German–Jewish 'Mischlinge,' 1933–1945," *Leo Baeck Institute Yearbook* 34 [1989], 300–301).
51. Friedrich Blach, *Die Juden in Deutschland* (Berlin: K. Curtius, 1911), 42.

mann—coined the much-quoted phrase: "the will to Judaism."[52] Seligmann presents an interesting example of the multilayered response
Nietzsche induced within circles of liberal Judaism. On the surface this
was a meeting of total opposites. Seligmann typified the liberal Bildungs
tradition of mainstream German Jewry. There was nothing less
Nietzschean than his emphasis on the quiet, settled, industrious, and
patriotic life. Yet as a liberal rabbi Seligmann felt it imperative to be
open to the currents of modern thought. Nietzsche, Seligmann had no
doubt, was central to this enterprise. He praised Nietzsche as an embodiment of modernity, a nondogmatic seeker of truth with no final or
closed system, a latterday prophet who could not be silenced or made
to die. Although he was quite aware of the more questionable dimensions of Nietzsche's version of Jewish history, he was more impressed
by the fact that not even the most chauvinist Jew had endowed Jews and
Judaism with greater significance than Nietzsche.[53]

For Seligmann encountering Nietzsche was itself a sign of Jewish
cultural openness. Ultimately, however, his Bildungs liberalism entailed
a rejection of the Nietzschean message. The problem, he wrote, was not
the prophetic idea of morality, as Nietzsche believed, but rather its lack
of fulfillment. For Judaism, unlike for Nietzsche, it was not man but the
Unmensch that had to be overcome.[54]

The prominent orthodox personality Rabbi N. A. Nobel also ultimately rejected Nietzschean illiberalism. Nietzschean immoralism and
contempt for the weak were unacceptable. "There is," wrote Nobel,
"only one morality and it is democratic, cultivates no disproportionate
cult of genius, advocates no romantic, mystic love of the distant but
says, 'Love thy neighbour as thyself.'"[55]

Nobel nevertheless went considerably further than Seligmann, and in
tandem with some Protestant formulations of the same period, in 1898
he expounded perhaps the first version of the German Jewish temptation to Nietzscheanize Judaism (and, at times, Judaize Nietzsche). For

52. On that phrase and Seligmann, see George L. Mosse, "The Secularization of
Jewish Theology," in *Masses and Man,* 257–259 and *German Jews Beyond Judaism*
(Bloomington: Indiana University Press, 1985), 74–75.
53. Cesar Seligmann, "Nietzsche und das Judentum," in his *Judentum und moderne
Weltanschauung* (Frankfurt am Main: J. Kaufmann, 1905), 69–70, 76–79. He especially
emphasized Nietzsche's love for the Hebrew Bible and his preference for it over the New
Testament.
54. Ibid., 86–89.
55. N. A. Nobel, "Friedrich Nietzsche's Stellung zum Judenthum," *Die Jüdische
Presse* 31, nos. 36, 37, 39 (7 September, 14 September, and 28 September 1900), 414,
373f.

Nobel the prevalent chronicling of what Nietzsche had said about the Jews and anti-Semitism did not penetrate to the core. Far more essential was the comparative inner relationship between these two structures.[56] Like Nietzsche, Nobel proclaimed, Judaism had always stressed the element of will. Indeed, it was precisely this volitional ingredient that had provided Judaism with its glory. Moreover, the Nietzschean call for Übermenschen, the notion of the development of humanity in terms of ever-higher goals, was the basis of the Jewish messianic faith. Here Nietzsche and the prophets were one.

As against the pessimistic Schopenhauerian worldview Judaism had always been characterized by a kind of affirmative Nietzschean Lebensphilosophie:

> Insofar as Jewish morality holds world-flight and renunciation to be immoral, it creates very immanent, very earthly moral values. The commandments of Judaism relate to life itself in all its details. It elevates the most common matters in the sphere of religion: it ennobles work and rest, food and drink. Every Jew who consciously fulfills one of the so-called ceremonial laws thereby enacts the transvaluation of values of which Nietzsche spoke.[57]

Such pontifications were not universally popular. It was one thing for Jews to study and confront Nietzsche, one critic complained, and quite another for rabbis of all people to transform Nietzsche into a Jewish prophet. The hysterical rabbinic attempt to "turn the German philosopher into a Hebrew" was nothing short of laughable, yet another misguided instance of Jewish "modernism."[58]

Still, the casuistic Nietzscheanization of Judaism became an ongoing temptation.[59] Writing in 1925 in the *Centralverein-Zeitung*, a journal

56. Ibid., 374.
57. Ibid., 413–414.
58. D. Neumark, "Die jüdische Moderne," *Allgemeine Zeitung des Judentums* 64, no. 45 (9 November 1900), 536.
59. We should note parenthetically that this equation of Nietzsche as ultimate Judaic prophet persists in the most unlikely incarnation in present-day Israel. Rebbe Arye Weissfisch, a pious *hared* from the highly orthodox Mea Shearim quarter in Jerusalem has made his life into an obsessive mission to spread the word. According to Weissfisch, Nietzsche's crowning love was Judaism and the Jews. This is a Nietzsche, indeed, who admires Judaism more than the Jews themselves do. For Weissfisch, in the post-Holocaust vacuum of faith, far from being a subversion, Nietzsche reveals to Jews the inner meaning and significance of their faith. Nietzsche rejected only "the God of Christianity" while in Judaism and Jews he perceived the "striving for morality, for the sanctity of man." His Nietzsche is patently a "holy man" whose wisdom has been touched by divinity. Weissfisch's ultra-Orthodox, anti-Zionist *Naturei Karta* community, opposed to all modernisms let alone Nietzscheana, has obviously taken exception to his idiosyncratic activities. For one of the few accessible English-language descriptions of Weissfisch's discovery of Nietzsche through his yeshiva training, and what others widely regard as slightly bizarre activities around Nietzsche, see Abraham Rabinovich, "Gathering of Foes," *Jerusalem*

identified with liberal German Jewry, Isaac Heinemann presented the Nietzschean model of the Übermensch as normative to Judaism and central to the philosophical–religious systems of Philo, Jehuda Halevi, and Maimonides. While maintaining Judaism's Übermenschlich dimension, Heinemann sought to temper it with a more human, less elitist face; Judaism softened and redirected the Übermenschlich mission, encouraging bonds between the leaders and the masses and linking the higher individuals with the people. Great knowledge, far from increasing distance, automatically entailed greater responsibility. Heinemann's resultant Jewish Übermensch was thus the synthesis of the Greek notion of the higher man with Jewish conceptions of responsibility and solidarity.[60]

Heinemann's was a critical application of Nietzschean categories to Judaism. Others were far less measured. In 1932 Heinrich Berl proclaimed Nietzsche to be nothing less than the "prophet of the Jewish spirit." Here was a relationship that had to be understood in terms of congeniality rather than consanguinity. Judaism and Nietzsche coincided in their psychology and ethics and shared the same paradigmatic mentality. Nietzsche had to be grasped in terms of the great Western cultural conflict between Greece (which he despised) and Judaism (which he admired). This, Berl argued in a moment of eccentricity extreme even amongst Nietzscheans, was reflected in Nietzsche's guiding categories: plastic and Apollonian Greece as against musical and Dionysian Judaism!

For Berl there were crucial Jewish–Nietzschean parallelisms. Jewish ethics was a *Gattungsethik* (species ethic) and Nietzsche was the first *Gattungsethiker*. Here was a morality, moreover, which—in its single-minded devotion to Yahweh—stood beyond good and evil. Nietzsche, Berl proclaimed, erred in his depiction of Jewish slave morality: throughout their history Jews had possessed primal Nietzschean characteristics! What Nietzsche had overlooked was that the slaves' will to domination was more powerful than the masters' because the masters already possessed external power while the slaves remained hungry for it.[61]

Post (26 April 1986). In a letter to Weissfisch (10 July 1980), Walter Kaufmann remarked that this position "strikes me as quite odd." I thank Rabbi Weissfisch for kindly providing me with a copy of this letter.

60. Isaac Heinemann, "Der Begriff des Übermenschen in der modernen Religionsphilosophie," *Der Morgen* 1 (1925).

61. Heinrich Berl, "Nietzsche und das Judentum," *Menorah* (1932), 59–61, 67–68.

While most of the presentations discussed above were surprising, given either their religious or establishmentarian provenance, they were nevertheless all variations on a conserving theme, identifying parallels and integrating Judaism and the Nietzschean thematic. They were all the products of circles concerned with the perpetuation, in some way or another, of normative Judaism. Like Nietzscheanism elsewhere, however, the real force of Nietzsche's impact was felt within non-conformist and dissident elements of the Jewish community. Amongst these groups Nietzsche became a galvanizing element in the post-traditional quest for regenerative Jewish forms and postliberal modes of identity.

It is hardly surprising that in the life and thought of Franz Rosenzweig (1886–1929), the most innovative German–Jewish theologian of the twentieth century, Nietzsche—the man and his mode of thinking if not his philosophy—stood as a shining beacon.[62] Impelled by the shattering experience of World War I, Rosenzweig's work, like so many other major cultural productions of the Weimar Republic, sought to rethink everything anew. Here was a theology of radical renewal characterized by its critical breakdown of accepted categories. As Gershom Scholem described it in 1930, there was an "obvious impossibility of recognizing the realms of orthodoxy or liberalism in Rosenzweig's world."[63] Rosenzweig described his work as "quite fantastic, entirely unpublishable, equally scandalous to 'Christians, Jews and heathens.'"[64] Nietzsche was central to Rosenzweig's rejection of Hegelian idealism and abstract academic scholarship, his discovery of a "living" Judaism, his epistemological emphasis on "becoming," and his insistence upon a personal philosophy in which humans had to be the start-

---

62. Recently Robert A. Cohen has suggested that as much as Rosenzweig praised Nietzsche he also sought to bury him. Whereas he admired Nietzsche's post-Hegelian and personal approach, there were basic points of disagreement. Rosenzweig, Cohen argues, regarded Nietzsche's individualism as inferior to Goethe's. Moreover, both Goethe's and Nietzsche's neopagan religious alternatives were inferior to Judeo-Christian options. Rosenzweig's post-Hegelian sense of subjectivity made him equate revelation with love since both implied the paradoxical meeting of heteronomy and autonomy. Nietzsche's radical subjectivity had missed this genuine meaning of subjectivity and divorced it entirely from truth. Of course, Rosenzweig's neo-Orthodoxy rejected key ingredients of Nietzsche. Nevertheless, Cohen's comments obscure the fact that, as Rosenzweig himself insisted, the influence was seminal ("Rosenzweig vs. Nietzsche," *Nietzsche-Studien* 19 (1990), 346–366.

63. Gershom Scholem, "On the 1930 Edition of Rosenzweig's *Star of Redemption*," in *The Messianic Idea in Judaism* (New York: Schocken, 1972), 320. See too his comments on *The Star of Redemption*'s profoundly revolutionary nature and impact.

64. Nahum N. Glatzer, ed., *Franz Rosenzweig: His Life and Thought* (New York: Schocken, 1976), 81.

ing point of thought.[65] In 1918 he wrote of Hegel: "It's a pity about
him! Only Nietzsche (and Kant) pass muster!"[66]

Quite independent of the content of his own theology, Rosenzweig
called for a theologian-philosopher impelled to translate "theological
problems into human terms" and to bring "human problems into the
pale of theology."[67] Nietzsche the heretic was precisely the embodiment
of such a vision. A Nietzschean rejection of dogma and formulae and an
affirmation of complete and concrete freedom of individual choice characterized Rosenzweig's project as did an underlying awareness of, and
temptation to, nihilism on the way to faith. As Rosenzweig put it, in his
1921 magnum opus, *The Star of Redemption,* Nietzsche

> was one man who knew his own life and his own soul like a poet, and
> obeyed their voice like a holy man, and who was for all that a philosopher.
> What he philosophized has by now become almost a matter of indifference.
> Dionysiac and Superman, Blond Beast and Eternal Return—where are they
> now? But none of those who now feel the urge to philosophize can any
> longer by-pass the man himself, who transformed himself in the transfor-
> mation of his mental images, whose soul feared no height, who clambered
> after Mind, that daredevil climber, up to the steep pinnacle of madness,
> where there was no more Onward. The fearsome and challenging image of
> the unconditional vassalage of soul to mind could henceforth not be
> eradicated. . . . For the philosopher, philosophy was the cool height to which
> he had escaped from the mists of the plain. For Nietzsche this dichotomy
> between height and plain did not exist in his own self: he was of a piece, soul
> and mind a unity, man and thinker a unity to the last.[68]

If Rosenzweig's work was a conscious part of the German-Jewish
impulse to renewal, it remained a densely personal endeavor independent of any larger social and political movement. For this we must turn
to Zionism and the role that Nietzsche played there.

Classical Zionism, that essentially secular and modernizing movement, was acutely aware of the crisis of Jewish tradition and its supporting institutions. Nietzsche was enlisted as an authority for articulating the movement's ruptured relationship with the past and a force in
its drive to normalization and its activist ideal of the self-creating Hebraic New Man. Unlike the circles mentioned above, Zionists were not

65. N. Glatzer, foreword to *The Star of Redemption,* by Franz Rosenzweig, trans.
William W. Hallo (Boston: Beacon, 1971); Glatzer, *Franz Rosenzweig,* ix–xxxviii.
66. Ibid., 81.
67. Paul Mendes-Flohr, "Franz Rosenzweig's Concept of Philosophical Faith," *Leo
Baeck Institute Yearbook* 34 (1989), 368. Mendes-Flohr gives an instructive analysis of
Rosenzweig's conception of the relation between philosophy and theology.
68. Rosenzweig, *Star of Redemption,* 9.

particularly interested in harmonizing Judaism with Nietzscheanism. What moved them was not Nietzsche's writings on Judaism but his radical antitraditionalism, his rebellious, transvaluative attitudes that they could bring to bear on their own Jewish experience. Zionism, to be sure, always bore an inherent tension—pressures for Jewish continuity as against the imperative to rebel—which muted this Nietzschean impulse or deflected it into more conserving directions.[69]

Nevertheless, until the end of World War I, the radical Nietzschean note functioned as a means for the expression of activist and redemptive Zionist hopes. In 1902, for instance, the future first president of the State of Israel, Chaim Weizmann, wrote from Switzerland to his then-sweetheart Vera Khatzman, "Vera, my joy, I am sending you Nietzsche: learn to read and understand him. This is the best and finest thing I can send you."[70] Weizmann never spelled out the reasons for his admiration, yet it was perhaps implicit in his earlier comment: "The French are incapable of understanding Nietzsche. They are too superficial for a revaluation of all values."[71] Presumably the Jews impelled by Zionism were not.[72]

Within German Zionism the attraction to Nietzsche was very much a generational affair.[73] The first Zionist generation, far from being a part of the revolt against liberal rationalism and positivism, embodied

69. For a superb analysis of this tension see Gershom Scholem, "Zionism: Dialectic of Continuity and Rebellion," in *Unease in Zion*, ed. Ehud Ben Ezer (Jerusalem: Academic Press, 1974).

70. Leonard Stein, ed., *The Letters and Papers of Chaim Weizmann*, collab. Gedalia Yogev, vol. 1 (London: Oxford University Press, 1968), 340–341.

71. Ibid., vol. 1, 95. "When you can read German," Weizmann promised Vera in a letter of 28 July 1902, "I'll get a *wonderful* edition of Nietzsche's 'Zarathustra' for you, but a really wonderful one. So go on, my sweet, and we shall read it regularly and without fail" (ibid., vol. 1, 326). Clearly this was the younger Weizmann; in later years he hardly mentioned Nietzsche.

72. The transvaluative task was admittedly vast and could only be gradual. As Weizmann wrote in his diagnosis of the Jewish problem:

The stench of decay hits one at every step. And years will pass, and many will still fall victims to these terrible conditions before creative, constructive work starts. Are we going to see all that? No, I doubt it. Our fate, the fate of a people who live in a time of transition, is to be given activities of a purely negative character. To understand and ponder over old Jewish values, to understand them only to discard them perhaps, and to reappraise them at a later stage—my God, this is agonising labour, agonising work, and we, the feeble and the weak, have to bear it on our shoulders.

Instructively, this passage did not mention Nietzsche, but the next paragraph (perhaps unconsciously) immediately passes on to the subject of Nietzsche—and his misuse by Socialists! (ibid., vol. 1, 122–123)

73. Mattenklott, "Nietzscheanismus und Judentum," 57.

its values. The official Zionist journal, *Die Welt*, remained unmoved by the Nietzsche cult at the turn of the century.[74] Theodor Herzl's close friend and the most famous Zionist of his time, Max Nordau, in his *Degeneration* had penned perhaps the most vociferous attack on Nietzsche. Herzl himself paid little attention to Nietzsche, referring to him, only once, as a "madman."[75]

The second German Zionist generation challenged the Zionism of their elders, defining it not as a philanthropic and diplomatic matter but as the imperative for personal metamorphosis and cultural rejuvenation. As Jewish renaissance was increasingly conceived as a question of personal realization, the Nietzschean moment entered German Zionism. The intellectual leadership of this generation no longer took the rationalist Enlightenment tradition for granted. The wider, antibourgeois, neo-Romantic mood of the day with its emphasis on the creative role of myth admirably fit the needs of a remodeled Zionism of collective regeneration and personal authenticity.[76]

The rhetoric of transvaluation was a staple in the intellectual diet of this generation.[77] On one level Nietzsche acted as a model of rebellious authenticity for what constituted the new secular Jew. Robert Weltsch cited the prevalent paradoxical contention that Nietzsche (and Hölderlin) would create stronger Jews than "a forced return to a ritual in which we do not believe."[78] In 1922 Hans Kohn—then still a Zionist—portrayed Nietzsche as the father of a new, less institutional, humanizing form of nationalism, one that was "becoming a question of personal ethics, personal shaping of life":

> Everywhere people feel the desperation of a time without faith or myth, the fatigue of termination, but people are trying to get away from these things. A new song of life affirmation and powerful courage is to begin. Nietzsche, the unique genius, as lonesome as a gigantic figure, who overshadows the

74. The only relevant article to appear was Ernst Müller's noncommittal "Gedanken über Nietzsche und sein Verhältnis zu den Juden," *Die Welt*, no. 40 (5 October 1900).

75. In a conversation with Leo Franckel, Herzl explained that he was "against the democracies": "'So you are a disciple of Nietzsche,' he [Franckel] said. I: 'Not at all. Nietzsche is a madman. But one can only govern aristocratically'" (Raphael Patai, ed., *The Complete Diaries of Theodor Herzl*, trans. Harry Zohn, vol. 1 [London: Herzl Press and Thomas Yoseloff], 191).

76. For a treatment of these generational differences see Aschheim, *Brothers and Strangers*, chaps. 4, 5.

77. See the collection by German and Czech Zionists, *Vom Judentum: Ein Sammelbuch* (Leipzig: Kurt Nolff, 1913), especially the articles by Moses Calvary and Moritz Goldstein. Even where Nietzsche was not specifically mentioned, the categories were his and the influence palpable.

78. Cited in George L. Mosse, "The Influence of the Volkisch Idea on German Jewry," *Germans and Jews*, 96.

decline of an era of faith, is the father of this desperate temerity, this endless hope for a new heaven.[79]

Some of this Nietzschean dynamism went beyond rhetoric into Zionist praxis. The radical Zionist youth movement *Hashomer Hazair*, founded in Vienna in 1916, clearly incorporated the Nietzschean thematic into its melange of influences including Hans Blüher, Freud, Gustav Landauer, and Gustav Wyneken. It actively aimed at creating a sexually and spiritually liberated, antibourgeois youth culture based upon voluntary and elitist communal forms, rejecting all "mechanical" relationships and party organization.[80] Transplanted into Palestine, this radical Central European youth ethos soon achieved notoriety. The Hashomer Hazair commune, Bitania, constantly clashed with party functionaries who sought to co-opt them into prevailing political structures. They loudly proclaimed their independence from all imposed ideology and organization. Their outspoken insistence upon establishing "agitated" (*t'sisa*) rather than settled modes of communal life as the basis for their central goal of perpetual self-creation, their strident cries for erotic and intellectual freedom were informed by the Nietzschean cloth they had packed into the cultural baggage they had brought from Vienna.[81]

Even within a less harsh environment it would have been difficult to maintain such a sectarian Nietzschean dynamic outside of a mediating ideological framework. It is hardly surprising that around 1926 the group adopted a revolutionary Marxist ideology. Nevertheless, their earlier insistence upon voluntarism and individual freedom remained strong.

All these Zionist circles were in one way or another affected by the most important intellectual influence on this generation of young Jews, Martin Buber (1878–1965). Through him, above all others, Nietzsche was assimilated into German Zionism. His particular mediation illustrates well both the possibilities and the limits which Nietzscheanism presented as it was incorporated into religious and national frameworks.

Buber maintained a passionate and changing relationship to

79. Hans Kohn, "Nationalism," in *The Jew: Essays from Martin Journal Der Jude, 1916–1928*, ed. Arthur A. Cohen, trans. Joachim Neugroschel (Montgomery: University of Alabama Press, 1980), 28. The essay appeared originally in *Der Jude* 6 (1921–1922), 674–686.

80. For a useful overview see Jehuda Reinharz, "Hashomer Hazair in Germany (I), 1928–1933," *Leo Baeck Institute Yearbook* 31 (1986), 173–174.

81. For a history of the group and its activities see Muki Tzur, ed., *K'hilateinu* (in Hebrew) (Jerusalem: Yad Ben Tsvi, 1988). The flavor of its thinking is most vividly expressed in the article by the remarkable spiritual leader of the group, Meir Ya'ari, "M'toch Hatsisa," 266–269. I thank Rina Peled and David Biale for this reference.

Nietzsche over the years, and Nietzsche had a profound impact on his work.[82] The young Buber found Nietzsche both intoxicating and threatening, but his public pronouncements were adulatory and his early work shot through with Nietzschean themes and language.[83] Nietzsche, wrote Buber in his 1900 eulogy, belonged to those "apostles of life" whose greatness was as undefinable as life itself. He was a visionary who could intuit future human forms in ways that went beyond everyday language and longings. He was the prophet of immanence and creative renewal: "out of dead cultures he gathered elements of new formations into light." He "erected before our eyes the statue of the heroic man who creates himself and goes beyond himself. . . . Against the God of Genesis he brought a great adversary: the God of becoming, in whose development we may share."[84]

It was precisely these values that informed Buber's influential fin-de-siècle vision of a Zionist Jewish renaissance, of a revivified nation composed of free and creative individuals:

> . . . the way out of medieval asceticism to a warm, flowing, life-feeling, out of the coercion of narrow-minded communities to freedom of the personality. The secret of the new, the rich sense of the discoverer, the free life of risks and the overflowing creative impulse (*Schaffenslust*) dominate this time.

The Jewish renaissance of 1900 was not a return to old traditions and practices but, Buber wrote, one conceived and led by people "possessed by a sense of the future (*Kommende*)."[85]

In Buber's Zionist vision, the historical precondition for Jewish rebirth entailed overcoming the "life-denying," disempowering abnormalities of *galut* (exile) and the distortions of the "unfree spirituality" of the ghetto. This would facilitate the reemergence of the "elemental" Jew, able once again to live a life of "unconditionality." The sources for

82. For a superb extended analysis of Nietzsche's influence on Buber, see Paul Mendes-Flohr, *From Mysticism to Dialogue: Martin Buber's Transformation of German Social Thought* (Detroit, Mich.: Wayne State University Press, 1989).

83. When he was seventeen, Buber later recalled, Zarathustra took possession of him "not in the manner of a gift but in the manner of an invasion which deprived me of my freedom, and it was a long time until I could liberate myself from it" ("Autobiographical Fragments," in *The Philosophy of Martin Buber*, ed. Paul Arthur Schilpp and Maurice Friedman, 3–39 [La Salle, Ill.: Open Court, 1967], p. 12). Buber's admiration—as well as fear—of Nietzsche's work was apparent throughout his work. While Buber's later works were dominated by critical comments, the influence remained, and in many ways his thought continued to be informed by the Nietzschean problematic.

84. Martin Buber, "Ein Wort über Nietzsche und die Lebenswerte," *Die Kunst im Leben* (December 1900), 13.

85. Martin Buber, "Jüdische Renaissance," in *Die Jüdische Bewegung: Gesammelte Aufsätze und Ansprachen, 1900–1914* (Berlin: Jüdischer Verlag, 1920), 10–11.

this recovery were contained in the still healthy materials and primal energies of the Jewish Volk. Buber's use of Nietzsche, like other nationalist appropriations, had to somehow reconcile the emphasis on activist transvaluation, on intensely lived *Erlebnis,* with the belief in the eternal, organic properties of the nation. Buber effected the compromise by arguing that only a dynamic movement such as Zionism would be able to tap the unbroken but historically repressed "life-feeling of the Jews."[86] Such an expansive life-feeling, the necessary antidote to "pure intellectuality" (*reine Geistigkeit*), urgently needed recovery. Exile had dislocated this vitality "from its natural expression, the free creation in reality and art."

Zionism, in this early Buberian rendering, was about the re-establishment of a proper, lived Jewish relationship to the cosmos, a project of Nietzschean renaturalization. Buber's youthful Nietzschean Zionism was an aesthetic, vitalist vision of "unconditionality" in which Jews would once again be able to lead freely creative, joyful, and healthy lives.[87] Even his conception of creative national life was replete with language that echoed *The Birth of Tragedy.* "The redemptive affirmation of an antagonism," he wrote, "is the essence of all creation."[88]

Buber's early *Erlebnis* Zionism of renaturalization never stressed the martial aspects of Nietzsche, nor did it elevate one national group over another in its will to power. It demonstrated that a nationalized Nietzsche could be pressed equally into humanist as well as antihumanist service. However, the activist Zionist impulse was increasingly tamed by the Buberian emphasis on sanctity and was seemingly deflected by Buber's sustained mythologization of Hasidism as a living model of heightened, authentic experience.

Nietzschean Zionist vitalism was maintained, however, in the writings of the controversial German–Jewish philosopher Theodor Lessing (1872–1933) during the late 1920s and early 1930s. But Lessing's theories were written under the shadow of nazism (of which he was an early victim) and as a last-ditch attempt to provide a Jewish answer. Lessing had already written a number of general works on Nietzsche as well as general critiques very much in the Nietzschean mode.[89] He now

86. Ibid., 13.
87. Ibid., 14ff.
88. Martin Buber, "Die Schaffenden, das Volk und die Bewegung," in ibid., 71ff.
89. Theodor Lessing's general works include *Schopenhauer—Wagner—Nietzsche: Einführung in moderne Philosophie* (Munich: C. H. Beck, 1906) and *Nietzsche* (Berlin: Ullstein, 1925). For a general critique see his *Geschichte als Sinngebung des Sinnlosen: Oder die Geburt der Geschichte aus dem Mythos,* 4th ed. (Leipzig, 1927).

applied many of these Nietzschean themes in his analyses and solutions for the contemporary Jewish condition. Lessing's diagnosis of Jewish self-hate—insights largely derived from his own share in the affliction— as well as his prescribed Zionist cure flowed from a kind of völkisch Nietzschean creed. Jewish self-hatred was a product of exile and an overly intellectual life alienated from the earth. In this unnatural situation, in a hostile environment, the Jews turned their own overspiritualized characteristics against themselves. The result was a pathological psychology.

How could the Jews move from their pathological state to one of healthy self-acceptance? Lessing explicitly invoked the Nietzschean injunction: "Become what you are."[90] For him, however, it was clear that becoming what one was would be far removed from conventional bourgeois Jewish self-acceptance. It meant rather a kind of Nietzschean process of renaturalization, the assertion of a Jewish will to power and a virile, even instinctual, activism. The exilic Jew had to be metamorphosed into the new Zionist Man, forged in the spirit of the "Old Testament, pagan *Naturmythos.*"[91]

Of course, Lessing's late, Nietzschean remedies were not animated by joy but by desperation. To see the really liberational Nietzschean Zionism one must turn to the East European Hebrew intelligentsia, for there he had the most sustained and radical impact. "No European thinker," the Israeli critic Menachem Brinker has recently pointed out, "had the same profound influence upon Hebrew literature during this period."[92]

The reasons for this should be immediately apparent. Western European Zionism was essentially a postassimilationist phenomenon, a project of return to forgotten Jewish materials.[93] In pre-emancipation Eastern Europe, Zionism instead functioned as a major secularizing force, a modernizing mode of escape from the constrictions of traditional Jewish life. Whereas Buber addressed a postassimilationist

90. Theodor Lessing, *Der jüdische Selbsthass* (Berlin: Jüdischer Verlag, 1930).
91. Theodor Lessing, "Jüdisches Schicksal," *Der Jude* 9 (1928), 17. *Machtwille* appears in his *Deutschland und seine Juden,* 14. See too Golomb, "Nietzsche and the Marginal Jews," 125–126.
92. Menachem Brinker, *Nietzsche and Soviet Culture: Ally and Adversary,* ed. B. Glatzer Rosenthal (Cambridge University Press, September, 1994). I am indebted to Prof. Brinker for providing me with a copy of this paper from which I freely draw for the following section.
93. Jehuda Reinharz, *Fatherland or Promised Land: The Dilemma of the German Jew, 1893–1914* (Ann Arbor: University of Michigan Press, 1975); Stephen M. Poppel, *Zionism in Germany, 1897–1933: The Shaping of a Jewish Identity* (Philadelphia: Jewish Publication Society of America, 1977).

audience who took the break with the past for granted, the Hebraic Nietzsche was designed for a public that had not severed the cord. The antitraditional Nietzsche made immediate sense to many Eastern European Jews precisely because they were still being actively shaped by that tradition.[94]

Historical coincidence enhanced Nietzsche's visibility: the Europeanization of these Hebraic East European Jewish intellectuals coincided with the period when Nietzsche was most in vogue. Nietzscheanism was thus easily channeled into some of the major thematics of the Zionist national revolt.[95]

The most famous and vocal East European Jewish Nietzschean was Micha Josef Berdichevsky (1865–1921; pseud. Bin Gorion).[96] The explicitly Nietzschean title of his collection of essays written between 1890 and 1896, *Shinui Arachim* (A transformation of values), proclaimed his agenda.[97] Berdichevsky enunciated nothing less than a Nietzschean Lebensphilosophie applied to the whole of the Jewish experience.[98] In his radical dismissal in his early writings of both diaspora life and the normative tradition with its anti-individualist

94. On the differences between the East and West European modes of Zionism see the introduction by Arthur Hertzberg in *The Zionist Idea* (New York: Atheneum, 1975) and Walter Laqueur, *A History of Zionism* (London: Weidenfeld and Nicolson, 1972). Some German Zionists were aware of these differences and warned against similar radicalism in their own deracinated context (Gerhard Holdheim and Walter Preuss, *Die theoretischen Grundlagen des Zionismus* [Berlin: Welt-Verlag, 1919].

95. See Brinker, "Nietzsche's Impact," for a list of such relevant luminaries as Shaul Tschernikovsky, David Frischman, and Hillel Zeitlin. Perhaps the most sophisticated and critical was Y. H. Brenner who was acutely sensitive to the Nietzschean themes of perspectivism and the fictionality of interpretations.

96. Needless to say, other Zionist writers opposed Berdichevsky's brand of Nietzscheanism. Yet in refuting him many critics themselves incorporated Nietzschean assumptions, themes, and categories into their own counterarguments. This was certainly true for Berdichevsky's most prominent critic, Ahad Ha-am (Asher Ginzburg). As Leon Simon remarked, Achad Ha-am in one essay "adumbrated a sort of Jewish version of Nietzscheism, with the substitution of morality for power as the ideal of the superman, and with the further postulate of the 'super-nation'" ("Judaism and Nietzsche," in *Ahad Ha-am: Essays, Letters, Memoirs,* ed. Leon Simon [Oxford: East and West Library, 1946], 76ff. See too "The Supremacy of Reason" in the same volume; "The Transvaluation of Values," in *Selected Essays of Achad Ha-am,* ed. Leon Simon (New York: Atheneum, 1970), 217–241.

97. These are not, alas, available in English (Micha Josef Berdichevsky, *Collected Essays* [in Hebrew; Tel Aviv: Dvir, 1960]).

98. Bin Gorion was reasonably well known in Germany. Many of his works were translated into German. It was above all Buber's journal that introduced him to a German–Jewish audience (Baruch Krupnick, "Micha Josef Berdyczewski: Seine Wahrheiten und Dichtung," *Der Jude* 3 [1918–1919]; Markus Ehrenpreis, "Gespräche mit Berdyczewski," *Der Jude* 6 [1921–1922]; Moritz Heimann, "Micha Josef Gorion: Seinem Gedächtnis," *Die Neue Rundschau* 33 [1922]).

constraints,[99] Berdichevsky posited a Zionist transvaluation of Jewish values based upon the perceived need for Jewish empowerment.

In Berdichevsky's view the Jewish religious and ideological establishment had rendered a pathetic powerlessness as a moral virtue. Lacking national power and the capacity to affect history, the Jews were simply "below good and evil." Only their re-establishment into a national entity based upon power and responsibility would render them again capable of doing good and committing evil.[100] Nietzscheanism was perhaps the most radical means by which this stream of Zionism could enunciate its drive towards empowerment and "normalization."

Nietzschean Lebensphilosophie also informed his radical rereading of the Jewish past, its enslavement to history, and its perpetual privileging of the "book" over the "sword."

> There is a time for men and nations who live by the sword, by their power and their strong arm, by vital boldness. This time is the hour of intensity, of life in its essential meaning. But the book is no more than the shade of life, life in its senescence.
> The blade is not something abstracted and standing apart from life; it is the materialization of life in its boldest lines, in its essential and substantial likeness. Not so the book.[101]

Berdichevsky began an important and ongoing shift in (mainly Zionist) historiography, placing renewed emphasis on Jewish power and sovereignty over its vaunted spirituality and political passivity. The priestly–rabbinic stranglehold on Jewish life, he wrote, had emasculated the vitality of the people by repressing its original, vital, natural religion—the "anti-natural" Torah of Moses was a later imposition—and transforming it into an abstract, spiritualized doctrine. The prophets had also contributed: their substitution of ethics for life had so weakened the national fiber that exile inevitably followed.

What Berdichevsky proposed, David Biale has perceptively suggested, was a Nietzschean counterhistory, a search for those vital ele-

---

99. In every other people, nationality is the single storehouse in which are preserved human individualities, and where the individual sees his achievements secured and his gains safeguarded. Among us, the individual finds in his Jewish nationality a power hostile to what is in his heart. Every one of us feels this opposition the moment he begins to improve himself and seek for culture. (Micha Josef Berdichevsky, "The Question of Culture," translated in Hertzberg, *The Zionist Idea*, 298).
100. Brinker ("Nietzsche's Impact") develops this point well and gives relevant sources.
101. Micha Josef Berdichevsky, "In Two Directions," translated in Hertzberg, *The Zionist Idea*, 295.

ments repressed in the distortive construction of a monolithic, antipluralist "historic Judaism."[102] He believed that within the rich reservoir of the Jewish tradition the materials for a vitalist recovery could be found, especially in those pre-Mosaic traditions of the sword and their orgiastic identifications with nature. Calling upon the Nietzschean insistence on destruction as precondition for creation, Berdichevsky maintained: "in order to build a temple, it is necessary first to destroy a temple."[103]

Yet even for the most enthusiastic nationalist Nietzscheans, there were inherent limits and inevitable ironies surrounding the Nietzschean revolt against normative tradition and the drive towards naturalization and empowerment. Despite Berdichevsky's deep longings for overcoming the unnatural distortions of ghetto and exilic life, he incarnated an ongoing and quite unresolved internal Zionist tension between normalcy and moral uniqueness, the traditional past and the open future:

> When we defeat the past, it is we ourselves who are defeated. But if the past conquers, it is we, and our sons, and the sons of our sons, who are conquered. . . . Elixir and poison in one and the same substance.[104]

Ultimately Berdichevsky accepted what his critics had argued: after the modern Jewish nation had been created and sovereignty restored, it would indeed be governed by the same moral spirit he had so castigated.[105] The later Berdichevsky turned to forgotten aspects of the Jewish tradition, including Hasidism, and neglected legends, sayings, and folklore.[106] These too may have been elements of his vaunted counterhistory, avenues to the lost alternatives of the Jewish past. Nevertheless, Berdichevsky increasingly regarded himself as a historian, a chronicler rather than a conscious mythologizer of the Jewish past, and in later collections of his early work he often deleted his references to Nietzsche.[107]

In 1934 a German Jewish commentator could write of Berdichev-

102. David Biale, *Gershom Scholem: Kabbalah and Counter-History* (Cambridge: Harvard University Press, 1979), 37–43.

103. Quoted in ibid., 40.

104. Micha Josef Berdichevsky, "The Question of Our Past," translated in Hertzberg, *The Zionist Idea,* 301.

105. Brinker, "Nietzsche's Impact," 23. Nevertheless, Berdichevsky insisted that being a holy people entailed a normal national livelihood and framework ("On Sanctity" translated in Hertzberg, *The Zionist Idea,* 301–302).

106. Micha Josef Berdichevsky, *Die Sagen der Juden,* published in 1913 and 1919, has appeared in English under the title *Mimekor Israel* (Bloomington: Indiana University Press, 1976).

107. Biale, *Gershom Scholem,* 43, 235, n. 23.

sky's and Buber's turn to Volksmärchen as not a conservative turning away from Nietzsche but a logical continuation of their interest in him. They had reached the point "where the extremes touch and the *Übermensch* is transformed into the *Volksgeist*. (The way from the Baalschem to Nietzsche and from Nietzsche to the Baalschem is possible, only that of the *Kommerzienrat* and the party functionary to the Baalschem or to Nietzsche cannot lead there.)" Moreover, there were clear commonalities: "With Nietzsche and Hasidism, Bin Gorion shared passion with passion, life-affirmation, . . . and the mistrust of all words, slogans, and programmes."[108] In fusing Nietzsche and Hasidism, the plasticity of Nietzscheanism was stretched to its utmost.

But then the whole history of Nietzscheanism abounds with unlikely combinations and politically ambiguous appropriations containing both novel radicalizing and, at times, unexpected conserving properties. The difficulties of classification become most evident once we turn to the quasipolitical, countercultural institutions that proliferated between 1890 and 1914 and to an examination of the Nietzschean impulse within the then nascent radical right.

It is not easy to classify the myriad of *Lebensreform* (life-reform) movements that mushroomed in pre–World War I imperial Germany. These groups—expressing, no doubt, the stresses of rapid industrialization—each had its own pet naturalist issue: vegetarianism; nudism and "body culture"; or abstinence from alcohol or smoking. These Lebensreform groups were animated by a strong regenerationist, indeed eugenic, impulse and were compatible with manifold anarchist, socialist, völkisch and racist visions of renewal.[109]

Nietzsche was easily integrated into this politics of anti-decadence. His affirmative vitalism, his eugenic critique of weakness and life-negating forces, the celebration of strength and health, were emblematic of these movements. There was even a Nietzsche Lebensreform iconography. Fidus (Hugo Höppener) drew a naked couple bound in marriage with a suitable Zarathustra quotation, and Alfred Soder pictured a nude Nietzsche in the elevated isolation of the high mountains (illus. 9 and 10). Early in the century a vegetarianist postcard—featuring a woodcut of Hans Olde's famous portrait of Nietzsche—carried an apocryphal

108. Hirsch, "Friedrich Nietzsche und der jüdische Geist," 189.
109. For a good discussion of these tendencies see Roy Pascal, *From Naturalism to Expressionism: German Literature and Society, 1880–1918* (New York: Basic, 1973), 172.

quote from Nietzsche: "I believe that the vegetarian with his prescription to eat less and more simply, has been more beneficial than all the new moral systems combined" (illus. 11).[110]

If the Lebensreform movement had a Nietzschean theorist it was Walter Hammer. His *Friedrich Nietzsche: The Life-reformer and His Culture of the Future* annexed Nietzsche to the movement's aspirations towards a simplification of life and its rejection of the urban, industrial, mechanistic mass culture of Western Europe. The culture of the future and the strengthening of personality was possible only by rising above the prevalent materialism.[111] Nietzsche was vital to this endeavor because of his ideas and his personal example: in Genoa, for instance, he ate neither soup nor meat but lived on fruit and vegetables, especially almonds! As Hammer told readers of *Healthy Life*, Nietzsche represented a purifying "will to health." With his regenerative ideal of the Übermensch he "gave back to us the will to life."[112] In another series of articles he argued that such a healthy life could be achieved by following the "foundations of a large-scale vegetarian *Kulturpolitik* in Nietzsche's sense."[113]

Similar regenerationist rhetoric characterized another important countercultural institution—the German Youth Movement.[114] It was there that the self-consciousness of a separate youth culture found its clearest expression. The slogan of one of its prophets, Gustav Wyneken—"Youth for Itself Alone"—encapsulated its rejection of parents, schooling, and bourgeois conventions and its drive for the free development of the spirit of youth.

Nietzsche's influence over their ethos was palpable, though of course never unalloyed. Uncovering the relevant strains is complicated by the movement's varied protopolitical tendencies. After World War I few observers bothered with these distinctions. Nietzsche was sweepingly

110. I consider the quotation apocryphal since I have been unsuccessful in locating its source; its very spuriousness only makes Nietzsche's myth-making import greater.

111. Walter Hammer, *Friedrich Nietzsche: Der Lebensreformer und seine Zukunftskultur*, 2d ed. (Leipzig: Karl Lentze, [1909] 1910).

112. Walter Hammer, "Nietzsche und sein Wille zur Gesundheit," *Gesundes Leben: Medizinpolitische Rundschau* (1910), 121–125.

113. Walter Hammer, "Nietzsche und der Vegetarismus," *Vegetarische Warte* 46, no. 7, (1913), 10–19.

114. For a general history see Walter Laqueur, *Young Germany: A History of the Youth Movement* (New York: Basic Books, 1962); Peter D. Stachura, *The German Youth Movement, 1900–1945: An Interpretation and Documentary History* (London: Macmillan, 1981).

described as the "Prophet of the German Youth Movement."[115] As one
of its historians put it in 1929, the philosopher had established

> the magically attractive, brilliant, new human goals, and called youth to its
> new arena of struggle (*Kampfbahnen*). . . . Nietzsche is the great prophet of
> the future who awoke in youth a consciousness of their worth and their
> calling to shape the future. His contempt of philistinism and . . . of societal
> lies and laziness penetrated deeply into the youth movement. . . . For he is the
> prophet of the undiscovered land that the youth movement seeks to build.[116]

The Youth Movement was the attempted incarnation of Nietzschean
transvaluative self-creation and responsibility as well as the attempted construction of culture through the development of leadership
qualities.[117]

Some later historians interested in rescuing a politically correct,
emancipatory Nietzsche have argued that Nietzsche only entered the
youth movement through the progressive Freideutsche youth after
1912. According to this view, both leaders and supporters of the original *Wandervogel*, with their increasingly völkisch and anti-Semitic
bent, considered the philosopher to be a dangerous and heretical
force.[118] This changed only in the quite different atmosphere of the
Weimar Republic when Nietzsche began to be retroactively portrayed
as the most significant of all influences on the Wandervogel.[119]

Nietzsche's influence on the Freideutsche youth and their mentor
Gustav Wyneken is uncontested. Wyneken's rejection of völkisch and
nationalist themes and his humanistic emphasis on achieving the highest
plane of individual creativity eclectically combined Nietzsche with Hegel and Johann Gottlieb Fichte.[120] Wyneken sought to integrate individualist creativity into the Youth Movement by forging an alternative
to völkisch conceptions of community. Here individual liberation was

115. Oscar Schütz, "Friedrich Nietzsche als Prophet der deutschen Jugendbewegung," *Neue Jahrbücher für Wissenschaft und Jugendbildung* 5 (1929), 64–74. Like
many of his contemporaries, Schütz shows Nietzsche's influence without distinguishing
the *Wandervogel* component from the *Freideutsche* one.
116. Else Frobenius, *Mit uns zieht die neue Zeit: Eine Geschichte der deutschen
Jugendbewegung* (Berlin: Deutsche Buch Gemeinschaft, 1929), 35ff.
117. Theo Herrle, *Die deutsche Jugendbewegung in ihren kulturellen Zusammenhang*, 14, quoted in Michael Jovy, *Jugendbewegung und Nationalsozialismus* (Münster:
Lit-Verlag, 1984), 53.
118. For an acute analysis of the völkisch aspect of the Youth Movement, see Mosse,
German Ideology, chap. 9.
119. This is the basic thrust of Hinton Thomas's argument, *Nietzsche in German
Politics*, chap. 8.
120. Gustav Wyneken, "Der Kampf für die Jugend," *Gesammelte Aufsätze* (Jena: E.
Diederichs, 1920). On Wyneken see Mosse, *German Ideology*, 184ff; Hinton Thomas,
Nietzsche in German Politics, 105ff.

regarded as the precondition for the creation of a truly free community. The blueprint for this community—as expressed in the pages of Wyneken's journal, *Der Anfang* (The beginning)—was filled with Nietzschean emphases on will, self-creation and worldly aspirations.[121]

Evidence of the philosopher's influence on the Wandervogel youth is ambiguous. Nietzsche clearly had his opponents. The founder of the movement, Karl Fischer, was indifferent to Nietzsche, enamored instead with the Youth Movement's other, virulently völkisch star, Paul de Lagarde.[122] The dedicated anti-Semite Theodor Fritsch also resisted Nietzsche's infiltration into youthful circles and desperately sought to erase him and his antinationalist, pro-Jewish orientation from its inspirational pantheon. Ironically, much of Fritsch's political vocabulary of will, masculinity, and heroism derived from the Nietzschean lexicon. Even the name of his journal—*Hammer*—had a Nietzschean resonance. Nevertheless, he regarded Nietzsche's ideas as sick, the source of a dangerous personal and national contagion. He too recommended de Lagarde instead as the proper and healthy guide to German youth.[123] The *Führerzeitung* of Herman Popert's *Vortrupp* similarly recommended that its members keep away from the mad philosopher and his wild landscape beyond good and evil.[124]

For all that, this exorcistic passion revealed an awareness of Nietzsche's attractiveness. Nietzschean rhetoric permeated the ambience of the Youth Movement, infiltrating the subtext even of his opponents. Indeed, the influence on the Wandervogel went considerably further. Amongst the leadership there were numerous explicit attempts to enlist him as a guiding force. Walter Hammer, for instance, sought to do for the Youth Movement what he had already done within Lebensreform circles. His *Nietzsche as Educator* (1914) aimed to provide them with a compatible and palatable account of the philosopher. His twenty letters to a Wandervogel member did, to be sure, advise that Nietzsche was not suitable for its younger recruits. For those, however, who had passed through the movement and had the courage for struggle he provided only the stable pole around which the culture of the time

121. See, for instance, Otto Braun's poem underlining humanity's self-creating, heroic, and willful powers, "Why Should There Be Gods?" in Mosse, *German Ideology,* 186. Orig. pub. in *Der Anfang* 12 (May 1909).

122. Hinton Thomas, *Nietzsche in German Politics,* 98–99.

123. Theodor Fritsch, "Nietzsche und die Jugend," *Hammer: Blätter für deutschen Sinn* 10, no. 29 (March 1911), 113ff.

124. *Führerzeitung,* no. 3 (1914), 66. Very shortly after, the Vortrupp made an abrupt and fundamental about-face; during the war it enlisted Nietzsche to its pantheon of Germanic thinkers.

what all groups doing it seems

revolved. One could now go beyond Nietzsche precisely because the time was so thoroughly permeated by his presence.[125]

This selective harnessing of Nietzsche was done by educational-reform circles as well. None other than Wyneken's nemesis, Ludwig Gurlitt,[126] the leading theorist of the völkisch school-reform movement and the first chair of the advisory council to the Wandervogel, described himself as a venerator of Nietzsche (*Nietzsche Verehrer*) and placed the philosopher at the center "of the new reformation in which we stand." Nietzsche was the great master who stressed the importance of self-discipline and will. Both the Wandervogel and the Freideutsche youth sought to awaken everything that was best "in our young Volk to a new life—all that is in Nietzsche's spirit."[127]

Nietzschean themes were built into Gurlitt's philosophy of education, which had to perceive and treat its charges as full human beings; education had to be made into a matter of "joy" and the free unfolding of "personality." Moreover, he rejected rationalism, decried the bourgeois age, and praised the creative and heroic dimensions. Hinton Thomas, while ignoring Gurlitt's pro-Nietzschean articles, has argued that "the reason why Gurlitt wanted pupils above all to enjoy themselves is the wholly un-Nietzschean one that they would then better love their country and be more naturally inclined to think and act patriotically."[128] But precisely this capacity for deployment within völkisch and other frameworks was a core property of Nietzscheanism and the basis of its broad influence.

This was not a hidden process. Leaders of the Youth Movement were well aware of the need to reconcile the tension between Nietzsche's individualist stance and the burgeoning drive to incorporate him within collective and national frameworks. Eugen Diederichs held that the tension could be resolved in a new kind of fusion. Diederichs's Nietzsche made sense only when transfigured into a larger whole. The Youth Movement and its self-redemptive impulses, he argued, derived from Nietzsche's prophecy of the Übermenschen. Personality was indeed important but the coming race (*Geschlechts*) could not exist

125. Walter Hammer, *Nietzsche als Erzieher* (Leipzig: Hugo Vollrath, 1914). The work, while admiring, was also critical, especially with regard to Nietzsche's views on social questions.

126. For details on Gurlitt see Mosse, *German Ideology*, 157ff.

127. Ludwig Gurlitt, "Friedrich Nietzsche als Erzieher," *Das Freie Wort* 14, no. 4 (May 1914), 131–132. Gurlitt also praised Hammer's *Nietzsche als Erzieher* in this article. For another example of his positive attitude see his "Friedrich Nietzsche als Philologe und Lehrer," *Die Hilfe*, no. 22 (1914).

128. Hinton Thomas, *Nietzsche in German Politics*, 100.

in isolated self-absorption; it had to be integrated into community. Nietzschean personal realization was thus made to meld into the nation (*Volkstum*).[129]

Oscar Schütz went so far as to regard the contradiction as a major source of the constant splintering within the Youth Movement. Common to the Wandervogel and Freideutsche youth, he wrote, was their Nietzschean individualist elitism and an antipathy to the masses. The entire history of the Youth Movement could be depicted as the swing of the pendulum between leadership through autocracy and through rebellion. Was this, Schütz asked, not attributable to Nietzsche's boundless individualism? The answer was negative, for Nietzsche understood that the autonomous personality was the possession of the few and that it was a great error to generalize it. The Youth Movement had gone beyond these boundaries and both socialist and völkisch leaders had sought to temper this with collective ideals that transcended the individual. It was precisely the relationship between elites and followers, individual and community which the Youth Movement had not resolved. If Nietzsche was the prophet of the Youth Movement, Schütz concluded, its later communitarian and völkisch ideas came from different sources.

Despite his acute analysis, in his conclusions Schütz could not resist harmonizing the tensions. He formulated a völkisch-Nietzschean answer to the dilemma! Only leaders, he proclaimed, had the right to create their own laws, but they had to be constructed in such a way that the good of the Volk would be the highest law.[130]

Most of the tendencies we have discussed thus far were dissident, unconventional ones. For the *traditional* right—a few exceptions notwithstanding[131]—Nietzsche remained anathema to conservatives, ruling elites, and nationalists alike.[132] Until 1914, establishment circles for

129. Eugen Diederichs, "Entwicklungsphasen der freideutschen Jugend," *Die Tat* 10 (1918–1919), 313–314.
130. Oscar Schütz, "Nietzsche als Prophet," n. 42, 74–80.
131. Maximilian Harden, editor of the influential *Die Zukunft,* for example, advocated a politics based on an activist will to power with Nietzsche as its theorist and Bismarck as its manifestation. *Die Zukunft* was crammed with Nietzscheana. A full listing can be found in Krummel, *Nietzsche.* Many proponents of the fusion of the Nietzschean will to power with the Hohenzollern Reich were not representatives of governing elites but members of the avant-garde—like Georg Fuchs who criticized the intellectual vacuum of the Kaiserreich and the critic Kurt Breysig, a member of the Stefan Georg circle.
132. This contradicts Arno J. Mayer in chapter five of his *The Persistence of the Old Regime: Europe to the Great War* (New York: Pantheon, 1981). He presents Nietzsche as the chief prop of Europe's aristocracy in their need to bolster a shaky old order in the face of democratizing threats. There is, in fact, little documentary evidence to support Mayer's assertion.

the most part continued to regard the philosopher as subversive and dangerous, despite the frenetic efforts of Förster-Nietzsche to endow Nietzsche with a patriotic pedigree. Count Kessler recounted in his diary that young people who were raised in conservative homes and had read the philosopher were "locked up with a priest for six months."[133] "The German aristocracy," its leading journal declared, "has not the slightest in common with Nietzsche and his aristocratism."[134]

Contemporaries, it is true, were surprised by this aversion. As one observer put it, the mountain air and absence of any industrial landscape in Nietzsche's thought was ideally suited to conservative representations. Their otherwise inexplicable neglect was a result of the celebration of Nietzsche in the liberal and democratic press![135]

The aristocracy obviously did not regard Nietzsche's aristocratic radicalism as referring to them nor did they identify with his radical critique of the traditional and churchly order. When Nietzsche did emerge as a spokesman for the right it was a new and radical right different from the traditionally conservative right that emerged after World War I. The embryonic outlines of this novel right wing were nevertheless already becoming visible in the 1890s. Here we trace the first steps of this new conjuncture.

We have already seen some of its diverse themes enunciated in the George Kreis, the Cosmics, aspects of Expressionism, and the Ascona project. But not all the building blocks that went into this construction derived from the avant-garde. Apart from the Youth Movement there were various nationalist and völkisch tendencies that went against the prevalent conservative grain and excavated useable Nietzschean nuggets for their own cause. For instance, a minority of nationalist and völkisch educators took issue with the prevalent picture of Nietzsche as an immoral, atheistic corrupter of youth; they proclaimed him "King of Pedagogy" and inspirer of a new living education to counter the deadening effects of official learning. Nietzsche, Martin Havenstein wrote in 1906, was to be welcomed as awakener and liberator of

133. Kessler, *Diaries*, 426.
134. Heinrich von Wedel, "Friedrich Nietzsche und sein Menschheitsideal," *Deutsches Adelsblatt* 20 (1902); quoted in Krummel, *Nietzsche*, vol. 2, 93. Between 1867 and 1918 this journal featured only three articles on Nietzsche, all negative. Jeannot Emil Grotthuss in "Das Christentum und Nietzsche's Herrenmoral" (*Deutsches Adelsblatt* 15 [1897], 270–275) stresses the connection between the aristocratic principle and the notion of divine authority. See too the anonymous "Friedrich Nietzsche und die Zukunft Deutschlands" (*Deutsches Adelsblatt* 15 [1902], 38–41), which seeks explanations for the popularity of this *Unsinndenker*.
135. Georg Biedenkapp, *Nietzsche und Naumann*, 44–45.

personality and the soul, a "Columbus of the inner world" opposed, as he later explained it, to superficial intellectualism and the spreading degenerating forces of Alexandrian rationalism and leveling democracy.[136]

Nietzsche's reception amongst the nationalist student fraternities is almost a study in cognitive dissonance. Because of their clear nationalist and Christian commitments they handily condemned him. Yet, as writers for the *Kyffhäuserverband* confessed, they also were drawn to his antiliberalism, antisocialism, poetic genius, and his critique of moral and religious hypocrisy.[137] Some sought to explain the contradictions by separating the early aesthetic, patriotic Nietzsche from the later sick, nihilistic one. These fraternities could safely identify with the early Nietzsche of *The Birth of Tragedy* and were increasingly attracted to his critique of rationalism and philistinism and his rhetoric of activist renewal. "A healthy culture," its leading journal proclaimed, "a healthy national life requires Dionysian devotion."[138]

Indefinable though he seemed, Nietzsche had become so central a new force within German culture that he had to be incorporated somehow into fraternity life. This was most easily done through articles recounting Nietzsche's own career as a fraternity member. These articles typically went on to argue for the selective use of a rather baffling thinker who was nevertheless "a phenomenon of the first range in European culture whose effects on the future could not yet be evaluated."[139] Even in apparently hostile quarters the Nietzschean influence was making itself felt.

Within the ideologically amorphous völkisch movement some of its most extreme and anti-Semitic members could be found on either side

---

136. Martin Havenstein, *Friedrich Nietzsche, ein Jugendverderber? Eine Verteidungsschrift* (Leipzig: J. Zeitler, 1906), 51. On p. 57, however, Havenstein warns that *Zarathustra* was not meant for unripe children, nor was Nietzsche intended for the general public. See also Havenstein's "Nietzsche als Erzieher," in the right-wing volume dedicated to Förster-Nietzsche on her seventy-fifth birthday, *Den Manen Friedrich Nietzsches*, ed. Max Öhler (Munich: Musarion, 1921), 93–94, 104.

137. Richert, "Ein Wort am Grabe Nietzsches," *Akademische Blätter: Zeitschrift des Kyffhäuser-Verbandes der Vereine deutscher Studenten* 15, no. 12 (16 September 1900); Reinhard Mumm, "Nietzsche und der Nationalismus im Kyffhäuserverband," *Akademische Blätter* 11 (1896/1897), 238f., 255ff. The positive comments appeared within a larger negative whole.

138. Johann Georg Meyer, "Friedrich Nietzsche als Aesthetiker und Patriot," *Burschenschaftliche Blätter* 10, no. 9 (1896), 234–240. The quote appears on p. 240.

139. A. Langguth, "Friedrich Nietzsche als Burschenschaftler," *Burschenschaftliche Blätter* 12, no. 1 (1 October 1897), 5–10. Quoted in Krummel, *Nietzsche und der deutsche Geist*, vol. 1, 200.

of the Nietzschean divide.[140] Through the mediation of Förster-Nietzsche, for instance, the influential völkisch novelist and founder of the open-air völkisch theatre, Ernst Wachler, enthusiastically created a Nietzsche that was the Germanic prophet of a newly born race of heroes.[141] To the publicist Wilhelm Schwaner, Nietzsche would have seemed the last possible candidate for his salvationary scheme that proposed to fuse Aryan racism and doctrines of superior blood with a purified and de-Judaized German Christianity. His insignia eclectically combined the cross with the swastika![142] Yet, as Schwaner announced in his 1900 eulogy, the widespread belief that Nietzsche was the enemy of religion and the Volk was an error. Nietzsche had dealt with the most profound human problems in abstruse language. When properly grasped, it was clear that he advocated what Christ had first preached on the Mount: the blessed creation of a kingly race and the transformation of earth into paradise.[143] Schwaner's *Germanen-Bibel*, a compilation of "the holy scripts of the German *Völker*," featured excerpts from Nietzsche's "holy" writings.[144]

Pre-1914 völkisch anti-Semites came to Nietzsche from a variety of different, interested angles. Franz Haiser, a later Nazi, wrote works with pointedly Nietzschean titles, such as *The Aristocratic Imperative*, that championed Nietzsche in the struggle against Christianity, plebian science, and the ressentiment "slave revolt" of 1789. Nietzsche, Haiser wrote, had understood and opposed those forces that had contributed to European cosmopolitanism and deracialization (*Entrassung*).[145]

The inveterate anti-Semite Adolf Bartels exemplified the direction of Nietzsche's future annexation into the völkisch camp. In Bartel's 1897

140. See another of Fritsch's attacks on Nietzsche's philo-Semitism written under the pseudonym of Thomas Frey, "Der Antisemitismus im Spiegel eines 'Zukunfts-Philosophen,'" *Antisemitische Correspondenz*, no. 19 (December 1887). The distaste of Dietrich Eckhart—a key influence on Hitler—for Nietzsche is recorded in Hans Göbel, *Nietzsche Heute: Lebensfragen des deutschen Volkstums und der evangelischen Kirche* (Berlin: Kranz, 1935).

141. For biographical details see Mosse, *German Ideology*, 80–82, 232, 296; Ernst Wachler, "Elisabeth Förster-Nietzsche," *Deutsche-Zeitung*, no. 388 (1918). Quoted in Krummel, *Nietzsche*, vol. 2, 647.

142. On Schwaner see Uriel Tal, *Christians and Jews in Germany: Religion, Politics, and Ideology in the Second Reich, 1870–1914*, trans. Noah Jonathan Jacobs (Ithaca, N.Y., and London: Cornell University Press, 1975), 273, 275, 323, 324.

143. Wilhelm Schwaner, "Friedrich Nietzsche," *Der Volkserzieher* 4, no. 35 (2 September 1900), 273.

144. *Germanen-Bibel: Aus den heiligen Schriften germanischer Völker*, ed. Wilhelm Schwaner (Berlin: Volkserzieher Verlag, 1904), 221–227. For details on this and later editions see Krummel, *Nietzsche*, vol. 2, 181–182.

145. Franz Haiser, *Der aristokratische Imperativ: Beiträge zu den neudeutschen Kulturbestrebungen* (Berlin-Seglitz: Politisch-anthropolog Verlag, 1913).

study of contemporary German poetry, he described Nietzsche simply as "the philosopher and poet of decadence."[146] A few years later he evaluated Nietzsche's positive and negative elements more thoroughly, condemning Nietzsche's Europeanism and his attacks on the German spirit but praising him as a perceptive cultural observer and a superb moral psychologist.[147] Nietzsche's appeal overcame the hesitations and qualifications, however, and soon after Nietzsche was thoroughly assimilated into Bartels's nationalist, anti-Semitic worldview. A people, Bartels wrote in "Friedrich Nietzsche and Germanism," had to hold on to their great men even as they sought to disengage themselves! Detachment was in any case impossible, for great men derived their treasures from the Volk and the bond between them was absolute. Great men were duty bound to tell their people the hard truth. They might transcend their contemporaries but not their own Volk. We will never, Bartels proclaimed, allow Friedrich Nietzsche to rob us of him![148] Bartels could thus present Nietzsche as a thoroughgoing German. He had turned away from Germanness only because he had not foreseen the "deeper and freer" nationalism which people like Paul de Lagarde had introduced. Nietzsche had penned a constructive, freedom-loving critique of Germany that had nothing in common with the vitriol of Ludwig Börne and Heinrich Heine who draped their racial hatred in the guise of love of freedom.[149] To be sure, Nietzsche's Europeanism was an error. Moreover, he did his own nation an injustice when he repeatedly sang Israel's praises while fully recognizing the real, pernicious nature of the Jews.[150] These qualifications aside, Bartels left no doubt as to which camp Nietzsche belonged.

Gradually, eugenicists, social Darwinians, and *Alldeutsch* nationalists began to relate to Nietzsche in kind. Some handled him gingerly, others dismissed him out of hand, and still others enthusiastically adopted him.[151] Early on, the social Darwinian Willibald Hent-

146. Adolf Bartels, *Die deutsche Dichtung der Gegenwart: Die Alten und die Jungen* (Leipzig: Eduard Avenarius, 1897); Krummel, *Nietzsche*, vol. 1, 183–184.

147. Adolf Bartels, *Geschichte der deutschen Litteratur*, vol. 2, *Das neunzehnte Jahrhundert* (Leipzig: Eduard Avenarius, 1902), 625–655. See Krummel, *Nietzsche*, vol. 2, 79.

148. Adolf Bartels, "Friedrich Nietzsche und das Deutschtum," *Deutsche Monatschrift für das gesamte Leben der Gegenwart* 2 (April–September 1902), 81–82.

149. Ibid., 86, 94.

150. Ibid., 89, 93.

151. Hinton Thomas (*Nietzsche in German Politics,* chap. 9) makes the rejection clear, mentions the ambivalence without fully examining it, and ignores the more positive appropriations and many of the völkisch and anti-Semitic personalities discussed above.

schel[152] forcefully dissociated himself from what he termed Nietzsche's "Jew-loving." Later, at a 1909 conference of German doctors and scientists, he made it clear that the notion of breeding a superman was idiocy.[153] Yet Hentschel eclectically appropriated elements from the Nietzschean sensibility into his conception of a regenerated racial nobility and his rural, utopian visions. Not surprisingly, the Nietzsche of *The Birth of Tragedy* attracted him; he admired the early pro-Wagner writings and Nietzsche's search for "pure spirituality."[154] More important, despite the surface contradictions, his Germanic eugenics resonated with Nietzschean themes: vitalism and "higher development," the breeding of a new and stronger people, a cult of strength, and the "succumbing of the weak" all figured prominently. He called for the establishment of a racially rejuvenative utopia called *Mittgart* designed to create an elite Aryan caste of nobles and warriors. Over its entrance one could "inscribe those words . . . with which Nietzsche linked the mystery of racial breeding with the name of Dionysus, 'The noblest clay, the most precious marble, is here moulded and chiselled, namely man.'"[155]

The leading racial theorist, Wilhelm Schallmeyer, also harnessed Nietzsche in a selective and critical manner. As someone interested in race, Schallmeyer regarded Nietzsche's emphasis on the individual as excessive. Nevertheless, he listed the philosopher amongst those who had contributed to the view that "we are on the way to progressive socialization, that is, increasing strength and efficiency of social organization . . . and that corresponds to a morality conducive to the development of the highest community powers."[156]

There were others, however, who made the link far more explicit. The *Political–Anthropological Monthly* of 1906, for instance, featured a long account by the well-known Leipzig Nietzsche scholar Raoul

---

152. Hentschel was the anti-Semitic associate of Theodor Fritsch, a founder of the extreme *Deutschsoziale* party, and author of the extremely popular racially anthropological 1907 work *Varuna* (George Mosse, *German Ideology*, 112–116).

153. Quoted in Hinton Thomas, *Nietzsche in German Politics*, 122.

154. Willibald Hentschel, "Irrende Spekulation oder wahre Geistes-Kultur?" *Antisemitische Correspondenz* no. 45 (17 February 1889), 4ff; quoted in Krummel, *Nietzsche*, vol. 1, 75–76.

155. Willibald Hentschel, *Vom aufsteigenden Leben ("Ziele der Rassen-Hygiene),"* 2d ed. (Leipzig and Hamburg: n.d.), p. 43; quoted in Hinton Thomas, *Nietzsche in German Politics*, 112–113.

156. Wilhelm Schallmeyer, *Vererbung und Auslese im Lebenslauf der Völker: Eine Staatswissenschaftliche Studie auf Grund der neueren Biologie* (Jena: Gustav Fischer, 1903); quoted in Krummel, *Nietzsche*, vol. 2, 106–107.

Richter. There Nietzsche was characterized as nothing less than the "philosopher of biological anthropology." In his unfolding cultural history Nietzsche had emphasized the breeding of the Übermensch and underlined the importance of ineradicable human inequality. Moreover, he had grounded individual differences in constant racial characteristics. In his evaluation of Aryans as a higher species whose blood was being poisoned by the lower races, Nietzsche, Richter insisted, was in line with Count Arthur de Gobineau, Richard Wagner, Houston Stewart Chamberlain, and their disciples! Nietzsche was the first "to advocate the close connection between racial anthropology (*Rassenanthropologie*) and biological ethics."[157] Richter's presentation was clearly racist but not anti-Semitic. He emphasized that the breeding of the Übermensch had to proceed according to the most favorable mixture of available anthropological types—most preferably a mixture of the Germanic–Slavic and Jewish components![158]

The most rabid Nietzschean in social Darwinian and pan-Germanic circles was Alexander Tille (1866–1912). Tille was a leading member of the *Alldeutsche Verband* after 1898 and an early and intense Nietzsche publicist.[159] He was also a major mediator of Nietzsche in Britain, teaching German for ten years at Glasgow University, and in 1895 became editor of an English translation of Nietzsche's works. He was also deputy director of the Organization of German Industrialists in Berlin and later became representative of an employers association in Saarbrucken.[160] Tille's Nietzscheanism stressed the philosopher's dismissal of humanism, equality, Christian ethics, socialism, and democracy, and was combined with a brutal social Darwinism.[161] Tille was in favor of "helping" nature by killing off unproductive elements of society (cripples, lunatics, and so on) and giving more food to its efficient

157. Raoul Richter, "Nietzsches Stellung zu Entwicklungslehre und Rassetheorie," *Politisch-anthropologische Monatsschrift* (1906), 544–564, reprinted in his *Essays*, ed. Lina Richter (Leipzig: F. Meiner, 1913), 137–177; quoted in Krummel, *Nietzsche*, vol. 2, 254. See also his *Friedrich Nietzsche, sein Leben und sein Werk* (Leipzig: Dürr, 1903) and his *Nietzsche-Aufsätze* (Leipzig: F. Meiner, 1917).

158. Richter, *Essays*, 173.

159. Alexander Tille, "Nietzsche und England," *Frankfurter Zeitung* 39, no. 289 (18 October 1894); "Nietzsche als Ethiker der Entwicklung," *Die Zukunft* 9, (10 November 1894); "Zarathustras Lehre," *Das neue Jahrhundert* 1, no. 5 (1898).

160. Biographical information on Tille may be found in Alfred Kelly, *The Descent of Darwin: The Popularization of Darwinism in Germany, 1860–1914* (Chapel Hill: University of North Carolina Press, 1981), 101ff; Hinton Thomas, *Nietzsche in German Politics*, 113–114; Krummel, *Nietzsche*, vol. 1, 134, n. 157.

161. Tille was Ferdinand Tönnies's central although rare embodiment of Nietzscheanism's central function: the justification of the most brutal aspects of capitalism (Tönnies, *Der Nietzsche-Kultus*, 109–110).

and gifted members. Slums were beneficial in that they purged the nation of its useless citizens.[162] His *From Darwin to Nietzsche* (1895) starkly rendered the connections. Nietzsche had provided ethics consonant with Darwin's evolutionary teachings and applicable to the development of humanity. Most crucial for Tille was the fact that, unlike Darwin, Nietzsche held that the new teaching was incompatible with the "christian–human–democratic ethic."[163] Only with Nietzsche did the realization emerge that a new morality had to distance itself from the traditional ethics of neighborly love. Nietzsche's fundamental lesson for the species was that people did not possess equal worth; while the strong represented upward development, the weak represented decay. To be sure, Nietzsche was not always aware that his Zarathustrian ideal grew out of the soil of evolutionary thought, yet there was no doubt that he drew the ethical conclusions of the Darwinian worldview: a physiologically higher form of human being was also the moral goal of mankind.[164]

Like most appropriators, Tille shaped Nietzsche into a worldview that entailed rejecting certain aspects of the master's vision. Tille as an active supporter of the industrialist cause believed that Nietzsche's ethic underestimated the intrinsic value of labor. He suspected that the shadow of feudalism still lingered in Nietzsche's aristocratic ideal and that he had not fully conceived of the aristocracy of merit. Moreover Nietzsche had not placed sufficient emphasis upon conflicts between tribes, nations, and races. He was also still partly bound to a traditional humanitarianism that was blind to the fact that only through service to one's own Volk could one serve humanity.[165]

These reservations notwithstanding, the conclusion reached by one recent commentator that with Tille "it was Nietzsche's faults that finally counted" is not only a gross exaggeration but also misses the central point.[166] Tille's whole career was a kind of extended and applied celebration of Nietzsche. From early in his career he called the master "The Herald of Modern Germany," and was perceived as a "furious

162. Marielouise Janssen-Jurreit, "Sexual-reform und Geburtenrückgang: Über die Zusammenhänge von Bevölkerüngspolitik und Frauenbewegung um die Jahrhundertwende," in *Frauen in der Geschichte*, ed. Annette Kuhn and Gerhard Schneider (Düsseldorf, 1979), 60–61.

163. Alexander Tille, *Von Darwin bis Nietzsche: Ein Buch Entwicklungsethik* (Leipzig: C. G. Naumann, 1895), vii, 10–11.

164. Ibid., 122–123, 214, 225.

165. Ibid., 239–241.

166. Hinton Thomas, *Nietzsche in German Politics*, 114.

Nietzschean."[167] His unlikely affair with Helene Stöcker was based upon their common passionate Nietzscheanism. The few reservations that Tille did voice only made sense in light of the overarching function Nietzsche performed in shaping Tille's social Darwinian and pan-Germanic goals.

Despite all their efforts the dissident Kaiserreich right did not produce a definitive version of Nietzsche commensurate with its own needs and worldview. It was only at the end of World War I that Ernst Bertram would produce a Nietzsche beautifully attuned to the changed circumstances and sensitivities of the new radical right. The conditions of the Wilhelmine era were obviously not conducive to the creation of an equivalently comprehensive, radical, and thus theoretically satisfying account (although the George Kreis, from which Bertram emerged, came closest to it). Most appropriations remained either too fractured, too factional, wed to the old order, or too selectively critical of the philosopher to permit an overall mythologization. Still, there were right-wing theoreticians who began to wrestle with the Nietzsche phenomenon. Already in 1899 Arthur Möller van den Bruck—later a cult figure of conservative revolutionaries—penned an exploratory appreciation that pointed to elements of the later radical appropriation.[168] This Nietzsche was valued for articulating the frustration that discontented circles felt for Wilhelmine society and the need to create a new culture. Nietzsche's culture of the future seemed at one with Möller-Bruck's demands: a future relieved of everyday mediocrity and selfish interests (code words in the völkisch lexicon for liberalism and divisive parliamentarianism). Nietzsche's proposal in *The Birth of Tragedy* to metamorphosize the present through the conscious employment of myth was comfortably endorsed by Möller-Bruck.

Ironically, the most sophisticated reading of Nietzsche consonant with the nascent right-wing interpretation came not from a völkisch activist but from the scholar Karl Joel (1864–1934) who, like Nietzsche, wrote in the detached, patrician tranquility of Basel. His *Nietzsche and Romanticism* (1905) sought to locate—and partially domesticate—Nietzsche within the German Romantic tradition. Both Nietzsche's life and thought were incomprehensible outside of the "in-

167. R. M. Wenley, "Nietzsche: Traffics and Discoveries," *Monist* 31 (January 1921), 136. Quoted in Krummel, *Nietzsche*, vol. 1, 134–135. Hinton Thomas himself quotes from this source.

168. Arthur Möller-Bruck, *Tschandala Nietzsche* (Berlin and Leipzig: Schuster and Löffler, 1899), 47. Although this analysis emphasizes his positive judgments, the pre-Weimar Möller-Bruck clearly still had reservations.

toxicated" Romantic frame; Joel's book was devoted to a sustained comparison. Nietzsche's life was depicted as the heroic struggle to emancipate himself from Romanticism while eventually returning to it in transmogrified form.[169]

The context in which Joel placed his quintessentially Germanic Nietzsche was one that could unintentionally provide the building blocks for a new political vision.[170] "One sees Nietzsche against the gloomy background of socialism, Darwinism and pessimism from which he freed himself. Without it Nietzsche appears as a fool and a criminal. With it he appears as a hero."[171] Joel prefigured many of the Nietzschean and Romantic themes that the radical right would later stress: the disregard for systems and the emphasis on dynamic movement; the attempt to fuse will and feeling; the praise of passion over reason; and, above all, the stress on "living dangerously" and "overcoming."[172]

Most critically, Joel enunciated the differences between early Romanticism and the later Nietzschean brand. Already in 1900 Nietzsche had been identified as symptomatic of the neo-Romantic mood,[173] but Joel did so in a sustained and persuasive fashion. There was, he pointed out, a world of difference between the early Romantic "feminine soul" and Nietzsche's "manly spirit." While for the early Romantics nothing was worse than exaggerated manliness, Nietzsche exhorted one to "become hard." Whereas Romanticism feminized to the point of sentimentality, Nietzsche sought manliness to the point of brutality. His main aim was the "masculinization of culture"—a theme that in later German developments was to become all too familiar.[174]

At an even deeper level, Joel intuited differences that were to become critical to the political appropriation of Nietzsche. There was nothing in the Romantic canon, he wrote, that even vaguely resembled Nietzsche's

169. Karl Joel, *Nietzsche und die Romantik* (Jena and Leipzig: Eugen Diederichs, 1905), 68.

170. Joel argues that Nietzsche's biting criticism of Germanness was itself a German characteristic. Nietzsche was thus no longer the antithesis of Germanism but its incarnation and prophet (ibid., 83–84). Joel's attitude toward both Nietzsche and Romanticism was critical as well as admiring: "We want to overcome Nietzsche, not scream him down" (ibid., 327). In the end, he argued, a mature synthesis between Classicism and Romanticism was desirable.

171. Ibid., 87.

172. Ibid., 133. Joel also stressed commonalities such as their Bacchanalian-Saturnalian mode and their fragmentary, aphoristic style.

173. Georg Tantzscher, *Friedrich Nietzsche und die Neuromantik* (Jurjew [Dorpat], 1900).

174. Joel, *Nietzsche und die Romantik*, 10–12.

intoxicated celebration of the intrinsic value of war and cruelty. While for the Romantic nothing was evil, Nietzsche regarded evil as humanity's best quality. The Romantic longed for the "moralization of nature"; Nietzsche sought the iced zones, the wild, raw power of destructive, dehumanized (*entmenschten*) nature. The Romantic was a backward-looking, dreamy creature, whereas Nietzsche emphasized forward-looking, activist creation: only the future was enchantment. History for the Romantic was applied morality and religion; Nietzsche was the great secularizer and philosopher of the profane and all its unbounded possibilities.[175]

Joel had portentously if unwittingly outlined the great Nietzschean themes that became enmeshed in the transformed right-wing politics of the future and in the unlimited profanity that was World War I.

175. Ibid., 57ff.

CHAPTER V

Zarathustra in the Trenches

The Nietzsche Myth, World War I, and the Weimar Republic

All power structures of the old society will have been
exploded—all of them are based on lies; there will be wars
the like of which have never yet been seen on earth.

Nietzsche, *Ecce Homo*

The present-day European requires not merely war but the
greatest and most terrible wars—thus a temporary relapse
into barbarism—if the means to culture are not to deprive
them of their culture and of their existence itself.

Nietzsche, *Human, All Too Human*

Soon after its beginning, a London bookseller dubbed the war of 1914
the Euro-Nietzschean War.[1] He was not only referring to the dramatic
increase in the sales of works by Nietzsche. He was alluding to the
widespread conviction of Germany's enemies that this thinker was
somehow directly responsible for its outbreak and especially brutal
conduct. In Britain and the Empire, in France and the United States,
Nietzsche was suddenly propelled into the limelight. He was constantly
discussed in the popular press, his name entering ordinary households
as perhaps *the* villain of the war. The legend that Nietzsche was a
thinker who generated dangerous acts was now internationalized. As a

---

1. James Joll, "The English, Friedrich Nietzsche and the First World War" in *Deutschland in der Weltpolitik des 19 und 20 Jahrhunderts,* ed. Imanuel Geiss and Bernd Jürgen Wendt (Düsseldorf: Bertelsmann Universitätsverlag, 1973), 305. This article contains a useful survey of English opinion during this period. I thank Prof. Joll for guiding me to other bibliographical sources.

later observer wrote, no other philosopher had been made responsible for a European war.[2]

Such convictions confirmed that by 1914 Friedrich Nietzsche had been transformed into a protean cultural symbol for many of the great issues of European life. The Nietzsche heritage was a shaping force that was itself constantly redefined by changing political needs and ideological circumstances. The Great War strikingly illustrates the workings of this heritage. Nietzsche's manly posture and his admonitions to live dangerously crucially affected turn-of-the-century attitudes towards a coming war; at the same time, the war itself spurred various groups, even nations, to re-create Nietzsche in terms consonant with their changing interests. Not surprisingly, World War I pushed Nietzscheanism deeper into the German nationalist and right-wing camps. As never before, reality seemed (or was made) to take on Nietzschean form as Nietzschean images fused with the ongoing conflagration. As a result, the deification and demonization of that thinker reached new extremes.

The simplest level of the Nietzsche war myth was his vilification by Germany's war enemies for propaganda purposes. It was convenient to equate Nietzschean extremism with the German condition itself and the foil on which to base the anti-German attack. As H. L. Stewart put it in his book-length tract, *Nietzsche and the Ideals of Germany* (1915), the war was between a Germany that stood for an unscrupulous "Nietzschean immoralism" and those who fought for the cherished principles of "Christian restraint." In tandem with the Prussian ruling class, Nietzschean notions had done their work: "I ask you . . . whether the creed of *Beyond Good and Evil* has left no mark in the smoking ruins of Ärschot and the mangled corpses of the women of Dinant?"[3] The negative equation of Nietzsche with Germany and the German mind was destined to become a tradition, and during World War II was successfully revived.[4]

Although dissenting voices opposed this vilification,[5] they were essentially overshadowed, especially at the beginning of the Great War.

---

2. See the comments by Eric Vögelin in "Nietzsche, the Crisis and the War," *The Journal of Politics* 6, no. 1 (February 1944), 177.

3. Herbert Leslie Stewart, *Nietzsche and the Ideals of Modern Germany* (London: Edward Arnold, 1915), 186, 228.

4. Eric Bentley, *The Cult of the Superman* (Gloucester, Mass.: Peter Smith, 1969), 248–250.

5. John Cowper Powys, *The Menace of German Culture* (London: William Rider and Son, 1915); Joll, "The English, Nietzsche, and the War," 305; Patrick Bridgwater, *Nietzsche in Anglo Saxony: A Study of Nietzsche's Impact on English and American Literature* (Leicester, 1972), p. 147.

Typical of the early mood were the letters of Thomas Hardy to the
English *Daily Mail* and the *Manchester Guardian:* "I should think there
is no instance since history began of a country being so demoralized by
a single writer."[6] Nietzschean notions were easily converted into German political characteristics. Hardy regarded the German leadership as
infected by the will to power. Moreover, Germany became identified as
a nation of rapacious supermen. Sophisticated thinkers, such as J. H.
Muirhead, were aware of Nietzsche's anti-Prussian, antinationalist posture. Nevertheless, he argued that Nietzsche's appropriation had produced explosive results:

> Let Nietzsche's *ego* be interpreted in terms of the nation and clothed with the
> power of the State; let it come to be taught in high places with all the flavour
> of prophecy that it was from the loins of the German nation that the Su-
> perman was destined to appear, while upon its chief enemies in the direction
> in which its hopes were set decay had already set her mark; finally let it be
> announced with all the authority of expert knowledge that the hour was
> about to strike, and it was not difficult to see what the harvest of this long
> sowing was likely to be.[7]

In France, too, intellectual luminaries began to perceive the German
enemy through the Nietzschean filter. Romain Rolland, for example,
argued that war developments were to some degree the product of
"what the masses make of the words of a sage. One superman is a
sublime spectacle. Ten or twenty supermen are unpleasant. But hun-
dreds of thousands who combine arrogant extravagance with mediocrity or natural baseness become a scourge of God ·which is ravaging
Belgium and France."[8] These pronouncements served to label all that
was negative and aggressive in the German heritage. It was certainly
World War I that spurred the Anglo–American tendency to read militarism and imperialism into Nietzsche's conception of power.[9] The very
titles of Ernst Barker's wartime Oxford pamphlet, *Nietzsche and
Treitschke: The Worship of Power in Modern Germany,* and Canon E.
McClure's *Germany's War Inspirers Nietzsche and Treitschke*[10] indicted Nietzsche simply for the nationalist and imperialist company he

6. *Daily Mail,* 27 September 1914; *Manchester Guardian,* 7 October 1914. Quoted
in Bridgwater, *Nietzsche in Anglosaxony,* 144.
7. J. H. Muirhead, *German Philosophy in Relation to the War* (London: J. Murray,
1915), 80–81, 78.
8. Romain Rolland, *Zwischen den Völkern: Aufzeichnungen und Dokumente aus
den Jahren 1914 bis 1919,* vol. 1 (Stuttgart: Dt. Vlgs.-Anst., 1954), 145.
9. Kaufmann, *Nietzsche,* 8.
10. Ernst Barker, *Nietzsche and Treitschke: The Worship of Power in Modern Germany* (Oxford: Oxford University Press, 1914); Canon E. McClure, *Germany's War-
Inspirers Nietzsche and Treitschke* (London, 1914).

was made to keep. In addition, he was often linked to the arch militarist and imperialist, General Friedrich von Bernhardi. Staid journals such as the *Athenaeum* explained how the Nietzschean web was spun throughout Germany:

> We find the principles of Nietzsche at work in the life of the German nation, in the teachings of her professors and schoolmasters, more startling than this, we find them embodied in the texts of the German Staff College—at least in Bernhardi—and, if not embodied, implied even in the conversation of diplomatists with foreign publicists. This deadly seriousness which can drag a professor from his lecture room and bear him in triumph through the land—for this may be said of Nietzsche—could not but end in explosion.[11]

But apart from the emblematic and decorative use of a Zarathustrian exhortation as the motto for Bernhardi's famous *Germany and the Coming War*[12] the relationship—as many indignant critics pointed out[13]—was extremely tenuous. Like all war propaganda, innuendo rather than accuracy characterized these discussions of Nietzsche. Indeed, at times such demonization reached the level of farce. Nietzsche's American popularizer, H. L. Mencken, was actually arrested and charged with being the war agent of "the German monster, Nietzsky."[14] Mencken's contemporary description (1915) of what he termed the "imbecile Nietzsche legend," satirically captured this popular trivialization of Nietzsche into a "high priest of diabolism" responsible for all the sins and butcheries of an anti-Christian war.[15]

Nietzschean immoralism, the symbolic antithesis of upright respectability, was smoothly transmuted into a metaphor for German immoralism. William Archer put it as bluntly as possible. The war was a war against the philosophy of Nietzsche. Not only did Nietzschean precepts

11. "Teutonismus," *The Athenaeum* (10 October 1914). Quoted in Joll, "The English, Nietzsche, and the War," 302–303.

12. Friedrich von Bernhardi, *Germany and the Coming War*, trans. Allen H. Powles (New York: Longsman, Green, 1914). This had already reached its 6th edition.

13. Numerous examples include Ernst Rolffs, "Treitschke, Nietzsche, Bernhardi," *Die christliche Welt* 30 (1916), 857–865, 882–888.

> The usual thing was to link together Nietzsche, Treitschke, and Bernhardi—a grotesque cacophony for the ear of all intellectual Germans, and not of the Germans alone. One might conceivably name Treitschke and General von Bernhardi in one breath, although there was a great injustice to Treitschke in this. But it was ridiculous that Nietzsche should be brought in to complete the symbol of German wickedness.

(Thomas Mann, "German Letter," *The Dial* 74 [1923], 610–611)

14. H. L. Mencken, "Introduction," in Friedrich Nietzsche, *The Antichrist* (New York, 1923). Quoted in Bridgwater, *Nietzsche in Anglosaxony*, 145–146.

15. H. L. Mencken, *The Smart Set*, quoted in ibid., 146.

and Prussian practice agree, but Nietzschean ideas also sanctioned the German soldier's brutality: "the average man hugs to his heart the philosopher's violently dogmatic asseverations, in semibiblical rhythms, that force, rapacity, unscrupulousness, pitilessness are indispensable parts of the ethics of the future."[16] These words represent the myth at its most basic level. There were, however, more complex perceptions tying Nietzsche to the war which went well beyond the elementary motivation of negatively labeling one's enemy.

One dimension of the history of prewar Nietzscheanism partly explains the later conjunction of Nietzschean themes with the war experience. For countless European intellectuals, Nietzsche's appeal before 1914 was closely bound to the widespread critique of decadence and a regenerative predisposition which glorified a future, cathartic, redemptive war.[17] There was no shortage of useable quotations in which Nietzsche celebrated war and martial virtues, regardless of their context. "War is the father of all good things."[18] Zarathustra's exhortations that war and courage had achieved things far greater than love of neighbor encouraged Nietzscheans to make courage a value regardless of the ends. "What is good you ask? To be brave is good." Nietzsche seemed to foster a conception of war as a means of transcending everyday banalities, as a purifying form of individual and collective action. From 1900 through 1945, Zarathustra's cry was endlessly invoked: "You say that it is the good cause that hallows even war? I say unto you: it is the good war that hallows any cause."[19]

Not all Nietzscheans were necessarily "war Nietzscheans" and not all intellectuals who advocated war did so on Nietzschean grounds. Nevertheless, the interrelation was clear. For many aesthetes, poets, and avant-garde intellectuals a Lebensphilosophie war, shorn of ideological trappings, seemed to answer to the great issues of the time as Nietzsche had diagnosed them. Would not war bring about Nietzsche's dictum to "live dangerously," facilitate the search for heightened, authentic experience, and overcome the pervasive decadence?

Such attitudes were spread throughout European intellectual circles. They were part of a new cultural and political style. Gabriele D'An-

16. William Archer, *Fighting a Philosophy* (Oxford: Oxford University Press, 1914–1915), 5, 3ff.
17. Ronald N. Stromberg, *Redemption by War: The Intellectuals and 1914* (Lawrence: Regents Press of Kansas, 1982).
18. Nietzsche, *Gay Science*, 145. This was an elaboration of Heraclitus's fragment 53: "War is the father of all."
19. Nietzsche, *Zarathustra*, 159.

nunzio, the aesthete dandy and an important mediator of Nietzsche to the Italian world, wrote in his famous novel, *The Virgins of the Rocks* (1894–1895),[20] about his ancestors whom he celebrated as a "noble race of warriors." Elsewhere he celebrated savage acts in a Nietzschean literary rhapsody over "the terrible energies, the sense of power, the instinct for battle and domination, the abundance of productive and fructifying forces, all the virtues of Dionysian man, the victor, the destroyer, the creator."[21]

The futurists contemporized this longing in their 1909 manifesto resonant with post-Nietzschean themes, images and passion:

> We want to exalt movements of aggression . . . the forced march, the perilous leap, the slap and the blow with the fist. . . . We want to glorify war—the only cure for the world—and militarism, patriotism, the destructive gesture of the anarchists, the beautiful ideas which kill, and contempt for women. . . . We want to demolish museums and libraries, fight morality, feminism and all opportunist and utilitarian cowardice.[22]

In France, Georges Sorel exemplified this new political aesthetic in expressing the hope that a great war would reawaken decadent energies and bring to the fore men who had the requisite will to power.[23] The emphasis on action and dynamism rather than stasis made it easy to acclaim war. The young Mussolini, for example, began in the socialist camp but his Marxism was always influenced by Nietzsche, integrated with the Lebensphilosophie of the time, and less concerned with ideology than heroic will and vitality. Here was a manly Marxism grounded in a warrior relationship to reality. These categories did not merely facilitate Mussolini's later move to fascism, they also conditioned his attitude toward the coming Great War. His pro-interventionism combined the socialist perception of war as a prelude to revolution with a less instrumental Nietzschean vitalism.[24]

Pre–World War I Nietzscheanism, then, proceeded independently of fixed national or political boundaries. Nietzsche adapted with some

20. Michael A. Ledeen, *The First Duce: D'Annunzio at Fiume* (Baltimore: Johns Hopkins University Press, 1977), 5.

21. Gabriele D'Annunzio, "Il Triofono della Morte," *Prose di Romanzi*, vol. 1 (Milan, 1954), 958. Quoted in Ernst Nolte, *Three Faces of Fascism* (New York: Mentor, 1969), 198, 606, n. 7.

22. Reproduced in Umbro Apollonio, ed., *Futurist Manifestos* (London: Thames and Hudson, 1973), 21–22.

23. Georges Sorel, *Reflections on Violence* (New York: Collier, [1908] 1974).

24. For the most thorough treatment of this question, see Ernst Nolte, "Marx und Nietzsche im Sozialismus des Jungen Mussolinis," *Historische Zeitschrift* 191 (1960), 249–335.

elasticity to a variety of ideologies. Indeed, he may even *have* had a role in the genesis of the Great War, for he penetrated the secret Young Bosnia Movement from whence came the assassins of the Archduke Franz Ferdinand. Its members, hotheaded Serb students, absorbed certain radical Nietzschean sentiments and sought to put them into action. Their intellectual mentor, Vladimir Cerina, taught them overtly transvaluative lessons:

> Thought, free thought, is the greatest and bravest ruler of the universe. It has huge space wings of the freest and most audacious bird, for which fear and danger do not exist.
>
> Its wild flight goes to infinity and eternity. It destroys today what was created yesterday. It destroys every dogma, every norm, every authority. It has no other faith but the faith in its power. It creates critics, subversives, rebels and wreckers.[25]

The assassin of the Archduke, Gavrilo Princip, who precipitated the crisis of 1914, was fond of reciting Nietzsche's short poem, *Ecce Homo:* "Insatiable as flame, I burn and consume myself."[26]

Whatever the degree of Nietzsche's influence upon the Serb students there is no doubt that Nietzsche's pre-war appeal to intellectuals throughout Europe made it easy for them to pack a copy of *Zarathustra* into their kitbags as they marched off into the Great War. Writers like Robert Graves in England,[27] d'Annunzio in Italy (the war transformed him into a military hero facilitating his takeover of the city of Fiume in 1919),[28] and the future Fascist Drieu La Rochelle in France[29] are only a few examples. They could all take Nietzsche into battle because Nietzsche transcended national distinctions and conventional political categorization. Like the anticipated war experience itself, Zarathustra symbolized the longing for transcendence, for the exceptional, and for the heroic.

While the Nietzschean sensibility helped to mold a positive disposition towards the coming war, the Great War reshaped the Nietzschean myth in terms of its own needs. Almost with the outbreak of hostilities, Zarathustra seemed to lose his individualistic and transnational char-

25. Vladimir Dedijer, *The Road to Sarajevo* (New York: Simon and Schuster, 1966), 232; Joll, "1914: The Unspoken Assumptions," in *The Origins of the First World War,* ed. H. W. Koch (London: Macmillan, 1972), 324.
26. Dedijer, *Sarajevo,* 238.
27. Bridgwater, *Nietzsche in Anglosaxony,* 10.
28. Ledeen, *First Duce,* 10–11.
29. Robert Soucy, *Fascist Intellectual: Drieu La Rochelle* (Berkeley, Los Angeles, and London: University of California Press, 1979), 45.

acteristics. Nietzscheanism underwent rapid politicization and nationalization that far outstripped its pre-war pace. Cosmopolitan and individualist motifs were increasingly drowned out by inflamed nationalist passions. Fraternal transnational moments, such as Herbert Read serenely discussing Nietzsche with a captured German, minutes after almost killing him in trench combat, became increasingly rare.[30] The French and Anglo-American demonization of Nietzsche was only one side of this coin. In Germany Nietzsche was linked to the war effort and celebrated as a national inspiration, the incarnation of the best within German culture. Some voices did contest this tendency—out of respect for Nietzsche or because they continued to despise him—but in the din of battle they were increasingly muffled.[31] Indeed, the changing content of the canonization of Nietzsche faithfully mirrored the various stages of the German war experience as it evolved from militant enthusiasm through bewilderment to despair and defeat.

At the beginning of the war British commentators blamed Nietzsche for its outbreak; German writers invoked him as the most effective way of fighting it. In Germany, too, there was a dramatic increase in sales of Nietzsche's works. Together with Goethe's *Faust* and the New Testament, *Zarathustra* was the most popular work that literate soldiers took into battle for inspiration and consolation. The "beautiful words" of Zarathustra, one author wrote, were especially apt for the Germans, who "more than any other Volk possessed fighting natures (*Kampfnaturen*) in Zarathustra's sense."[32] About 150,000 copies of a specially durable wartime *Zarathustra* were distributed to the troops.[33] Even Christian commentators were struck that *Zarathustra* had taken its place alongside the Bible in the field.[34] Indeed, this very combination

30. Jon Glover and Jon Silkin, *The Penguin Book of First World War Prose* (London: Viking, 1989). Quoted in C. J. Fox, "Bondservants of Destruction," *Times Literary Supplement* (February 16–22, 1990).

31. Some academic and nationalist figures remained unconvinced of the desirability of this annexation and Nietzsche's patriotic credentials. Nietzsche, Ernst Tröltsch told Friedrich Meinecke in a wartime conversation, was like rat poison in the guts (Meinecke, *Erlebtes, 1862–1901* [Leipzig: Koehler-Amelang, 1941], 184f). See also Karl Lamprecht, *Krieg und Kultur* (Leipzig: Hirzel, 1914); Adolf Dryoff, *Was bedeutet "Kulturvolk"? Nietzsche und der deutsche Geist* (Bonn: Peter Hanstein, 1915).

32. Rektor P. Hoche, "Nietzsche und der deutsche Kampf," *Zeitung für Literatur, Kunst, und Wissenschaft* 39, no. 6 (12 March 1916); Krummel, *Nietzsche*, vol. 2, 607.

33. Robert G. L. Waite, *The Psychopathic God: Adolf Hitler* (New York, 1977), 279; Rolffs, "Treitschke, Nietzsche, Bernhardi," 859. In 1917 alone 40,000 copies of *Zarathustra* were sold (Peters, *Zarathustra's Sister*, 205).

34. Edelbert Kurz, *Nietzsche der Deutsche und wir Christen* (Munich-Gladbach, 1918). See Krummel, *Nietzsche*, vol. 2, 645–646.

was a key way for interpreters to integrate the notorious author of the *Antichrist* into respectability. Ernst Wurche, the hero of Walter Flex's highly successful Nietzschean war novel, *Wanderer Between Two Worlds* (1917), claimed that such apparently contradictory books were like people in the trenches. They could be as different from one another as they liked: "they must only be strong and honorable and be able to hold their own; that makes for the best comradeship."[35] In his war tract Karl Joel declared that the fact that German soldiers went to battle with the Bible, *Faust* and *Zarathustra* constituted the best possible evidence to demonstrate the "idealist" nature of the German people and the best reproof to those who reproached the Germans as "barbarians."[36] Others exalted *Zarathustra* as eminently suitable for German troops. So much a part of national life, it surely fitted one's potential hour of death.[37]

Beyond this, of course, Nietzsche's emphasis on heroism and will suited the challenge posed by war. What Ernst Wurche most admired about Zarathustra, for instance, was the constant reminder that man was "something to be overcome." The war was the Zarathustrian abyss and the ultimate test of self. This, at least, was how the makers of the German Nietzschean war myth presented it to their readers.

We simply do not have accurate evidence indicating how many soldiers in fact read that book. Critics of the nationalist appropriation argued that they did not do so in great numbers.[38] Whatever the case, one may legitimately be skeptical about how many soldiers in the field really experienced *Zarathustra* as a living guide to an ecstatic war experience. A preliminary perusal of war letters, diaries, and memoirs indicates that in the harsh reality of the trenches the Zarathustrian theme did not always strike a major chord. It was not easy to blend the sordidness of the Somme with the elevated Nietzschean mountain landscape.[39] The Zarathustrian praise of war for its own sake, one caustic critic observed, had been a disastrous recipe. Had the troops not been told that the German cause was a good one and that the struggle

35. Walter Flex, *Der Wanderer zwischen beiden Welten: Ein Kriegserlebnis* (Munich: C. H. Beck, 1918), 9. The book went through thirty-nine editions and sold 250,000 copies in less than two years.
36. Karl Joel, *Neue Weltkultur* (Leipzig: Karl Wolff, 1915), 88–89.
37. Richard Gröper, "Nietzsche und der Krieg," *Die Tat* 8 (1916–1917), 25.
38. Oscar Levy, "Nietzsche im Krieg," *Die Weissen Blätter* (1919), 277ff.
39. Laqueur comments that Nietzsche's "ecstatic rhymes did not stand up too well to the great test. Those who had been through the holocaust of Flanders and the mud and ice of the Eastern front knew all they needed to know about the spirit of tragedy" (*Young Germany,* 9).

constituted its own justification they would never have embarked upon the war.[40]

Some soldiers did experience a species of Zarathustrian transportation.[41] Usually, however, when they perceived the war through Nietzschean lenses they tended to do so in a rather trivialized and detached way. A 1915 field letter written by a student of theology describing his Superman commander demonstrates the personalization of such perceptions. Here was a fearless officer who regarded Christianity as a religion of the weak and who was supremely indifferent to the opinions of others: "I don't know much about Nietzsche, but I should think that he must have been just like that. I don't want to set myself up as a judge, but when I am with him it is quite plain to me that I am one of the weaklings."[42] If there was a superman most soldiers did not regard themselves as such; he was displaced onto more remote figures. Alternatively, Nietzschean categories filtered perceptions according to more idiosyncratic criteria. The painter Franz Marc, for instance, domesticated Nietzsche for his own professional purposes. The idea of the eternal recurrence became the metaphor for Marc's wartime observation that there were only a few standardized human types that kept on reappearing.[43] This was hardly heady ideological stuff.

It is probably safe to conclude that in the field *Zarathustra* was not as popular as proponents of the Nietzschean myth claimed. But this very claim is crucial to an understanding of Nietzschean discourse both during and after World War I, for it centrally informed public mythmaking and political symbolic mobilization. This propaganda facilitated the adaptation of Nietzscheanism for the essentially nationalist and establishmentarian goal of winning the war. Equally significantly, Nietzscheanism gradually became incorporated into an emergent, radicalized right-wing politics.

This was a new development. As we have seen, prior to 1914 most Nietzscheans were not particularly patriotic in their outlook. Indeed, virtually the only connecting link between the pre-war strands of

---

40. Ruthardt Schuhmann, "Der Nietzsche Kult und der Krieg," *Bühne und Welt* 17 (1915), 354.

41. Hans Leip, *Der Widerschein: Eine Rückschau, 1893–1943* (Stuttgart: Cotta, 1943), 42. After reading *Zarathustra* in 1915 he noted: "*Beim Lesen des Zarathustra schreien wir manchmal auf vor Entzuekken. Ich bin erhoben und wieder niedergeschmettert, so dass mir die Seele weh tut*" (Kummel, *Nietzsche*, vol. 2, 597).

42. Phillip Witkop, *German Students' War Letters*, trans. A. F. Wedd (London: Methuen, 1929), 42–43.

43. Franz Marc, *Briefe, Aufzeichnungen, und Aphorismen* (Berlin: Cassirer, 1920), 41.

Nietzscheanism was an anti-establishment, anti-Orthodox stance. The war provided the grounds for a more plausible construction of a nationalist Nietzsche. Moreover, it rendered the progressive version less appealing. It became increasingly difficult for liberationist circles to believe that Nietzsche was after all a suitable champion for their cause.[44]

Arnold Zweig is an interesting case in point. Before the war he was a confessed Nietzschean. Nietzsche had been his aid in the expression of discontent with Wilhelmine materialism and philistinism and provided the hope for a Dionysian deliverance from this plight. Moreover, with the outbreak of war Zweig regarded himself as a militarist on Nietzschean grounds.[45] In the midst of the war he wrote that the German spirit was distinguished by its essentially "musical–political" nature, which Nietzsche exemplified. The greatness of the war was that it reawakened this creative spirit.[46] But Zweig did not stay with these notions for very long. The massive destruction and waste of human life transformed him into one of the great antiwar critics in Germany. He correspondingly changed his attitude towards Nietzsche. As he wrote later to Sigmund Freud: "You know that ever since the end of the war I have turned bitterly away from this idol of my youth."[47]

Zweig recognized what was common to Freud and Nietzsche: the daring new perspective on antiquity, the reversal of values, the critique of Christianity, and the thoroughgoing reevaluation of civilization. But, in Zweig's postwar view, what distinguished Freud was his fusion of such insights with humanism and rationalism. The war made such a fusion essential for it had brought into relief the problem of the release of the instinctual without the mediating control of the rational. Zweig

---

44. The liberationists never entirely abandoned him. In his address to the assembled Munich workers', peasants', and soldiers' councils, Ernst Toller memorialized his revolutionary colleague Kurt Eisner with a tellingly ironic quote from Zarathustra:

> Behold the good and the just! Whom do they hate most? The man who breaks their tables of values, the breaker, the lawbreaker; yet he is the creator. Behold the believers of all faiths! Whom do they hate most? The man who breaks their tables of values, the breaker, the lawbreaker; yet he is the creator. (Kaufmann, *Portable Nietzsche*, 135–136)

See *Der Fall Toller: Kommentar und Materialen,* ed. Wolfgang Frühwald and John M. Spalek (Munich and Vienna: Carl Hanser, 1979), 54.

45. Arnold Zweig, *Werk und Leben in Dokumenten und Bildern,* ed. Georg Wenzel (Berlin and Weimar: Aufbau Verlag, 1978), 61. See Krummel, *Nietzsche,* vol. 2, 358–359.

46. Zweig, *Werk und Leben,* 66.

47. Ernst L. Freud, ed., *The Letters of Sigmund Freud and Arnold Zweig* (New York: Harcourt, Brace and World, 1970), 74.

put it thus to Freud: "you have avoided his [Nietzsche's] distortions and follies, just because you have invented analysis and not Zarathustra."[48] When the Nazis came to power, Zweig argued that in the war the future national-socialist elite had received their vulgarized Nietzschean education. The acoustics of battle had provided resonance for Nietzsche's ideas of the

> glorification of "the blonde beast"; his struggle against ratio, enlightenment and reason; . . . his highly charged negation of bourgeois ideals, Christian morality, and the slow ascent of the socialist masses; and above all his hysterical discarding of mercy and neighborly love.[49]

French predictions during the Great War were now realized: whoever philosophized with a hammer destroyed all values.

Contemporaries were aware that events were pushing Nietzsche in a new symbolic direction. As Erwin Piscator, the radical producer of German political theater, lamented, before the war Nietzsche had been the "scourge of the middle classes," helping him shed his "petit bourgeois background." The war, however, produced a new Nietzsche in the wave of mass nationalist hysteria:

> The entire intellectual elite of Europe rose as one man in the defense of their "Cherished Heritage" which they had till then viewed with some skepticism: . . . They rose against "enemies" like Tolstoy and Dostoevsky and Pushkin and Zola and Balzac and Anatole France and Shaw and Shakespeare, and went to war with Goethe and Nietzsche in their knapsacks. And so this generation set the seal on its own spiritual bankruptcy. Whatever they may have thought and whatever they may have done it became evident on August fourth that all they had thought and done was as nothing.[50]

In this jingoistic atmosphere, *opposition to the war on Nietzschean grounds* was unlikely to evoke an enthusiastic response. In any case, how was it possible to oppose the war from a Nietzschean viewpoint? The example of certain German expressionists is instructive. Prior to 1914 their Nietzsche was the artistic creator who was a law unto himself and quite removed from conventional social and patriotic considerations. Thus, in Gustav Sack's 1914 drama *Der Refraktair* (The objector), the hero Egon, a penniless writer, refuses to leave Switzerland and join the German army when war is declared. Egon's objections, as

48. Ibid.
49. Arnold Zweig, *Bilanz der deutschen Judenheit 1933: Ein Versuch* (Amsterdam: Querido, 1934), 290–291.
50. Erwin Piscator, *The Political Theatre: A History, 1914–1929* (New York: Avon, 1978), 11.

Walter Sokel has reminded us, are not Quaker, socialist, or Tolstoyan but Nietzschean and are explicitly opposed to humanitarian pacifism. His objections center entirely around the artist's self. Egon has only contempt for the masses to whose fate he is indifferent; he believes they deserved this war. Here the Nietzschean objection is not to war as such but against this petit-bourgeois one based upon the demeaning search for profit.[51]

Before 1914 expressionists welcomed visions of a Nietzschean apocalyptic war arising out of a combination of boredom and nihilistic disgust. Such a war would presage the death of bourgeois society from whose ashes a nobler world would arise. In Sacks's first novel, *Ein verbummelter Student* (1910), his protagonist loudly proclaims: "Let war come! It's lurking about in glittering spires of clouds—: let a star awaken and arouse it from its lurking slumber . . . ! Nation against nation . . . nothing but one raging storm, a twilight of mankind, a rejoicing destruction—! oh, perhaps then something higher [will be born]."[52] Expressionists of this ilk came to regard the Great War as a capitalist enterprise, not the Nietzschean one they had anticipated.

More significantly, as the war's grotesque realities became clearer, many expressionists became leading opponents of the war, adopting increasingly pacifist and humanitarian positions. It was thus consistent that the radical expressionist journal *Die Aktion* passionately objected to the wartime Germanization of Nietzsche. Its editor, Franz Pfemert, lashed out at this transformation of the philosopher into a great patriot, this Nietzsche "whose Prussian and German hate cannot be outdone by any foreigner."[53]

Stefan George had also spoken longingly of a future holy war. In his 1914 poem, "Der Stern des Bundes," he elaborated on how such a war would purify the spiritually moribund society of his time. Yet the same poem made it clear that the impending European war was far removed from George's heroic, Nietzschean vision of regeneration. Nietzsche is portrayed as the man who labored mightily to avert the coming catastrophe:

> One man arose who, sharp as lightning, cracked
> open the clefts and steel-like, severed camps,
> creating a Beyond, inverting your old Here—

51. Walter Sokel, *The Writer in Extremis*, 67.
52. Quoted in ibid., 68.
53. Franz Pfemert, "Die Deutschsprechung Friedrich Nietzsches," *Die Aktion: Wochenschrift für Politik, Literatur, Kunst* 5, no. 26 (1915), 321.

who roared your madness into you so long
with so much force that his throat burst. And you?
Some dumb, some clever, false or genuine,
perceived and looked as if nothing had happened—
You go on speaking, laughing and conspiring.
The warner went—the wheel that hurtles down
toward emptiness no arm attempts to tackle.[54]

George's 1917 war poem, "Der Krieg," unmistakably recognizes that this was no holy Nietzschean war. There the "hermit on the mountain" (George, Nietzsche, and Zarathustra rolled into one) looks askance upon the battle and declares, "I take no part in the struggle as you experience it."[55]

These, however, were marginal responses. Far more important was the mobilization of Nietzsche for nationalist and military purposes. Of course, many who opposed this appropriation did so not because they thought the war was too sordid for Nietzsche but rather that Nietzsche was too sordid for the war! Hinton Thomas has argued that Nietzsche was actually *not* generally welcomed as part of the war effort, that nationalists, annexationists, and propagandists continued to make anti-Nietzsche pronouncements and that therefore the Nietzsche legacy remained safely in the hands of progressives throughout the war.[56] While Nietzsche was never the exclusive preserve of one political faction, Hinton Thomas's view simply does not hold up: Nietzsche's nationalization and annexation by an increasingly radicalized right during World War I is unmistakable. Indeed, this tendency was confirmed and bitterly opposed both by certain progressive intellectuals,[57] some pro-Communist circles[58] and, more significantly, unrelenting anti-Nietzscheans of the right. Theodor Fritsch, for example, protested in terms more outraged than ever. Nietzsche himself, he declared in ironic Nietzschean language, "must be overcome."[59] But Fritsch's ob-

54. Stefan George, "Der Stern des Bundes," in Walter Kaufmann, *Twenty German Poets* (New York: Random House, 1962), 167.

55. Patrick Bridgwater, "German Poetry and the First World War," *European Studies Review* 1, no. 2 (April 1971), 155–156.

56. Hinton Thomas, *Nietzsche in German Politics,* 126ff.

57. Pfemert, "Deutschsprechung"; Levy, "Nietzsche im Krieg"; Zweig, *Bilanz der deutschen Judenheit,* 290–291, 50–52.

58. F. Schwangart describes the German nationalist war propaganda around Nietzsche as "an unforgettable misdeed" ("Was ist uns Nietzsche?" *Heimstunden: Proletarische Tribune für Kunst, Literatur, Dichtung* no. 5 [May 1925], 145).

59. See Fritsch's article under the pseudonym F. Roderick-Stoltheim, "Nietzsches Macht-philosophie und der Deutschenhass," *Hammer: Blätter für deutschen Sinn* 14, no. 301 (1 January 1915), 3.

jection was a barely audible response to an overwhelmingly celebratory tendency.

The war finally bestowed success on the long-term project of Förster-Nietzsche and her associates at the Weimar Archives. She was, after all, the foremost proponent of a patriotic, conservative version of Nietzsche. At the beginning of the war her sanitized image at last fell on fertile ground. Her articles appeared throughout the war.[60] Significantly, one of her first contributions appeared in the important *liberal* newspaper, the *Berliner Tageblatt,* in September 1914. "The 'Genuine Prussian' Friedrich Nietzsche," written in support of Werner Sombart's piece in the same paper, reinforced the perception of Nietzsche as the embodiment of all that was finest in the Prussian tradition.[61] His ideals incorporated the noble Prussian values of discipline, breeding, order, and duty. This was the "true" Nietzsche who had little to do with the version that riff-raff coffeehouse intellectuals were purveying.

Beginning with the biography of her brother (1904),[62] Förster-Nietzsche tirelessly presented him in terms of the Prussian experience. Nietzsche was a patriot and a martial man—very much a reflection of Förster-Nietzsche's own penchant for marching soldiers and bright uniforms. It was perhaps portentous that an extremely völkisch Ernst Wachler summed up Förster-Nietzsche's contributions to the Nietzschean heritage in Germany. If the nation, he wrote, had become increasingly permeated with Nietzsche's spiritual treasures (*Geistesschätze*), this was due to Förster-Nietzsche's noble efforts.[63] Wachler's Nietzsche as mediated by Förster-Nietzsche was not all that far from the heroic, political, nazified Nietzsche that Alfred Bäumler and others were soon to construct.[64]

60. A far from exhaustive list of Förster-Nietzsche's writings includes: "Nietzsche und der Krieg," *Tag* 212 (10 September 1914); "Nietzsche im Kriege 1870," *Der Neue Merkur* 1 (1914); "Nietzsche und Deutschland," *Berliner Tageblatt* 44, no. 453 (5 September 1915); "Nietzsche, Frankreich, und England," *Neue Freie Presse* (11 June 1916). Krummel, *Nietzsche,* has a complete list of Förster-Nietzsche's publications.

61. Elisabeth Förster-Nietzsche, "Der 'echt-preussiche' Friedrich Nietzsche," *Berliner Tageblatt* (16 September 1914). Sombart's comments appeared in the same paper, 6 September 1914.

62. Elisabeth Förster-Nietzsche, *Das Leben Friedrich Nietzsches,* vol. 2 (Leipzig: Naumann, 1904). Here she argues that Nietzsche derived his conception of the will to power from an incident in the Franco-Prussian war. Nietzsche had witnessed a spirited attack by a Prussian regiment despite its grave fatigue, persuading him, we are told, that not Darwin's struggle for survival but the will to power was the proper conception of life (682ff).

63. Ernst Wachler, "Elisabeth Nietzsche (Zur Begründung des Nietzsche-Archivs)," *Deutsche-Zeitung* 388 (1918).

64. Alfred Bäumler, *Nietzsche der Philosoph und Politiker* (Leipzig: Reclam, 1931).

Militant nationalism at the beginning of the war coincided with Nietzsche's seventieth birthday. This provided a convenient forum in which to rapidly absorb Nietzschean categories into the new war reality. These reflections appeared regularly not simply in academic and fringe journals but in the popular and national press. They presented a Germanic Nietzsche attuned to the needs of a nation at war.

Rhetoric linking Germanic with Nietzschean heroism emanated from the liberal press. What linked them was an affirmative philosophy of struggle and heroism in which discipline and suffering (rather than the superficial English utilitarian goal of happiness) could lead to Geist and greatness. These difficult tasks demonstrated that Nietzsche's "famous and defamed 'Superman' bears a thoroughly German imprint."[65] The same author, while nationalizing the Nietzschean superman, also quoted from *The Twilight of the Idols* in order to also provide the requisite anti-English, antiliberal and antidemocratic ideology:

> And war educates for freedom. For what is freedom? That one has the will to assume responsibility for oneself. That one maintains the distance that separates us. That one becomes indifferent to difficulties, hardships, privation, even to life itself. That one is prepared to sacrifice human beings for one's own cause, not excluding oneself. Freedom means that the manly instincts which delight in war and victory dominate over other instincts, for example, over those of "pleasure." The human being who has become *free*— and how much more the *spirit* who has become free—spits on the contemptible type of well-being dreamed of by shopkeepers, Christians, cows, females, Englishmen, and other democrats. The free man is a *warrior.*[66]

Nietzsche, it was stressed, was not an academic thinker but one who dealt with larger issues intimately bound with German destiny.[67] One such vital question was the meaning of individual and national death. It was easy to harness Nietzsche to this theme. He was typically portrayed as "the philosopher of the World War" because he had educated a whole generation towards "a life-endangering honesty, towards a contempt for death, . . . to a sacrifice on the altar of the whole, towards heroism and quiet, joyful greatness."[68] These emphases socialized Zarathustra and, consonant with the galvanizing for war, transformed

65. August Messer, "Nietzsche und der Krieg: Zum 70 Geburtstag des Philosophen, 15 Oktober," *Frankfurter Zeitung* 286 (15 October 1914).

66. Kaufmann, *Portable Nietzsche*, 541–542.

67. Kurt Singer, "Nietzsches Vermächtnis: 15 Oktober 1844–15 Oktober 1914," *Hamburgischer Correspondent* 184, no. 524 (15 October 1914).

68. Theodor Kappstein, "Nietzsche der Philosoph des Weltkriegs: Zu seinem 70 Geburtstag am 15 Oktober," *Strassburger Post* 1028 (1914).

Nietzschean overcoming into a moral glorification of personal and collective death.

This Nietzsche was diffused to soldiers and the public in a flood of publications. He was one of the first figures in the *Illustrated Library of Heroes;*[69] special war issues of various journals carried readings from Nietzsche and the *Will to Power.*[70] Poems were written exhorting people to imitate his martial Germanism.[71] At least 20,000 copies of Hermann Itschner's Nietzsche anthology, presented as an inspirational guide for great times, were distributed.[72] The themes of heroism, patriotism, and will were meshed with Nietzsche as the great yea-sayer and prophet of a great postwar regeneration.

For certain radical right, völkisch and Youth Movement circles, the war fused martial values with the vision of a grand, national cultural, and spiritual transformation. Nietzschean metaphors crucially informed this vision which became integral to the armory of Weimar's conservative revolution. Here Nietzsche could function as an effective counterfoil to Marx by emphasizing the cultural over the material and the spiritual over the economic. To be sure, in certain circles this emphasis predated the war. Eugen Diederichs's neo-Romantic group centered around *Die Tat,* for example, had from its beginnings based its ideal of German cultural renaissance upon the Nietzschean influence.[73] The war simply heightened their expectations. Its commentators insisted that through the crucible of the war the breakthrough to a new national Nietzschean authenticity was indeed possible.[74]

For other important völkisch groups, however, it was the war itself which prompted a new attitude towards Nietzsche. Hermann Popert's youth movement, the Vortrupp, which had dismissed Nietzsche as pro-

69. O.te Kloot, *Nietzsche,* Illustrierte Helden-Bibliothek 30 (Berlin: Ed. Rose, 1914).
70. "Friedrich Nietzsche: Vom Kriege," *Insel-Almanach* (Kriegsalmanach, 1915). [Leipzig: Insel Verlag].
71. For instance, Elizabeth Gnade, "Zu Friedrich Nietzsches 70 Geburtstage, 15 Oktober 1914," *Tägliche Rundschau* 241 (14 October 1914)

> Uns bleibt nur Zeit,
> Um deutsch zu sein, deutsche, wie du selber warst—
> Damals—vom Lehrstuhl aus der sich'ren Schweiz
> Herzugeeilt beim Schall der Kriegsfanfare!

72. Hermann Itschner, *Nietzsche-Worte: Weggenossen in grosser Zeit* (Leipzig: Alfred Kröner, 1915).
73. On Diederichs's activities see Gary D. Stark, *Entrepreneurs of Ideology: Neoconservative Publishers in Germany, 1890–1933* (Chapel Hill: University of North Carolina Press, 1981). The full title, of *Die Tat: Wege zu Freiem Menschentum,* had obvious Nietzschean overtones. The first issue (April 1909) had a heroic bust of Nietzsche on its opening page.
74. Gröper, "Nietzsche und der Krieg."

foundly dangerous to a healthy national outlook, made a total about-face. The war transformed Nietzsche into their guiding völkisch star. Paul Schulze-Berghof (later an active disseminator of the Nazi Zarathustra myth)[75] exemplified the Vortrupp's new attitude by naming Nietzsche "The Culture Prophet of German World Empire." Nietzschean self-redemption, in the last resort, was "the self-redemption of German humanity as a nation." Zarathustra's tablets were to the Germans what the Mosaic tablets represented for the Israelites. The war was the baptism of fire that had revealed Zarathustra to be "the great storm song of our time, the Eroica of our Volk-soul, Germany's own *Heldenlied*."[76]

The radical right, nationalist revolutionaries who mushroomed during the Weimar Republic, was by no means an obvious force before 1918. Still, during the war signs of its presence began to dot the cultural landscape. The war, of course, provided the basis for its main themes and goals. Nietzschean images emphasizing masculinity, will, heroism, and struggle permeated their political vocabulary. Commentators like Max Brahn combined these values with an emphasis on Nietzsche as "a teacher of organization." This politicized Nietzsche stressed the state as a vital means towards the realization of the ultimate Nietzschean goal, the Übermensch.[77] While this alliance was later characteristic of annexations by the right, their emphasis was still upon ideals of a new culture steeled by the war experience. In certain esoteric right-wing journals Nietzsche influenced a germinating proto-Fascist outlook. *Der Panther: Deutsche Monattschrift für Politik und Volkstum*, for instance, consistently presented Nietzsche as the champion of cultural totality resulting from the fusion of aesthetic and heroic values, as opposed to the splintered, liberal, intellectualist and moralistic world. This cultural totality, moreover, could only be created through struggle and strength. *Der Panther*'s Nietzsche foreshadowed the Nietzsche of the postwar radical right, transformed politics into the problem of will, and sought to nationalize Nietzsche's will to power into a fearless German will to power and self-assertion.[78]

75. Paul Schulze Berghof, "Der Zarathustra Dichter als Mystiker," *Die musische Erziehung* 9 (1942).
76. Paul Schulze Berghof, "Der kulturprophet des deutschen Weltreichs," *Der Vortrupp* 5 (1916); Schulze Berghof, "Zarathustra-Deutsche-Mystik-Deutscher Glaube," *Der Vortrupp* 5 (1916). Schulze Berghof also formulated a Nietzschean religion.
77. Max Brahn, *Friedrich Nietzsches Meinungen über Staaten und Kriege* (Leipzig: A. Kröner, 1915).
78. Lenore Ripke-Kühn, "Nietzsches Kulturanschauung," *Der Panther* 3 (1915), 420–456; Ripke-Kühn, "Nietzsches Willenserziehung," *Der Panther* 5, no. 4 (April 1917), 519–535.

Nietzsche was domesticated into national respectability through his incorporation into the patriotic war experience. Karl Joel, not unexpectedly, argued that Nietzsche's pro-French orientation was misleading and that "in reality" he was part of the German "manly" line characterized by the unity of thought and deed.[79] In this vein the subtle links between Bismarck and Nietzsche were stressed. Both favored the warrior spirit and struggle; "blood and iron" and the Übermensch were complementary not contradictory.[80] Similarly, Max Scheler's *The Genius of War and the German War* and *Ressentiment*, both from 1915, praised ennobling aspects of war written in the spirit of Nietzschean Lebensphilosophie.[81] Scheler sought to reconcile the Christian with the warrior ethic; it was not the Christians who, as Nietzsche claimed, were carriers of the slave morality or of despised ressentiment ideas but the bourgeoisie.

The critique of the bourgeoisie was never a monopoly of the left in German political culture. From Wilhelmine times traditional conservatives as well as the disaffected völkisch right participated. This was an idealized national self-representation in a society not yet reconciled to its own capitalism.[82] Before 1914 and after 1918 the Jewish–bourgeoisie equation channeled this discontent. During the war itself, however, it was the English who were often cast as the real bourgeoisie, merchants who embodied the negative traits of a ressentiment mentality. Nietzsche thus became a convenient hook on which to hang this negative labeling of the enemy. No one did this to greater effect than Werner Sombart in his extremely popular *Merchants and Heroes* (1915).[83] Sombart, like many other champions of the conservative revolution, reduced empirical socioeconomic phenomena to hypostatizations of Geist.[84] *Merchants and Heroes* merely transposed onto the English what Sombart had previously written about the

79. Joel, *Neue Weltkultur*, 55–56.
80. Gröper, "Nietzsche und der Krieg," 30.
81. Max Scheler, *Der Genius des Krieges und der Deutsche Krieg* (Leipzig: Weissen Bücher, 1915); Scheler, "Das Ressentiment im Aufbau der Moralen," in Scheler, *Abhandlungen und Aufsätze* 1, 39–274 (Leipzig: Weissen Bücher, 1915). Translated as *Ressentiment*, trans. William W. Holdheim, intro. Lewis A. Coser (New York: 1976).
82. Fritz Stern, "Money, Morals, and the Pillars of Society," in his *The Failure of Illiberalism: Essays on the Political Culture of Modern Germany* (Chicago and London: University of Chicago Press, 1971).
83. Werner Sombart, *Händler und Helden: Patriotische Besinnungen* (Munich and Leipzig: Duncker and Humblot, 1915).
84. Herf, *Reactionary Modernism*, 133–134.

Jews.[85] The juxtaposition of merchant and heroic spirits was not, according to Sombart, a mere question of individual temperament but reflected the distinction between the English and the German *Volkseele* (national soul). This conceptual framework had clear Nietzschean resonances. Sombart's Nietzschean emphasis on the centrality of will and heroism slid easily into his hypostatized types; while the English represented merchant types, the Nietzschean spirit imperceptibly metamorphosized into the German heroic spirit.

> When foreigners philosophize over the present war, strangely they always return to the same thought: the 1914 war is Nietzsche's war. Germany had called him forth and Germany's soul was filled with the Nietzschean spirit. This, apart from the lie that we alone desired the war, is correct, but only partially. As much as one calls this Nietzsche's war, one can also call it Frederick the Great's, Goethe's, Schiller's, Beethoven's, Fichte's, Hegel's, or Bismarck's: for it is the German war. And Friedrich Nietzsche was only the latest singer and visionary who, coming from heaven, brought us the tidings that from us the son of God would be born, which in his language he called the *Übermenschen*.[86]

For Sombart, German militarism was only the outward expression of an internal heroic spirit, Potsdam and Weimar in the highest unity, and the "*Faust* and *Zarathustra* and Beethoven-Partitura of the trenches," as he called it.[87] Yet he also had to deal with Nietzsche's putative antinationalism. He argued that the Nietzschean heroic life necessarily led to a nationalist, völkisch outlook, for there could be no heroism without a fatherland and the superman was a condition of national existence. Indeed, did not Nietzsche's own Zarathustrian teachings contradict his doctrine of the transnational "good European"? A metanational Übermensch was an absurdity.[88]

All proponents of the nationalist Nietzschean war myth were equally constrained to explain away Nietzsche's many anti-German diatribes. Typically, distinctions between the real or the deep and the merely apparent Nietzsche were made. In contradistinction to Fritsch, radical

---

85. Sombart's most famous prewar work on the Jews was *Die Juden und das Wirtschaftsleben* (Leipzig, 1911). After the war he returned to the topic of Jewish geist. For a critical analysis see Paul R. Mendes-Flohr, "Werner Sombart's 'The Jews and Modern Capitalism': An Analysis of Its Ideological Premises," *Leo Baeck Institute Yearbook* (1976). See too Steven E. Aschheim, " 'The Jew Within': The Myth of 'Judaization' in Germany," in *The Jewish Response to German Culture*, ed. Jehuda Reinharz and Walter Schatzberg (New Hampshire: University Press of New England, 1985), 212–241.
86. Sombart, *Händler und Helden*, 53.
87. Ibid., 84–85.
88. Ibid., 141.

Nietzschean anti-Semites argued that it was necessary to discover the true Germanic Nietzsche whom Jews had systematically hidden from public consciousness by monopolizing his mediation within Germany. They had distorted him into a nihilist and internationalist consonant with their own destructive interests.[89] Others argued that 1914 would have marked a drastic transformation in Nietzsche's attitude toward the fatherland. One critic believed Nietzsche would have turned out to be a second Fichte, grasping the greatness of the struggle and rising in passionate defense of Germany.[90] For others, Nietzsche's vitriolic criticism implied love and passionate commitment. Like the Jewish prophets, he was an organ of his Volk, driving it to ever greater heights by his castigations.[91]

Nietzsche was a major resource for the creation of charged and changing political meanings as events unfolded. His changing canonization mirrored the stages of the war. At first, as we have seen, he was the great mobilizer providing the heroic rationale and triumphalism necessary for battle.

As the war drew to its end and defeat seemed imminent, bewilderment and anxiety replaced that buoyant triumphalism. German reflections of 1918 were characterized less by self-confident proclamations of the unity of thought and deed than by consciousness of national insecurity, failure, and incompletion. The traditional spectre of culture (*Kultur*) threatened by an alien Western civilization was realized. Nietzsche became the central figure in the attempt to provide a consoling and galvanizing account of the moment. This new Nietzsche was at once the embodiment of the torn German condition itself and testament to its still-evolving nature.

The most sophisticated constructions of Nietzsche to emerge from the war were Thomas Mann's *Reflections of a Nonpolitical Man* and Ernst Bertram's *Nietzsche: An Attempt at a Mythology,* which both appeared in 1918. They articulated a mood and pointed to a shared vision characteristic of many intellectuals of the time.[92] While both men recognized their affinities, they later went their separate ways: Mann

---

89. Lenore Ripke-Kühn, "Nietzsche der ewige Deutsche: Zu Ernst Bertrams 'Nietzsche, Versuch einer Mythologie,'" *Deutschlands Erneuerung* 6 (1919), 420, 424.

90. Brahn, *Friedrich Nietzsches Meinungen,* 29.

91. See Moritz Heimann's 1915 essay, "Nietzsche und sein Volk" in his *Prosaische Schriften,* 3 vols. (Berlin: S. Fischer, 1918), vol. 1, 180–184.

92. Bernhard Böschenstein, "Erlösung und Beglaubigung: Thomas Manns *Betrachtungen eines Unpolitischen* und Ernst Bertrams *Nietzsche: Versuch einer Mythologie,*" *MLN* 90 (1975).

revised his antidemocratic posture and became a champion of the Weimar Republic; Bertram turned increasingly to the right, to the point of sympathizing for a time with the National Socialists. During the war and its aftermath, however, the men were close friends and in agreement about Nietzsche's Germanic and symbolic significance.[93] As Mann recorded in his diary:

> After supper finished Bertram's *Nietzsche.* Gratifying to think that without *Tonio Krüger* and *Death in Venice* this book would not have been possible, neither in certain specific turns nor certainly as a whole. Moving to see how it stands as something dignified, prudent, magisterial, unassailable, irreproachable, yet brotherly alongside my imprudent, untutored, stammering, and compromising artist's book. . . . Truly I am as proud of this work as if I had written it myself.[94]

It is Germany's looming defeat that both these works capture and seek to transcend. Mann's outraged polemic, as he later reported,[95] was informed by a desperate defense of his own conservative burger heritage in the full knowledge that the cause he opposed would be victorious. Bertram's far more lyrical work portraying Nietzsche as a tortured cultural hero did not even mention the great conflagration. Yet his lofty reflections were clearly a coded, sublimated product of that event at its critical turning point. His declared neo-Romantic, antirationalist aim was to create a "mythology of the last great German," to grasp Nietzsche "in the historical moment of the present."[96]

Our post facto knowledge of the "good" Thomas Mann should not blind us to his virulently antidemocratic, anti-Western posture prior to the Weimar Republic or, indeed, its complex ambiguities well after.[97] In

93. Their relationship is recounted in *Thomas Mann und Ernst Bertram: Briefe aus den Jahren 1910–1955,* ed. Inge Jens (Pfullingen: Neske, 1960).

94. Entry for September 18. Thomas Mann, *Diaries, 1918–1939,* selected by Hermann Kesten, trans. Richard Winston and Clara Winston (London: Robin Clark, 1983), 6. See too the entries for 14 September and 15 September 1918.

95. Thomas Mann, *Briefe, 1889–1936* (Frankfurt: S. Fischer, 1961), 291; H. Stefan Schultz, "Thomas Mann's *Betrachtungen eines Unpolitischen:* Some Observations," *MLN* 90 (1975), 431.

96. Bertram, *Nietzsche,* 6.

97. Even after the Nazi takeover, aspects of the earlier Mann remained, voiced only in private. They too were related to Nietzsche and his Jewish malappropriation.

But for all that, might not something deeply significant and revolutionary be taking place in Germany? . . . It is no calamity after all that Alfred Kerr's brazen and poisonous Jewish-style imitation of Nietzsche is now suppressed, or that the domination of the legal system by Jews has been ended. Secret, disquieting, persistent musings. Come what may, much will remain that in a higher sense, is repellent, base, and unGerman. But I am beginning to suspect that in spite of everything this process is one of those things that have two sides to them. (Mann, *Diaries,* 150).

Reflections of a Nonpolitical Man Nietzsche was the central justifying figure around which he built his anticivilization arguments. His overtly political use of the philosopher was especially ironic given his constant berating of those "Latins" who had politicized Nietzsche: "The politicization of Nietzsche is nothing else than the disfiguring of Nietzsche, and if this war has actively brought about anything intellectual at all, it is this: the inability of the Latins to keep philosophy and politics apart."[98]

But Mann himself clearly had some difficulty keeping them apart: "The colossal manliness of his [Nietzsche's] soul, his antifeminism, his opposition to democracy—what could be more German? What could be more German than his contempt for 'modern ideas,' for eighteenth century ideas, for 'French ideas' which, he insisted, had English origins?"[99]

For Bertram, Germanism was essentially a different aesthetic and psychic mode of being expressed through the metalinguistic medium of musicality:[100]

> The identity of music and Germanism which the young Nietzsche sensed everywhere enabled him to perceive this Germanism as the most serious and eternal opponent of everything that was mere civilization. . . . (The idea of the polarity between civilization and culture is as typically Nietzschean as it is typically German.)[101]

Both Mann's and Bertram's Nietzsche transcended the more static representations of the past. In the face of defeat both stressed paradox, process, and duality. Thus Mann's Nietzsche (in many ways a reflection of his own ambivalences) possesses complex and contradictory attractions: Nietzsche is split into "aesthetic" and "power" components as opposed to his "ethical" and "ironic" sides. (Mann clearly opted for the latter qualities.) His Nietzsche, moreover, becomes complicit in the conflicting heritages over which the war was being fought.

> Without detriment to the deep Germanness of his spirit, Nietzsche, with his deep Europeanism, has contributed more than anyone else to Germany's education in criticism, to her intellectualization, psychologization, literarization, radicalization, or, not to shun the political word, to her democratization. . . . The powerful strengthening of the literary-critical element in

98. Thomas Mann, *Reflections of a Nonpolitical Man,* trans. Walter D. Morris (New York: Ungar, 1983), 152. See also chap. 11.
99. Ibid., 57; see also pp. 18, 58.
100. See the instructive reading of Bertram in Joel Golb, "Celan and Hölderlin: An Essay on the Problem of Tradition" (Ph.D. diss., Princeton University, 1985), 119ff.
101. Bertram, *Nietzsche,* 108.

Germany that Nietzsche brought about signifies *progress* in the most dubious, most political sense, in the sense of "humanization,"—progress toward Western democracy, and that to be educated by him is not exactly what one could call an education in the spirit of preserving German tradition.[102]

Nietzsche's personal example was even more important for Mann; "the ethical tragedy of his life, of this immortal European drama of self-conquest, self-discipline, and self-crucifixion with the intellectual, sacrificial death as a heart-and-brainrending conclusion."[103] Bertram's *Nietzsche* was similarly characterized by this *Zwiespalt*. The work is structured in a pre-set pattern of polarities (culture versus civilization, the North versus the South, and so on). Nietzsche becomes the epic embodiment of Germanic destiny, its soul caught between opposing spiritual states. These conflicts were encapsulations of the German experience at its most sublime; as a result Nietzsche's Germanism paradoxically achieved its most profound expression at the moment of radical self-critique.[104]

For all the commonalities between Mann and Bertram their differences provide a key to the distinction between the old and the emerging new right. Mann's was a transitional document, torn by contradictions, filled with ambivalence, but nevertheless molded by and committed to the old, vanishing order. His vision remained quietist, ironist, and profoundly conservative. "Radicalism," he wrote, "is nihilism. The ironist is conservative." Not surprisingly Mann depicted Nietzsche's radicalism as antiradicalism "in a sense and to a degree that was up to then unheard of." Here his "German character came to an unparalleled primeval eruption. For antiradicalism . . . is the specific distinguishing, and decisive quality or peculiarity of the German spirit."[105]

But those radical power elements rejected by the ironic, conservative Mann characterized the emerging new German right. Irony was the last thing that interested these Weimar radicals. While Mann was unable to resolve the contradictions he felt so acutely as the historical epoch drew to a close, Bertram pointed forward, resolving conflicts by integrating Nietzsche into the framework of a rounded and positive völkisch mythos.[106] Standing at the threshold of a new age, Bertram's work was

102. Mann, *Reflections*, 60–61.
103. Ibid., 104.
104. See Golb, Celan and Hölderlin, 118–120, for a more detailed literary analysis of this structure.
105. Mann, *Reflections*, 419, 57–58.
106. For an illuminating analysis of Bertram's role within the völkisch tradition see Mosse, *German Ideology*, 204–209.

crucial to the post-1918 nationalist appropriation of Nietzsche and his
transfiguration into what Bertram called the climactic German, the embodiment of *Überdeutschtum*.[107] His Nietzsche transcended duality and
became both metaphor and agent of the redemptive hope of Germany
itself.

Authentic Germanism, according to Bertram, lay in a kind of continuous Nietzschean process of transcendence and creative becoming.
Nietzsche was the deepest expression of Germanness and its longing for
self-realization at ever-higher levels. In the midst of defeat and bewilderment here indeed was a consoling message. Transcendence was still
possible and the intensity of despair and suffering was part and parcel
of the redemptive process.

This regenerating breakthrough (*Durchbruch*) could be achieved
through the Nietzschean power of will. Here both Nietzschean ideas
and Nietzsche as heroic personality served to fuse the mythos with the
aspirations of the *Volk*. Nietzsche, Bertram exclaimed, represents "the
self-knowledge of the *Volk* at the moment . . . of its greatest inner
danger—and is simultaneously an awakening and development of the
saving instincts and the saving will."[108]

Bertram's *Nietzsche* also exemplified the frankly irrationalist epistemology which was to become a hallmark of the Weimar radical right.
Like the elitist, antidemocratic Georg Kreis of which he was an associate, Bertram insisted that history had to be made into an explicitly
mythmaking task. Objectivity was both unattainable and undesirable:
only intuition and activating knowledge were of value. "All events
strive towards image, everything living towards legend, all reality toward *Mythos*."[109] Nietzsche now became the incarnation of the time-
less Nordic experience, a metaphysical presence transcending historical
limitations and a continuing metaphor for the ongoing German confrontation with the world. Bertram and Mann emphasized Nietzsche's
love for Albrecht Dürer's famous painting *Knight, Death, and Devil*,
which in the völkisch worldview symbolized the Nordic plight and
exhorted heroic action.[110] The Nietzschean mythos became fused with

---

107. Bertram, *Nietzsche*, 250. His construction also received much popular attention
beyond radical and völkisch circles. See Curt Hotzel, "Nietzsches Deutsche Aufgabe,"
Der Türmer 28, no. 10 (July 1926).
108. Ibid., 79.
109. Ibid., 6.
110. See Bertram's chapter "Ritter, Tod und Teufel," in *Nietzsche*, 42–63; Mann,
Reflections, 399.

the Germanic knight. His qualities of will, endurance, and courage were precisely those needed in the Germany of 1918.

It was hardly surprising that as the war ended and Germany's plight became visible the radical right seized upon this mythologized Germanic Nietzsche.[111] He was to dominate German representations from the beginning of the Weimar Republic through the end of nazism.

This political marriage was novel, made possible only by the transformation of both Nietzsche and the right. While Nietzsche had undergone widespread nationalization, the right underwent a corresponding radicalization to become modernized and loosened from its traditional moorings with church, monarchy, and aristocracy. They adopted an oppositionalist dynamic whose agenda could then be enriched by selective scavenging of the Nietzschean universe.[112] The war and its immediate aftermath had indubitably accomplished this interdependent transformation. The old tension between the establishmentarian right and the subversive Nietzsche was wiped out. Both were now radical dissidents disdainful of the status quo and in search of a revolutionary and yet unclassifiable future. Both contributed to and reflected the increasingly brutalized atmosphere of the Weimar Republic.

We need waste little time establishing the centrality of Nietzsche for the Weimar radical right between 1918 and 1933. A few dissenting voices notwithstanding, he was its most authoritative and inspirational source. As its sympathetic chronicler Armin Mohler put it, the "conservative revolution" would have been "unthinkable" without Nietzsche.[113] In his protean works the new right discovered a remarkably plastic, almost inexhaustible, source for enunciating a radical worldview and for locating both its enemies and positive ideals. In 1931 Friedrich Hielscher, an active publicist on the radical right, summed up Nietzsche's multiple functions for this political universe: "Nietzsche stands as questioner, as fighter, as the solitary one. He stands for the Reich as protector of the past, as crusher of the present, as transformer of the future."[114]

Nietzsche provided essential tools for the themes that distinguished

[margin annotation: Consv. opp to Weimar]

---

111. Ripke-Kühn, "Nietzsche der ewige Deutsche," 420–421.

112. For the sake of historical exactitude it should be clear that we are referring to a tendency, a cluster of attitudes, rather than an ironclad law. There were pre-1914 outlines of the right-wing Nietzsche just as there was always some opposition within the radical right after this annexation.

113. Armin Mohler, *Die konservative Revolution in Deutschland, 1918–1932: Ein Handbuch* (Darmstadt: Wissenschaftliche Buchgesellschaft, 1972), 29, 87.

114. Friedrich Hielscher, *Das Reich* (Berlin: Das Reich, 1931), 200.

the new right from the traditional Bismarckian and Wilhelmine right: an insistence on activism and a self-propelling dynamic; a masculine, soldierly, nationalist ethic to contrast with prewar static patriotism;[115] a virulent critique of Weimar liberalism, Marxism, and mass culture; and contours for its heroic, post-bourgeois, New Man of the future.

Perhaps most critically, Nietzsche furnished the right with the most fecund arsenal for a Lebensphilosophie undergoing unprecedented politicization. The radical right constantly reiterated a transvalued Nietzschean vision of a postrationalist, post-Christian social order "beyond good and evil." Nietzsche moreover provided the vitalist criteria for identifying healthy, life-affirming forces and diagnosing those decadent and degenerate anti-life (*Lebensfeindlich*) elements deemed unworthy of propagation.

In a period of radical dislocation and polarization, detailed blueprints of the ideal future Nietzschean order mushroomed. Friedrich Mess's massive 1930 work, *Nietzsche: The Lawgiver,* was only the most systematic of many attempts. "Just as canonical law derived from the Bible and the writings of the Church fathers," Mess proclaimed, "so must the *lex Futurana Europearum* be built upon Nietzsche's wisdom."[116] In such commentaries—and in later Nazi ones—a new conception of law and morality was formulated. Nietzschean jurisprudence, Mess insisted, was neither abstract nor a codification of immutable reason but a function of what enhanced life. Both law and morality were represented as instruments in the life of the Volk, placed at the service of the nation's (or race's) needs. The struggle for national self-assertion and the heightening of power was the source of both law and morality and shifted according to changing needs. Nietzschean law was dynamic, not static.[117] In every such rendering Nietzschean society was presented in antitranscendent terms: immanent, renaturalized, and demoralized.

This anticultural Nietzsche immediately rendered anachronistic Hermann Hesse's 1919 invoking of a different understanding of the philosopher. His "Zarathustra's Return" was couched in the prewar cultivated language of Bildung, appealing to German youth through that

---

115. For a good discussion of the new right's themes, see Karl Prümm, *Die Literatur des Soldatischen Nationalismus der 20er Jahre (1918–1933)* (Kronberg: Scriptor Verlag, 1974). Eugen Schmahl's *Der Auffstieg der nationalen Idee* ([Berlin, Leipzig: Union Deutsche Verlagsgesellschaft, n.d.], 143–144, 103) is a Nazi work that held that Nietzsche had already anticipated all expressions of the new nationalism.

116. Friedrich Mess, *Nietzsche: Der Gesetzgeber* (Leipzig: Felix Mainer, 1930), vii.

117. Kurt Kassler, *Nietzsche und das Recht* (Munich: Ernst Reinhardt, 1941).

tradition of critical thought.[118] But in Weimar's highly politicized, polarized postwar climate the old nonconformist, libertarian, and internationalist Nietzsche had lost his resonance. Despite some counterindications (a perturbed Förster-Nietzsche noted that when the revolution broke out some 25,000 copies of the cheap edition of *Zarathustra* were sold in four weeks!)[119] a quite different Zarathustra of the right had already replaced him.

The new Zarathustra must be seen within the context of a certain brutalization that spilled over from the war and became an inbuilt part of postwar attitudes. The subsequent cheapening of life, the infusion of greater linguistic and physical violence into the public realm, and the depersonalization may have been a generally European phenomenon, but in Germany it was exacerbated by defeat, revolution, and the persistent socioeconomic crisis. It increasingly provided the space for politically extremist alternatives.[120]

It goes without saying that both the radical right and this brutalization would have emerged without Nietzsche. Social Darwinism, doctrines of violence, anti-Semitism, and racism were quite independent influences. But Nietzsche could supply both the philosophical legitimacy and the larger vision with which to channel such sentiments. This also involved a process of constant selective scavenging and reinterpretation—a casting of Nietzsche into the required brutalized mold.

From 1918 to 1933 the Right comprised over 550 clubs and 530 journals.[121] The radical right was never monolithic and ranged from the supposedly conservative *Deutschnationalevolkspartei* to the Nazis, but it was never limited to any single political party. While it was a malleable sensibility compatible with a large number of organizational affiliations and ideologies, even in its more modest and conservative forms, Nietzsche played a guiding role. There were always some who remained suspicious.[122] Nevertheless he remained crucial for numerous

118. Hermann Hesse, "Zarathustra's Return: A Word to German Youth," in Robert C. Solomon, ed., *Nietzsche: A Collection of Critical Essays* (New York: Anchor, 1973). For a previous work that Hesse wrote in this spirit see *Faust und Zarathustra* (Bremen: Otto Melchers, 1909). Ernst Thiel also applied what he considered high Nietzschean standards to the political and intellectual leaders of the time and found them wanting in his *Die Generation ohne Männer* (Berlin: Paul Neff, 1932).
119. Peters, *Zarathustra's Sister*, 206–207.
120. George L. Mosse, *Fallen Soldiers: Reshaping the Memory of the World Wars* (New York: Oxford University Press, 1990), chap. 8.
121. Mohler, *Konservative Revolution*, 539–554.
122. Karl Kynast, "Der Fall Nietzsche im Lichte rassenkundlicher Betrachtung," *Die Sonne* 2 (1925), 534–535. Those of the "northern race," Kynast warned, had to be wary of the ressentiment views of this "Mongolmischling."

völkisch circles; Dionysian irrationalists; certain expressionists; cultural and political regenerationists associated with Eugen Diederichs and Hans Freyer; various offshoots of the German Youth Movement; and even elitist Christian radical rightists such as Edgar Jung.[123]

The Weimar Archives played a pivotal role within this radical-right construction.[124] Its Nietzscheanism was disseminated through its publications and festivities featuring luminaries like Oswald Spengler.[125] One dismayed observer aptly summarized the result in 1932: "Inside the Archive everyone from the doorkeeper to the head is a Nazi."[126] But Nietzsche's penetration into German political culture was always far wider and more spontaneous than this single institutional expression. We must, therefore, return to the most radical and symptomatic of these postwar new-right eruptions.

These eruptions were most clearly evidenced in their positive notions and ideal types. For Hitler and Mussolini, for example, war and conflict became normative, the model for everyday life and politics. Political circumstances now provided real outlets for violence. In a sense the Freikorps, made up of soldiers who fought on after the war had ended, was the earliest political manifestation of an updated nationalist–nihilist Nietzschean praxis. It embodied Zarathustra's cry that the good war hallowed the cause. Members of the Freikorps described themselves in caricaturistic Nietzschean terms: a band of ruthless men enamored of struggle and action for its own sake whose task it was to "become hard" and "live dangerously." Intensely nationalist and anti-Bolshevist, they nevertheless regarded themselves as bereft of ideology. "What we wanted we didn't know," wrote Ernst von Salomon, the minstrel of the Freikorps and an accomplice to Walther Rathenau's murder, "and what we knew we didn't want. War and adventure, insurrection and destruc-

123. For völkisch commentaries see Paul Schulze Berghof, "Nietzsches historisch-mythische Sendung," *Der Volkserzieher* 34 (1930); Hans Kern, "Nietzsche und die romantischen Theorien des Unbewussten," *Zeitschrift für Menschenkunde* 3 (1927). Ludwig Klages (*Der Geist als Widersacher der Seele* [Leipzig: Barth, 1926]) exemplifies the irrationalist position. Gottfried Benn is the outstanding expressionist example. For Benn's pre-Nazi reflections see "Akademie-Rede" in his *Gesammelte Werke*, vol. 1. See also Eugen Diederichs, "Das Kommen des Dritten Reiches" and "Entwicklungsphasen der freideutschen Jugend" *Die Tat* 10 (1918); Jerry Z. Muller, *The Other God that Failed: Hans Freyer and the Deradicalization of German Conservatism* (Princeton, N.J.: Princeton University Press, 1987); and Edgar Jung, *Die Herrschaft der Minderwertigkeiten: ihr Zerfall und ihre Ablösung durch ein neues Reich* (Berlin: Deutsche Rundschau, 1927).
124. Peters, *Zarathustra's Sister*, chaps. 22–24.
125. Max Öhler, ed., *Den Manen Friedrich Nietzsches* (Munich: Musarion, 1921); Oswald Spengler, "Nietzsche and His Century," in his *Selected Essays*.
126. Kessler, *Diaries*, 426.

tion, and an unknown, agonizing . . . yearning."[127] They portrayed themselves as a uniquely constituted community in a novel form of human bonding and steeled by the trench experience. The postwar era, Salomon declared in 1930, had "created a unique new race, a new type of warrior. No order can tolerate them but none can be created without them."[128] The prewar quest for moral and personal purification, for overcoming the bourgeois malaise and its accompanying hypocrisy, was increasingly replaced by a vision of the unleashing of the instincts.[129]

In 1930 Werner Best, later to become an important functionary in the extermination of European Jewry, formulated this Nietzschean vision in terms of what he believed would be the judicial norm of the future. War, he wrote, was not a sin against nature nor was there a universal law transcending the rights of nations as the liberal rationalist would have it. War did not contradict life but was, indeed, its most essential element. Life after all had no ultimate goal—and here Best invoked Nietzsche's dictum, "If the world had a goal, it must have been reached."[130] What remained was only the eternal, dynamic struggle and the need in the face of this nihilist predicament to adopt an attitude of "heroic realism."[131] That attitude, overcoming nihilism through will, formed the center of Bäumler's 1931 Nazi transmogrification of Nietzsche into the thinker of great politics, whose will to power ushered in the great postliberal, postbourgeois age.[132] It also formed the philosophical basis of Heidegger's attachment to the radical right during the early 1930s.[133]

The multiplicity of calls for a tough, masculine elite to solve the postwar predicament was saturated with Nietzschean vocabulary. Oswald Spengler's unfolding vision of a neobarbarian elite, his 1931 call for a "beast of prey" (*Raubtier*) whose will had not yet been castrated by the feminizing impact of bourgeois and Christian morality, was only one variation on that theme.[134]

127. Ernst von Salomon, *Die Geächteten* (Gütersloh: C. Bertelsmann, 1930), 83.

128. Ernst von Salomon, "Der verlorene Haufe," in *Krieg und Krieger,* ed. Ernst Jünger, 103–126 (Berlin: Junker and Dünnhaupt, 1930), 122–123.

129. George L. Mosse, *Nationalism and Sexuality: Respectability and Abnormal Sexuality in Modern Europe* (New York: Howard Fertig, 1985), 125.

130. Nietzsche, *Will to Power,* 546.

131. Werner Best, "Der Krieg und das Recht," in Jünger, ed., *Krieg und Krieger.*

132. Alfred Bäumler, *Nietzsche der Philosoph und Politiker* (Leipzig: Reklam, 1931).

133. Jürgen Habermas, "Work and Weltanschauung: The Heidegger Controversy from a German Perspective," *Critical Inquiry* 15, no. 2 (Winter 1989), 438–440.

134. Oswald Spengler, *Der Untergang des Abendlandes,* 2 vols. (Munich: C. H. Beck, 1918); trans. Charles Francis Atkinson, *The Decline of the West,* 2 vols. (New York: Alfred Knopf, 1926). Beginning with this work Spengler gradually developed and radi-

Yet the Weimar radical right tempered this appropriation in two characteristic and interrelated ways. In the first place, it fundamentally transmuted Nietzschean individualism. Nietzsche's New Man ceased to be solitary or even possess unique characteristics and was instead almost utterly typologized. This depersonalization was another symptom of the aforementioned brutalization. In the second place, Nietzsche's dynamic was also regimented, subordinated to the service of a tightly controlled nation. These framing processes were essential before Nietzsche could be made serviceable to the radical right.

Ernst Jünger best illustrates these tendencies. He articulated a vision of the naked Nietzschean dynamic, of combat waged as an aesthetic and redemptive masculine form of creation. In very popular works—most notably his 1919 *Storm of Steel*[135]—he portrayed his vision of violence. Jünger moreover transposed the thrill of violence from the battlefield into civilian life.[136] But, like all German radical-right Nietzscheans, he poured his aesthetic of postwar Nietzschean man into an abstract mold and tamed him within larger containable frameworks. When Jünger's Zarathustra emerged from the trenches, his unique face had been transfigured into an interchangeable cog. There is little disparity between this and Hitler's physical description of the newly emergent storm pioneer that would constitute the elite of central Europe. This is an abstracted new race characterized not only by its tough will but also by its own stereotyped physiognomy: "Lithe, lean, sinewy body, strong-featured face, eyes hardened by a thousand shocks under the helmet [in battle]."[137]

The individualistic Nietzschean dynamic recedes as Jünger places his fighter into a national and industrial frame, into a mobilized society where the energy and dynamism of war is defused through disciplined, obedient subordination.[138]

This subordination occurred within an explicitly modernizing industrial context, quite removed from older conservative images of a backward-looking, rustic pastoralism. Jeffrey Herf has perceptively demonstrated how the Weimar radical right incorporated the new industrial

calized this theme. On Raubtier see his *Der Mensch und die Technik* (Munich: C. H. Beck, [1931] 1971), 10–17.

135. *In Stahlgewittern* (Hannover, 1920) sold well over 244,000 copies, went into twenty-six editions, and was translated into seven languages.

136. Ernst Jünger, "Über die Gefahr," *Widerstand* 3 (1931).

137. Quoted in Prümm, *Soldatischen Nationalismus*, 155. On the theme of will see Jünger's *Der Kampf als inneres Erlebnis* (Berlin, 1922), 76.

138. Ernst Jünger, "Der Arbeiter," in his *Werke*, vol. 6 (Stuttgart: E. Klett, 1964).

and technological dimension into its worldview.[139] Nietzsche—despite his utterly unindustrialized Zarathustrian landscape—was crucial to this exercise.[140] Jünger put it thus:

> Yes, the machine is beautiful; its beauty is self-evident to anyone who loves life in all its fullness and power. Nietzsche might well have been writing of the machine (though it did not yet have a place in his Renaissance landscape) when he argued that life was more than Darwin's wretched struggle for existence, but a will to higher and deeper goals. The machine must be made more than a mere means of production to satisfy our pitiful basic needs; it should provide us with a higher and deeper satisfaction. When it begins to do so, many a question will be resolved; the creative artist will suddenly perceive the machine not as a pragmatic collection of iron parts but as a totality; and the strategist will be released from the spell of the war of production. These men will be as active as any technician or socialist in this process of solution.[141]

The most sustained example of the attempt to render Nietzsche as the philosopher of both the technical and even the post-technical age was contained in Georg Förster's 1930 tome, *Machtwille und Maschinenwelt*. There was no aesthetic Renaissance landscape here. Nietzsche was not a tragically torn, lonely thinker but a burningly relevant "mediator of technology, pioneer of the machine, herald of a new *übernaturhafter* reality." Förster explicitly aimed to modernize and collectivize the Nietzschean will to power within an industrial frame, tying the birth of the Übermensch to a creative mastery of technology and the possibility of planetary control. The material basis of the Übermenschen "is not pale, self-referential . . . thought but the iron world of technology."[142] Jünger's worker similarly had nothing to do with the traditional feudal order in the nineteenth-century sense. Jünger envisaged him as a

---

139. Herf, *Reactionary Modernism.*
140. Nietzsche blessed technology to the degree that it served the interests of Übermenschen, condemned it insofar as it advanced the interests of the *letzten Menschen* and their *Machtwillens* associated with the leveling, Christian, democratic, socialist society (Reinhart Maurer, "Nietzsche und die kritische Theorie," *Nietzsche-Studien* 10/11 [1981/ 1982], 61).
141. Ernst Jünger, *Feuer und Blut* (Berlin, 1929), 82. Quoted in Klaus Theweleit, *Male Fantasies*, vol. 2, trans. Chris Turner et al. (Minneapolis: Polity, 1989), 197–198.
142. Georg Förster, *Machtwille und Maschinenwelt: Deutung unserer Zeit* (Potsdam: Alfred Protte, 1930). 67, 78; see too p. 12. Linking Nietzsche to the industrial world had to be an intensely selective exercise. Aphorisms 218 and 220 of his *Human, All Too Human*, for instance, did acknowledge the energizing and centralizing power of machine culture but also warned against its regimenting, deindividualizing effects. Aphorism 288 was wholly unambiguous, as its title indicates: "To what extent the machine abases us" (pp. 366–367, 383).

new man who would not experience himself as an end, but only as a
means, a carrier of the elemental will to power.[143]

Such reflections appeared throughout the Weimar Republic despite
the criticisms that the Nietzsche–technology marriage elicited. Early on,
skeptics noted that one could not have it both ways. One had "the
choice to live (or rather to die) in a Dionysian way without technology
or to live a technologically ordered life without the Dionysian. No
synthesis is possible here."[144]

But this was not an optimal time for skeptics. Indeed, Nietzsche not
only informed the right's positive revolutionary images of a rejuvenated
humanity but, perhaps more fatefully, also its antitheses. A politicized
Nietzschean Lebensphilosophie could easily be employed to identify
ressentiment and antilife enemies and to prescribe appropriately ruthless measures for dealing with them. It possessed a new salience in a
dislocated society where the notions of regeneration and degeneration
had become common coinage and where the demand for corrective
action against external and internal enemies grew ever more shrill.

The better-known figures of the radical right, theoreticians such as
Spengler and Möller van den Bruck, usually labeled the enemy arche-
typally and left it at that. Jünger's omnipresent *bourgeois* is the most
obvious example. What we need to note, however, is the veritable
explosion of lesser-known *Rassehygiene*, anti-Semitic and anti-Commu-
nist literature that circulated at all levels of Weimar society and which
was diffused not just by the Nazis. It appeared not only as crude,
paranoid street pamphlets[145] but also in more sophisticated form, penetrating the supposedly elevated world of scholarship. Many of these
sentiments would doubtless have emerged in any case, but the
Nietzschean rationale gave it a broader meaning and a certain legitimacy. For those who needed it, Nietzsche supplied a vocabulary that
rendered Weimar's dehumanizing impulses respectable.

The new practice of labeling political enemies, unwanted outsiders,
and deviants as *Untermenschen* provides one linguistic example of such

143. Jünger, *Arbeiter*, 118ff and the section "Die Ablösung des Bürgerlichen Indi-
viduums durch den Typus des Arbeiters."
144. Rudolf Paulsen, "Dionysische Politik?" *Der Türmer* 22 (October 1919–March
1920), 59–60. Paulsen's dismissive remarks presumably referred to Spengler's fusion of
technology with apocalypse and decline. *Der Türmer* had always evinced an interest in
Nietzsche; most of the July 1926 issue was filled with right-wing Nietzscheana.
145. This paranoid literature also addressed the theme of Nietzsche's death. One
anonymous article in a crackpot journal identified the secret forces who tried to steal
Nietzsche's work and poison him ("Zarathustra's Überang: Ein Verbrechen der Geheim-
cheka an Nietzsche?" *Ludendorff's Volkswarte* 3, no. 24 (1931).

dehumanization. The word, it is true, derived from the late eighteenth century, and Nietzsche used it infrequently and in quite another context. Within the Weimar Republic, however, its brutalized connotations and connections to a related Nietzschean Übermensch and anti-egalitarianism were clear. These connections were indeed brought to their logical conclusion under the Nazis a few years later.[146]

Vitalist immoralism was eminently suited to the postwar ground swell advocating racist and eugenicist options. Ernst Mann's 1920 pamphlet, *The Morality of Strength,* typified the trend in its most blatant form. "What is good," he wrote in tandem with Nietzsche, "is what increases the mental and physical strength of [the] people. Evil is that which weakens [such] strength."[147] Here Nietzsche's exhortations to prevent procreation of anti-life elements and his advocacy of euthanasia is restated as crudely as possible.[148] "All the weaklings and the sick," Mann wrote, "must be exterminated." He included tuberculosis and mental patients, all cripples, and the blind; all those who lent society a pessimistic tone and were unable to contribute to the society would have to give up their lives. Their destruction was the precondition for the development of healthy, strong people. "Manly men" were the most valuable members—homosexuals thus had to be wiped out. As in nature, the human beast of prey had to act as "health police" (*Gesundsheitspolizei:*) the exterminatory instinct of the strong would have to reassert its morality over its weak, ressentiment underminers.[149]

Brutalization meant both extending and radicalizing the scope of exclusion. The title of Franz Haiser's 1926 Nazi work, *The Jewish Question from the Standpoint of Master Morality,* is self-explanatory. It advocated a literal and operationalized reading of what Nietzsche had said in *The Antichrist* and *The Genealogy of Morals* about the Jewish denaturalization of all values, of morality itself.[150] The degeneration and racial chaos of Weimar and Europe was the result of Jewish rule

146. For a discussion of the *Untermensch* and its various uses see Alex Bein, "The Jewish Parasite," *Leo Baeck Institute Yearbook* 10 (1964), 27–28.

147. Ernst Mann, *Die Moral der Kraft* (Weimar: Gerhard Hofmann, 1920), 7.

148. Such passages abound in Nietzsche's works (*Will to Power,* 389, also 246, 740; *Gay Science,* 73; "On Free Death," in *Zarathustra,* 36; *Genealogy of Morals,* 120–125).

149. Mann, *Moral der Kraft,* 43ff, 41, 47. Mann never mentions Nietzsche but his categories and spirit permeate the work, as reviewers recognized. See the reviewers' comments reprinted on the back cover of the book.

150. Franz Haiser, *Die Judenfrage vom Standpunkt der Herrenmoral: Rechtsvölkische und linksvölkische Weltanschauung* (Leipzig: T. Weicher, 1926). See too Nietzsche, *Antichrist,* 592–595.

and the concomitant weakening of the *Herrenmensch*. The return of the original Herrenmensch and his elevation to the status of worldly Übermensch was a biological imperative. To achieve this a massive Nietzschean conflagration between Aryan Nordics and their Jewish and other enemies was necessary.

Works like these and Arno Schickedanz's 1927 *Socialparasitism in the Life of the Nations* rendered such a Lebensphilosophie war ever more stark and apocalyptic. The world was poised between the forces of healthy Aryan light and Semitic darkness. The Nietzschean imperative to "be oneself" was invoked as the holy cornerstone of a fundamental confrontation: "We stand," wrote Schickedanz, "at the point of world change. If the nature of Judaism is continuous destruction, ours is uplifting life. There is only one 'holy' law of being, to be what we are!"[151]

The degree to which late-Weimar anti-Semitism resonated with Nietzschean themes and inspiration was quite extraordinary, one startled Jewish commentator noted.[152] Discussions of the Jewish question included heavily edited selections (naturally from *The Antichrist* and *The Genealogy of Morals!*) accompanied by comments that these passages proved that Nietzsche was the most radically anti-Jewish thinker imaginable.[153]

These tracts were typically associated with head-on attacks on traditional and Kantian notions of morality. Dependence on ethical conscience, wrote one Rudolf Klages in 1918, is "the stigma of those . . . whom Nietzsche called 'slave men.' . . . The anthropologist recognizes in the phenomenon of morality only one factor: the spiritual expression of inferior blood. . . . But the principle of all sin against life is the so-called categorical imperative. The teacher of morality is unconsciously a systematic sinner against life."[154]

This kind of thinking also penetrated more scholarly circles. One journal saluted Nietzsche as a founder of racial hygiene and for his usefulness in the class struggle. As E. Kirchner put it, Nietzsche's "enmity against the proletariat" was a vital and healthy response, for

151. Arno Schickedanz, *Sozialparasitismus im Völkerleben* (Leipzig: Lotus-Verlag, 1927), 177.
152. See Arthur Prinz, "Diskussion der Judenfrage," *Jüdische Rundschau* (20 April 1932).
153. *Klärung: 12 Autoren Politiker Über die Judenfrage* (Berlin: Wilhelm Kolk, 1932). The Nietzsche excerpts are entitled "Rome versus Judea, Judea versus Rome" (pp. 57–65). For an analysis of the importance of Nietzsche as an anti-Semite see Ernst Johannsen, "Über den Antisemitismus als gegebene Tatsache," 15–17.
154. Rudolf Klages, *Briefe über Ethik*, quoted in Bein, "Jewish Parasite," 29.

"the growth of the traditionless proletariat leads to degeneration of the race."[155] In 1920 Karl Bindung and Alfred Hoch published *The Release of Unworthy Life in Order that it Might be Destroyed* (*Die Freigabe der Vernichtung Lebensunwertes Leben*), a work applauded by one commentator as the "creative solution" to problems posed by Plato, Thomas More, and Nietzsche. It provided an answer to Nietzsche's observation that "the sick person is a parasite of society."[156] From then until its Nazi implementation, the Nietzschean celebration of euthanasia was constantly invoked by its proponents and its later practitioners as an essential ingredient in the creation of a healthy society.[157]

When the Nazis came to power, the building blocks of a Nietzsche-inspired vitalistic, renaturalized, elemental society had been implanted, in many cases by sources that remained outside or even opposed to national socialism. Having taken over the machinery of the state, these positive and negative messages could be removed from the realm of rhetoric and put into practice.

World War I and the experience of Weimar graphically illustrated that the Nietzsche heritage both molded and was molded by the dominant cultural, political, and ideological perceptions of the day. Nietzsche was also bound to interact with the other great unresolved issues of the time: socialism, religion and, thereafter, nazism.

155. E. Kirchner, "Nietzsches Lehren im Lichte der Rassenhygiene," *Archiv für Rassen und Gesellschaftsbiologie* (1926), 380. This adulatory article nevertheless takes issue with Nietzsche's emphasis on will and creation of the Übermensch and argues for a more strictly biological approach. This racist, eugenicist journal was not anti-Semitic, though when the Nazis came to power its editors were enthusiastic supporters.

156. E. Kirchner, "Anfänge rassenhygienischen Denkens in Morus 'Utopie' und Campanellas 'Sonnenstadt,'" *Archiv für Rassen und Gesellschaftsbiologie* (1927); Robert N. Proctor, *Racial Hygiene: Medicine under the Nazis* (Cambridge: Harvard University Press, 1988), 179.

157. See for instance Margarete Adam, "Unwertiges Leben und seine Überwindung bei Nietzsche," *Monistische Monatshefte* 14 (June 1929), 140–145. On practitioners, see Ernst Klee, *"Euthanasie" im NS-Staat: Die "Vernichtung lebensunwerten Lebens"* (Frankfurt am Main: S. Fischer, 1983), 16ff.

CHAPTER VI

Nietzschean Socialism:
Left and Right

Poor, poor Nietzsche . . . these Messrs. Socialists are trying
to pull their little red cap on that giant genius's head.

Chaim Weizmann

Socialism is a moral question inasmuch as it provides the
world with a new way of judging all human actions, or—to
use Nietzsche's famous expression—with a total revaluation
of things.

Georges Sorel, "Bases de critique sociale"

Nietzsche's biting, elitist contempt for leveling and despotic socialism as
well as for the masses and their life-negating ressentiment morality is
well known.[1] The enemies of socialism were certainly aware of it and
often employed Nietzsche for their attack on the left. As one conservative British commentator put it in 1909: "John Bull is a patient just
now. Nietzsche is the only doctor who can help him, for his greatest
disease is socialism. . . . Dr. Nietzsche either cures his patients radically
or kills them."[2] In the 1890s Franz Mehring began a tradition that
stated the orthodox Marxist attitude just as clearly.[3] Nietzsche was the
anti-egalitarian "philosopher of advanced capitalism," both symptom
and spokesman of an irrationalist post-Hegelian philosophy that re-

---

1. There are countless examples including Nietzsche's *Human, All Too Human*, 173–
174; *Beyond Good and Evil*, 115–118; and *Will to Power*, 77–78, 123–124, 186, 397,
398, 460–463.
2. J. M. Kennedy, *The Quintessence of Nietzsche* (London: T. W. Lawrie, 1909),
79–80. Quoted in Joll, "The English, Nietzsche, and the War," 296.
3. Franz Mehring, *Kapital und Presse: Ein Nachspiel zum Falle Lindau* (Berlin: Kurt
Brachvogel, 1891); "Zur Philosophie und Poesie des Kapitalismus," "Nietzsche gegen den
Sozialismus," and sec. 9 of his "Aesthetische Streifzüge," in vols. 9, 11, and 13 of his
Gesammelte Schriften (Berlin: Dietz, 1961). For an overview of early German socialist
responses, see Ernst Behler, "Zur Frühen Sozialistischen Rezeption Nietzsches in
Deutschland," *Nietzsche-Studien* 13 (1984), 503–520.

flected the interests of the bourgeoisie and capitalism in its most aggressive forms. Totally ignorant of scientific socialism, he was the great enemy of the proletariat.

In this light, what possible meaning could the expression *Nietzschean socialism* possess? The answer will reveal a snapshot of a highly volatile political consciousness which, after 1890, routinely regarded itself as being in crisis. Throughout the political culture, distinctions between left and right were constantly challenged and blurred; perceptions of political and mental boundaries were rendered increasingly permeable by activists and thinkers in search of novel modes of identification. Nietzschean categories contributed to the general sense of fluidity, loosened traditional moral and intellectual definitions, and helped to construct more elastic political postures.

These developments affected socialist self-understanding as much they did other sectors of the cultural and political spectrum. Throughout Europe the strict Marxist definition of socialism was challenged by various dissident tendencies within the left. Determinedly anti-orthodox, anarchist, syndicalist, and revisionist formulations mushroomed on the political landscape. The idea of socialism—outside of a generalized identification with the working classes and some form of egalitarian commitment—became ever more vague and susceptible to external influences and counterinterpretations. Nietzsche often served in these exercises as an important resource for articulating many of these dissident concerns.

We should not forget that in the minds of some of his early detractors, as Count Kessler recalled, Nietzsche "was reckoned as a revolutionary and almost as unpatriotic a fellow as the Socialists."[4] In popular consciousness the two were sometimes simply equated. In the relatively obscure play *Kinder* by Robert Misch (1906), for instance, one character declares: "Nietzsche is nonsense . . . [he is a] Social Democrat!"[5]

Some of Nietzsche's celebrators made equally loose connections. Reporting from Moscow for the French Communist daily *L'Humanité* in Spring 1921, Isadora Duncan prefaced her report on the revolution with Zarathustra's "I love the man who creates higher than himself and perishes in this way." She concluded that this was the "shining vision of the future. The prophecies of Beethoven, of Nietzsche, of Walt Whit-

4. Kessler, *Diaries*, 426.
5. Robert Misch, *Kinder: Eine Gymnasiasten Komödie* (Berlin: Harmonie, 1906), 12. I thank Robert Holub for this reference.

man are being realized. All men will be brothers, carried away by the great wave of liberation that has just been born here in Russia."[6]

To many the Nietzsche–socialism association seemed entirely natural and unproblematic. Helene Stöcker's Nietzscheanism accompanied not only her feminism but also her unaffiliated leftist and increasingly pacifistic stance. For her, Nietzsche and socialism shared the ultimate goal of an "emancipated humanity." Each, she did admit, had their own particular bias. Social reformers were so busy with everyday life that they neglected the heights, while Nietzsche from "his perspective of eternity" had perhaps not paid enough attention to external conditions. Nevertheless, she asked, would "it not be insane to demand of the prophet of the Superman that he should also study economics and social science in order to identify the exact path that one must take to reach his goal?"[7] In her 1939 autobiographical fragment she explained her lifelong conception of the relationship:

> The two poles of human evolution, the striving for social justice and the urge for the highest personal development, for me always remained inextricably connected. This for me has for perhaps the last half-century been expressed by the words "Nietzsche *and* Socialism."[8]

Radicals were attracted to Nietzsche because of his devastating indictment of the bourgeoisie and because he provided a counterlanguage, a rhetoric of total regeneration of the New Man which could channel the revolutionary impulse, while keeping the content of that impulse vague and unclassifiable.

When the radical right sought to appropriate socialism for their own purposes, Nietzsche was a central enabling force in the transition. That the new right chose to designate itself as socialist was perhaps a paradox, but it did reflect an awareness that the term had become an essential catchword in modern mass politics. In the eyes of the radical right, it was extremely important to wrest both the socialist constituency and its definitional monopoly from the left. In forging its own notion of socialism it stripped the concept of almost all Marxist landmarks and made any precise grasp of its contours even more elusive.[9]

6. Duncan, *Isadora Speaks*, 65–66.
7. Helene Stöcker, "Friedrich Nietzsche und die Frauen," *Das Magazin für Literatur* 67 (1898), 156–157; trans. in Hackett, "Helene Stöcker," 117.
8. Cited in Hackett, "Helene Stöcker," 117.
9. Adherents were aware of the vagueness and made use of it. (Werner Sombart, *Deutscher Sozialismus* [Charlottenburg: Buchalz & Weisswange, 1934]. Translated by Karl F. Geiser as *A New Social Philosophy* [New York: Greenwood Press (1932), 1969], 45–109).

The right now offered a national socialism as a counterweight to the Marxist idea of international proletarian revolution. Its ideologues could proclaim themselves socialists not only because they assigned to the state authoritarian powers to regulate socioeconomic life along quasicorporate lines but also because they couched their analysis of society in a biting critique of the bourgeoisie and accorded to the lower classes a major role in their visions of national regeneration. Nietzsche provided a fruitful source for these themes. His radicalism was easily molded into the framework of a new right that, unlike its older conservative counterpart, put a premium on the national mobilization and integration of the working classes. *Socialism* here referred to the conflation of the national with the social. It aimed at inclusiveness and participation of the working masses within the broader whole. Dedication to the nation would create a socialism of the *Volksgemeinschaft*, a viable substitute for the socialism of class.

The Nietzschean impulse in the socialism of both the left and right can only be understood within the context of this crisis of political revaluation. Although it took on numerous guises and was often the work of opposed circles, these were all nonconformist expressions of dissent from conservative tradition, bourgeois respectability, or left-wing orthodoxy. Nietzschean socialism was part of an ongoing quest for new forms of politicocultural integration, providing suggestive images of an idealized future transcending conventional class categories.

Although we will only be concerned here with the German case, variants of Nietzschean socialism appeared throughout Europe. It ranged from the individualist ethics transcending obligatory norms and emancipatory communism beyond good and evil, as expounded by prerevolutionary Russian Marxists such as Anatol Lunacharski and Stanislav Volsky,[10] to the Zionist socialism of Bitania. It informed Viktor Adler's infusion into Austrian social democracy of Dionysian impulses designed to arouse the nascent proletariat to a willful consciousness of its own power[11] It vitally influenced syndicalism and its transmutation of Marxism into a glorification of violence and dynamic activism. Georges Sorel, transposing Nietzsche's elitism to a new aristocracy of revolutionaries who would lead the proletariat first to class

---

10. Eugen Kamenka, *The Ethical Foundations of Marxism* (London: Routledge and Kegan Paul, 1962), 178–179; George L. Kline, "'Nietzschean Marxism' in Russia," in *Demythologizing Marxism*, vol. 2, ed. Frederick J. Adelmann (Chestnut Hill and The Hague: Boston College and Martinus Nijhoff, 1969), 166–183.
11. J. McGrath, *Dionysian Art*, chaps. 2 and 8.

war and thereafter into a heroic, postdecadent civilization, is perhaps
the most famous example of this trend.[12] It encompassed Mussolini's
pre-1914 Lebensphilosophie Marxism with its emphasis on will, energizing vitality, and its warrior relationship to reality.[13]

We must, however, concentrate on Germany. Nietzsche's presence
began to manifest itself seriously within German social democracy in
the 1890s, coinciding with his general popularization and the emergence of various Nietzsche cults. Nietzschean language and categories
then became part of the vocabulary of the organized socialist world.
Regardless of their political separatism, neither the socialist movement
nor the working class were immune to broader cultural influence. It is
true that certain elements of Nietzschean terminology became part of a
system of negative catchwords, a mode of condemning one's political
enemies. Socialist propaganda increasingly disparaged opponents for
their self-aggrandizing "will to power," labeling the bourgeoisie as
ruthless Übermenschen or Gewaltmenschen, beasts of prey and the
like.[14]

But Nietzschean terms also began to assume more affirmative meanings. Positive socialist goals of worker emancipation were formulated
within a Nietzschean frame. J. Karmeluk's 1904 Proletarian Sermon
from the Mount: An Intermezzo from the Transvaluation of Values,
for instance, was a socialist counterliturgy based upon explicitly
Nietzschean inspiration.[15] Here was a socialist gospel affirming the
worker's will to power and arguing that only struggle and rebellion
would bring about the worker's paradise. Socialism and the Antichrist
in tandem were the keys to the new earthly liberation.

The degree to which the Nietzschean presence infiltrated actual
working-class communities is unclear due to the paucity of evidence.
Nevertheless, some scattered indications are available. That Nietzsche
had begun to make inroads at least among literate workers is demonstrated by an 1897 survey of Leipzig workers' libraries. Its author reported that Nietzsche's works had been far more widely borrowed than

    12. J. L. Talmon, The Myth of the Nation and the Vision of Revolution: The Origins
of Political Polarization in the Twentieth Century (Berkeley, Los Angeles, and London:
University of California Press, 1981), 468–469. See too Sternhell, Neither Right nor Left,
56, 87, 89.
    13. Nolte, "Marx und Nietzsche."
    14. Vivetta Vivarelli, "Das Nietzsche-Bild in der Presse der deutschen Sozial-
demokratie um die Jahrhundertwende," Nietzsche-Studien 13 (1984).
    15. J. Karmeluk, Die Proletarische Bergpredigt: Ein Intermezzo aus der Umwertung
aller Werte (Zurich, 1904); Vivarelli, "Nietzsche-Bild," 564–565.

those of Marx, Lasalle, or even Bebel.[16] In 1914 Adolf Levenstein produced the results of a survey complete with letter-interviews in which he
sought to examine both the scope and nature of the influence. His
Friedrich Nietzsche in the Judgment of the Working Classes[17] demonstrated not only that many educated workers were acquainted with the
philosopher but that, in the overwhelming majority of cases, Nietzsche
fulfilled a positive function. Only two of the interviewees rejected
Nietzsche but even they admitted to being stimulated by him. Levenstein suggested that in their lives, their tragic isolations, and their com-
pensatory attempts to cultivate an "inner life" there was an unexpected
affinity between workers and Nietzsche.[18] Both were quintessential outsiders. This explained the paradox, as one reviewer put it, that the most
centrifugal of all philosophies worked so strongly and bindingly on the
most neglected core of society.[19] For our purposes the responses to
Levenstein's questions demonstrated a degree of proletarian familiarity
with Nietzsche; whether positively or negatively received, Nietzsche
had become a recognized point of reference. Nevertheless, the historical
importance of Nietzschean socialism does not depend upon Nietzsche's
purported impact on daily working-class attitudes. Rather, its significance derives from how it functioned for leading activists and theoreticians as both a critical and visionary tool, a mode of advancing alternative, postorthodox representations of socialism. The adventures of
the Nietzschean idea within the German Social Democratic party almost always manifested itself as a form of dissent—whether leftist or
rightist. Its numerous versions were expressions of the developing crisis
within Marxism. Defenders and attackers of the faith were quite aware
that Nietzschean impulses within social democracy were almost by definition heretical.

The very articulation of the orthodox line by Franz Mehring declar-
ing Nietzsche to be "the philosopher of capitalism" was in reaction to
the importation of Nietzsche into the Social Democratic party during
the 1890s by a group of radicals who became known as the Jungen. Led
by Bruno Wille, this circle accused the party of accommodationist *em-*

16. A. H. T. Pfannkuche, *Was liest der deutsche Arbeiter* (Tübingen and Leipzig,
1900), 23; Vivarelli, "Nietzsche-Bild," 521.
17. Levenstein reported that thirty-seven metal workers, sixteen textile workers, two
miners and fifty-four workers in other professions had occupied themselves with
Nietzsche's Zarathustra (*Friedrich Nietzsche im Urteil der Arbeiterklasse* [Leipzig: F.
Meiner, 1914]).
18. Ibid., 2d ed. 1919, iii.
19. Max Adler, "Arbeiterbriefe über Nietzsche," *Wissen und Leben* 14 (1921), 430–
433.

bourgeoisement, which committed the party to a parliamentary rather than a revolutionary course. The party was ossifying, its bureaucratic institutions growing ever further removed from the masses. In the end, the Jungen articulated nothing less than a critique of the authoritarian dangers within Marxism.

The utopian and anarchist strains within this critique were inspired and legitimized by a Nietzschean-based individualism. Wille's play *An Enemy of the People,* produced by the Freie Volksbühne in 1890, and a series of polemic works[20] forcefully brought home the Jungen's point: Nietzsche was the ideal champion for a critique of party mindlessness and conformity which stifled all possibilities of creative expression. This individualism did not, the Jungen claimed, entail a repudiation of socialism. Nietzschean ideals had to be universalized, made integral to the socialist endeavor. Proletarians did not have to be part of an anonymous mass; they too could be "higher men." Personal freedom and socialism were reconcilable.

The Jungen's direct attack on the party leadership inevitably resulted in a struggle that could only lead to their defeat.[21] Many of its adherents left the party and became independent socialists. Their journal, *Der Sozialist,* soon took on an anticentralist, antistatist hue. Nietzschean volition informed their anarchic socialist vision of the future. No one worked out the bases of this Nietzschean anarchism more radically than the one-time editor of *Der Sozialist,* Gustav Landauer (1870–1919).

Landauer, as Eugene Lunn has demonstrated, was able to harness Nietzschean irrationalism and voluntarism and point them leftward.[22] He created an anarchism based on a form of vitalism and the notion of an individual and collective willful self-transformation. Landauer filtered Nietzsche's negation of human solidarity and community out of his system while incorporating the philosopher's critique of materialism and suspicion of the state. Landauer insisted that social questions could best be solved through willful transformations of consciousness. As Landauer put it in his *Aufruf zum Sozialismus* (1911): "Socialism is possible and impossible at all times; it is possible when the right people are there to will it and to do it; it is impossible when people either don't

---

20. These polemic works began with Bruno Wille's "Der Mensch als Massenmitglied," *Freie Bühne* (1890), and culminated with his *Philosophie der Befreiung durch das reine Mittel: Beiträge zur Pädagogik des Menschengeschlechts* (Berlin: S. Fischer, 1894).

21. Hinton Thomas (*Nietzsche in German Politics,* 7–16) has a useful account of this episode.

22. Eugene Lunn, *Prophet of Community: The Romantic Socialism of Gustav Landauer* (Berkeley, Los Angeles, and London: University of California Press, 1973).

will it or only supposedly will it, but are not capable of doing it."[23] Nietzschean anarchic socialism thus served as an alternative to a cold, determinist Marxist orthodoxy. Landauer explicitly upheld the Nietzschean insistence that life and culture required illusion.[24] Viewed from this perspective, socialism was a consciously generated antihistoricist myth of perpetual self-creation.

Although the Jungen affair caused a great outcry at the time, its only lasting effect was to reinforce the party leadership's skepticism toward fashionable intellectuals. Mehring approvingly quoted Kurt Eisner's characterization of the Jungen (and the naturalism they often espoused) as "decadent youth, exploiters of rot, and rummagers in ruins," the kind of people who "boast about syphilis to prove their manhood."[25] In his 1892 tome on Nietzsche, Eisner perceptively observed that the radical chic of these Nietzsche cults rendered the older radicalism of socialism trivial, dull, and outmoded.[26]

Yet the Jungen and Landauer were not freak phenomena. Although they never became normative, the history of German socialism was punctuated by such challenges from various directions. While Landauer and the Jungen forged a leftist radical critique, a similar Nietzschean impulse emanated from a particular section of the revisionist right. In 1893 Eduard Bernstein did dismiss the literary Nietzscheans and the Jungen as elitist advocates of a simple Nietzschean *Herren-Anarchismus*.[27] Nevertheless, reformists aligned with the independent *Sozialistische Monatshefte*, and its editor, Joseph Bloch, annexed Nietzsche as principal authority and inspiration for their brand of socialism (illus. 12). Again Nietzschean images and metaphors guided another internal socialist heresy, and one quite different from the Jungen's. The *Monatshefte*'s Nietzsche legitimized a new conception of working-class integration in Germany and abroad.[28] There was little of the fiery,

---

23. Quoted in Martin Buber, "Landauer," *Paths in Utopia,* trans. R. F. C. Hull (Boston: Beacon Press, 1958), 47.

24. Landauer's emphasis on illusion was clearest in his *Skepsis und Mystik* (Berlin: E. Fleischel, 1903). See Lunn, *Prophet of Community,* 160.

25. Franz Mehring, "Der heutige Naturalismus," *Die Volksbühne* 1, no. 3 (1892–1893), 9–12. See Mehring's review of Eisner in "Literarische Rundschau," *Die neue Zeit* 10 (1892), 669; translated in Vernon T. Lidtke, "Naturalism and Socialism in Germany," *The American Historical Review* 79 (1974), 28–29.

26. Eisner, *Psychopathia Spiritualis,* 87.

27. See Bernstein's review of W. Weigand's *Friedrich Nietzsche* in *Die neue Zeit* 11, (1892–1893). Quoted in Vivarelli, "Nietzsche-Bild," 530.

28. Roger Fletcher has written a useful history of this circle stressing Nietzsche's role in their politics (*Revisionism and Empire: Socialist Imperialism in Germany* [London: George Allen and Unwin, 1984]).

revolutionary rhetoric that had attended Wille's and Landauer's Nietzscheanism. The *Monatshefte* fostered a revisionist Nietzschean nationalization of the masses.

This nationalization was to be achieved in two ways. Domestically it entailed a Nietzschean individuation that would gradually differentiate a too homogenous and isolated working class and provide it with an opportunity to enter the mainstream of national life. As Willy Hellpach wrote in 1900, this was the stage of socialist and proletarian development in which Nietzsche could be crucial.[29] Despite Nietzsche's own dissociation, he had to be regarded as a prophet of socialism. Hellpach was indulging in a casuistic exercise familiar to all branches of Nietzscheanism. Just as feminists feminized him, Jews Judaized him, and völkisch circles nationalized him, so too did Hellpach seek to demonstrate Nietzsche's incipient socialism.

Nietzsche had opposed political democracy, Hellpach argued, because it only encouraged herd feeling and mass leveling. Economic democratization, however, would simply amount to the application of the Nietzschean principle of Individualität to proletarians, making them aware of the feeling of selfhood. Slowly, individuals would be able to rise through their own efforts, which would increase class mobility. Socialists had to adopt Nietzsche's aristocratic principle as their own. To the degree that the working class became differentiated, proletarians too would be able to qualify for membership in that elite that Nietzsche idealized as lawgivers of the future.

The *Monatshefte* reserved its martial Nietzsche and the associated imagery evoking conflict, courage, and hardness for the propagation of an expansionist foreign policy. The worker was also to be integrated into German society through Germany's imperialism. The journalist Karl Leuthner was the energetic spokesman for this line. Leuthner schooled his readers in the ecstatic Nietzschean language of the will to power, forging and collectivizing it into a national instrument. He harnessed Nietzsche's vitalism and emphasis on struggle to form a socialist politics of imperial expansion linked to the interests of the working class.[30]

Just as party leaders dissociated themselves from the leftist Nietzscheans, so too did they distance themselves from such notions. Leuthner's name, wrote Karl Kautsky, had become a byword for "German

29. Hellpach wrote under the pseudonym Ernst Gystrow ("Etwas über Nietzsche und uns Sozialisten," *Sozialistische Monatshefte* 4 [1900]).

30. Karl Leuthner, "Herrenvolk und Pöbelvolk," *Sozialistische Monatshefte* 13 (1909). Fletcher (*Revisionism*, 199–200) has a full list of Leuthner's publications in this journal.

völkisch arrogance" and a "pan-German outlook, which in him out-
weighs other considerations." Otto Bauer accused Leuthner of "con-
taminating broad sectors of the people with a cynical nationalist ideology
of the overlord (*Herrenideologie*) which flies in the face of all ethics."[31]

During the Weimar period, the *Monatshefte* published one more
excursus metamorphizing Nietzsche into a "socialist imperialist" but in
a quite different spirit. There was no doubt, Regina Barkan wrote, that
Nietzsche's will to power was grounded in an imperialist philosophy.
But his imperialism had nothing in common with the aggressive national politics of conquest and expansion. It was grounded in his conception of the world as one, his affirmation of a *Gesamtnatur* and the
desire to overcome all dualities. This was not an imperialism of material
acquisition, of having more but rather of becoming more. This was
Nietzsche's great politics: a conception of European and world unity
bound by a project of common human creativity. Consolidated world
economic and political structures, Barkan declared, were mere forms
serving the realization of deeper Nietzschean creative processes. "With
such an imperialism before our eyes one should define the will to power
in social life as a will to community. . . . Such an imperialism is one with
the foreign politics of applied socialism. (Despite everything, Nietzsche
already darkly intuited the connection.)"[32]

Still other sections of the party assumed fluid and evolving Nietzschean positions. Before World War I men like Max Maurenbrecher
(1874–1930) sought practical ways of reaching the working classes
through the establishment of a post-Christian socialist Nietzschean
faith.[33] Maurenbrecher was both a Protestant pastor and a political
activist. Both his politics and religion were extremely volatile. He was
prominent in Friedrich Naumann's *Nationalsozialer Verein* until it dis-
banded in 1903 when he joined the Social Democrats. He left the evangelical church in 1907 and linked up with the new free religious communities that, although independent of the official socialist apparatus,
attempted to wean the workers away from traditional sources of religious inspiration. Nietzsche was Maurenbrecher's paradigm for a modernist secular religiosity, and Zarathustra the model of godlike self-
creation of the world.

31. Quoted in Fletcher, *Revisionism*, 101, 99.
32. Regina Barkan, "Nietzsche der Imperialist," *Sozialistische Monatshefte* 30
(1924), 506–507.
33. Albert Kalthoff was another Protestant pastor who also took this form of
Nietzschean socialist religion to the workers but gave it a decidedly Christian bent.

Significantly, Maurenbrecher conceived of his Nietzscheanism as a complement to the Communist vision. As he put it, his work was dedicated "to the interflow between Marx and Nietzsche."[34] Maurenbrecher stressed their common secular components. Both Marx and Nietzsche shared the anticlericalism of the Enlightenment, rejected Christianity, and strongly maintained the idea of worldly redemption.

But that was the Maurenbrecher of the pre–World War I era. During the war he rejoined the Church and veered from Marx and social democracy to a Deutschnational position. Yet all these changes did not entail a lesser commitment to Nietzschean values. Heroism, will, and tragedy all sat comfortably on either side of the political fence.[35]

Maurenbrecher was by no means the only Nietzschean socialist to change positions, often on explicitly Nietzschean grounds. We have already discussed the Nietzschean feminism of Lily Braun. As an active member of the Social Democratic party, Braun originally came to feminism from within Marxism. To the chagrin of the party leadership, her Marxism was always highly unorthodox, reformist, and based not on Kantian, Christian, nor Hegelian but on Nietzschean grounds. She opposed dogma, bureaucratic control, and regimentation and emphasized creativity. Whether or not Alfred Meyer is correct in regarding Braun as a major radical forerunner of a post–World War I Western Marxism, she undoubtedly sought a species of humanist socialism and a heroic "self-transcendence through revolutionary praxis" that derived from Nietzsche.[36] "Socialism," she wrote, "is the necessary precondition for individualism just as much as individualism must be the necessary complement to socialism."[37] The emphasis on human community was never to subordinate but rather to underpin the free development of the human personality.[38] Her emphasis on aesthetics similarly lent a Nietz-

34. Max Maurenbrecher, *Das Leid: Eine Auseindandersetzung mit der Religion* (Jena, 1912).

35. For this Protestant and Germanized Nietzsche see Max Maurenbrecher, *Über Friedrich Nietzsche zum deutschen Evangelium: Gottesdienste, Andachten und religiöse Auseinandersetzungen* (Dresden: Verlag, Glaube und Deutschtum, 1926). Hinton Thomas's argument that as Maurenbrecher moved increasingly toward nationalism he tended to ignore Nietzsche is incorrect. Nietzsche served people throughout the political spectrum even when they individually expressed several political views (Hinton Thomas, *Nietzsche in German Politics*, 128).

36. Meyer, *Lily Braun*, chaps. 7, 8.

37. Lily Braun, " 'Bürgerliches' und 'proletarisches' Erziehungsprinzip," *Neue Gesellschaft* 3, no. 8 (1906), 93–94. Quoted in Meyer, *Lily Braun*, 102.

38. The final goal of any work for the well-being of the community, for the liberation of humanity from every form of intellectual and personal slavery, can be nothing else than the freedom of development for the individual, the right of everyone to his or her personality. But whoever is engaged in the struggle for these

schean tinge to her Marxism. Although she did not ignore socioeconomic oppression, the coming revolution was to be equally spiritual and aesthetic: the working classes were to share the joy of aesthetic appreciation and creation.

Braun insisted upon the "spirit of negation" (*Geist der Verneinung*) as the principle for a rejuvenated socialism. That spirit explicitly excluded Kantianism as a guide to socialism. Nietzsche was to be its prophetic force for "he gave to socialism what we need: an ethical foundation."

> All his great ideas live in us: the drive to personality, the transvaluation of all values, the yea-saying to life, the will to power. We need the flashing weapons from his armory. . . . With the ideal of the greatest happiness for the greatest number . . . we create only a society of phlegmatic petit-bourgeois. . . . Do you not sense the spirit of negation in everything that today is vital and seeks forward movement? . . . If your flags were fully unfurled the cowards would be separated from the courageous, the strong from the weak and everything with youthful spirit, that has a future within it, would flow towards you. We will only find the way to our goal when the idea of a moral revolution lends wings to the idea of economic transformation.[39]

As with Maurenbrecher's, Braun's Nietzsche was compatible with both a Marxist–cosmopolitan and a nationalist–patriotic purpose. The same categories of heroism, will, aestheticism, and self-transcendence that informed her radicalization of orthodox Marxism animated her later intense nationalist commitment to World War I; her antipacifism and support for German annexationist aims; and even her turn to an authoritarian cult of the state and the yearning for an inspired young leader.[40] Braun's wartime Nietzsche was not very different from the themes of the previous chapter: the philosopher of heroism, the collective and individual mobilizer, the visionary of a culture that went beyond everyday bourgeois concerns, and the affirmer of martial, virile values.[41]

Although she remained consistently anti-Christian, the war aroused religious longings within her. In quite un-Marxist fashion she now

---

goals must be doubly careful not to lose his own ego in this struggle, but must preserve it. (Lily Braun, "Abseits vom Wege," *Neue Gesellschaft* 4, no. 4, 126. Quoted in Meyer, *Lily Braun*, 102–103)

39. Lily Braun, *Memoiren einer Sozialisten*, vol. 2, *Kampfjahre* (Munich: Albert Langen, 1911), 653–654.

40. Meyer, *Lily Braun*, 182ff.

41. For Braun's affirmation of war, feminism, and Nietzsche see her *Die Frauen und der Krieg* (Leipzig: Hirzel, 1915).

called for a Nietzschean hero who would bring with him a Nietzschean religion commensurate with the needs of the ongoing war:

> If a new savior were to come who found the right word to give form to all our longing, in order to proclaim—right now, in the face of death—a religion of life (I do not mean this in the usual trivial sense of a religion for daily life, but one of creative, eternal life forever—giving new birth to itself), it would be the axe which would cut Christianity out at its root.[42]

Braun's fluid Nietzscheanism was not entirely the work of an isolated eccentric. In 1903 she and her husband Heinrich formed an independent institutional base, the controversial journal *Die Gesellschaft*, in which they and their circles expressed their iconoclastic views. In the face of party opposition (which may account for its sporadic and short-lived nature) dissidents formulated alternative and sometimes unexpected positions. In "The Tactics of the Weak and the Tactics of the Strong" by Franz Laufkötter, Nietzscheanism was employed both as a radicalizing and a moderating factor. In this application of Nietzschean ideas to the class struggle, Laufkötter portrayed a proletariat characterized by its strength, courage, and preparedness for struggle. It possessed such characteristics because it was a rising not a decadent class, embodying life and the will to power. But Laufkötter's guidelines for militant trade unions and party tactics within Germany also advocated scrupulous dealings with the class enemy. Workers had to be honest, for dishonesty was a ressentiment weapon of the weak. The proletariat sought the Nietzschean goal of a higher, nobler culture: their behavior had to conform to this ethic.[43]

Even where it did not explicitly invoke Nietzsche, the journal diffused attitudes that dovetailed with his emphases: its disbelief in the iron laws of historical materialism; its greater emphasis on the role of the individual in history; its growing skepticism towards the masses; and its stress on will.[44]

The topic of "Nietzsche and Marx" or "Nietzsche and socialism," however, went well beyond these relatively organized Social-Democratic streams. Throughout the history of Nietzsche-reception, the ep-

42. Lily Braun to Otto Braun, 17 January 1916, quoted in Meyer, *Lily Braun,* 177–178.

43. Franz Laufkötter, "Die Taktik des Starken und Taktik des Schwachen," *Die Neue Gesellschaft* 4 (July 1906).

44. Dieter Fricke, "Zur Rolle der revisionistischen Zeitschrift *Die neue Gesellschaft* in der deutschen Arbeiterbewegung, 1905–1907," in *Beiträge zur Geschichte der deutschen Arbeiterbewegung* 17 (1975); Hinton Thomas, *Nietzsche in German Politics,* 35.

ochal and somehow interrelated nature of these two thinkers has been recognized.[45] *Kulturkritik* reflections have become almost a separate genre whose quality and depth ranged from the philosophically differentiated to the vacuous.[46] Critics and practitioners across the political spectrum have sought either to highlight the negative[47] or positive affinities—the revolutionary thrust, the anticlericalism, the unflinching critique of ideology, the antibourgeois impulse, the common goal of a free humanity—or to accentuate their unbridgeable differences.

From early on certain socialist intellectuals were aware that Nietzsche had posed some of the ultimate questions concerning modern culture. He represented a crucial post-Marxist modernist challenge that would help to deepen socialism. Nietzsche, wrote Samuel Lublinski in 1905, belongs among those "genuinely valuable enemies who force us to ever more sharply and finely formulate our problems and thereby deepen and lend them even greater force and strength of conviction." Nietzsche had to be internalized while being overcome: "It would be a noble and powerful revenge of socialism on Nietzsche if it proved to be his only heir."[48]

Indeed, traces of this irony were visible even in socialist exercises specifically designed to dismiss Nietzsche. The best example lies in Kurt Eisner's *Psychopathia Spiritualis*, written many years before he became a leader of the ill-fated, postwar, Bavarian revolution. On the one hand, Eisner's criticisms were clear enough. Nietzsche provided nothing more

45. For the most recent comparison in light of modernity, see Nancy S. Love, *Marx, Nietzsche, and Modernity* (New York: Columbia University Press, 1986).

46. In a series of works the neo-Hegelian Emil Hammacher sought to establish a synthesis out of the major modern antinomies—labor and capital, the individual and mass society—through a critique of Marx and Nietzsche, and by redefining the meanings of socialism and individualism. See his "Marx und Nietzsche," *Kölnische Zeitung*, no. 58, Beilage (17 January 1909); "Nietzsche und die soziale Frage," *Archiv für Sozialwissenschaft und Sozialpolitik* 31 (1910); *Hauptfragen der modernen Kultur* (Leipzig and Berlin: B. G. Teubner, 1914). See too Albert Dietrich, "Marx' und Nietzsches Bedeuting für die deutsche Philosophie der Gegenwart," *Die Dioskuren* 1 (1922). On the vacuous side, Max Falkenfeld in his foreword to *Marx und Nietzsche* (Leipzig: Wilhelm Friedrich, 1899), stresses the common German origins of both thinkers and argues that the German Volk had the strength and courage to overcome the apparent incompatibilities.

47. During the Weimar period Hugo Bund insisted on the despotic aims of both (*Nietzsche als Prophet des Sozialismus* [Breslau: Trewendt and Grenier, 1919]). Nietzsche's fundamental class division between masters and slaves had the same leveling effect as the socialism he so lambasted, for both called for a devaluation of personality. There have been numerous permutations around this negative theme, especially amongst conservative and religious critics (Eduard Schreiber, "Nietzsche und Marx im sozialen Kampfe," *Deutsche Arbeit* 8, no. 6 [June 1923]). The rise of bolshevism, nazism, and fascism sharpened these criticisms.

48. Samuel Lublinski, "Nietzsche und der Sozialismus," *Europa: Wochenschrift für Kultur und Politik* 1, no. 22 (15 June 1905), 1085, 1092.

than a romantic dream while socialism was rational and practical.[49] Nor could this Kantian socialist accept the Nietzschean ethic.[50] One could not, Eisner remarked, build an ideology on an egocentric lack of compassion nor on purely negative notions such as antifeminism or anti-Semitism. Moreover, the Nietzschean imperative to become hard caused degeneration. The philosopher of the future would, unlike Nietzsche, cry: "Become tender (*weich*)!"[51]

Yet even more significant than the criticisms was the fact that this work was written as an explicit act of self-liberation from Nietzsche, almost as an exorcism. Eisner quite openly admitted Nietzsche's powerful and almost uncanny influence. Nietzsche was an obsessive temptation of the time: only through direct confrontation, he wrote, could "the Nietzsche problem" be mastered (bewältigen können). He was attracted to Nietzsche's magical lyricism, intoxicating speech, and "narcotic style," and respected his insightful criticism of contemporary shallowness and mediocrity. Eisner's skepticism concerning historical materialism must have helped to make Nietzsche more compelling than the dogmatic certainties of the party line.[52] His Kantianism, rather paradoxically, drew him to sympathize with Nietzsche's stress on free and maximal individual development.[53]

This ingredient rendered Eisner's exorcism only partially complete, for in the end his critical vision of socialist self-liberation retained a Nietzschean core. Socialists, Eisner believed, could still selectively learn from Nietzsche. While Nietzsche's overbearing cult of egocentricity had taken him beyond socialism, it was nevertheless necessary to fuse the Nietzschean aristocratic principle and the imperative of selfhood with democracy and socialism. Eisner's socialism called for the democratization of Nietzsche's aristocratic principle—an aristocratization of the masses. Democracy would become a "pan-aristocracy" in which the meaning of aristocracy would reveal itself as altruism rather than ruthlessness and selfishness.[54]

Eisner's thinking was part of a larger endeavor. The 1890s marked

49. Eisner, *Psychopathia Spiritualis*, 86.
50. On the Kantian side of Eisner see George L. Mosse, "Left-Wing Intellectuals in the Weimar Republic," in *Germans and Jews*, 179–180.
51. Eisner, *Psychopathia Spiritualis*, 58, 95–99.
52. Ibid., 6, 9, 11, 94. Eisner's work was in part written as a response to Mehring's interpretation of Nietzsche. Mehring's subsequent review of *Psychopathia Spiritualis*, while lauding Eisner's eventual rejection of Nietzsche, takes him to task because only the historical-materialist viewpoint was admissible (*Neue Zeit* 10, no. 2, 668f).
53. Ibid., 78–86.
54. Ibid., 79.

the beginning of a project amongst European socialist theoreticians and activists to fashionably synthesize Nietzsche with Marx.[55] Its most common form revolved around the perceived need to reconcile the imperatives of community with selfhood, the free development of the individual with the just society.[56] Nietzsche had, to be sure, specifically warned against such efforts:

> One should not judge the solitary type in terms of the herd; and the herd in terms of the solitary. Seen from above: both are necessary, in the same way their antagonism is necessary, and nothing should be more outlawed than the "desirability" to develop a third way out of both.[57]

Needless to say, those interested in effecting such a union blithely ignored the warning.

This exercise operated on numerous levels and at times within quite unexpected circles. As late as 1925 in an article entitled "What Is Nietzsche to Us?" the journal *Heimstunden* lyrically adopted Nietzsche as a latterday Communist prophet. His psychologically grounded insights, his atheism, and his affirmation of life were at one with socialism. Most important, his aristocratic type, whose task it was to overcome nihilism, resembled not the traditional elites but the "proletarian aristocracy" of which Leon Trotsky had spoken. Was not Lenin far more the embodiment of Nietzschean "personality" than the old feudal oligarchies? There was a world of difference between the pseudo-individualism (*Schein-Individualismen*) of the hereditary aristocracy and the plutocracy and that of the "worker's aristocracy" which emerged from the skilled sectors of the proletariat, genuine individualists who were to play the future, decisive, revolutionary role.[58] Moreover, although Nietzsche was officially frowned upon, he also occasionally insinuated himself into the Socialist Democratic

55. Chaim Weizmann describes that atmosphere:

On Monday Mlle Axelrod, from Berne, is giving a lecture here on Nietzsche and soc[ialism]. Poor, poor Nietzsche, what ugly lips will be uttering his words, and these Messrs. Soc[ialists] are trying to pull their little red cap on that giant genius's head. It seems clear enough that no one liked that fraternity less than Nietzsche. They might have left him in peace, they might have let him lie peacefully in his grave instead of bandying his name about, and to what purpose? Mlle A will presumably prove that Nietzsche was wrong, that had he known her, he would have been much wiser. Pack, Pack, Pack! (*Papers and Letters,* 123)

56. Franz Servās, "Nietzsche und der Sozialismus: Subjektive Betrachtungen," *Freie Bühne* 3 (1892), 85–88, 202–211.

57. Quoted in Reinhart Maurer, "Nietzsche und die Kritische Theorie," *Nietzsche-Studien* 10/11 (1981–1982), 46.

58. F. Schwangart, "Was ist uns Nietzsche?" *Heimstunden: Proletarische Tribune für Kunst, Literatur, Dichtung* no. 5 (May 1925), 141–148.

party's authorized publications. In a 1911 anthology they published, he was included in a collection of revolutionary bourgeois and proletarian poets.[59] The self-conscious proletarian novelist Karl Henckell dedicated an adulatory poem to the philosopher[60] and introduced a militantly Nietzschean tone in his call to arms against the bourgeoisie.[61] In a work—dedicated to Franz Mehring!—Alfred Klineberg proclaimed that Nietzsche's criticism had made him next to Marx "perhaps the greatest intellectual midwife of our German present" whose work had helped prepare for the future classless society.[62] Even Mehring acknowledged a certain function for Nietzsche as "a transition to socialism."[63]

In some cases, Mehring's description was perfectly apt. With individuals like Clara Zetkin and Erich Mühsam, for instance, the Nietzsche fascination was merely a passing phase in their development.[64] Similarly, Georg Lukacs's early Lebensphilosopie and his advocacy of a tragic worldview was influenced by and mimicked the master he was later to reject. Ironically, he espoused precisely the same kind of Nietzschean romantic anticapitalism that he later so virulently condemned in the philosopher.[65]

For other unorthodox socialists, however, the Nietzschean impulse was longer lasting, crucial in the construction of free-wheeling post-Marxist visions. We examined Kurt Hiller's Nietzschean Expressionism in chapter 3. For Hiller it was not so much individualism as a frankly espoused elitism that had to be wed to socialism. His journal, Das Ziel, was populated by radicals of all kinds critiquing the absence of Geist in bourgeois society and calling for a social revolution. Its main aim was

---

59. Nietzsche's poem "Vereinsamt" was included in Von unten auf: Das Buch der Freiheit, ed. Franz Diederich, 3d ed. (Dresden: Verlag Kaden, 1928), 365. See Holub, 1.
60. See Karl Henckell, Deutsche Dichter seit Heinrich Heine (Berlin: Bard-Marquardt, 1906), 112–120, for a discussion of the poet and the poem. See too Krummel, Nietzsche, vol. 2, 264.
61. George L. Mosse, "Literature and Society in Germany," in Masses and Man, 26.
62. Alfred Klineberg, Die deutsche Dichtung in ihren sozialen, zeit- und geistesgeschichtlichen Bedingungen (Berlin: J. H. W. Dietz, 1927), 397–398. Quoted in Hollub, 1.
63. Mehring, "Literarische Rundschau," 668–669.
64. David Bathrick and Paul Breines, "Marx und/oder Nietzsche: Anmerkungen zur Krise des Marxismus," in Karl Marx und Friedrich Nietzsche, ed. R. Grimm and J. Hermand, 119–135 (Königstein: Athenäum Verlag, 1978), 127–129. This article has been useful in suggesting some important themes for this chapter.
65. For a detailed review with bibliography see Henning Ottmann, "Anti-Lukacs: Eine Kritik der Nietzsche-Kritik von Georg Lukacs," Nietzsche-Studien 13 (1984). Henning makes the psychological speculation that the extreme vehemence of Lukacs's Nietzsche critique is explicable as an attack on himself or his youthful self (pp. 571–572).

to abolish the barriers erected against the constitution of a necessary elite, the natural aristocracy of intellectuals which would be replenished by fresh proletarian blood.[66] He founded the short-lived Council of Brain Workers at the end of 1918 in order to further the combined goals of socialism, pacifism, and intellectual aristocracy. Nietzsche was central to his eclectic "logocratic" vision: "It is the mission of the century to allow the intellectual line that leads from the Sermon on the Mount to the *Communist Manifesto* to converge with that other mighty line: Plato–Nietzsche."[67]

For some, the socialist–Nietzschean temptation did not die even after the experience of nazism. Thomas Mann, in typically sublimated and conserving form, advocated a variation as late as 1947. His new Nietzsche, no longer champion of the old antidemocratic order, now became a guide to Mann's own patrician and spiritualized conception of socialism.[68] He declared Nietzsche's aestheticism to be ultimately incompatible with the ethical outlook of socialism. Nevertheless, he insisted, there were points of significant contact, which the predemocratic Mann would not have been particularly interested in making. Nietzsche, wrote Mann, had been concerned about making "private property more moral," was aware how "dangerous is the man who possesses too much," had called for the international powers to "practice world perspective," and had, indeed, predicted as unavoidable the future unified economic administration of the earth.

> The socialist flavor in his vision of the post-bourgeois life is just as strong as the one we might call fascist. What is it after all when Zarathustra exclaims: "I beseech you, my brethren, remain true to earth! No longer bury your heads in the sand of heavenly things, but carry it freely, ahead of this earth, creating the sense of earth! . . . Guide our dissipated virtue back to earth as I do—yea, back to life and love: that it may give a sense to the earth, a human sense!" It means the will to pervade the material element with the human one, it means materialism of the spirit, it is socialism.
> Here and there his concept of civilization shows a strongly socialist,

66. Kurt Hiller, "Logokratie," *Das Ziel* (1920), 220. Cited in Mosse, "Left-Wing Intellectuals," 188ff. Mosse emphasizes the Kantian rather than the Nietzschean influence. "Ratio dissolves into the human will, and Kurt Hiller wrote that from rationalism the will rises, liberated from the shackles that intellectualism has fastened upon it"; the quote smacks as much of Nietzsche as of Kant.

67. Hiller's *Leben gegen die Zeit* (Hamburg: Rowohlt, 1969), 141; Krummel, Nietzsche, vol. 2, 102, n. 86.

68. On this characteristically Mannian—and German—problematic see Mann's 1928 essay "Kultur und Sozialismus" in his *Essays*, vol. 2, *Politik*, ed. Hermann Kurzke (Frankfurt am Main: Fischer Taschenbuch, 1977).

certainly no longer a bourgeois coloring. He stands against the cleavage
between educated and uneducated, and his youthful discipleship of Wagner
signifies this above all: the end of the Renaissance civilization, that great age
of the bourgeoisie, an art for high and low, no more delights that would not
be common to the hearts of all.

It does not testify of enmity against the workers, it testifies to the contrary
when he says: "The working men should learn to feel like soldiers: a
recompensation, a salary, but not payment. They shall live one day like
the middle-class now, but *above* them, distinguishing itself by its lack of
needs, the *higher* caste, i.e., poorer and simpler, but possessed of the
power."[69]

Mann's idiosyncratic thinking, however, remained dislocated from
the traditional political or ideological frameworks of Marxism and
socialism no matter how broadly conceived. In order to discover the
most important post–World War I traces of the leftist Nietzschean impulse we must therefore turn to what has become known as Western
Marxism. In that body of cultural and increasingly postorthodox
thought—especially in the work of Ernst Bloch and the Frankfurt
school—Nietzsche played a crucial role. In a far more sustained and
sophisticated manner than the piecemeal prewar challenges we have
examined thus far, and in the light of multiple crises (October 1917; the
abortive German revolutions; the unanticipated consolidation of advanced capitalism; totalitarianism in its Fascist, Stalinist, and Nazi
forms) this diverse heterodoxy both challenged and sought to revise
normative Marxism. Nietzsche was part inspiration and part beneficiary of an "essential readiness," as Martin Jay has put it, "to draw on
non-Marxist intellectual currents to make up deficiencies (or develop
incipient leads) in the inheritance from the nineteenth century."[70]
Whether such eclectic cross-fertilizations enriched and rejuvenated the
tradition from within, as its adherents claimed, or whether it undermined or superseded it, transforming it into a quite different non-
Marxist animal as its critics claim, must remain here unanswered. Certainly, however, this became a Marxist tradition ever more critical of its
own naive rationalist and progressive underpinnings. Its warily sophisticated ruminations, its premises and epistemology, sense of break-

69. Thomas Mann, "Nietzsche's Philosophy in the Light of Contemporary Events,"
in *Thomas Mann's Addresses, 95–96.* On the antagonism between amoral aestheticism
and moral socialism see 98ff.

70. Martin Jay, *Marxism and Totality: The Adventures of a Concept from Lukacs to
Habermas* (Berkeley, Los Angeles, and London: University of California Press, 1984),
9–10. This fine work has been extremely suggestive for the present theme.

down, and sometimes desperate search for renewal cannot be fully comprehended outside of its tortured dialogue with Nietzsche.[71]

The case of the maverick Ernst Bloch (1885–1977), "the German philosopher of the October Revolution," was sui generis.[72] Whereas the Frankfurt school's central trauma revolved around the dark years of the 1930s, Bloch's 1917 revolutionary ardor remained steady throughout his life. This fervor fueled his need to create a "warm" Marxism, inspired, very often, by antipositivist, neoromantic, bourgeois sources.[73] These currents, he argued, had always been part of the Marxist heritage, but they had previously been suppressed or ignored. Religious and irrationalist dimensions of experience had a legitimate place in the tradition. Bloch's search for repositories of utopian hope in the modern world, his eagerness to scavenge for materials in the least likely of Marxist places—a system and sensibility which Lukacs wryly declared to be a fusion of left-wing ethics and right-wing epistemology[74]—not surprisingly drew him also to Nietzsche. This philosopher of the "principle of hope" constructed a Nietzsche diametrically opposed to the archaic Dionysianism of Klages with its backward turn and refusal to countenance the possibility of a qualitatively transformed utopian future.[75] Bloch explicitly dismissed the notion of eternal recurrence as profoundly static and antiutopian. Unlike Klages, his Nietzschean will to power was determined to avoid castration by such archaism. Instead it would be galvanized by a dynamic Dionysian impulse of an "unfinished nature," possessed of open and explosive revolutionary possibilities.[76] While Bloch also admired Nietzsche's critique of con-

71. Some of this complexity emerges from Terry Eagleton's admiring evocation of Walter Benjamin. Benjamin's "views of cultural revolution, his anti-historical insistence on the ruptures, recyclings, and reinsertions" were deeply influenced by Nietzsche:

Benjamin's writings are in a crucial sense post-Nietzschean, unthinkable without that astonishing iconoclasm; yet he knew also that there are traditions of political struggle, "earlier meanings" that, if only they could be remembered, would blow Nietzsche's own crass politics into the historical rabble he had himself created. (*Walter Benjamin: Towards a Revolutionary Criticism* [London: Verso, 1985], 66).

72. Oskar Negt, "Ernst Bloch: The German Philosopher of the October Revolution," *New German Critique* 4 (Winter 1975); for an overview see Wayne Hudson, *The Marxist Philosophy of Ernst Bloch* (London: Macmillan, 1982).

73. Jay, *Marxism and Totality*, chap. 5.

74. Ibid., 179–180.

75. For this criticism of Klages's Nietzscheanism see Ernst Bloch, "Romanticism of Diluvium," *Heritage of Our Times*, 304–311.

76. For Bloch's pre–World War I utterances, see his "Über das Problem Nietzsches" and "Der Impuls Nietzsches" in his *Durch die Wüsste: Kritische Essays* (Frankfurt: Suhr Kamp, 1964), 108–112. Translated as "The Impulse of Nietzsche," in Bloch, *Heritage of Our Times*, 325–331.

temporary culture and his essentially musical sensibility, it was
Nietzsche's willful "overcoming," the critical-revolutionary impulse,
that he integrated within his esoteric Marxism.[77] In Bloch's vision, the
Dionysian dynamic was radicalized into "a subversive countermovement of the subject" against alienating objectivity and became a universal symbol of human redemptive capacity.[78]

Unlike Bloch, the Frankfurt school grew increasingly skeptical of
these totalized redemptive possibilities. The experience of their generation perhaps rendered them suspicious of inclusive ideologies and systems, a Nietzschean predilection. Their post-Marxist *Ideologiekritik*
and sensitivity to Nietzschean epistemology disallowed easy schemes of
a progressive historical teleology and rendered assumptions of an ultimate object–subject union problematic. The Frankfurt school was able
to place the critique of ideology at the center—rare in the history of
politicized Nietzsche appropriation—because they increasingly distanced themselves from total political programs. Instead, they regarded
themselves as engaged in the salvaging project of critical theory. Such
emphasis on critical negation bespoke not the days of fiery hope that
animated Bloch, but the dark years of the 1930s and 1940s. Critical
theory was preoccupied with opposing the constant falsity of the whole,
although they did clutch at the slim hope of eventual universal human
emancipation. Less concerned with the mechanics of progress than with
the sources of an all-encompassing modern barbarism and increasingly
skeptical of finding human agents of redemption, the Frankfurt school
nevertheless also operated, as one scholar recently put it, with a paradoxical hope for the saving of the hopeless.[79] The road to its realization,
of course, became increasingly blurred, and the signposts to utopia were
presented in increasingly abstract terms—transformed, in the words of
Martin Jay, into "a nuanced defence of theory as itself a form of non-
resigned practice."[80]

There were, of course, a range of influences working on the Frankfurt school (the humanist Marx, Hegel, Freud, Heidegger, and so on).
Nevertheless, theirs was, as Reinhart Maurer has recently persuasively
argued, a Nietzschean neo-Marxism.[81] Both the creators of critical theory and later scholars have been aware of the relationship. Certainly, it

77. Bathrick and Breines, "Marx und/oder Nietzsche," 125ff.
78. Bloch, "The Impulse of Nietzsche," 325.
79. Reinhart Maurer, "Nietzsche und die kritische Theorie," 41–42. This is a brilliant and provocative study.
80. Jay, *Marxism and Totality*, 8.
81. Maurer, "Nietzsche und die kritische Theorie," 35–36, 43–44.

was a very revised Marxism that could prompt the later Max Horkheimer (in an interview with the Italian paper *L'Espresso*) to declare
that Nietzsche was most probably a greater thinker than Marx.[82]

Nietzsche played a complex role within critical theory, fulfilling both
manifest and latent functions. At the most obvious level, he was attractive to the Frankfurt school precisely because he challenged all orthodoxies, because he insisted upon the necessity and complexity of interpretation, and because of his refusal to countenance partisan and
simplified formulae. "God knows," Theodor Adorno chided the more
orthodox Walter Benjamin, "there is only one truth. . . . Ultimately
there is more of that one truth in Nietzsche's *Genealogy of Morals* than
in [Nikolay Ivanovich] Bukharin's *ABC of Communism*."[83] They also
admired Nietzsche's unflinching critical spirit and his dissociation, as
Adorno put it, "from complicity with the world."[84] Indeed, for Adorno,
Nietzsche's negativism exemplified the mission that critical theory had
set for itself: it was a "unique demonstration of the repressive character
of occidental culture" and "expressed the humane in a world in which
humanity had become a sham."[85]

The Frankfurt school's admiration for Nietzsche was often expressed
through their comments about his vulgarizing, reactionary disciples.
"Nietzsche's hymn to the human beast of prey," Horkheimer noted in
1933, "always maintains a socially critical (*gesellschaftkritischen*) un-
dertone . . . . Several tendencies of the Enlightenment remain alive in
him."[86] His endorsement was even more powerful in 1937 when he
wrote of Nietzsche: "The independence that is expressed in his philosophy, the freedom from enslaving ideological powers is the root of his
thought."[87]

Such critical independence was crucial for a Marxism minus a pro-

82. *Der Spiegel* 37 (8 September 1969), 164. See too Peter Pütz, "Nietzsche Im Lichte
der kritischen Theorie," *Nietzsche-Studien* 3 (1974).

83. *Aesthetics and Politics* (London: NLB, 1977), 131.

84. Theodor Adorno, "Spengler after the Decline," in *Prisms* (Cambridge: MIT Press,
1986), 65. Adorno made this point in relation to his negative appraisal of Spengler.

85. Theodor Adorno, review of Ernst Newman's Wagner biography in *Kenyon Review* 9 (no. 1, Winter 1947), 161; Martin Jay, *The Dialectical Imagination: A History of
the Frankfurt School and the Institute of Social Research, 1923–1950* (Boston and Toronto: Little, Brown, 1973), 311, n. 41.

86. Horkheimer's comments were similarly made in relation to his distaste for Spengler (review of Spengler's *Jahre der Entscheidung*, *Zeitschrift für Sozialforschung* [1933],
423).

87. Max Horkheimer, "Bemerkungen zu Jaspers' 'Nietzsche,'" *Zeitschrift für Sozialforschung* (1937), 414.

letariat in which theory itself became praxis.[88] Even the pessimistic Herbert Marcuse of *One-Dimensional Man* could regard this as "the liberating air of Nietzsche's thought, cutting into Law and Order."[89] In his earlier—and for critical theory quite uncharacteristically optimistic—*Eros and Civilization* (1955), Marcuse provided a concrete demonstration of such liberational Nietzschean possibilities. That work, with its emphasis on the liberating power of remembrance,[90] contained the critical seeds for socially redemptive action—something which the Freudian concept of repression as a psychic need to forget individual pain and trauma could not.[91] Nietzsche's conception of repression as a response to life-negating external social pressures, however, gave it a clearly sociohistorical and therefore reversible character:

> Nietzsche saw in the training of memory the beginning of civilized morality—especially the memory of obligations, contracts, dues. This context reveals the one-sidedness of memory-training in civilization: the faculty was chiefly directed toward remembering duties rather than pleasures; memory was linked with bad conscience, guilt, and sin. Unhappiness and the threat of punishment, not happiness and the promise of freedom, linger in memory.[92]

Marcuse's Nietzsche "had exposed the gigantic fallacy on which Western philosophy and morality were built—namely, the transformation of facts into essences, of historical into metaphysical conditions"; the Nietzsche whose "total affirmation of the life instincts, repelling all escape and negation" represented "a reality principle fundamentally antagonistic to that of Western civilization."[93] Marcuse's critique of Western civilization included the official manifestations of Marxism. Indeed, he regarded its orthodox assault on Nietzschean and other "bourgeois irrationalisms" as revelatory of "traits common to the Soviet and Western rationality, namely, the prevalence of technological elements over humanistic ones." Schopenhauer, Nietzsche, the vitalists, and so on explode

88. Chapter 2 of Susan Buck-Morss's work is tellingly entitled "Marx Minus the Proletariat: Theory as Praxis" (*The Origin of Negative Dialectics: Theodor W. Adorno, Walter Benjamin and the Frankfurt School* [Hassocks, Sussex: Harvester, 1977]).

89. Herbert Marcuse, *One-Dimensional Man* (Boston: Beacon, 1966), 216.

90. Nietzsche, *Genealogy of Morals*, 57–62.

91. Jay, "Anamnestic Totalization: Memory in the Thought of Herbert Marcuse," chap. 7 in *Marxism and Totality*.

92. Herbert Marcuse, *Eros and Civilization: A Philosophical Inquiry into Freud* (Boston: Beacon, 1966), 232.

93. Ibid., 121, 122. See too pp. 119–124.

the technological rationality of modern civilization. They do so by pointing up the psychical and biological forces beneath this rationality and the unredeemable sacrifices which it exacts from man. The result is a transvaluation of values which shatters the ideology of progress—not by romanticist and sentimental regression, but by breaking into tabooed dimensions of bourgeois society itself. This transvaluation acts upon precisely those values which Soviet society must protect at all cost: the ethical value of competitive performance, socially necessary labor, self-perpetuating work discipline, postponed and repressed happiness.[94]

Though Nietzsche's positive programme was never central to critical theory, it did thus play a certain role. Horkheimer also occasionally hinted at the affirmative social content of Nietzsche's vision and not just his individualistic critical thrust. Through a greater control over nature Nietzsche's goal for the future consisted of the liberation of an indeterminate number of human powers. His notion of Übermenschen designated such a situation and was not as individualistic as may have appeared. "Despite everything," Horkheimer wrote, "he [Nietzsche] knew that there would be many 'Übermenschen' or none at all."[95]

We cannot elaborate here on the multiple parallelisms. Those of style and form are patently obvious. Adorno's *Minima Moralia*, for instance, clearly replicated the aphoristic Nietzsche of the middle period. His frame of reference was similarly Nietzschean: there Adorno characterized his "negative dialectics" (in which the negation of the negation did not lead to a new positive position but rather to an inclusive nonidentity of subjects) as "melancholy science," an explicit contrast to Nietzsche's *Gay Science*.[96] The relationship of critical theory to Nietzsche must, however, also be identified at a deeper, latent level: in relation to the underlying *Fragestellung*, its operating categories, and its methodological and philosophical assumptions and concerns.

The Frankfurt school's overwhelming interest in superstructure and culture derived from numerous sources in addition to Nietzsche. Nevertheless its analysis of the philistine, dehumanizing, and leveling nature of modern mass culture possessed an indelible if updated Nietzschean

94. Herbert Marcuse, *Soviet Marxism: A Critical Analysis* (New York: Columbia University Press, 1958), 228–229.

95. Horkheimer remarks that Nietzsche's means to achieving his Übermensch society, especially his stress on eugenics, were a result of his own isolation ("Bemerkungen zu Jaspers," 409). Nietzsche's ideas on socialism and the classless society were formed by his exposure to the Social Democrats, not to Marx. He did not, Horkheimer wryly commented, so badly misjudge the Social Democrats!

96. Theodor Adorno, *Minima Moralia: Reflections from Damaged Life,* trans. E. F. Jephcott (London: NLB, 1974), 15.

stamp.[97] There was too a Nietzschean element in the determined aestheticism and individualism—rather than class-centered nature—of critical theory. "If art 'is' for any collective consciousness at all," Marcuse opined, "it is that of individuals united in their awareness of the universal need for liberation—regardless of their class position. Nietzsche's *Zarathustra* dedication 'Für Alle und Keinen' [For All and None] may apply also to the truth of art."[98]

Together with the critique of mass culture and aestheticism went a certain sympathy for Lebensphilosophie. It represented, Horkheimer argued, a genuine protest against advanced capitalism with its inexorable leveling of individual existence and growing rigidity of abstract rationalism. The Frankfurt school, unlike Lukacs, made distinctions between various kinds of irrationalism. They sought to identify useful critical potentials amongst these doctrines and separate these from reactionary versions. Nietzsche's vitalism was an example of the former, and the Lebensphilosophie of the 1930s, designed to reconcile people to the irrationality of the prevailing order, an example of the latter.[99]

Moreover, the Frankfurt school's awareness of the breakdown of the moral and epistemological certainties of the Western tradition and its central insight into the "dialectic of enlightenment" owed much of its acuity to Nietzsche. He most radically applied the subjective relativism and perspectivism of the Enlightenment and turned it against the Enlightened subject.[100] Critical theory radicalized this even further by applying it in an undifferentiated manner to the dark totalitarian experiences of the 1930s and 1940s: Stalinism, fascism, and American consumer capitalism. Critical theory considered itself an overall *Ideologiekritik,* conceived as "an enlightenment of enlightenment"[101] and

97. This link has been forcefully argued by George Friedman (*The Political Philosophy of the Frankfurt School* [Ithaca, N.Y., and London: Cornell University Press, 1981], chap. 3). Such analyses of the Frankfurt school also incorporated socioeconomic and capitalist factors more than Nietzsche did.

98. Herbert Marcuse, *The Aesthetic Dimension: Toward a Critique of Marxist Aesthetics* (Boston: Beacon, 1978), 31.

99. Max Horkheimer, "Materialismus und Metaphysik," *Zeitschrift für Sozialforschung* 2, no. 1 (1933), 3–4; "Zum Rationalismusstreit in der gegenwärtigen Philosophie," *Zeitschrift für Sozialforschung* 3, no. 1 (1934), 9. Jay notes that in regarding "the irrationalism of the thirties basically as an ideology of passivity, Horkheimer neglected its dynamic and destructive sides, which the Nazis were able to exploit" (*Dialectical Imagination,* 48–49).

100. Nietzsche, *Beyond Good and Evil,* 44; *Genealogy of Morals,* 3, 24. Maurer has a sustained analysis of this issue ("Nietzsche und die kritische Theorie," 36).

101. Ibid.

radically critical of culture criticism! Adorno was obsessed with the ironic, inner dynamic of these processes.[102]

Despite these influences, the Frankfurt school also voiced a certain critical ambivalence toward Nietzsche (most clearly expressed in the *Dialectic of Enlightenment*). This ambivalence served as a reminder of the Marxist origins of critical theory. In this mood Nietzsche remained, despite all, a bourgeois philosopher unable to recognize the importance of society in his analyses, and one who did not develop sufficiently his insights into the dialectic.[103] Horkheimer's materialist yet respectful 1935 critique clearly exemplifies this argument:

> The only great spirit who, in the face of the gross thickening of this fog which has taken place since the middle of the last century, has achieved the freedom from illusion and the comprehensive view which are possible from the standpoint of the big bourgeoisie, is Nietzsche. It must indeed have escaped him that the intellectual honesty with which he was concerned did not fit in with this social standpoint. The reason for the foulness against which he fought lies neither in individual nor national character, but in the structure of society as a whole, which includes both. Since as a true bourgeois philosopher he made psychology, even if the most profound that exists today, the fundamental science of history, he misunderstood the origin of

---

102. Adorno wrote:

Among the motifs of cultural criticism one of the most long-established and central is that of the lie: that culture creates the illusion of a society worthy of man which does not exist; that it conceals the material conditions upon which all human works rise, and that, comforting and lulling, it serves to keep alive the bad economic determination of existence. This is the notion of culture as ideology, which appears at first sight common to both the bourgeois doctrine of violence and its adversary, both to Nietzsche and to Marx. But precisely this notion, like all expostulation about lies, has a suspicious tendency to become itself ideology. This can be seen on the private level. Inexorably, the thought of money and all its attendant conflicts extends into the most tender erotic, the most sublime spiritual relationships. With the logic of coherence and the pathos of truth, cultural criticism could therefore demand that relationships be entirely reduced to their material origin, ruthlessly and openly formed according to the interests of the participants. For meaning, as we know, is not independent of genesis, and it is easy to discern, in everything that cloaks or mediates the material, the trace of insincerity, sentimentality, indeed, precisely a concealed and doubly poisonous interest. But to act radically in accordance with this principle would be to extirpate, with the false, all that was true also, all that, however impotently, strives to escape the confines of universal practice, every chimerical anticipation of a nobler condition, and so to bring about directly the barbarism that culture is reproached with furthering indirectly. In the cultural critics after Nietzsche this reversal of position has always been obvious: Spengler endorsed it enthusiastically. But Marxists are not proof against it either. (*Minima Moralia*, 22; see also 18, 38–39, 43–44).

103. For an enumeration of these criticisms see Pütz, "Nietzsche im Lichte der kritischen Theorie," 187ff.

spiritual decay and the way out, and the fate which befell his own work was therefore inevitable.[104]

Evaluations of critical theory and its Nietzschean connection, of course, differ drastically. Some like Maurer have accused it of lacking the courage of its Nietzschean convictions. For Maurer, Nietzsche represents the ultimate antiutopian whose *Ideologiekritik* sets everything into question including the muffled utopianism of the Frankfurt school. In this view Nietzsche remains more consistently radical than critical theory.[105] This, in a sense, may illuminate George Friedman's comment that the Frankfurt school was "too Nietzschean without being Nietzschean enough."[106] For other critics the problem with critical theory was not an insufficiency but rather a hopeless overdose of Nietzsche. As J. G. Merquior has recently put it:

> Underlying most of Adorno's subsequent ideal of a negative dialectic was the shadow of Nietzsche, the master of misology, i.e., of the attack on logic and reason. In his *Genealogy of Morals* (1887) Nietzsche contended that "only that is definable which has no history"; now, as has been noticed, Adorno tried to make the same point about society, the medium of history. Consequently he denied himself the stability of a conceptual grasp of social structure and cultural process. Therefore his negative dialectic lacked not only direction but even content, in [Siegfried] Kracauer's shrewd remark.[107]

It is instructive that in Jürgen Habermas's endeavor to reconstruct socialist humanism, a respectful criticism of the Frankfurt school has been combined with a fundamental rejection of its Nietzschean component.[108] This relates above all to Habermas's search for a coherent rationality that the Frankfurt school—succumbing to the Nietzschean temptation—had conspicuously failed to provide: "Horkheimer and Adorno . . . surrendered themselves to an uninhibited

---

104. Max Horkheimer, "On the Problem of Truth," in *The Essential Frankfurt School Reader*, ed. Andrew Arato and Eike Gebhardt, intro. Paul Picone, 407–433 (New York: Continuum, 1985), 442.

105. Maurer, "Nietzsche und die kritische Theorie," 46–49.

106. Friedman, *Political Philosophy*, 300.

107. Siegfried Kracauer, *History: The Last Things Before the Last* (New York: Oxford University Press, 1969), 201. It had already been recognized in Gillian Rose, *The Melancholy Science: An Introduction to the Thought of T. W. Adorno* (London: Macmillan, 1978), 22, 24. See J. G. Merquior's scathing *Western Marxism* (London: Paladin, 1986), 134.

108. Jürgen Habermas, *Autonomy and Solidarity*, ed. Peter Dews (London: Verso, 1986). The critique of both Nietzsche and the Frankfurt school is stressed in Habermas's attempt to go beyond them (pp. 49, 103, 133, and chap. 6). This is most substantially analyzed in his *The Philosophical Discourse of Modernity*, trans. Frederick Lawrence (Cambridge: MIT Press, 1987).

scepticism regarding reason, instead of weighing the grounds that cast doubt on this scepticism itself."[109]

Twenty years ago, Habermas commended Nietzsche's linkage of "knowledge and interests," without accepting the philosopher's inclination to psychologize such connections and radicalize skepticism to encompass all knowledge, especially the most refined conceptions of reason. This was *Ideologiekritik* that went well beyond its traditional, redeeming functions. "Nietzsche carried to its end the self-abolition of epistemology inaugurated by Hegel and continued by Marx, arriving at the self-denial of reflection."[110] For Habermas this was no longer dialectic of enlightenment but simply a form of late bourgeois irrationalism; he has of late updated his conviction to include the most recent "Nietzscheanisms" manifested in neo-Heideggerianism, Foucaultian poststructuralism and Derridean deconstructionism.[111]

Despite Habermas's efforts, it is dubious whether at this late stage of postmodernist consciousness Nietzsche can indeed be simply written out of radical, leftist, or even Marxist formations.[112] He is certainly at the justifying center of current French radical conceptions of culture characterized by heterogeneity, an emphasis on play and laughter, pluralism, contradiction, desire, *difference,* and a belief that the erosion of belief in a stable and unified truth constitutes a form of liberation.[113]

---

109. Jürgen Habermas, "The Entwinement of Myth and Enlightenment," in *Philosophical Discourse.*

110. Jürgen Habermas, *Knowledge and Interests,* trans. Jeremy J. Shapiro (Boston, 1971), 290.

111. Nietzsche is an all-pervasive haunting presence in Habermas's response to the current Nietzschean "irrationalist" wave contained in *Philosophical Discourse.* Although Habermas places Adorno in Jacques Derrida's and Michel Foucault's company (all employed "a playful–subversive element of a critique of reason which is conscious of its own paradoxical self-referentiality"), Adorno still "remains true to the idea that there is no cure for the Enlightenment other than the radicalized Enlightenment itself." See Habermas, *Autonomy and Solidarity,* 157–158.

112. This is the burden of James Miller, "Some Implications of Nietzsche's Thought for Marxism," *Telos* 37 (Fall 1978). There are, of course, Marxists who persuasively resist this syncretism.

> The daringly "radical" recourse to Nietzsche turns out to land one in a maturely liberal Democrat position, wryly sceptical but genially tolerant of the radical antics of the young. . . . What is at stake here . . . is nothing less than the dialectical relation of theory and practice. For if practice is defined in neo-Nietzschean style as spontaneous error, productive blindness, or historical amnesia, then theory can of course be no more than a jaded reflection upon its ultimate impossibility. (Terry Eagleton, "Capitalism, Modernism, and Postmodernism," in *Against the Grain: Selected Essays* [London: Verso, 1986], 137).

113. Prominent representatives of this trend include Gilles Deleuze, Derrida, Jean Lyotard, and Foucault. For an example of the Nietzschean component of this thinking see

Like so many other Nietzschean projects their political pedigree is elusive. While Habermas has denounced these currents as forms of political irrationalism, they have variously been pronounced as post-Marxist continuations of leftist radicalism, as nihilist anarchism, and even as conservative quietism incapable of envisaging even the possibility of meaningful change.[114]

The often-confused attempt to combine Nietzsche with Marx still continues, but as far as the organized socialist movement of the left is concerned, the Nietzschean influence was never central. Although it bore various manifestations and functioned as a protean and re-evaluative irritant, it could not become part of the mainstream.

This was not true for the numerous ideologies of German socialism developed by polemicists of Weimar's radical right. There Nietzsche was pivotal in an attempt by conservative revolutionaries to reappropriate the socialist monopoly from the left and put it to right-wing ends. In this exercise Nietzsche acted as the authoritative counterfoil to Marx and as a prophet who both incarnated and enunciated authentic German Geist and values. The authors of this exercise, of course, ferreted only those images, categories, and metaphors from the Nietzschean storehouse which suited their purpose. They formulated a transfigured conception of socialism which left behind all its Marxist associations. Many of the makers of German socialism regarded only Nietzsche as prophetic and revolutionary enough and capable of providing the armory of necessary concepts, the idiom of heroic struggle and power, to give shape to an attractive and modern counterconception of socialism.

Although there were differing strands in the German Nietzschean socialism of the right, a few basic commonalities can be identified. It too had to indulge in casuistry. Nietzsche's hatred for social goals, wrote one commentator early in the Nazi period, was mere foreground. In reality he prescribed a union between socialist strivings and masterful leadership: moreover, he would welcome the fact that the struggle between the classes was over, making way for the tasks of a great politics. In essence he distinguished between "a good and bad socialism. Democracy is socialism elevated to a goal in itself, while for Nietzsche

---

the anthology edited by David B. Allison, *The New Nietzsche: Contemporary Styles of Interpretation* (Cambridge: MIT Press, 1985).

114. See Jay's masterful "Epilogue: The Challenge of Post-Structuralism," in *Marxism and Totality*, 510–537.

socialism is a means, a necessary fundament from which great leaders could erect new peoples out of stratified structures."[115]

These Nietzschean socialisms of the right were enamored with an explicitly irrationalist Lebensphilosophie that depicted the abstract rationalism of Marxism and liberalism as hopelessly unsuited to capturing the authentic sources of life. Since the right was held to embody life, it stood above rational scrutiny. Politics was viewed as essentially an aesthetic matter. Fused with a volitional conception of action, politics became transformed and socialized into a national Nietzschean will to power. This conception of socialism was inextricably tied to the themes and mythology of World War I. It sought to replace the language of class with that of the masculine community at war. This was to be the basis of a new integration of the worker into society for which Nietzscheanism was eminently suited.

In 1919 as a direct response to the German revolution and as an attempt to redefine its goals, Arthur Möller van den Bruck announced the union of Nietzsche and socialism. He first enunciated the bases of this viewpoint in the popular magazine *Illustrierte Zeitung* in an article appropriately entitled "Nietzsche and Socialism." Nietzsche, van den Bruck asserted, had begun to sense that socialism had a positive as well as a negative potential. When socialism was properly understood, it could be the "will to affirmation of life." All revolutions when properly steered could be creative and result in new human powers that could strengthen the nation. This too could be applied to present events. Van den Bruck quoted Nietzsche's prediction (the same one later invoked by Thomas Mann): "One day the worker will live like the bourgeois; but above him, the higher caste characterized by its frugality: thus poorer and simpler, but in possession of power."[116]

Nietzsche's vision, the elitist van den Bruck wrote, was already partially true for the workers. But at this stage of the revolution they had to decide which values to choose: either the materialism of a merely political socialism, or an idealist, "spiritual socialism" whose ethical consequences Nietzsche had made clear.

In 1923, when the threat of a workers' takeover seemed to have waned, van den Bruck published his famous *Das dritte Reich* in which he formulated a less-urgent conception of German socialism and ex-

115. Friedrich Wurzbach, *Nietzsche und das deutsche Shicksal* (Berlin and Leipzig: Deutsches Verlaghaus Bong, 1933), 19–20.

116. Arthur Möller van den Bruck, "Nietzsche und der Sozialismus," *Illustrierte Zeitung* 152, (1919), 233. The Nietzsche quotation is from *Will to Power*, 399.

panded upon his previous ideas. Van den Bruck's socialism combined individualist and corporatist notions of a more open social structure with a massive dose of anti-Marxism and a clearly patronizing view of the working classes he sought to liberate. Nietzsche, van den Bruck insisted, sought to bring new individuals from the proletariat into the nation. Presently they were undeniably without ideals, material people in an economically regulated world who were part of a proletariat that still lived an animal existence. Despite their materialist and amorphous condition, they could be gradually incorporated into the life of the nation through shaping and spiritualization. Was not Nietzsche thinking of worker dignity when he proclaimed: "There must be no relation between pay and accomplishment. Each individual according to his gifts must be so placed that he does the best that is in him to do."[117]

Nietzsche's was a nobler interpretation of communism, van den Bruck declared, for he substituted the leveling idea of equality with that of equality of rights on a higher moral plane. He recognized only one measure of human values and demanded that the proletariat attain it. Van den Bruck's conception of socialism was also inextricably linked to the nation; when workers placed themselves within its framework their actions would be transformed from mere force into creative power. Socialism acquired meaning only when it embraced the whole people and their economic necessities. Worker inclusion was the basis of national regeneration: "This New Socialism must be the foundation of Germany's Third Empire." His socialism began where liberalism and Marxism ended, one that was indissolubly tied to a national regeneration couched in explicitly Nietzschean terms: "The manpower of sixty million," van den Bruck wrote, "must be transformed into the will to power of sixty million. . . . This will is the only thing we can surely count on."[118]

Nietzschean socialists of the right also employed Nietzsche for the analysis of decadence and the road to recovery. Hugo Fischer, an associate of the radical conservative circle around Hans Freyer,[119] commended both Marx and Nietzsche as analysts of the decadence of bourgeois society: nevertheless, Nietzsche was the superior thinker. He had placed decadence at the very center and, unlike Marx, was able to

117. Arthur Möller van den Bruck, *Germany's Third Empire*, trans. E. O. Lorimer, (London: Allen and Unwin, 1934), 151–154. The Nietzsche quotation is from *Will to Power*, 399.
118. Ibid., 76, 136, 221.
119. Jerry Z. Muller, *The Other God That Failed*, 149–150, 288–289.

distinguish between merely symptomatic and real decadence.[120] The socialism of the right was engendered by the search for a healthy, post-decadent, and anti-bourgeois New Man.

Nietzschean values of heroism, struggle, and power were paramount to a solidarity based not on factory lines but on the community of the trenches. Perhaps the most repeated quote emphasizing this form of socialism was Nietzsche's dictum regarding the future of the worker: "Workers should learn to feel like soldiers. An honorarium, an income, but no pay!"[121]

Werner Sombart argued that there was a fundamental distinction between materialistic Marxist socialism marked by a calculating merchant spirit and an idealistic and heroic German socialism that preferred being a lion for the day to being a sheep for the century. It was the antithesis of the labor cult whose whole ideology rested upon a foundation of thorough ressentiment.[122]

This socialism of the right was meant to counter Western hedonism, progress, and utility, values associated with the rejected Marxist and liberal worldviews. These values were to be replaced by a tragic Nietzschean antihistoricist vitalism that would encourage a socialism of duties as well as rights and that stressed sacrifice for a supra-individual goal. Typically this goal was transposed from the international proletariat to the nation.

Not all advocates of some form of national socialism were Nazis. Yet the attempt to reduce the social to the national and vice versa increasingly characterized all segments of the German radical right. As Hitler put it in 1932:

---

120. Hugo Fischer, *Nietzsche Apostata oder die Philosophie des Ärgenisses* (Erfurt: Verlag Kurt Stenger, 1931), 11–17.

121. Nietzsche, *Will to Power*, 399. Strangely, few latched on to the following:

Soldiers and leaders still have far better relationships with each other than workers and employers. So far at least, culture that rests on a military basis still towers above all so-called industrial culture: the latter in its present shape is altogether the most vulgar form of existence that has yet existed. Here one is at the mercy of brute need; one wants to live and has to sell oneself, but despises those who exploit this need and *buy* the worker. Oddly, submission to powerful, frightening, even terrible persons, like tyrants and generals, is not experienced as nearly so painful as is this submission to unknown and uninteresting persons, which is what all the luminaries are. What the workers see in the employer is usually only a cunning, bloodsucking dog of a man who speculates on all misery. (Nietzsche, *Gay Science*, 107).

122. Sombart, *New Social Philosophy*, 72, 81–82. His *Deutscher Sozialismus* typified the trends summarized here. The outlines of this thinking were already contained in his war tract, *Händler und Helden*.

Every true national thought is in the last analysis social. . . . [H]e who devotes himself wholly to his people . . . he who comprehends our great anthem "Deutschland, Deutschland über alles," that nothing in the world stands higher for him than this Germany . . . is a socialist. That was and is the socialism of the Front, of Adolf Hitler, and was and is the socialism of the Steel Helmet.[123]

The various versions of this socialism were able to substitute Prussian for Marxist traditions as constitutive of "true" socialism. Their major socialist virtues were courage, discipline, order, and obedient subordination. Nietzsche provided an updated masculine vocabulary for such values. But even further, he was also able to provide what one commentator described as the dynamic "revolutionary element in socialism" while discarding its "democratic-economic element." What was valuable above all in socialism and in need of diversionary tapping was its revolutionary energy.[124] Moreover, suprahistorical Nietzschean values of life and the will to power were integrated into a socialism that centered on the working classes without explicitly attacking the institution of private property or promising an end to economic inequality.

Nietzschean socialists of the right began their analyses with diagnoses of present decadence, stating that Germany was sinking into a state of hopeless degeneration; only radical, even apocalyptic socialist measures could bring about the required revitalization. The exceedingly popular Oswald Spengler—Nietzsche's "clever ape," as Thomas Mann dubbed him[125]—articulated both these themes.

It is significant that in his first volume of *The Decline of the West* (1918) Spengler combined his analysis of socialism as a cultural phenomenon with the book's only full discussion of Nietzsche.[126] At this stage, Spengler exhibited an ambivalent and critical attitude toward both Nietzsche and socialism. Socialism was portrayed as part of the late Western condition, a universal and ultimate expression of Faustian ethics in its declining and negative stage. Like science, it lacked the creativity of the Faustian ethic as it manifested itself during the high period of Kultur; it was practical, soulless, and lacking all metaphysical qualities. It reduced everything to an external, social character, intolerantly intent on socializing everything into its own mold. As such it was a universal, inescapable part of modernity:

---

123. Adolf Hitler, *Ring*, 30 (1933). Quoted in Sombart, *New Social Philosophy*, 49.
124. Friedrich Mess, *Nietzsche: Der Gesetzgeber* (Leipzig: Felix Mainer, 1930), 216.
125. Mann, "Nietzsche's Philosophy," 94.
126. For an analysis of Spengler's ongoing relationship with Nietzsche see Zumbini, "Untergänge und Morgenröten."

If we allow that socialism (in the ethical, not the economic, sense) is that world-feeling which seeks to carry out its own views on behalf of all, then we are all without exception, willingly or no, wittingly or no, socialists. Even Nietzsche, that most passionate opponent of "herd morale" was perfectly incapable of limiting his zeal to himself in the classical way. He thought only of "mankind," and he attacked everyone who differed from himself. . . . The Nietzschean Zarathustra—though professedly standing beyond good and evil—breathes from end to end the pain of seeing men to be other than as he would have them be. . . .

Socialism—in its highest and not its street-corner sense—is, like every other Faustian ideal, exclusive. . . . When Nietzsche wrote down the phrase "transvaluation of all values" for the first time, the spiritual movement of the centuries in which we are living found at last its formula. . . . It is just this, the general transvaluation, that makes . . . —using the word in a novel and deep sense—socialism.[127]

Nietzsche, wrote Spengler, did not have the courage to draw his own conclusions. It was left to George Bernard Shaw, he claimed, to complete the argument that Zarathustra had been too fastidious to make. His *Man and Superman* and *Major Barbara* gave practical and precise forms to these vague Nietzschean impulses. Shaw pursued Nietzsche's notion of breeding the superman. In doing so he recognized the Darwinian nature of the project; he also perceived that Nietzsche had in essence demanded "the transformation of mankind into a stud-farm." Ironic as it may have seemed, Spengler argued, Nietzsche's master morality with its scheme of systematic breeding—"a completely materialistic and utilitarian notion"—"derived . . . from that source of all intellectual modernity, the atmosphere of the English factory."[128]

Such heady, critical stuff entirely changed the conventional meanings of socialism. Yet already Spengler hinted here at the positive evaluation he would later give to Nietzschean socialism. Frederick William I of Prussia, he declared, was "the prototype of the socialist in the grand sense."[129] Socialism, moreover, was

not a system of compassion, humanity, peace, and kindly care, but one o will-to-power. Any other reading of it is illusory. The aim is through anc through imperialist; welfare, but welfare in the expansive sense, the welfare not of the diseased but of the energetic man who ought to be given *freedom to do*, regardless of obstacles of wealth, birth, and tradition.[130]

127. Oswald Spengler, *The Decline of the West*, vol. 1, *Form and Actuality*, 342, 351.
128. Ibid., 371, 370–372.
129. Ibid., 347.
130. Ibid., 361–362.

Although Spengler did not mention the relevant passage, Nietzsche had indeed outlined a similar conception:

> Socialism is merely a means of agitation employed by individualism: it grasps that, to attain anything, one must organize oneself to a collective action, to a "power." But what it desires is not a social order as the goal of the individual but a social order as a means for making possible many individuals: this is the instinct of socialists about which they frequently deceive themselves.[131]

Spengler's socialism becomes the freedom to rise beyond one's own class and allow the suitably gifted the opportunity to express the will to power. In the second volume of *The Decline of the West* (1922) he went considerably beyond this position. He depicted a cosmic struggle in which capitalism played the role of the destructive money powers. Socialism was instead the hard-working, self-sacrificing, caring servant of the state, "suddenly the focus of immense life-forces."[132] It was, indeed, nothing less than "the will to call into life a mighty politico-economic order that transcends all class-interests, a system of *lofty* thoughtfulness and duty-sense that keeps the whole in fine condition for the decisive battle of its history."[133]

The Decline of the West was, however, a quasi-scholarly tome, and the theme of socialism was apt to get lost in its labyrinthine meanderings. This was not the case with Spengler's 1920 polemic *Preussentum und Sozialismus*. There, socialism becomes simply identical with the Prussian virtues of leadership, courage, discipline, and obedience. These were the keys to the integration of the working class into the wider community and the basis for national regeneration. In this volume Nietzsche is hardly mentioned by name, yet his spirit, language, and values permeate Spengler's vision. Socialism, wrote Spengler, had nothing to do with the contradiction between rich and poor but with the capacity to dominate life:

> I turn to the youth. . . . Become men! We do not need ideologues any more, no speeches of *Bildung* and the spiritual mission of the Germans. We need hardness, we need a fearless scepticism, we need a class of socialist mastermen. Once again: socialism means power, power, and yet again power.[134]

---

131. Nietzsche, *Will to Power*, 411.
132. Oswald Spengler, *Decline of the West*, vol. 2, *Perspectives of World History*, trans. Charles Francis Atkinson (New York: Alfred A. Knopf, 1980), 464.
133. Ibid., 506.
134. Oswald Spengler, *Preussentum und Sozialismus* (Munich: C. H. Beck, 1925), 99.

It was in Ernst Jünger's *Der Arbeiter* (The Worker, 1932) that this tendency found its apotheosis. Jünger's lines between left and right became quite blurred. In the late 1920s, he had expressed sympathy for the Communists and their positive, militant will to power. During the 1930s he became associated with national bolshevism and the search for common ground with Russia against the West. *Der Arbeiter*, that radical attempt to foresee the coming order and rethink the meaning of the worker, was to have been the manifesto of the National Bolsheviks.[135] Precisely because of their capacity for total mobilization and for creating a new order, Jünger could admire both Italian fascism and bolshevism.

Jünger's *Der Arbeiter* took to its limits a radical vision where a novel conception of labor becomes the principle of all of society. In his transmutation of Nietzsche and his peculiar image of nationalized socialism, the worker becomes the center of all life—the very basis of existence and its capacity for regeneration. Yet Jünger's worker in no way resembles the familiar, everyday proletarian. He is a stylized prototype. The worker is regarded not through socioeconomic categories but as a metahistorical type, a deindividualized gestalt. This gestalt had its basis in a kind of aesthetic politics and was beyond good or evil, neither false nor true.[136] Rather, it was a phenomenon comprehensible only in its own terms. One either experienced its dynamic or did not.

In unmistakably Nietzschean language, Jünger's postwar Weimar vision of the future worker society sought to make the Kriegserlebnis part of everyday modern life. The worker and the new order emanated a pure will to power, one that was quite removed from all previous bourgeois expressions. Indeed, the worker represents the antithesis of the bourgeois whose whole project had been to deny the elemental and the dangerous as essential to life. The war, wrote Jünger, had reestablished their centrality and had relegated the bourgeois order to the past. The new order of the future could already be apprehended: "It has become unnecessary to occupy oneself with the transvaluation of values—it is sufficient to see the new and participate in it."[137]

The new age seemed nothing less than the actualization of Nietzsche's exhortation to live dangerously. Jünger without Nietzsche is unimaginable. As he put it in *Das Wäldchen 125:* "Almost everything

135. For details of the National Bolshevik connection see J. P. Stern, *Ernst Jünger: A Writer of Our Time* (Cambridge: Bowes and Bowes, 1953), 10–13.

136. Ernst Jünger, "Der Arbeiter" in *Werke*, vol. 6, *Essays II* (Stuttgart, 1964), 47.

137. Ibid., 61, 26ff, 53ff.

that most strongly moved us . . . we owed to the lonely Nietzsche."[138]
His entire corpus breathes the spirit of Nietzsche, updated in a peculiarly impassioned way. *Der Arbeiter* seemed to herald the Nietzschean
age, a society created in Nietzsche's dynamic and nihilistic image.

Yet Jünger tamed that dynamic by socializing the worker into a
highly disciplined world. He typologized and collectivized his
Nietzschean man and harnessed him to an impersonal national and
industrial framework. Nietzsche was put on the workbench, transforming Zarathustra into a faceless cog in an industrial machine bent on
total mobilization. The primitive and the sophisticated came together in
Jünger's fantasy by making will the mediating force. The sense of power
and discipline were combined through the willed control of technology
and production. Labor was always a key to the totality of things.
Through their elemental capacities and their labor, workers were destined to become the regenerative and ruling force.[139]

The creation of a new humanity was the goal of the worker. This had
nothing to do with classical Marxist ideas. Based upon the principle of
heroic realism, the new order represented the death of the individual
and the rise of the type. Jünger's New Man would not experience
himself as an end but only as a means, a carrier of the elemental will to
power. As in war, where individual character counted for less than
collective, mechanized action, the new age would render individual
character obsolete.[140] The apparatus of the modern industrial state
would be an expression of the worker's will to power.[141]

In this new society, the laws of war and total mobilization were to be
applied to all areas of life and the distinction between combatants and
noncombatants expunged. Freedom was no longer conceived as an expression of individual independence but as an act of becoming part of
the totality. It was a world in which the workers' will to power made
freedom and obedience identical.[142] In the final version of a right-wing
Nietzschean socialism, Nietzsche's individualism was entirely sub-
merged by its postwar brutalization. On the eve of the rise of the Nazis,
both Nietzsche and socialism underwent their ultimate transfiguration.

138. *Das Wäldchen 125: Eine Chronik aus den Grabenkämpfen, 1918*, 3d ed. (Berlin, 1926), 154. I should like to thank Millard Griffin for this reference.
    139. Jünger, "Der Arbeiter," 154.
    140. Ibid., 118ff.
    141. Ibid., 164ff.
    142. Ibid., 159.

DER RIESE
FRIEDRICH NIETZSCHE
«Meine Brüder», sagte der älteste Zwerg,
in Gefahr. Ich verstehe die Attitüde dieses Riesen.
ist im Begriff, uns anzurieseln. Wenn ein Riese
giebt es eine Sandfluth. Wir sind verloren, wenn er
Ich rede nicht davon, in welch affreusem Elemente
da ertrinken.»
«Problem», sagte der zweite Zwerg, «wie
man einen Riesen am Rieseln?»
«Problem», sagte der dritte Zwerg, «wie
man einen Grossen, dass er etwas Grosses gross
«Ich danke», antwortete der älteste Zwerg mit
«Hiermit ist das Problem philosophischer genommen,
Interesse verdoppelt, seine Lösung vorbereitet.»
«Man muss ihn erschrecken», sagte der vierte
«Man muss ihn kitzeln», sagte der fünfte Zwerg.
«Man muss ihn in die Fusszehe beissen», sagte
sechste Zwerg.
«Thun wir Alles zugleich», entschied der Älteste.
sehe, wir sind dieser Lage gewachsen. Dieser Riese
nicht rieseln.»
Turin, 21. April
GROSSEN

1. Ernst Moritz Geyger's illustration of Nietzsche's parable "The Giant" (1895). *Pan* 1, no. 2 (1895/96), p. 91.

2.   Etching by Hans Olde (1899). *Pan* 5, no. 4 (1899/1900), p. 233.

3. Anonymous. Nietzsche with a crown of thorns.
Bookplate for Georg Lapper (ca. 1900). Courtesy of the
Goethe-Schiller Archive, Weimar.

4. Nietzsche writing a testimonial for Bersons. *Die Fackel,* no. 5–6 (January 1914), pp. 391–392.

5. House in Darmstadt by Peter Behrens: vestibule mosaic with four stylized eagles. Tilmann Buddensieg, "Das Wohnhaus als Kultbau," in *Peter Behrens und Nürnberg* (Munich: Prestel, 1980), p. 39. Courtesy of the Germanisches National Museum, Nürnberg.

6.   Bruno Taut, *Alpine Architektur* (Hagen: Folkwang, 1919).

7. Fritz Schumacher, design for Nietzsche Monument (1898). Fritz
Schumacher, *Studien* (Leipzig: Baumgärtner, 1900), table 1.

8.   Arnold Kramer, sculpture of Nietzsche in sick-chair (1898). Exhibition in the renovated Nietzsche archive. In the background is an unknown work featuring Nietzsche with Zarathustrian symbols of the snake and the eagle. Courtesy of Goethe-Schiller Archive, Weimar.

9. Fidus (Hugo Hoeppener), marriage ceremony combined with a Zarathustra citation (1906). *Jugend* 11 (1906), p. 369.

10. Alfred Soder, picture of Nietzsche naked in the mountains. Bookplate for Friedrich Berthold Sutter (1907). Courtesy of the Goethe-Schiller Archive, Weimar.

11. Anonymous. Postcard with vegetarian citation. Woodcut of Nietzsche after Hans Olde (ca. 1900). Courtesy of the Goethe-Schiller Archive, Weimar.

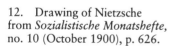

Ich glaube, daß die Vegetarier mit ihrer Vorschrift, weniger und einfacher zu essen, mehr genützt haben, als alle neueren Moralsysteme zusammengenommen.

Nietzsche.

12. Drawing of Nietzsche from *Sozialistische Monatshefte*, no. 10 (October 1900), p. 626.

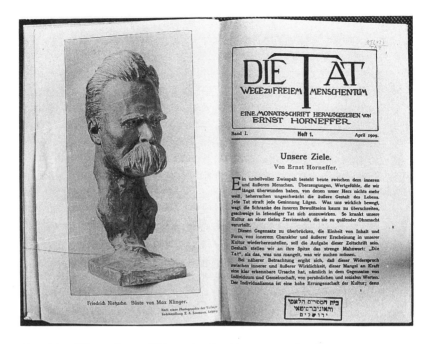

13.   Max Klinger, bust of Nietzsche. *Die Tat* I, no. 1 (April 1909).

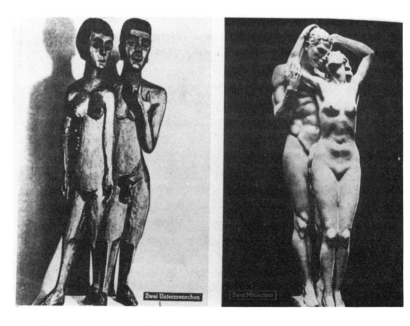

14.   "Two Subhumans" (*Untermenschen*) and "Two Humans." *Der Untermensch* (Berlin, 1942).

15. Hitler next to a bust of Nietzsche, 1934. Courtesy of the Goethe-Schiller Archive, Weimar.

16. The eighty-eight-year-old Elisabeth Förster-Nietzsche receiving Hitler at the entrance of the Nietzsche archives. Courtesy of the Goethe-Schiller Archive, Weimar.

17. "The Return of a Philosopher: Nietzsche the Thinker, Hitler the Perpetrator." Cover of *Der Spiegel* 35, no. 24 (8 June 1981). Courtesy of *Der Spiegel: Das Deutsche Nachrichten-Magazin*.

CHAPTER VII

After the Death of God

Varieties of Nietzschean Religion

> And how many new gods are still possible! As for myself, in
> whom the religious, that is to say god-forming, instinct
> occasionally becomes active at impossible times—how
> differently, how variously the divine has revealed itself to
> me each time! . . . Is it necessary to elaborate that a god
> prefers to stay beyond everything bourgeois and rational?
> And, between ourselves, also beyond good and evil?
>
> Nietzsche, *The Will to Power*

It is a commonplace that Nietzsche and his disciples were key contrib-
utors to a fundamental crisis of Christian faith in Europe from the
nineteenth century onward.[1] No one, however, has as yet charted the
complex ways in which generations of Nietzscheans simultaneously
sought to surmount that crisis by redirecting and regenerating the religious impulse rather than obliterating it. The creation of a number of
alternative counterreligious conceptions constituted an essential ingredient in the assimilation of Nietzscheanism into European, especially
German, culture. Our task here will be to present an anatomy of these
surrogate faiths, to place them within an ideological context, and to
examine some of their political implications in Germany from the 1890s
through the Third Reich.

Nietzscheanism was part creator and part beneficiary of a general
erosion of traditional belief and dissatisfaction with the established
church. For many this dissatisfaction, far from quenching the thirst
for religion, gave it renewed impetus. In fin-de-siècle Germany there

---

1. The classic exposition of this crisis of the "Bourgeois-Christian world" is in Karl
Löwith, *Von Hegel zu Nietzsche: Der revolutionäre Bruch im Denken des neunzehten
Jahrhunderts* (Zürich: Europa, 1941). Translated as *From Hegel to Nietzsche: The
Revolution in Nineteenth Century Thought,* trans. David E. Green (New York: Holt,
Rinehart and Winston, 1964).

were diverse attempts to either rejuvenate or graft a self-consciously secular form upon religious consciousness. The growing discredibility of dogma and the resultant spiritual loss—exacerbated by the process of rapid and intense industrialization—spawned a multitude of reformist tendencies (both within the Church and without), naturalist religions, and occult and mystic societies.[2] Many of these had a crackpot, fringe quality about them,[3] but they pointed to the existence of new configurations of faith in which the religious and the political realms increasingly intermingled. The forms and content of these alternative religions were inevitably eclectic and, like other areas of Nietzschean endeavor, blurred traditional lines of political demarcation. Acolytes of the new cults, groping for new forms of spiritual self-representation, were thus often ideologically ambiguous and politically mobile.[4]

The fact that those in search of religious faith often took their inspiration from the most radical of all atheists was an irony that typified Nietzsche appropriation. Nevertheless, the construction of Nietzschean religiosity was never entirely arbitrary—plausible projections could be selectively mined from the master's works, as the opening quote of this chapter demonstrates. The death of God, Nietzsche argued in places, did not necessarily presage the age of nihilism and the end of religion as such. "It seems to me that the religious instinct is indeed in the process of growing powerfully—but the theistic satisfaction it refuses with deep suspicion."[5]

Those who sought a religious Nietzsche could find allusions throughout his work.[6] The very language and style of *Also sprach Zarathustra* (by consensus one of the great lyrical achievements in the German tongue) breathed the biblical spirit.[7] The religious dimension, of course, far transcended matters of language and style. It informed Nietzsche's

2. For an overview of these groups, see Roy Pascal, "Religion and the Churches," chap. 7 in his *From Naturalism to Expressionism*.

3. For a marvelously insightful satire depicting the charlatan, Nietzschean, and demonic character of these groups, see Thomas Mann's 1904 story, "At the Prophet's," in his *Stories of Three Decades*, trans. H. T. Lowe-Porter (New York: Alfred A. Knopf, 1936). For the later period see Ulrich Linse, *Barfussige Propheten: Erlöser der zwanziger Jahre* (Berlin, 1983).

4. Between 1880 and 1910 dozens of free-thought organizations sprang up. In 1909 they coalesced into the Weimar Cartel, claiming as many as 60,000 members. Given their vast differences, little came from the coalition (Kelly, *The Descent of Darwin*, 91ff).

5. Nietzsche, *Beyond Good and Evil*, 66.

6. For a discussion of Nietzsche's views on religion, see Dieter Henke, *Gott und die Grammatik: Nietzsches Kritik der Religion* (Pfullingen: Günther Neske, 1981).

7. *Zarathustra*'s religiosity accounts too for the unofficial consecration during World War I of that work as a holy national document, which was made official in the Third Reich when it was placed in the vault of the Tannenburg Memorial.

entire project. His insistence on the creation of new tablets, his elevation of Dionysian divinity in direct juxtaposition to (and at the end, in combination with) the crucified, his doctrine of eternal recurrence, and his vision of the Übermensch as an earthly inheritor of the old God, all encouraged Nietzschean religious constructions.

These constructions spanned the politico-ideological spectrum. Nietzschean religious themes appeared in various left-wing guises, inspiring the imagery of countless neoromantic and völkisch groupings as well as purportedly apolitical spiritualist, literary, and intellectual circles.

For all the variety, some basic elements made up most Nietzschean religions. All fostered a humanist Nietzschean universe of voluntarism, will, vitalism, myth, and heroism. All sought to disseminate to different Christian or post-Christian constituencies a regenerative sensibility in which Nietzsche was the central presence.

The dissemination began in a startling way. The escapades of Nietzschean religion in Germany began as a force *within* the faith, seeking to revitalize not to destroy Christianity! Essentially a Protestant phenomenon, it was spearheaded by a number of critical but committed pastors and theologians who invoked the Nietzschean religious impulse in the struggle to revive the authentic Christian message.

We know how most Christians viewed Nietzsche. Was he not the man who had savaged their faith and defined himself as the antichrist? Much of his infamy derived from his ruthless condemnation of Christianity as a life-negating force and fount of an ongoing and debilitating ressentiment slave morality. In place of the effeminate, decadent ethics of Christianity which had poisoned the innards of Western civilization, he proposed an immoralist world beyond good and evil.

Not unexpectedly many Christians responded in kind. Nietzsche, they argued, was an immoral man advocating doctrines that were blasphemously anti-Christian and socially dangerous. His proclamation that God was dead and that all was now permitted possessed demonic dimensions. His teachings, like his mind, were insane, destructive, and diseased.[8]

There were, however, significant others who dissented. At a time of great inner malaise, a number of Protestants found the Nietzschean

8. For a differing overview of Nietzsche's reception in theology, see Peter Köster, "Nietzsche-Kritik und Nietzsche-Rezeption in der Theologie des 20 Jahrhunderts," *Nietzsche-Studien* 10/11 (1981/1982), 615–685; Joelle Phillipi, "Das Nietzsche-Bild," chap. 9, "Nietzsche als Feind der Religion und der Moral."

language of regeneration and life-affirmation particularly appealing. Protestantism, itself the product of a break with a powerful normative tradition, had always been especially receptive to external, modern influences. This capacity for innovation notwithstanding, the incorporation of Nietzsche into Christianity demanded even more than the usual casuistry. The numerous attempts testify to the attraction of the Nietzschean vision and shed some light on the extremes of Protestant self-representation since the 1890s.

As early as 1896 the theologian Hans Gallwitz provided Protestantism with a clear Nietzschean thrust. For him, Nietzsche's manly, warrior values were not only worthy of emulation but also constituted the heart of original, authentic Christianity. The masculine, heroic virtues of Nietzscheanism and "real" Christianity were virtually indistinguishable. So close were they, indeed, that Gallwitz (writing in that bastion of respectable German opinion, the *Preussiche Jahrbücher*) propagated "Friedrich Nietzsche as Educator towards Christianity."[9]

If one penetrated the "paradox" of Nietzsche's thinking and arrived at the core of his ethics, Gallwitz proclaimed, one would discover that Christ and the antichrist had advocated the same values and truths. Armed with quotes from the New Testament and the Nietzschean one, Gallwitz demonstrated the affinity. In this exegesis Christ was metamorphized into a Nietzschean. The savior's own conduct was characterized by the equation of goodness with feelings of power while the bad was identical with weakness. When Christ proclaimed (in Matthew 10:34): "Do not think that I have come to bring peace on earth; I have not come to bring peace, but a sword," he was fully in accord with the Nietzschean vision. Their commonalities were there for all to see: both had sought to awaken their exhausted age with new life energy; both had loved truth; and their affirmation of self and distaste for cowardice bound them together.

Of course Nietzsche had been wrong in his assessment of Christianity; it was not at all a pitiful ressentiment religion. Far from fostering egalitarianism and sickly mediocrity, original Christianity had posited recovery from a false, sterile reality to one based on nature, strength, and beauty. Paul's attack on pagan reason and Jesus's scorn for pharisaic legalism, in Gallwitz's view, were akin to earlier versions of Nietzsche's Lebensphilosophie, part of the return to the Sinn der Erde.[10]

9. Hans Gallwitz, "Friedrich Nietzsche als Erzieher zum Christentum," *Preussische Jahrbücher* 83/84 (1896).
10. Ibid., 336.

In an age where manliness was increasingly identified with normalcy and national definition, Gallwitz's attempt to refashion Christianity in terms of a Nietzschean ethic of power, heroism, and masculinity becomes more comprehensible.[11] Outraged Catholic critics regarded this Nietzscheanization of Christianity as a reflection of the Protestant condition. Lacking any mission and bereft of authority, it was quite understandable that Protestants would begin to regard themselves as Übermenschen. This overturning of traditional morality for a vitalism which produced a creature beyond sin and to whom nothing was forbidden was radically evil.[12]

There were other ways in which the attempt to Nietzscheanize Protestantism—and to Protestantize Nietzsche—proceeded. There was a growing recognition of Nietzsche's indispensability as a critic who raised issues of fundamental importance for modern culture. Protestants who borrowed from Nietzsche usually did so as part of their critical sense of the Protestant condition. They applied the neoromantic language of decadence and regeneration to their own Christian predicament. Nietzsche's role was here conceived as lulling Christianity out of its deceptive sleep, alerting it to its own situation and shortcomings, and thus paving the way towards a more authentic, rejuvenated religiosity. Nietzsche was harnessed to Protestantism in crisis.

In order to do this effectively, Nietzsche required a legitimate pedigree. The philosopher, a Protestant critic wrote in 1900, could teach Christians important lessons because his whole life was suffused with spirituality.[13] His pietist background, his lifelong engagement with theological issues, and his own unswervingly religious nature made him an important source for modern Christians. Nietzsche's purported atheism betrayed a palpable yearning for faith: had not Zarathustra cried out that God himself had converted him to Godlessness?[14] Nietzsche's countermessage of eternal recurrence was unacceptable to Christians, the Nuremburg pastor F. Rittelmeyer declared, but his message remained profoundly religious. Was not his invocation of a correspon-

11. Mosse, *Nationalism and Sexuality*.

12. G. Grupp, "Nietzsches Bedeuting für unsere Zeit," *Historisch-politische Blätter für das katholische Deutschland* 122 (1898); Adelbert Düringer, *Nietzsches Philosophie und das heutige Christentum* (Leipzig: von Velt, 1907).

13. Eduard Grimm, "Wie wurde Friedrich Nietzsche ein Feind des Christentums, und was können wir von ihm lernen?" *Protestantische Monatshefte* 4, no. 7 (1900).

14. Eberhard Arnold, "Nietzsches Ringen um Gott," *Der Geisteskampf der Gegenwart: Monatsschrift für christliche Bildung und Weltanschauung* 52, no. 10 (1916), 380.

dence between thought and being an implicit admission of belief in a "hidden God" who brought order to the world?[15]

In appropriating Nietzsche, Protestants followed the familiar pattern employed by all who yoked the philosopher to a particular cause: the real, the deep Nietzsche had to be discovered. Thus, as the theologian Theodor Odenwald insisted, a true Christian harnessing of Nietzsche entailed differentiating it from the myriad of shallow, sensationalist cults surrounding him. Nietzsche, he argued, could not be exploited as a symbol of a general anti-religiosity; his negation of Christianity flowed from his yearning for it. Indeed, Nietzsche was comprehensible, Odenwald delighted in arguing, only in "that totality of European spirituality that was always bound up with Christianity." In Nietzsche's system of thought the Catholic, Protestant and mystic streams of Christian experience all found their place.

This domestication of Nietzsche into an expression of the European religious intellectual tradition served an important function. Once integrated, Nietzschean goals could be legitimately pursued. Odenwald could thus fuse Christianity into the overall process of transvaluation (*Umwertungsprozess*). Nietzsche could be a central figure inspiring Christianity's own transvaluation process, its struggle to treat faith in worldly terms, and its move from dogma and fixed forms to an emphasis on dynamic deeds. Nietzsche's confrontation with Christianity, Odenwald insisted, was one with "our struggle for a new understanding of Christianity." Nietzsche's quest for regeneration had to become normative for those concerned with the future of a viable religion. His struggle against his own time and the Christianity of his age constituted "the anticipation of our own struggle, Nietzsche's inner tension, from which his spirit sprang, is our tension."[16]

The most influential and active purveyor of Nietzsche in the Protestant church was the colorfully idiosyncratic Bremen pastor Albert Kalthoff (1850–1906).[17] As one critic discerned, here was a man, supposedly serving an evangelical community, who subversively smuggled Nietzsche and Nietzscheanism into the Church.[18] The critic was referring to Kalthoff's series of addresses that he gave to his congregation

15. Friedrich Rittelmeyer, *Friedrich Nietzsche und die Religion: Vier Vorträge* (Ulm: Heinrich Kerler, 1904), 88.

16. Theodor Odenwald, *Friedrich Nietzsche und das heutige Christentum* (Giessen: Alfred Töpelmann, 1926), 17, 23.

17. On Kalthoff's career see Friedrich Steudel, "Lebensskizze," in A. Kalthoff, *Zukunftsideale* (Jena, 1907).

18. Düringer, *Nietzsches Philosophie*, 150.

and which he published under the title *Zarathustra Sermons*.[19] Kalthoff talked wherever possible to working-class audiences. Although he remained within the Protestant fold, his activities resembled those free-religious preachers fashionable in the 1890s who founded congregations outside the Church.

Kalthoff's eclectic thinking and career were symptomatic of those seekers attracted to Nietzschean religion in one form or another. He fused monism, socialism, and Nietzscheanism without too much anguish. Like other Nietzscheans, he dissented from mainstream positions and indulged in a free-floating radicalism that expressed itself through heretical positions. Given their Marxist bent, his writings on Christianity created sensations. The primitive Church, he wrote, had given the world "the widest communist manifesto ever framed" while Jesus had never in fact existed. He was rather the mythical embodiment of the needs and desires of the underclasses of the ancient world.[20]

Kalthoff's Marxist-based rejection of Jesus was linked to Nietzschean vitalist antihistoricism. A man who had lived in another historical period could not be made into an absolute law for one's own time. Those who looked to the past for salvation, Kalthoff asserted, were misguided. Only future-oriented solutions that merged religious consciousness with the imperatives of modern life would bring deliverance. Like most Nietzscheans, he adumbrated the myth of the man as an integral part of redemptive Nietzschean ideas. Nietzsche, Kalthoff wrote, was the embodiment of his age and its possibilities, its disease, and potential for recovery. Consciously or not, Kalthoff proclaimed, "we all carry part of him within us."[21]

The Church could appropriate its greatest enemy, Kalthoff held, once it realized that this thinker had "more morality, this antichrist more Christianity than those who blaspheme him."[22] The basis for the recovery of Christianity was the recovery of its original radicalism. Primitive Christianity had shared with Nietzsche such a radical drive. It too had transvalued all the old values of faith and morality. Had Christianity remained true to itself it too today would have been dissatisfied with the divine, it too would have become a "conspirator of the future."

19. Albert Kalthoff, *Zarathustrapredigten: Reden über die sittliche Lebensauffassung Friedrich Nietzsches* (Leipzig: Eugen Diederichs, 1904).
20. Albert Kalthoff, *Entstehung des Christentums* (Jena, 1904); James Bentley, *Between Marx and Christ: The Dialogue in German-Speaking Europe* (London: Verso, 1982), 36–41.
21. Kalthoff, *Zarathustrapredigten*, 4.
22. Ibid., 9.

Kalthoff formulated an explicitly modern religious sensibility virtually interchangeable with Nietzschean categories. It had to be liberated from the shackles of debilitating history. Free individual appropriation, not external proscription, was the way to both a positive life and an affirmative Christianity in which the Church too would become free. Following Nietzsche's example, the new religion would have to be entirely "untheological, unchurchly" and take its stand "beyond belief and unbelief." It would emerge not out of sterile scholasticism but from the creative sources of one's own life.

Most dissenting fin-de-siècle ideologies projected their positive visions onto an idealized New Man of the future. Kalthoff found his model in a Nietzscheanized Protestant Übermensch who would incarnate a new religious consciousness affirming the interconnectedness of the world and overcoming the fragmentation of bourgeois-commercial society. The new person would achieve an integrity that went beyond the usual individualist or socialist categories.[23]

Kalthoff's Nietzsche—the prophet of this new man and new culture—was emancipationist. Nietzsche had foreseen a culture that promised the realization of the still-unfulfilled potential of a free humanity. This new Christianity would take on an essentially Nietzschean shape, positing humanity its goal, beauty as its form, and life as its law, creating eternity in the present.

Like many other progressive Nietzscheans Kalthoff integrated what we today view as a more problematic eugenic element. His new Protestant sought a world "in which everything unliving, unfree, dying, weakly, and sick in man is eliminated."[24] Here was a Christian utopia with subversive premises designed to render older conceptions of Christian morality and action outmoded. It sought to inculcate into Protestant life a vitalist, Lebensphilosophie aesthetic that would overturn the "sterile, life-negating ethics" of scholastic Christianity.

The harmonization of Nietzsche with Protestantism took on a more clearly defined political direction, however, when the Nietzschean impulse became selectively integrated into that part of the völkisch movement concerned with the construction of a specifically Germanic form of Christianity. Nietzsche thus became a force in the wider nationalist annexation and redefinition of religion.

Nietzsche was by no means an obvious candidate for sainthood in

23. Albert Kalthoff, *Die Religion der Modernen* (Jena and Leipzig: Eugen Diederichs, 1905), 88, 310.
24. Kalthoff, *Zarathustrapredigten*, 19–20.

the thrust to create a Germanic Christianity. He appeared, after all, to
oppose both the Germanic and the Christian components. Paul de Lagarde was a far more likely champion.[25] Yet Nietzsche, assuming increasing cultural authority, expressed enough useable and inspirational
themes to become part of that pantheon. His unmatched radical critique
of contemporary culture, his emphasis on the play of mythical and
irrational forces, and his concern with vital, regenerative impulses appealed to central figures in the Christian völkisch revival.

Key popularizers, such as Arthur Bonus, infused Germanic Christianity with a Nietzschean texture that they did not always fully acknowledge. Germanic religion, Bonus declared, opposed the Jewish–Greek
emphasis on knowledge. It was instead predicated upon the centrality of
shaping and creating (*Schaffen*). It was concerned with the individual
and with the freedom of the personality; its very essence was contained
in the Nietzschean title of one of Bonus's books, *Religion as Will*.[26] The
basis, Bonus argued, for the Germanization of Christianity was masculine. This nationalization of religion would replace the old, timid, and
cowardly spirit of Christianity with that of a "courageous, just, and
free" Germanism (*Deutschtum*).

Bonus, to be sure, was critical of various Nietzschean notions.
Nietzsche's Übermensch was informed by an essentially Roman worldview. The German alternative, embodied in Dietrich of Bern, represented a quite different ideal.[27] But even if he questioned the content of
the Übermensch ideal, the idea remained central and was integrated into
a conception of religion where Nietzschean will was the primary loco-
motive. Indeed, Bonus's almost taken-for-granted, pre-reflective use of
Nietzschean categories and terms for his own purpose marked the depth
of Nietzsche's impact.

Bonus's Übermensch construction buttressed his own point of view.
Inverting the accepted understanding of the term, he argued that it was
really only the Übermensch who could engage in a proper relationship
with God. Far from being the incarnation of the breakdown in belief,
his Übermensch now became the exemplar of authentic belief! For Bo-

25. On de Lagarde see Fritz Stern, "Paul de Lagarde and a Germanic Religion," part
1 in *The Politics of Cultural Despair: A Study in the Rise of Germanic Ideology* (Berkeley
and Los Angeles: University of California Press, 1961), 3–94.

26. Arthur Bonus, *Religion als Wille: Grundlegende zur neuen Frömmigkeit* (Jena:
Eugen Diederichs, 1915). These ideas were given some impetus by World War I but they
had developed some time before. See Bonus's series of articles on the Germanization of
Christianity in *Die christliche Welt: Evangelisches Gemeindeblatt für Gebildete aller
Stände* 13 (1899).

27. Bonus, *Religion als Wille*, 106.

nus, Luther and Ernst Moritz Arndt represented such a human type. "The German Christian," Bonus wrote, "does not fear even the most boisterous Übermenschen. Overflowing with defiant strength he feels himself an Übermensch and because of that loves and fears God, whom he knows has given him strength."[28]

This emerging faith entailed a new moral-religious determination designated by Bonus as an "unbending will to power" that would create the disposition to experience God as an ally rather than as an enemy. Germanic Christianity would be based not on fear but on feelings of power and strength.[29] Even God in this view was invested with Nietzschean characteristics. There had to be a symmetry, Bonus declared, between the personality of the Germans and the God they worshipped. They would either discover a strong and free God who in turn would make them strong and free or they would turn entirely from him. German atheism was thus not godless. It was, rather, only rent from that God who willed slavish self-renunciation and who denied the power of will and creative this-worldly affirmation.[30]

All these religions had to channel Nietzsche's potentially anarchic notions of will, vitalism, immoralism, and individualism into manageable sociopolitical and intellectual frameworks. The adherents of a völkisch Germanic Christianity did this by placing the Nietzschean dynamic within the bounds of the nation. Interestingly, this provided room for both the expression and the containment of the radical drive.

The Germanic Christian Nietzsche was linked to his general domestication, as typified by Karl Joel's *Nietzsche and Romanticism.* As he put it, Nietzsche's life work was a sustained expression of conscience, written as the "inheritor of German religiosity of the millennia."[31] Mirroring his nationalization, the Germanic Christian Nietzsche became ever more dominant as a result of World War I. The consecration of Zarathustra as a holy national book went together with commentaries like Paul Schulze-Berghof's describing the "metaphysical ether of Zarathustra" as fully in tune with German mystic Christianity.[32]

Völkisch circles often argued that such a German mysticism provided access to a higher reality beyond superficial reason and mechanistic

28. Arthur Bonus, "Der neue Geist," *Die christliche Welt* 13 (1899), 173.
29. Arthur Bonus, *Zur Germanisierung des Christentums* (Jena: Eugen Diederichs, 1911), pp. 66–67.
30. Bonus, "Der neue Geist," 173.
31. Karl Joel, *Nietzsche und die Romantik* (Jena: Eugen Diederichs, 1911), 143.
32. Paul Schulze-Berghof, "Zarathustra—Deutsche Mystik—Deutscher Glaube," *Der Vortrupp* 5 (1916).

Enlightenment thinking. Schulze-Berghof not only assimilated Nietzsche into that tradition but also recast that mysticism into fundamentally Nietzschean molds. Thus the great German mystic Jakob Böhme
(1575–1625), like Nietzsche, had denied the absolute distinction between good and evil. He too had affirmed life in all its wild beauty.
Indeed, even before Böhme, Schulze-Berghof maintained, the mediaeval
mystic Meister Eckhart (1260–1327) had in Nietzschean fashion located divine creativity within humanity. German Christian mysticism,
Schulze-Berghof wrote, unlike biblical religion, recognized that human
powers constituted the basis of redemption. Nietzsche had to be understood as the apotheosis of this tradition. His ideal of the Übermensch
was an expression of this emphasis on the godly humanity.

The process linking Meister Eckhart with Nietzsche, another commentator wrote, was part of the unfolding secularization of God or the
deification of man.[33] This fostered a far deeper religiosity characterized
by a love for the dangerous which sought to come to grips with life-
in-itself. Those who formulated such a Nietzschean Germanic Christianity, then, did not divert the Nietzschean dynamic into quietistic mystical forms. They tried rather to tap its "revolutionary" implications
while channeling this neo-irrationalism within the nationalist frame for
völkisch purposes.

Not surprisingly, Ernst Bertram made full use of the Nietzschean
religious theme in his war-associated, mythmaking *Nietzsche*.
Nietzsche's religious problematic, according to Bertram, was central to
his whole project. The great man was a "believing doubter, . . . a
God-seeking blasphemer," and "an extraordinary phenomenon within
the history of Nordic Christianity."[34] Here Nietzsche even becomes an
integral part of Church history. Hero of the Volk, he was the climactic
expression of all its positive, immanent forces. Or, at least, everything
in Nietzsche that was creative and good derived from his "Lutheran,
reformational, Nordic, Romantic heritage." Intoxicated though he may
have been with the classical and southern worlds, Bertram wrote,
Nietzsche's entire ethical impulse flowed from his Nordic Christianity.
He was the last and quintessential expression of Protestantism.

The Lutheran and Zarathustrian heritages, Bertram proclaimed,
were opposed in superficial, external ways; at a deeper level there was
a profound inner relationship. Who more than Nietzsche exemplified

33. Joseph Bernhart, "Meister Eckhart und Nietzsche," *Blätter für Deutsche Philosophie* 3, no. 4 (1930).
34. Bertram, *Nietzsche*, 8, 53.

protest? An examination of his work would demonstrate, moreover, that this great atheist had by no means completed his odyssey with Christianity. Was not his paradoxical vision of Dionysius on the Cross evidence? Nietzsche's life and work was nothing but "the last fulfillment of an eternal Nordic yearning for a Yes-saying Christianity." The eternal Dionysian Yes of the recurrence teaching was of Pascalian, not Greek, origin. It was the Yes of the Christian to an endlessly prolonged wager and an ever-renewed self-overcoming. Both the man and his thoughts were legendary representations of a faith which assumed external betrayal but which in fact constituted a saving of the divine through the murder of God, at least in his Eastern-Jehova aspect.[35]

In Bertram's view, if Nietzsche incarnated the conflict between the Socratic, individualist, and destructive drives on the one hand with the prophetic, communitarian, and mystic will on the other, he also glimpsed their resolution, his own being elevating these antinomies into a higher transpersonal reality.[36] Ultimately Bertram's Nietzsche assumed mythical, even Christlike dimensions.

Clearly, not all those involved with the Nietzschean religious impulse confirmed the death of God. Those who enunciated the numerous shadings of a Protestantized Nietzscheanism sought not to bury but to resuscitate the Christian God and to provide him—and his followers—with a transvalued face etched with Nietzschean features. These exercises typically were made possible only by uncovering his deeper, hidden essence. In this way Nietzsche was co-opted as a crucial agent of Protestant regeneration, which had a double effect. It integrated Nietzsche as a respectable part of German culture and tradition while allowing the purveyors of this current to facilitate the seepage of radical and irrationalist ideas into various Protestant forums.

Nietzsche performed a crucial function precisely because there was a sense of crisis and because he seemed to provide both the appropriate diagnosis and means for recovery. These Protestant circles were indeed living refutations of Nietzsche's own dictum that: "All the possibilities for a Christian life, the most single-minded and the most superficial, the silliest and the best thought out, have been tried out: it is time to discover something new."[37]

Nietzschean Christians were overwhelmingly Protestant, but some Catholics also felt the temptation. We have already mentioned the case

35. Ibid., 125–135.
36. Ibid., 280–363.
37. Quoted in Löwith, *From Hegel to Nietzsche*, 327.

of Max Scheler. The Munich bohemian Ludwig Derleth and his circle
provides perhaps the most exotic example. Derleth proposed the creation of a latterday Übermensch monastery.[38] This, of course, was not
intended to be an ordinary community. His 1904 *Proclamations* envisaged a new world-renouncing, elite order based upon a strong Caesarian principle in which a strict dichotomy between leader and followers would obtain.[39] The Caesarian principle was important, as Derleth
regarded himself as the realization of Nietzsche's definition of the Übermensch as "the Roman Caesar with Christ's soul."[40] Munich wags did
not take Derleth seriously and made up verses about the "Jesus
Bonaparte!"[41] Nevertheless, his *Proclamations* earnestly advocated a
transvaluation of values on Christian soil and the creation of a Dionysian Catholicism.[42] One contemporary described Derleth as "a religious
Catholic with Nietzschean ideas! His dream was to reform and purify
the church and to shape a new theocracy in which he himself would
occupy a high position."[43] Idiosyncratic as they may have been, Derleth's activities demonstrated that even believing Catholics were not
entirely immune to the Nietzschean temptation.

The other side of Nietzschean religion was concerned with those who
accepted Nietzsche's onslaught against Judeo-Christianity while seeking
to recapture the redemptive impulse outside of traditional supernaturalism and the familiar modes of monotheistic religion.

By no means all of the post-Christian surrogate faiths that had mushroomed since the 1890s amongst scientific monists, anarchists, socialists
of various hues, neoromantic prophets of national cultural regeneration,
naturalists, bohemians, and völkisch racists were Nietzsche inspired.
Yet, as one avant-garde journal put it, Nietzsche's work was particularly
satisfying to the contemporary longing for a genuine religiosity that
transcended conventional denominational and confessional religion.[44]

38. Hubert Treiber, "Nietzsches 'Kloster für freiere Geister,'" in Antes and Pahnke,
Die Religion von Oberschichten, 149–150.
39. Ludwig Derleth, *Die Proklamationen* (Leipzig: Insel, 1904). See too Krummel,
Nietzsche, vol. 2, 182–183.
40. Nietzsche, *The Will to Power,* 513.
41. H. Kreuzer, *Die Boheme: Beiträge zu ihrer Beschreibung* (Stuttgart, 1968), 334.
42. Dominik Jost, *Ludwig Derleth: Gestalt und Leistung* (Stuttgart, 1965), quoted in
Krummel, *Nietzsche,* vol. 2, 183, n. 156.
43. Pieter van der Meer de Walcheren, *Heimweh nach Gott* (Freiburg i.Br: Herder,
1937), 52, 58ff, 93. Quoted in Krummel, *Nietzsche,* vol. 2, 183, n. 156.
44. Hans von Liebig, "Nietzsches Religion," *Die Umschau* 4, no. 42 (13 October
1900); H. Driesmans, "Friedrich Nietzsche und die Religion," *Ernstes Wollen* 6, no. 113
(1 August 1904).

For the many emergent harbingers of renewed spiritual meaning, those "barefoot prophets" of the time, Nietzsche could fulfill a variety of functions. Most such prophets disappeared into obscurity, although some achieved enduring fame, such as Rudolf Steiner (1861–1925). His anthroposophy has been so attractive because it appears to democratize spiritualism by removing its initiate quality. Steiner argued that the supersensible, spiritual world behind the material world was as real as the material world and that it was generally accessible through simple training. Nietzsche, as Steiner's biographer Colin Wilson has noted, would hardly have countenanced this notion of separate but equally real physical and metaphysical worlds.[45] Steiner was nevertheless powerfully drawn to the philosopher, working for a time at the Nietzsche Archives (and inevitably wrangling with Förster-Nietzsche).[46] In Nietzsche the young Steiner probably perceived himself.[47] The title of his early, full-length work on the master described equally well his self-conception and sense of mission: *Friedrich Nietzsche, A Fighter against His Time.*[48] Steiner regarded Nietzsche as both critic and visionary, a man who like himself understood that people created their own realities and had foreseen the future of human existence devoid of religious illusions.

Steiner's encounter with the ill philosopher in Naumberg confirmed everything he had previously intuited about the nature of the spiritual world; Nietzsche embodied its deeper truth:

45. Wilson, *Rudolf Steiner*, 18, 86–90. Wilson's account of Steiner is sympathetic.

46. The power of the attraction is evident in the huge amounts of published writings beginning already in 1892 that Steiner devoted to Nietzsche, including: "Nietzsche-anismus," *Litterarischer Merkur* 12, no. 14 (2 April 1892), 105–108; "Nietzsche in frommer Beleuchtung," *Das Magazin für Litteratur* 67, no. 33 (20 August 1898), 769–772; "Tolstoi und Nietzsche," *Das Magazin für Litteratur* 70, no. 45 (1901), 1068–1071. A more complete list can be found in both volumes of Krummel's *Nietzsche*. On his conflict with Förster-Nietzsche, see "Das Nietzsche-Archiv und seine Anklagen gegen den bisherigen Herausgeber: Eine Enthüllung," *Das Magazin für Litteratur* 69, no. 6 (10 February 1900), 145–158; "Frau Elisabeth Förster-Nietzsche und ihr Ritter von komischer Gestalt," *Die Gesellschaft* 16 (May 1900), 197–212.

47. Steiner's admiration did not last long. Perhaps because he had prophet-like aspirations, he wrote very critical, psychologizing pieces on Nietzsche, arguing that Nietzsche could not be the leading spirit for the future. Some of these writings are collected in *Friedrich Nietzsche ein Kämpfer gegen seine Zeit* (Dornach: Rudolf Steiner, [1895] 1983): "Die Philosophie Friedrich Nietzsches als psychopathologisches Problem"; "Friedrich Nietzsches Persönlichkeit und die Psychopathologie"; and "Die Persönlichkeit Friedrich Nietzsches." Steiner's anthroposophic followers were even more convinced that it was not Nietzsche but Steiner who was the real inheritor of the future (Diana Beckenhaupt, "Nietzsches Sehnsucht nach einem neuen Menschheitsführer," *Die Drei* 10 [1930], 352–370, 430–445; Beckenhaupt, *Nietzsche und das gegenwärtigen Geistesleben* [Leipzig, Strassburg, Zürich, 1931]).

48. Steiner, *Nietzsche ein Kaempfer*.

The inner shock I experienced led to what I can only describe as an insight into the genius of Nietzsche whose gaze, though directed towards me, did not meet mine. The very passivity of this gaze, resting upon me for a long time, released my inner comprehension. . . . In inner perception I saw Nietzsche's soul as if hovering over his head, infinitely beautiful in its spirit-light, surrendered to the spiritual worlds it had longed for so much but had been unable to find before illness had clouded his mind. . . . Previously I had *read* Nietzsche. Now I saw the actual bearer of ideas from the highest spirit realms, ideas that even here shone in their beauty despite having lost their original radiance on their way. A soul who had brought from former lives on earth golden riches of great spirituality but was unable to let it shine fully in the present life. I admired what Nietzsche had written; now I saw his radiant spirit behind what I so greatly admired.[49]

The various cults and surrogate faiths of the time were linked to a widespread perception that the age was particularly empty, materialistic, and despiritualized. Many defined their projects as directly Nietzschean in nature, responses to the famous proclamation that God was dead. These post-Christian Nietzschean faiths have been labeled "religious atheism," "secular polytheism," and "pan-cosmic religion without transcendence."[50] However one defines them, they abounded in number and demonstrated an adaptability to a range of divergent political and cultural tendencies.

Even where Nietzsche came under bitter attack his categories formed the basic assumptions of discourse for progressive intellectuals in search of new forms of religiosity. Julius Hart's *The New God* provides an excellent example.[51] His analysis of the crisis and supersession of Christianity, his construction of a New Man to replace the old divinity, his emphasis on dynamic becoming and human creativity, and his style were all, as a contemporary critic hastened to point out, inseparably part of the Nietzschean heritage.[52]

The content of Hart's new religion, however, was at times defined in explicit contradistinction to Nietzsche. Like Nietzsche Hart rejected Nazareth, but he also decisively dismissed Hellas. Nietzsche, Hart argued, was backward-looking while the new religion had to be dynamic, progressive, and based on a unifying, pantheistic principle. This was, Hart claimed, the very opposite of the Dionysian principle that, far

49. Cited in Wilson, *Rudolf Steiner*, 87–88.
50. Lukacs, *Destruction of Reason*, 362; Miller, "Some Implications of Nietzsche's Thought for Marxism," 30; Pannwitz, *Einführung in Nietzsche*, 9–13.
51. Julius Hart, *Der neue Gott: Ein Ausblick auf das kommende Jahrhundert* (Florence and Leipzig: Eugen Diederichs, 1899).
52. Richard Meyer, review of Julius Hart's *Der neue Gott*, in *Deutsche Literaturzeitung*, no. 14 (8 April 1899).

from uniting God, nature and humanity, stood for chaos and negation. Nietzsche's Übermensch in addition represented the "southern Aryan" principle of ruthless egoism, which was antithetical to the "northern Aryan" or Germanic morality that free and joyful spirits possessed. These men would create a blooming, harmonious culture, rather than a Nietzschean wasteland, in which the strong would not dominate but sustain the weak. Ironically, Hart's northern Aryans replicated the Nietzschean ideal. They were men of deeds, "men of will, happy in struggle and work, affirming Life and Earth . . . sensing its tragedy but overcoming it."[53] The new culture would overcome the fragmentation of the nineteenth century and replace it with constant creativity and transformation.

The Nietzschean influence was palpable. Hart declared, "Why do you seek the thing in itself and then declare it inscrutable, unfathomable? You are the thing in itself! You are God—the hub of the universe—the center of the sun—the core of matter—substance!"[54] Paul Mendes-Flohr has demonstrated that this was in essence a Dionysian–Heraclitean outlook culled from Nietzsche.[55] Through the notion of eternal flux Hart, like Nietzsche, sought to overcome the debilitating duality of the world by fusing unity and multiplicity. In the recognition of the infinite fluidity of the world itself, as in the vision of the eternal recurrence, unity and plurality became as one. In Hart's vision, this in no way implied a passive stance:

> You should know that you are not created spirits, but rather you are creating spirits. . . . We are always nature, and in that we create, we reveal and disclose the essence of matter—and the wine of substance flows into the goblets of creative forms (*Gestalten*). . . . In that we [create], we need not seek truth, for we are truth.[56]

Hart's views reflected those of the Neue Gemeinschaft, an intellectual circle he founded with his brother Heinrich. Here was a group of searching, radical, bourgeois intellectuals imbued with the desire to refound a meaningful community outside of conventional liberal, Marxist, or Social Democratic paths. They blended their inchoate long-

53. Hart, *Der neue Gott*, 92.
54. Hart, "Der neue Mensch," *Das Reich der Erfüllung* 2 (1901), 21. Quoted in Mendes-Flohr, *From Mysticism to Dialogue*, 56.
55. See Mendes-Flohr's excellent discussion of the Hart brothers, the Neue Gemeinschaft, and Nietzsche in chap. 3, "Buber's *Erlebnis*-Mysticism," in *From Mysticism to Dialogue*.
56. Hart, "Der neue Mensch," 27. Quoted in Mendes Flohr, *From Mysticism to Dialogue*, 57.

ings for Gemeinschaft with a receptivity to Nietzsche and the antipositivist, neoromantic currents of the time. Many of the group's associates (which included the anarchist Erich Mühsam and the Zionist Martin Buber) had vague leftist instincts that combined with a humanist völkisch nationalism. What united them and gave their activities a clearly Nietzschean tinge—which they couched in self-consciously liberational terms—was their insistence on dynamic process and the centrality of each individual's self-determining role as creator.

One member of this circle was the socialist, völkisch anarchist Gustav Landauer.[57] His anarchistic communitarianism incorporated elements of a left-leaning, humanist, Nietzschean religious vision. We have already discussed the outlines of Landauer's Nietzscheanism. Here we must merely emphasize the centrality of religion and will to Landauer's vision. God, wrote Landauer, was not an external, transcendental being but rather the goals that people set for themselves. The God we believe in is the "God we want to become and will become."[58] This was nothing if not a clear appropriation of the Nietzschean Übermensch mission combined with a conception of religion as an active, transformative process of constant becoming.

Landauer was also attracted to the Nietzschean call for myth as an energizing factor of culture and history. His socialist anarchism thus incorporated elements of Nietzsche's skeptical epistemology, a perspectivism, that expelled objective truth. New and self-created illusions, Landauer wrote, were preconditions for the constant revitalization of human activity. Whereas the Marxist tradition emphasized demystification, Landauer's Lebensphilosophie of the left posited illusion as the rejuvenating principle of social life. In words resonant with Nietzsche's proclamation in *The Birth of Tragedy* on the renewing capacity of myth, Landauer wrote: "Illusion—an idea in which we believe, a holy goal—has up to now created the spell of all *Vöelker*, of all *Kultur*."[59]

While Landauer harnessed the Nietzschean religious impulse to enunciate a clearly non-Marxist socialism, Ernst Bloch employed it as one necessary current for the salvaging of the Marxist tradition. Bloch insisted that the mythical, mystic, and religious dimensions all had a legitimate place in that tradition. This Marxist metaphysician with his

57. Landauer considered the Hart brothers superficial, interested in empty word games, and their search for community rhetorical rather than a genuine search for living alternatives (Lunn, *Prophet of Community*, 142–147).

58. Gustav Landauer, "Die religiöse Jugenderziehung," *Freie Bühne* (February 11, 1891). Quoted in Lunn, *Prophet of Community*, 32.

59. Landauer, *Skepsis und Mystik*. Quoted in Lunn, *Prophet of Community*, 160.

messianism of "forward hope" and his visions of "a strangely vibrant and explosive eternity"[60] was obviously drawn to Nietzsche for at least part of his apocalyptic dream. Within his system, Nietzsche, Dionysius, and Christian heresy combined to form a powerful message of potential human redemption:

> The true "Antichrist" in the Dionysian sense, of the Escrit sicut Deus ["You will become like God," Gen. 3:5], is—Jesus. This is "Dionysus, the crucified one," it is on this that the only realization insists, from the depths of Christian heresy, and in fact of the oldest, "ophitic," snake-informed one, which does justice to the "resurrection and the life." This Christ is the preacher of an unknown human glory. . . . He is the conquest of the human glory even behind the smallest and most unexpected window, and precisely there, precisely in the paradox of the utterly unexpected, not in the contented measure of the already appeared, ruling, and satiated into which the Church has falsified and defused him. The Jesus of the heretics . . . in this image of Jesus there is also the life of Dionysus or the draught of a kingdom which is neither of this (become) world nor of that (far from human, fateful) one. Such allusions and "ophitic" memories, hostile to St. Paul, suppressed in the history of "victorious" Christianity, were highest of all in Nietzsche's last visions, in "Dionysus, the crucified one."[61]

But the idiosyncratic visions of intellectuals like Bloch and Landauer were not likely to have a major impact on organizations. There were other circles, however, that actively sought to instill Nietzschean religion in the socialist movement. This innovative thrust was not limited to Germany.

In fact, in Russia between 1903 and 1913 the most elaborate form of Nietzschean socialist religion emerged in the left-wing of the Bolshevist faction of the Marxist Russian Social Democratic party. This counter-faith, as formulated by Maxim Gorky (1868–1936) and Anatoli Vasilyevich Lunacharsky (1875–1933), bore the unmistakably Nietzschean name of *God-building*.[62]

Gorky and Lunacharsky argued that socialism should harness the positive and creative aspects of historical religion while jettisoning what socialists regarded as ideologically false. In socialist religion traditional supernaturalism would have no place, but followers would retain a

60. Quoted in George Steiner, "Sojourns in the Wondrous," *Times Literary Supplement* (4 October 1985), 1087.
61. Ernst Bloch, "The Impulse of Nietzsche," *Heritage of Our Times*, 331.
62. George L. Kline, "The 'God-Builders': Gorky and Lunacharsky," chap. 4 in his *Religious and Anti-Religious Thought in Russia* (Chicago and London: University of Chicago Press). I am grateful to Prof. Jonathan Frankel for this reference.

sense of communion with the world and incorporate the yearning for self-transcendence.[63]

There was a clear Feuerbachian element here, but the collectivized Nietzschean dimension was both explicit and seminal. God was to be replaced by a self-conscious and creative humanity, the individual Übermensch transmuted into a Marxist *Übermenschentum*. The true creator of God was the proletariat and the revolution was regarded as a fundamental emancipationist act of God-building. Lunacharsky proposed an act of faith in the self-created collective future in which the working class became "a co-participator in the life of mankind, a link in the chain which stretches towards the overman, towards a beautiful creature, a perfected organism."[64]

Lenin, needless to say, rejected these approaches: "The Catholic priest who seduces young girls is far less dangerous than a priest without a frock . . . a democratic priest who preaches the building and creating of God."[65] His centralism and hard-boiled emphasis on social engineering brooked none of this neoromantic fantasy. Therefore, after 1917 few traces of Nietzschean God-building remained in the new Bolshevik order.

Clearly, all socialist Nietzschean religions were also expressions of dissent. In Germany, the closest equivalent to a fully developed Nietzschean socialist religious alternative came from Max Maurenbrecher who created what amounted to a revisionist socialist Nietzschean religion and who, as we have seen, sought to spread the word to working-class, free-thinking congregations.

His most systematic formulation of this theology appeared in *Das Leid* (1912). Like other advocates of a nontranscendental Nietzschean religiosity, Maurenbrecher argued for both the redefinition and retention of the creative essence of religion. For Maurenbrecher, religion was essentially tragi-Dionysian, inextricably tied to the human condition of pain and suffering. Life, in all its hardness, he argued in clearly Nietzschean terms, had to be lived and loved.[66] The test of authentic religion was its ability to creatively transform suffering into active joy, into an affirmation of life in all its fullness. Maurenbrecher explicitly

---

63. See Leszek Kolakowski's succinct analysis of the God-builders in his *Main Currents of Marxism*, vol. 2: *The Golden Age*, trans. P. S. Falla (Oxford and New York: Oxford University Press, 1985), 446–447.

64. Kline, *Religious and Anti-Religious Thought*, 119.

65. Ibid., 124.

66. Max Maurenbrecher, *Das Leid: Eine Auseinandersetzung mit der Religion* (Jena: Eugen Diederichs, 1912), 5–6.

juxtaposed facile Enlightenment optimism with his religion couched in a tragically affirmative Lebensphilosophie.

In this view churchly religion had lost its capacity for authenticity. What was now at issue was which religion was most suited to satisfactorily replace it. The measure of authenticity was also conceived in quasi-Nietzschean terms. The age of axiomatically accepted tradition, Maurenbrecher declared, with its objective, historical, and communal character, had dissolved. Now, self-conscious individuals had to appropriate beliefs that were consistent with obviously Nietzschean standards: "Every myth, every ethic, every cult has significance for us, only as it leads us towards the shaping and energy of our will to life."[67] Only a myth or religion freely chosen and personally lived could be valid in the twentieth century. Informing such choices, Maurenbrecher declared, was a new, secular tradition: the thought of men like Goethe, Spinoza, Marx, and Nietzsche. They had achieved the great insight that struggling human beings were themselves the goal of life.[68]

Nietzsche occupied a special role in this religion partly because of his heroic transcendence of Schopenhauerian pessimism. The socialist dimension of such affirmation was linked to the fact that pessimism could never be transcended fully when regarded purely as a private, individual matter, but only "when we regard the social process as the real content and essence of all that happens."[69] Technology, science, and organization had provided the basis for hope in a better future for which one could now work. Existence now had a will.

For all that, Maurenbrecher warned, suffering and tragedy were inevitable, part and parcel of development itself. One could escape suffering by denying willing and becoming, but, as a Nietzschean voluntarist, Maurenbrecher dismissed such an alternative. Instead, he argued, the affirmation of suffering, allowing life to develop, constituted the true transcendence of pessimism. Unlike the first generation of socialists, Maurenbrecher proclaimed, the new generation understood that their hopes of instant utopia would have to be deferred, that the process of social transformation would last a long time.

This socialist religion, Maurenbrecher emphasized, required no sacraments, churches, priests, or holy places. It needed rather a Nietzschean heroic mode and the daily exercise of will. The new breed of socialist, far from experiencing the end of suffering, would "not want

67. Ibid., 9.
68. Ibid., 133.
69. Ibid., 168.

to experience it, either for himself or for some conceivable future for humanity, because for him suffering is none other than the precondition for creative strength and growing will."[70]

We have already noted Maurenbrecher's political and religious mobility and his usage of Nietzsche as an inspirational guide within all these guises. His Nietzsche, however, consistently stressed suffering and hard values, which clearly facilitated Maurenbrecher's transference from left to right. Prior to World War I, to be sure, his post-Christian Nietzschean religious reflections had been noticeably free of völkisch content (for which he was castigated by fellow Nietzschean neopagans).[71] Still, all his other biases pointed to the masculine, hard Nietzsche. His socialist emphasis on the need to breed the Übermensch could be reconciled equally with radical-right and with socialist notions.[72] That same masculine, antiliberal postrationalist Nietzsche accompanied Maurenbrecher when he returned to the Protestant church. His sermons to his Dresden congregation—perhaps a trifle apologetically after his years of godlessness—restated these themes but now very much in the nationalist Protestant Nietzschean idiom with which he began.[73]

Maurenbrecher's Nietzschean religion had either allied socialism with radical anti-Christianity or advocated völkisch nationalism in tandem with a regenerated Protestant piety. He never articulated a religion that was simultaneously nationalist, anti-Christian, and avowedly pagan. This nationalist pagan turn was significant, and some variations were later associated with a Fascist and National Socialist outlook.

Prior to World War I, it was around Die Tat (established in 1909), that fount of neoromantic thought, that this nationalist pagan tendency was most systematically advanced. The Die Tat circles were associated with the doyen and publisher of the fin-de-siècle neoromantic revival, Eugen Diederichs.[74] A writer and activist, Diederichs advanced the ideas of diverse groups interested in national regeneration, especially in its religious and spiritual forms. Indeed, he published many of

70. Ibid., 182.

71. Ernst Horneffer, "Die Deutschen und die Religion: Eine Ergänzung und Entgegnung," *Die Tat* 2, no. 7 (1910).

72. Max Maurenbrecher, *Christentum oder Monismus* (Annaberg i. Sa: Grasers, 1914), 10.

73. Max Maurenbrecher, *Offenbarung: Eine Probepredigt* (Langensalza: Wendt and Klauwell, 1919); Maurenbrecher, *Über Friedrich Nietzsche zum deutschen Evangelium: Gottesdienste Andachten und religiöse Auseinandersetzungen* (Dresden: Verlag Glaube und Deutschtum, 1926).

74. On Diederichs see Stark, *Entrepreneurs of Ideology*.

the Nietzscheans discussed here: Kalthoff, Bonus, Maurenbrecher, Joel, Julius Hart, and others. Diederichs had no doubt that Nietzsche constituted an inspiring, prophetic presence for these spiritual purposes.[75] Imbued with the mystic and mythical realm, indeed, the force and role of the "irrational" itself, Diederichs's ideas fused völkisch themes with an almost dazzling variety of "creative" cultural and religious regenerative projects.[76] His own un-Christian metaphysical ideas were adopted by the enthusiastic youth who formed the Sera circle in Jena and who, under the publisher's guidance, engaged in heathen rituals, celebrated the changing of the sun, reveled in pseudoclassical settings, and indulged in wild Dionysian dance.[77]

It was, however, the brothers August and Ernst Horneffer—fervent Nietzscheans and editors at the Nietzsche Archive—who were the foremost champions of a neopagan Germanic Nietzscheanism.[78] In their hands, *Die Tat*'s Nietzsche was decisively heroic, simultaneously the scathing critic of a fragmented and decadent bourgeois culture and a prophet who promised its overcoming on the basis of a new and higher

75. Eugen Diederichs, "Sils Maria und Friedrich Nietzsche," *Berliner Tageblatt* (8 August 1906); see too his autobiographical comments in his festschrift, *Eugen Diederichs: sein Leben und sein Werk* (Leipzig: Eugen Diederichs, 1927).

76. On Diederichs's völkisch posture and connections see Mosse, *Crisis of German Ideology*, chap. 3. For a different, more sympathetic perspective, see Hinton Thomas, *Nietzsche in German Politics*, 116ff, and Green, *Mountain of Truth*. The scathing reflections of Theodor Adorno from 1945 provide yet another angle:

> One need only glance through the books published by Eugen Diederichs or those of a certain kind of cantingly emancipated theologian. The vigorous vocabulary makes one wonder about the fairness of these wrestling bouts arranged and contested by inwardness. The expressions are all taken from war, physical danger, real destruction, but they describe mere processes of reflection, which may indeed have been connected with a fatal outcome in the cases of Kierkegaard and Nietzsche, whom the wrestlers are fond of quoting, but certainly not in their unsolicited followers, who claim to be at risk. While they take the credit twice over for sublimating the struggle of existence—for their intellect and their courage, they neutralize the element of danger by internalization, reducing it to an ingredient in a complacently rooted, hale and hearty *Weltanschauung*" ("Wrestling Club," in *Minima Moralia*, 133–134).

77. Mosse, *Crisis of German Ideology*, 59–60.

78. For the history of the Horneffers' relationship to the Archive, see Peters, *Zarathustra's Sister*, 168–169. Their writings on Nietzsche were legion. Here is a small sample: both brothers published *Das klassische Ideal: Reden und Aufsätze* (Leipzig: J. Zeitler, 1906) in which Nietzsche is prominent; August Horneffer, *Nietzsche als Moralist und Schrifsteller* (Jena: Eugen Diederichs, 1906); Ernst Horneffer, *Nietzsches Lehre von der Ewigen Wiederkunft und deren bisherigen Veröffentlichungen* (Leipzig: C. G. Naumann, 1900); *Vorträge über Nietzsche: Versuch einer Wiedergabe seiner Gedanken* (Göttingen: Franz Wunder, 1901).

totality. The lost classical unity of form and content would again be captured.[79]

It is no coincidence that *Die Tat*'s premier issue, subtitled "Paths to a Free Humanity," featured a heroic bust of Nietzsche by Max Klinger on its frontispiece (illus. 13).[80] The Nietzschean drive was explicit, but so too was the drive to frame him within social and national form. As Ernst Horneffer (1871–1945) posited, Nietzsche was to be the cornerstone of religious and cultural renewal, but his one-sided individualism had to be overcome. The realization of genuine Nietzschean values required a collective framework: "The detached individual whose values and aspirations find no echo in the greater whole," he wrote, "is not the strong but the weak individual."[81] This new, "strong" individual would be self-determining and appropriate a personal religion, but within a larger, meaningful whole.[82]

In his "Pagan Life Course" August Horneffer made the nationalist, masculine nature of the new religion even more explicit.[83] The state was the proper basis for the proposed neopaganism, he argued, because it believed not in God but in itself and, unlike organized Christian religion, its activities were earthbound. Nietzsche's invocation to remain true to the earth was possible only when anchored in community life. The community that Horneffer envisaged had Nietzschean contours. It would be a community not of "'compassion' for the poor and the sick, . . . not that of Christian neighborly love, but rather the community of creation, brotherhood in arms, and mutual elevation and fructification."[84] It was thus only within a special community that the Nietzschean vision could be realized. Seldom was the socialization of Nietzsche into the German *Männerbund* tradition, that predilection for male friendship and association, more clearly spelled out.

In his *Religion of the Future*, Ernst Horneffer laid bare the underpinnings of his worldview.[85] Europe, he proclaimed, had been alienated

---

79. It should be pointed out that *totality* permeated the rhetoric of the neoromantic right. Although the notion lacked the rich theoretical nuances it had on the left (as Martin Jay has shown in his *Marxism and Totality*), it was a prime evocative category for the right as well. Again Nietzsche was the authoritative formulator of this idea and the counterfoil to Marx.

80. *Die Tat: Wege zu Freiem Menschentum* 1, no. 1 (April 1909), 2.

81. Ernst Horneffer, "Unsere Ziele," *Die Tat* 1, no. 1 (April 1909), 2.

82. Martin Green distinguishes nicely between Diederichs's support for individuality and his opposition to individualism (*Mountain of Truth*, 220). This distinction applied equally well to the Horneffers and others whom Diederichs supported.

83. August Horneffer, "Der heidnische Lebensweg," *Die Tat* 3 (1911–1912).

84. Ibid., 30.

85. Ernst Horneffer, *Der künftige Religion* (Leipzig: Werner Klinkhardt, 1909).

by Christianity. Matching Nietzsche's withering scorn, Horneffer declared that Christianity, far from molding the European spirit, constituted its very violation. Only recently through secular philosophy was Europe beginning to discover itself after a long process of self-estrangement.

For Ernst Horneffer, again echoing Nietzsche, the genuine European spirit resided in the Greeks. Their emphasis on movement, change, and freedom stood in marked contradistinction to Oriental, and therefore Christian, immobility, stagnation, fatalism, and fanaticism. Only slowly were Europeans awakening to their own inner truth. Luther had freed the layman from the yoke of the priests and the external compulsion of the Church while he had retained the idea of divine revelation. Kant had greatly furthered the process by freeing moral law from religious faith, arguing that faith was instead dependent upon the categorical imperative. But Kant still held that morality remained a self-sufficient law of reason, its content set.[86]

With Nietzsche, Ernst Horneffer wrote, the European revolution of ethics was accomplished and the struggle for theoretical and practical freedom was realized. This was Nietzsche's historical deed: he had provided the conditions by which men could forge their own ideals in accordance with their own nature. People could now form and follow their own morality, determining the content of the law out of their own free will. Nietzsche was the last and most radical German "liberator of conscience" (*Gewissenbefreier*).[87]

Ernst Horneffer's Nietzschean—a self-determining creator of an unshackled naturalistic morality—thus appeared to radically unleash the dynamic while placing it clearly under national control. The turn away from organized religion, he argued, did not leave one in a void. For in the construction of an alternative, the materials were to be found in "the great creations of our *Volksgeist* . . . the heroic acts, the manifold struggles in which the *Volk* have been put to the test."[88] Such a religion looked upon life as a wager. Essentially pagan and Nietzschean, it was constructed for heroes and the strong, not for cowards, the weak, and the broken who had ruled for too long. Such neopaganism, Horneffer maintained, consisted of the fundamental belief in the self-redemptive capacity far removed from traditional notions of religion.

86. Ibid., 29ff.
87. Ibid., 30.
88. Ibid., 70.

Though willed self-redemption was based upon the Greek example, Ernst Horneffer rendered the Nietzschean will to power subordinate to what he termed the "will to form."[89] The Nietzschean will, Horneffer maintained, could not really affirm joyously when its essence was one of eternal struggle, ceaseless movement, and even mutual enslavement. Such a will willed only its own development, and so was devoid of clarity and order. Form was required which would provide will with a stable framework. The will did have a goal after all: shaping itself into form. It sought to bring unity, sequence, and consequence out of chaos.

This did not necessarily mean that the Nietzschean dynamic was to be tamed or "aestheticized," rather that it would have to be nationally channeled and politically structured. As Horneffer put it: "Only through concentration, ordering, and organization can the will come to its fullest expression, can it fully exhaust itself."[90]

The Horneffers' prewar Nietzschean neopaganism with its radical anti-Christianity, its unshackling of morality from traditional constraints, and its heroic national mode, while integrating older, conventional notions of the *Volk*, also incorporated a modernist thematic similar to futurism. The New Man became part of the nation to the degree that he achieved "personal self-realization" and "self-determining" freedom. This nationalism purportedly aimed at providing space for individuality and personality, Nietzschean priorities.[91] Ernst Horneffer and his successors made sure, however, that these requirements were contained within the framework of the spirit of Germanism. Indeed, when the National Socialists came to power, Horneffer welcomed it as an embodiment of his vision, proclaiming Nietzsche to be the movement's central prophet.[92]

The Horneffers' brand of Germanic religion, however, never took off as an independent movement. With the rise of the Third Reich they sublated their neopaganism into nazism itself. This was not so for the Deutsche Glaubensbewegung (German Faith movement). At least during the early years of the Reich, this movement sought to sustain and express the anti-Christian, Nietzschean, German religious impulse. In-

89. Ibid., 103–105.
90. Ibid., 120.
91. George L. Mosse, "The Political Culture of Italian Futurism: A General Perspective," *Journal of Contemporary History* 25, nos. 2–3 (May–June 1990), 256.
92. Ernst Horneffer, *Nietzsche als Vorbote der Gegenwart* (Düsseldorf: A. Bagel, 1934).

deed, here was a movement that claimed to represent the authentic spiritual arm of the Nazi revolution.[93]

Under the leadership of yet another Protestant-trained theologian, Jakob Wilhelm Hauer (1881–1962), this movement was made up of a wide variety of circles and groups. These included the highly nationalist Germanische Glaubenschaft and the Deutschgläubige Gemeinschaft as well as the free-thinking Bund frei-religiöser Gemeinde, a large anticlerical organization which included Marxists in its ranks who joined the movement partly as shelter (from the Nazis). In Scharzfeld in 1934 they merged.

In the early years of the Reich, the Glaubensbewegung's membership grew impressively; its high point occurred in 1935. Gatherings were held throughout Germany climaxed by a mass meeting held at the Berlin Sports Palace in April. It never again achieved such prominence. The movement's mixed fortunes were only partly a function of its heterogeneity. Its fate ultimately depended upon the Nazi party's attitude towards it. It thrived only when the party wanted to counter Church influence. Hitler was prepared to make political use of the organization, but it could not weather his well-known antipathy to cultist cliques. Of the Glaubensbewegung he is reported to have said: "These professors and mystery men who want to found Nordic religions merely get in my way. Why do I tolerate them? Because they help to disintegrate, which is all we can do at the moment."[94] More fundamentally, national socialism was itself a total political faith and was not prepared to tolerate an independent confessional counterpart, even one that regarded itself as the religious arm of nazism. The Glaubensbewegung was thus gradually brought under National Socialist control, in effect losing its separate identity.[95]

93. For the history of this movement, see Hans Buchheim, *Glaubenskrise im Dritten Reich: Drei Kapitel nationalsozialistische Religionspolitik* (Stuttgart: Deutsche Verlag, 1953); J. Conway, *The Nazi Persecution of the Churches, 1933–1945* (London: Weidenfeld and Nicholson, 1968).

94. Hermann Rauschning, *Hitler Speaks: A Series of Political Conversations with Adolf Hitler* (London: Thornton Butterworth, 1939), 59. Rauschning's account must be taken with a dose of healthy skepticism. Its validity has been brought into question by Wolfgang Hänel (Karl-Heinz Janssen, "Kümmerliche Notizen: Rauschnings 'Gespräche mit Hitler'—wie ein Schweizer Lehrer nach 45 Jahren einen Schwindel auffliegen liess," *Die Zeit* [19 July 1985], 16). There is nevertheless general agreement about Hitler's impatience with this kind of cultist activity.

95. The movement was transformed into a propaganda arm under Nazi supervision through the journal *Durchbruch*. Even after Hauer was stripped of effective control he continued to preach his religion and was a leading proponent of Aryanization at the University of Tübingen (Uwe Dietrich Adam, *Hochschule und Nationalsozialismus: Die Universität Tübingen im Dritten Reich* [Tübingen: J. C. B. Mohr, 1977]).

Despite Nazi disavowals there were numerous ideological affinities, especially concerning the absurdity of trying to Germanize Christianity. Whatever the similarities and differences, the Glaubensbewegung regarded itself as the spiritual expression closest to the new reality of national socialism. The movement, Hauer wrote, was "an eruption from the biological and spiritual depths of the nation." It was brought about by those "primal forces whose nature is symbolized by the words Blood, Soil, Empire. Thus the German Revolution is for us an event born of the nation's primal will, an event in which eternal powers are revealing themselves by the accomplishment of newer and greater things."[96]

The ideologues of the Glaubensbewegung (including Ernst Bergmann[97] and Hans Günther) created a Germanic religion that transposed Nietzscheanism onto a racial–national base. Nietzschean qualities were simply projected onto idealized depictions of the Nordic race. Indo-Germanic religion was the antithesis of Judeo-Christianity, and was purely a worldly affair. Its ethic, devoid of fear and anxiety, produced men who embodied Nietzsche's vision of grand health and who affirmed life in all its tragic reality.[98]

Nietzsche permeated every aspect of the Glaubensbewegung's counter-religion. He was the central authority behind its attack on Enlightenment reason, liberalism, and socialism.[99] But he was also the major force behind its positive vision for the future. For Hauer (who discovered Nietzsche in a dentist's waiting room!)[100] he was simply the decisive destiny, the model for the inner breakthrough that every German had to accomplish. This Germanic racial religion simply nationalized the familiar Nietzschean counterfaith of immanence, heroism, and vitalism. Nietzschean morality was transposed into Germanic religious morality. Good and evil were still measured by their life-enhancing capacities but the Volk rather than the individual had become its repository. What was good, Hauer insisted, was that which

96. Wilhelm Hauer, "The Origin of the German Faith Movement," in Wilhelm Hauer, Karl Heim, Karl Adam, trans. T. S. K. Scott-Craig and R. E. Davies, Germany's New Religion (New York: Abingdon, 1937), 29, 36.

97. Ernst Bergmann, 25 Theses of the German Religion: A Catechism (London, 1936).

98. Hans Günther, Frömmigkeit nordischer Artung (Jena: Eugen Diederichs, 1937), 24.

99. Almost endless references to Nietzsche and Nietzschean themes can be found in the numerous works of Hauer and in the movement's journal, Deutscher Glaube (Hans Kern, "Die Umwertung aller Werte," Deutscher Glaube 3 [1936]; Hans Endres, "Aussprache: Der Erlösungsgedanke bei Nietzsche," Deutscher Glaube 5 [1938]).

100. Wilhelm Hauer, "Meine Begegnung mit Nietzsche," Deutscher Glaube 2, no. 11 (1935), 569.

corresponded to the highest wishes of the Volk, and that which went against its will was evil. Such a Germanic morality was inevitably juxtaposed to its Christian equivalent. As one example of the differences between the two, Hauer cited the issue of sterilization. Whereas Christians regarded it as a violation of the divine law, German faith looked upon it positively: "Can there be a higher value than the health of a Volk which unconditionally demands the extermination of bad instincts and criminal drives?" The Volk, Hauer proclaimed, "according to its deepest will wants to be pure, strong, and good."[101]

The Glaubensbewegung's nationalized vitalism went naturally with a form of dynamic Nietzschean ethics. Good and evil were malleable instruments serving life and therefore in need of constant renewal. This was the meaning, Hauer preached, of Nietzsche's breaking of the old tablets. His dynamic conception had thus facilitated the liberation of Germanic genius from its chains. Nietzsche could never himself have founded a new Decalogue, for that went against the grain of German being. But he did provide the conditions for Germans to recognize anew their proper mode: only on the basis of this particular racial makeup could German morality develop.[102]

Such open-endedness was evident in the way Hauer constructed his new German liturgy. In his formulation of the Germanic religion's modes of worship he did invoke the German past and ancient Germanic myths, but he gave greater emphasis to the dynamic by which Germanic being and blood constantly renewed itself. Germanic religion was based upon a pagan inheritance revolving around sun and nature festivals, but it moved ever more from lower to higher forms in which the heroic and creative Dionysian elements were increasingly central.[103]

With the demise of Hauer's movement the harnessing of Nietzsche for specifically religious purposes exhausted itself. Nietzsche, as we shall presently see, influenced and penetrated national socialism in a number of crucial and complex ways, but his annexation had to be direct, and cut off from any independent religious impulse. This was made clear by a Nazi ideologue, Hans Schröder, in his critique of the

101. Wilhelm Hauer, *Deutsche Gottschau: Grundzüge eines Deutschen Glaubens* (Stuttgart: Karl Gutbrod, 1935), 110.

102. Ibid.

103. Wilhelm Hauer, *Fest und Feier aus deutscher Art* (Stuttgart: Karl Gutbrod, 1936). Hauer wrote prolifically during this period. His works systematically traced the connections between religion and race (*Glaube und Blut: Beiträge zum Problem Religion und Rasse* [Karlsruhe and Leipzig: Bolze, 1938]).

Glaubensbewegung.[104] Had Nietzsche been alive, Schröder wrote, he
would have scoffed at Hauer-like cults, much as he had in 1873 at
David Friedrich Strauss's New Faith in his *Untimely Meditations*.[105]
Hauer had merely advocated changes in faith and dogma. But national
socialism did not limit itself to confessional matters; it was bringing
about total revolution. One of its great tasks was the overcoming of
decadence and Christianity, opposed as they were to the healthy,
völkisch life principle. Hauer had regarded Christianity simply as racially alien (*rassenfremd*). But this was to misunderstand Christianity;
Christianity was not the expression of a different race principle but
rather the antithesis of the principle itself. Christianity, argued Schröder
in a fusion of the racial with the Nietzschean worldview, threatened the
very fabric of the race principle because it exemplified *Unrassigkeit*—
race mixing and ensuing decline and decadence. Only the harnessing of
a Nietzschean heroic, masculine, biocentric culture, imbued with the
German racial mission, would overcome it.

Few of the makers of the various Nietzschean religions took seriously
Rudolf Pannwitz's elitist admonition that Nietzsche was "no prophet
for the Volk but rather a prophet for the prophets."[106] They all sought
to channel these new configurations of faith into wider communal and
ideological settings and to fuse the religious and political realms. If
Nietzsche's writings were inherently elitist, this was lost upon his acolytes. Cognizant of the great crisis of religion, they sought to harness,
socialize and institutionalize Nietzscheanism. Nietzschean religion, by
definition, was a culturally and politically mediated affair, for only thus
could its constituencies be reached.

Significantly, the attempt to create a "pure" Nietzschean religion,
unsullied by ideology and resistant to all annexation, was forged not in
Germany but in France, by Georges Bataille (1897–1962) where it
assumed a politically deconstructive, disintegrational character. Bataille's religious vision, which like the rest of his Nietzscheanism instinctively sought the extreme edge, pursued the unconditional and
unconditioned dynamic for its own sake. For Bataille violence, death,
sexuality, and evil became central ingredients in humanity's immanent
search for "sovereignty" and "totality" as a completely unsubordinated

104. Hans Eggert Schröder, *Nietzsche und das Christentum* (Berlin: Widulind, 1937), 50ff, 74ff.
105. Nietzsche, *Untimely Meditations*.
106. Pannwitz, *Einführung in Nietzsche*, 4.

realm.[107] In this guise, Nietzsche was not the philosopher of the will to power, but "the philosopher of evil" conceived as a liberating agent, as "concrete freedom, the troubling break with taboo." Bataille's Nietzschean religion was explicitly designed not as one of self-realization but rather a "signal dissolution in totality. . . . 'the man whose life is an unmotivated feast'; it celebrates in every sense of the word, a laughter, a dance, an orgy which knows of no subordination, a sacrifice heedless of purpose, material, or moral."[108] In his conception of that "atheological god which denies the transcendental, logocentric formations represented by Western deities"—Bataille's Nietzschean religion found its suitable and most inappropriable expression.[109]

There were no such expressions of Nietzschean religious nihility in Germany: there it inevitably attached itself to mediating positive external and political goals. Nevertheless, it would be an error to explain away Nietzschean religion in Germany by reducing it purely to its political functions. Its wide-ranging nature (including its penetration into various Marxist streams) renders dubious Georg Lukacs's assertion that Nietzschean religious atheism functioned to preserve "the vague religiosity that mattered to the preservation of capitalist society" and as such constituted "another manifestation of indirect apologetics."[110] This reduction of religiosity to the imperatives of capitalism bypassed the major historical impetus behind the Nietzschean religious moment: the great crisis of Protestantism and the search for alternatives.[111]

A quite disproportionate percentage of those who articulated the various versions of Nietzschean religion were Protestants or ex-Protestant pastors and theologians. They all took the crisis of religion seriously and sought to resolve it in a quasi-Nietzschean redemptive idiom. But, of course, Nietzschean religions were also designed to go beyond Protestantism. They constituted one of the important vehicles by which Nietzschean notions entered the political marketplace. Völkisch, nationalist, and right-wing groups harnessed it, but progressive, avant-

---

107. For an excellent overview see Allen S. Weiss, "Impossible Sovereignty: Between *The Will to Power* and *The Will to Chance*," *October* 36 (Spring 1986).

108. Georges Bataille, "On Nietzsche: The Will to Chance," *October* 36 (Spring 1986), 51, 56.

109. Weiss, "Impossible Sovereignty," 130.

110. Lukacs, *Destruction of Reason*, 359.

111. This criticism was correctly leveled at Lukacs by George Lichtheim: "Nowhere does Lukacs come to grips with the notion that Nietzsche's shattering impact upon an entire generation of Germans may have had something to do with the dissolution of the Protestant faith. The religious dimension simply does not seem to exist for him" (*Lukacs* [London: Fontana, Collins, 1970], 114).

garde and leftist intellectuals also found its thematics compelling. Like so many aspects of the Nietzsche legacy, the cultural significance of the Nietzschean religious impulse cannot be simplistically dismissed as an expression of "reactionary irrationalism" as against "progressive rationalism."

Various critics have argued a deeper point. It was, they claim, precisely the pseudoreligious language of the antichrist, its naturalistic view of man, and its accompanying desacralized amoralism which stood at the core of the murderous and genocidal impulse of our times.[112] Nietzsche's atheism, George Lichtheim has insisted, "had nothing whatever in common with that of pre-Marxians such as Feuerbach, for whom humanism had replaced theism."[113] This argument holds that, unlike Marxism, the Nietzschean critique of organized Christian religion was made not in protest against its historical inhumanities but rather because it had not been cruel enough.

Whatever the merits of this position, insofar as Nietzsche contributed to Europe's brutalization, he did so in inevitably mediated guise. "The liturgical language of the religion of the antichrist" was always canalized and expressed within larger organizing political frames. Nietzscheanism was effective as a public force only when it was structured by mediating systems and ideologies. No naked or pure Nietzschean nihility existed. All the versions we have discussed in some way nationalized or socialized the Nietzschean thematic, placing it at the service of other goals. This had the effect of taming or limiting its dynamic or selectively controlling and deploying it. Such ideologies, far from dispensing with transcendence, simply redefined it, and stayed firmly within their self-created sacred boundaries.[114]

These processes applied especially to the Nazi case. We must now therefore proceed to a direct examination of the multiple mediations and the complex deployments by which the Nietzschean and the Nazi universes were made to meet.

112. Roger Scruton, "The Philosopher on Dover Beach," *Times Literary Supplement* (23 May 1986), 565–566.

113. George Lichtheim, *Europe in the Twentieth Century* (London: Cardinal, 1974), 186.

114. Considerable scholarship on nazism denies the nihilism thesis. Ernst Nolte's interesting view that nazism represented a kind of Nietzschean naturalistic revolt against bourgeois theoretical and practical transcendence has a great deal of plausibility (*Three Faces of Fascism* [New York: Mentor, 1969]). He does not, however, allow that nazism constructed its own form of transcendence that, while allowing radical action, also carefully defined its limits. See George L. Mosse's interesting review of Nolte's *Three Faces* in *Journal of the History of Ideas* 27, no. 4 (1966), 621–626.

CHAPTER VIII

Nietzsche in the Third Reich

From now on there will be more favorable preconditions
for more comprehensive forms of dominion, whose like has
never yet existed. And even this is not the most important
thing; the possibility has been established for the production
of international racial unions whose task it will be to rear a
master-race, the future "masters of the earth." The time is
coming when politics will have a different meaning.

Nietzsche, The Will to Power

"Nothing is true, all is permitted": thus I spoke to myself.
Into the coldest waters I plunged, with head and heart . . .
Alas, where has all that is good gone from me—and all
shame, and all faith in those who are good?

Nietzsche, Thus Spoke Zarathustra

Because both Nietzsche and national socialism are central to the
twentieth-century experience and because both retain their symbolic
explosiveness, the disputed nature of their relationship has become a
defining part of the cultural and ideological landscape, one index to our
perceptions of the modern world. The controversial history of their
imputed connection well predates the Nazi takeover. From the beginning some regarded the affinity as natural (or at least comprehensible)
while others were appalled at the very suggestion. Since then and
through our own time, various divergent readings and judgments of
Nietzsche have determined the preparedness to implicate him in nazism.
Conversely, particular interpretations of national socialism have governed the readiness to include him within its contours. The issue, with
its ideologically vested interests and shrill tones, has generated endless
controversy.

What, at this late stage, can the historian contribute to this vexed question? Most useful, perhaps, would be clarification: identifying and critically analyzing those levels most relevant to claims concerning this relationship. In this chapter we deal with the most straightforward yet strangely underexamined empirical dimension of the relationship: locating and analyzing the ways in which Nietzsche was integrated into or banished from Nazi discourse, and the various functions Nietzsche-anism fulfilled within the Third Reich.

That Nietzsche was incorporated into the Nazi pantheon of Germanic giants and that he became an integral part of National Socialist self-definition is a matter of empirical record. There is no way, of course, to accurately assess the degree to which his integration affected everyday popular attitudes. It is certain, however, that Nietzsche assumed importance in the official culture of the Third Reich. We need to examine the connections between this construction and the regime's own self-image.

Recognition and analysis of Nietzsche's role within the realm of Nazi culture, ideology, and indeed policy must proceed independently of whether or not we believe that this usage distorts Nietzsche's thought or faithfully reflects it. This typically has been the level at which the issue has been discussed. As we have been emphasizing throughout this book, however, ideological appropriation itself becomes the major relevant datum—not the question of the truth or falsity of such appropriation.[1] That this entailed selective reading, casuistic interpretation, and even frequent suppression and expurgation of potentially embarrassing material makes an understanding of the process even more imperative. If Nietzsche's nazification—and the Nietzscheanization of nazism—is well known, the internal strategies involved in this transmutation and the extent of its diffusion have to date still not been systematically analyzed.[2]

The Nazi Nietzsche was facilitated by the broader postwar annexation of the philosopher by the radical right; the "philosophical" nazi-

1. H. Langreder, in "Die Auseinandersetzung mit Nietzsche im dritten Reich: Ein Beitrag zur Wirkungsgeschichte Nietzsches" (Ph.D. diss., Christian Albrechts University, Kiel, 1971), has argued for a similar method although he is inconsistent. The title, moreover, promises more than it delivers. The work limits itself to a few major examples without studying in detail either the multilayered diffusion or content of the Nazi Nietzsche. The suggestion that, as time went on, Nietzsche's importance waned, is asserted, not demonstrated, and contradicted by some of Langreder's own evidence.

2. Already in 1942 and within the context of nazism, Franz Neumann called for an examination of "the actual dissemination of Nietzsche's ideas among the various groups of the German people and the transformation of his ideas during this process of popularization" (*Behemoth: The Structure and Practice of National Socialism* [New York: Oxford University Press, 1944], 490, n. 93).

fication of Nietzsche well predated the takeover of power. By 1931 Alfred Bäumler—later to become the Reich's authorized Nietzsche scholar and professor of philosophy at the University of Berlin—had spelled out the major thematics of Nietzsche's Nazi transmogrification. Bäumler emphasized the power components of the philosopher's thought. His Nietzsche was essentially a political thinker, a man who foresaw the postliberal, postbourgeois age of Great Politics. The Nietzsche that Bäumler emphasized was the one who in *Beyond Good and Evil* had written:

> *To acquire one will* by means of a new caste that would rule Europe, a long, terrible will of its own that would be able to cast its goals millenia hence—so the long-drawn-out comedy of its splinter states as well as its dynastic and democratic splinter wills would come to an end. The time for petty politics is over: the very next century will bring the fight for the dominion of the earth—the *compulsion* to large-scale politics.[3]

Bäumler explicitly rejected what he regarded as the passive doctrine of eternal recurrence. He dismissed it as an unfortunate and philosophically irrelevant whim. The authentic Nietzsche was interested in the unlimited flux of becoming; the notion of eternal recurrence denied that possibility. Nietzsche was the philosopher of the will to power, a dynamically Heraclitean rather than Dionysian thinker. He was the philosopher of heroic realism whose politics no longer accepted the idea of a stable world of norms and values but posited in its place a universe of constant flux and conflict. This entailed a turn from rationalist consciousness, objectivist ethics, and traditional transcendental logic, and the rejection of the decadent forms of democracy and "theoretical man." He promoted a naturalized "aesthetic of the body," a reassertion of warlike, heroic male values and community, and a vitalist ethos of struggle.[4]

Bäumler was never alone in this enterprise. Well before 1933, official

---

3. Nietzsche, *Beyond Good and Evil,* 131; see also *Ecce Homo, 327:*

    For when truth enters into a fight with the lies of millenia, we shall have upheavals, a convulsion of earthquakes, a moving of mountains and valleys, the like of which has never been dreamed of. The concept of politics will have merged entirely with a war of spirits; all power structures of the old society will have been exploded—all of them are based on lies: there will be wars the like of which have never yet been seen on earth. It is only beginning with me that the earth knows *great politics.*

4. Alfred Bäumler, *Nietzsche der Philosoph und Politiker* (Leipzig: Reklam, 1931). For other relevant essays from before the Third Reich, see the reprints of his "Bachofen und Nietzsche" (1929) and "Nietzsche" (1930) in his *Studien zur deutschen Geistesgeschichte* (Berlin: Junker und Dünnhaupt, 1937).

Nazi organs were proclaiming Nietzsche as their own.[5] By the time of the Nazi takeover, it seemed self-evident to portray Nietzsche as a central forerunner of the movement. Gottlieb Scheuffler's 1933 *Friedrich Nietzsche in the Third Reich* was typical of this genre, portraying the great "natural aristocrats," Mussolini and Hitler, as Nietzsche's spiritual descendants.[6] Of course, he was not considered the sole ideological pillar of national socialism. Paul de Lagarde and Houston Stewart Chamberlain were just as apt to be invoked as immediate precursors.[7]

These other purported forerunners did not, however, possess anything like the stature that Nietzsche had come to possess. The particular Nazi emphasis on Nietzsche derived from his peculiar capacity to legitimate them. Of course, the Nazis also relentlessly enlisted other cultural giants—Herder, Schiller, Goethe—for similar purposes. The difference, however, was that Nietzsche's uses went beyond the merely occasional or decorative. Here was a German thinker with what appeared to be genuinely thematic and tonal links, who was able to provide the Nazis with a higher philosophical pedigree and a rationale for central tenets of their weltanschauung. As Franz Neumann noted in 1942, Nietzsche "provided National Socialism with an intellectual father who had greatness and wit, whose style was beautiful and not abominable, who was

5. See for example J. Günther, "Nietzsche und der Nationalsozialismus," *Nationalsozialistische Monatshefte* 2, no. 21 (December 1931), 560–563.

6. Gottlieb Scheuffler, *Friedrich Nietzsche im dritten Reich: Bestätigung und Aufgabe* (Erfurt: E. Scheuffler, 1933).

7. Dr. Gross, "Die Propheten: Friedrich Nietzsche, Paul de Lagarde und Houston Stewart Chamberlain in ihrer Bedeutung für uns," *Nationalsozialistische Monatshefte* 1 (1930), 29–33. For listings of Nazi forerunners see Alfred Rosenberg, "Gegen Tarnung," *Völkischer Beobachter* (3 December 1933); Fritz Peuckert, "Chamberlain und Nietzsche," *Nationalsozialistische Monatshefte* 5, no. 49 (April 1934); Rosenberg, *Gestaltung der Idee* (Munich: F. Eher Nach. F., 1938), 18. Richard Wagner was another prominent precursor. Pro-Nietzsche Nazi commentaries variously dealt with the Nietzsche–Wagner antagonism: disregarding it, casuistically explaining it away, or overcoming it by the higher synthesis of nazism. For one expression of the recaptured unity between Weimar and Bayreuth—manifested by Hitler's visit to the Nietzsche Archives and proceeding to the opening of the Bayreuth festival—see Richard Öhler, *Friedrich Nietzsche und die deutsche Zukunft* (Leipzig: Armanen, 1935), 11. Winifred Wagner and Förster-Nietzsche did indeed bury the hatchet. Michael Tanner has described the reconciliation in strong language: "Nietzsche's unspeakable sister presided over a luncheon party in Weimar given for Winifred Wagner, when the two vicious ladies could revoke the regrettable feud between their long-dead brother and father-in-law respectively" ("Organizing the self and the world," *Times Literary Supplement* [16 May 1986], 519). See too Hans Kern's account of the Wagner–Nietzsche relationship and their attempt to create a tragic German myth (*Schöpfersiche Freundschaft* [Jena: E. Diederichs, 1932]). Indeed, well before the Third Reich some attempted to locate their commonality in their struggle against the nineteenth century (Kurt Hildebrandt, *Wagner und Nietzsche: Ihr Kampf gegen das 19 Jahrhundert* [Breslau, 1924]).

able to articulate the resentment against both monopoly capitalism and the rising proletariat."[8]

His protagonists insisted that Nietzsche's placement within the pantheon went well beyond cosmetic legitimation. The visionaries of national socialism, one commentator made clear, could not be conceived passively and distantly. For a "movement" possessed by an "idea" there were no "forerunners," only creators, cocombatants and active participants.[9] In his 1934 *Nietzsche as Portender of the Present,* the veteran Nietzschean Ernst Horneffer (now suitably decked in Nazi garb), couched this in ultimate mythopoeic form: Nietzsche does not belong to his own "but our time. It is as if he lingered (on) living amongst us."[10] In the new social reality Nietzsche was resurrected into a living, active presence.

An appropriately fashioned Nietzsche was diffused not only explicitly but also subliminally—and thus, perhaps, more powerfully—through the integration of Nietzschean slogans into everyday Nazi rhetoric. National Socialist vocabulary was saturated with a suitably transfigured Nietzschean phraseology. Since Nietzsche was often not mentioned as their author, the slogans could assume a natural, taken-for-granted quality. This heroic language of will doubtless had its (politically activating) effect.[11] So too did its opposing, dehumanizing nomenclature. Heinrich Himmler, for instance, regularly described Russians and Slavs as bestial *Untermenschen* and the Jews as the "decisive leader of the Untermenschen."[12] These notions, moreover, received

8. Neumann, *Behemoth,* 490, n. 93. See too Rudolf E. Künzli, "The Nazi Appropriation of Nietzsche," *Nietzsche-Studien* 12 (1983), 429–430.

9. Hans Herbert Reeder, "Leidenschaft um das Reich: Hölderlin, Kleist, Nietzsche," *Die Westmark* 4, no. 10 (July 1937), 493.

10. Ernst Horneffer, *Nietzsche als Vorbote der Gegenwart* (Düsseldorf: Abagel Aktiengesellschaft, 1934), 12. Horneffer was not the only Nietzschean to continue pro-Nietzsche activities during the Third Reich. So did Gottfried Benn, Richard Gröper, Paul Schulze-Berghof, and Kurt Hildebrandt.

11. There are countless instances. In Baldur von Schirach's Nazi youth journal, *Wille und Macht,* for example, there was little explicitly Nietzschean, nor was the title the same as *Wille zur Macht.* Yet the tones and categories employed, even if parodistic, partial, or unconscious, were derived from the Nietzschean storehouse. For the most systematic attempt to account for the role of Nietzschean rhetoric (centered especially around the notion of will) within the Nazi world, see J. P. Stern, *Hitler: The Führer and the People* (London: Fontana, 1984), chaps. 7, 8. Because Stern's intelligent analysis is inferential, however, it does not sufficiently document the direct or transmitted levels of influence. On the changes in language during the Third Reich, see Viktor Klemperer, *Notizbuch eines Philologen* (Berlin: Aufbau, 1949).

12. Nietzsche did employ the term *Untermensch* (in *The Gay Science* and the prologue to *Zarathustra*), as Kaufmann points out in his translation of *The Gay Science* (192, n. 30). But the word was not Nietzsche's invention; it was first used at the end of the eighteenth century, and besides was very marginal for Nietzsche. The Nazis used it far

enormous coverage in *Schutzstaffel* (SS) publications such as *Der Untermensch*. This pamphlet was translated into fifteen languages and four million copies were printed (illus. 14).[13] These forms of subliminal influence doubtless played a role, but because they are notoriously immeasurable, we should return to safer ground and examine the more explicit ways in which Nietzscheanism was mediated in the Nazi world.

Nazis transformed Nietzsche into a prescient prophet—the isolated individual who in the period of hopeless liberal decline alone embodied the spirit of true Germanness that was so powerfully unfolding in the new Reich.[14] Nietzsche was presented as the genius who began to think in new, comprehensive ways and who presaged both the coming crisis and the way out of it. For many he was the major presager of national socialism, foreseeing in the realm of ideas what nazism was to realize in practice. In critical matters of policy and sensibility, Nietzsche was to serve as guide and inspiration.

At the same time, these National Socialist mediators proffered a reciprocal sociology of knowledge: if Nietzsche had enunciated Nazi ideas, he himself had become comprehensible only because of a particular unfolding of historical events and the creation of a new social reality. It took World War I and the advent of national socialism to reveal his proper meaning. As a revolutionary struggling against his own time, Nietzsche was bound to be misunderstood, proclaimed Alfred Rosenberg; only "in our time" was true appreciation possible.[15] Moreover, a positive commitment to national socialism appeared to be the prerequisite for such an understanding: "Whoever stands outside of this revolution," wrote Hans Kern, "and does not know what it wants and where it comes from, will never be able to grasp Nietzsche."[16] "I am convinced," an authorized spokesman wrote, "that only a conscious National Socialist can fully comprehend Nietzsche."[17]

---

more frequently after transforming it. Still, the term and its application took on its particular resonance within a familiar Nietzschean frame of association—emphasis on Übermenschen implicitly evoked images of Untermenschen (Alex Bein, "The Jewish Parasite," *Leo Baeck Institute Yearbook* 10 [1964], 27–28).

13. Josef Ackermann, *Heinrich Himmler als Ideologe* (Göttingen: Musterschmidt, 1970), 210–214.

14. Dietrich Beitzke, review of Hans Endres's *Rasse, Ehe, Zucht und Zuchtung bei Nietzsche und heute, Deutscher Glaube* 4 (1939), 183.

15. Alfred Rosenberg, *Friedrich Nietzsche* (Munich: Zentralverlag der Nationalsozialistische Deutsche Arbeiter Partei [NSDAP], 1944), 3.

16. Hans Kern, "Nietzsche und die deutsche Revolution," *Rhythmus: Monatschrift für Bewegegungslehre* 12 (1934), 146.

17. Heinrich Härtle, *Nietzsche und der Nationalsozialismus* (Munich: Zentralverlag der NSDAP, 1937), 6.

What did this "proper Nazi grasp" of Nietzsche entail? What were the crucial Nietzschean materials that had either given birth to national socialism or from which, at least, it could creatively draw? How was nazism itself understood as a Nietzschean project? What were the minimal, necessary contours, the agreed content of his nazification?

Almost all presentations portrayed him as defining nazism's major goals, both its affirmations and negations. First of all, the philosopher radically rejected bourgeois society, liberalism, socialism, democracy, egalitarianism, and the Christian ethos. His antiuniversalist themes were constantly hammered home, finding their way into almost every nook and cranny of the Nazi world. Equally important, however, was the emphasis on Nietzsche as a crucial force of regeneration and central to the construction of the movement's promise of a thoroughly transvalued world.[18] These aims were typically represented as total alternatives to the world that both Nietzsche and nazism had rejected. The decadent and feminized nineteenth century was to give way to a new masculine warrior age, one that regarded Nietzsche as a pioneer of the "German rediscovery of the body."[19] Such an age would exchange materialist and mechanical conceptions for organic, healthy ones. They explicitly hoped to supersede the libertarian Nietzschean conception of the body as focus of social and erotic emancipation, with that of a physical regeneration channeled into a disciplined völkisch and soldierly framework.[20] An instinctual, renaturalized, vitalistic, and tragic culture would replace the "transcendental" (and therefore life-threatening) rationalist worldview. The old bourgeois ethos of security was to be rendered anachronistic by the emergence of hard personalities animated by the joy of living dangerously. Here the individual and collectivized Übermensch acted as a countertype (*Gegenbild*) to shallow post-Enlightenment humanity.

It goes without saying that Nietzsche was harnessed to the struggle against Marxism and bolshevism which, as Richard Öhler put it, Nietzsche regarded as his greatest future opponent, the very embodiment of nihilism. Nietzsche's solution to that nihilism—the creation of higher men of the future animated by the will to power—had already

18. K. O. Schmidt, *Liebe dein Schicksal! Nietzsche und die deutsche Erneurung: Ein Überblick und ein Ausblick* (Pfüllingen: Johannes Baum, 1933).

19. Hans Kern, "Die deutsche Wiederentdeckung des Leibes," *Rhythmus* 12, nos. 5/6 (May/June 1934); Rudolf Luck, "Nietzsches Lebenslehre des Leibes," *Rhythmus 14* (1936), 97–105.

20. For an illuminating discussion of political interpretations of the rediscovery of the body, see Mosse, *Nationalism and Sexuality,* chap. 3, especially p. 53.

become real under national socialism. Nazism was the great protecting wall against nihilism, the proposed Nietzschean counterweight. "Nietzsche, like Hitler, sees the only possibility of countering the will to destruction of nihilism in the renewal, intensification, and creation of the healthy, out of the source of the great, naturally produced values."[21]

In a spate of publications, nazism was variously depicted as the realization of the Nietzschean vision, as crucially inspired by it, or as thematically parallel. Had the master not called for the creation of a biologized, hierarchical, Lebensphilosophie society; the breeding of a higher, soldierly New Man unfettered by the *ressentiment* chains of traditional morality and an antilife rationalist intellect? Was not the present reality the fulfillment of Nietzsche's vitalist vision? Nazism was, after all, a regenerationist, postdemocratic, post-Christian social order where the weak, decrepit and useless were to be legislated out of existence.[22]

The marriage between Nietzsche and national socialism was authorized and consummated at the highest of levels and accompanied by fanfare and publicity. Together with Hitler's *Mein Kampf* and Rosenberg's *Myth of the Twentieth Century*, *Zarathustra* was placed in the vault of the Tannenberg Memorial (commemorating Germany's victory over Russia in the Great War).[23] Much to the delight of its minions, the union was publicly sanctified within the official home of the cult—the Nietzsche Archives. "We are drunk with enthusiasm," wrote Förster-Nietzsche in May 1933, "because at the head of our government stands such a wonderful, indeed phenomenal, personality like our magnificent chancellor Adolf Hitler."[24] Already by 1932, those entrusted with the Nietzsche legacy at the Archives—from the head to the doorkeeper—were, according to Count Kessler, overwhelmingly and enthusiastically Nazis.[25] Förster-Nietzsche had, of course, always advocated a rightist, patriotic Nietzsche, and vehemently opposed the Republic. When in 1923 she heard of the nascent national resurrection led by Ludendorff and Hitler, she declared that had she been younger she would have joined them in their march on Berlin. Just prior to the

21. Öhler, *Nietzsche und die deutsche Zukunft,* 18.
22. Mine is a composite picture of representations to be found in virtually all of the Nietzschean sources quoted in this chapter. Öhler's *Nietzsche und die deutsche Zukunft* contains almost all of these components.
23. Peters, *Zarathustra's Sister,* 221.
24. Elisabeth Förster-Nietzsche to Ernst Thiel, 12 May 1933; quoted in ibid., 220.
25. Kessler, *Diaries,* 426.

Nazi power takeover, it is true, she regarded herself more nationalist than Nazi. At first she admired Hitler as a religious rather than as a political leader, although this would soon change. Elisabeth's right-wing proclivities were in any case never all that finely tuned. She openly identified with Mussolini and his Fascist regime.[26] (Mussolini responded more tangibly in 1931 with his gift of twenty thousand lire.)[27] Hitler visited the Archives in autumn 1934 and posed next to a bust of Nietzsche of which only one half of the head, ironically, was visible (illus. 15). He agreed to provide money for the construction of a Nietzsche memorial auditorium to be constructed by Schultze-Naumburg. Albert Speer, who accompanied Hitler on this visit, reported that the chemistry between Hitler and Förster-Nietzsche was quite unsatisfactory: "This solitary, eccentric woman obviously could not get anywhere with Hitler; an oddly shallow conversation at cross-purposes ensued" (illus. 16).[28]

The unsatisfactory private meeting counted far less than the public validation. Förster-Nietzsche's funeral in November 1935 was conducted with great pomp and circumstance and was attended by local and national dignitaries, including Hitler,[29] and she was gushingly eulogized in official Nazi sources.[30] Such authorized participation continued. The 1944 Nietzsche centenary, for instance, was held under the patronage of Rosenberg, acting as Hitler's official representative.

Nietzscheanism in the Third Reich went well beyond these high-level rituals. It would be a mistake to simply focus on these and the efforts of its better-known proponents such as Bäumler and Rosenberg, and miss the dense and broad diffusion through which suitably adapted Nietzschean notions became a differentiated and integral part of Nazi self-definition. For its proponents, the Nazi–Nietzschean vision was meant no less than to remold the order of things. Suggestive blueprints for its detailed implementation were to be found at myriad levels of social organization.

In the first place Nietzsche was made an integral part of Nazi ideological training, becoming the primary legitimating champion of the new education. Nietzschean illiberalism, antihumanism and a politicized Lebensphilosophie were placed at the center of the new educa-

26. Peters, *Zarathustra's Sister*, 211, 212; see too chap. 23, "The Fight against the Weimar Republic."
27. Kessler, *Diaries*, 426.
28. Albert Speer, *Inside the Third Reich* (London: Sphere, 1971), 109.
29. Peters, *Zarathustra's Sister*, 222, 224.
30. *Völkischer Beobachter* (11 November 1935).

tional philosophy. Innumerable and sometimes critical discussions applying Nietzschean principles of renewal were sprinkled throughout the
educational journals. The philosopher's critique of traditional education, academic antiquarianism, and life-destroying rationalism; his imputed linking of the Greek principle of *paidea* with that of political
education; and his emphasis on life and cultural totality became pillars
of the proposed pedagogical revolution.[31]

These notions applied also to revised conceptions of science and
knowledge in general. In his rectoral address at Königsberg in October
1933, the philosopher Hans Heyse proclaimed that "we are standing at
a fateful turning point of the ages," one that demanded a Nietzschean
transvaluation of all values and that would overcome the modern conception of science, "that expression of a broken existence which, as an
untrue existence, leads by necessity into catastrophe."[32] Nietzsche, another commentator wrote in *Volk im Werden,* had demonstrated the
tyranny of objectivity and the "sick sovereignty" of smug, self-satisfied
science. He had shown that there was no absolute truth, only the need
to create one's own culture.

> If we take Nietzsche as the intellectual *Führer* to a new culture, we should,
> yes we must, say: German culture must be a unity: that is, all its components
> must be German. And that also includes *Wissenschaft.* The first steps to a
> new culture are education to struggle and education to unity through blood
> and deed.

Was not the political soldier at the university the first step to the heroic,
conception of knowledge of which Nietzsche spoke?[33]

The elevation of Nietzsche to the status of jurisprudential reformer,

31. Hans Donndorf, "Friedrich Nietzsche und die deutsche Schule der Gegenwart,"
Deutsches Philologen-Blatt 43 (1935); Heinrich Weinstock, "Die Überwindung der 'Bil-
dungskrise' durch Nietzsche," *Der Erziehung: Monatschrift für den Zusammenhang von
Kultur und Erziehung in Wissenschaft und Leben* 10 (1935), 469–470; Gerhard Budde,
"Nietzsche und die höhere Schule," *Monatschrift für höhere Schulen* 37 (1938); Friedrich
Meyer, "Die aktuelle Bedeutung der Gedanken Nietzsches über Kultur und Bildungsform
im Schlussabschnitt seiner 'Zweiten Unzeitgemässen,'" *Nationalsozialistisches Bildungswesen* 5, no. 8 (August 1940); Erich Weisser, "Der Erzieher Nietzsche und die nationalsozialistische Schulerneurung," *Nationalsozialstische Bildungswesen* 6 (1941), 125–134,
356–367; F. Beck, "Nietzsches Philosophie unter nationalsozialistischer Blickrichtung,"
Der deutsche Erzieher (1942).
32. Hans Heyse, *Die Idee der Wissenschaft und die deutsche Universität* (Königsberg:
Gräfe and Unzer, 1935), 3, 9. Quoted in Hans Sluga, "Metadiscourse: German Philosophy and National Socialism," *Social Research* 56, no. 4 (Winter 1989), 812. I thank
Menachem Brinker for this reference.
33. Hans-Joachim Falkenberg, "Nietzsche und die politische Wissenschaft," *Volk im
Werden* 2 (1934), 455–460.

legislator, and prophet of a new legal order went back well into the
Second Reich.[34] While not racist in the National Socialist sense,
Friedrich Mess's 1930 *Nietzsche: The Lawgiver* was explicitly
acknowledged as seminal by later Nazi commentaries. Like Mess, they
argued that future European social structures had to be built upon
Nietzschean foundations. Who better provided the outlines for the
desired post-Christian, post-Enlightenment, anti-Kantian society?
Nietzsche had to be considered the legislator of the future, wrote
H. Specht in the 1939 journal of the Criminal Biological Society.[35]
Unlike the sick Christian–Jewish mode, his was no closed system. The
Nietzschean legal mode was designed to restore one to life, predicated
on the non-Christian assumption of the innocence of being (*Unschuld
des Daseins*) and upon fundamentally transvalued conceptions of good
and evil. Nietzsche did not seek to abolish punishment but to
demoralize it and loosen it from the stranglehold of priestly law.
Punishment existed only to serve the life-enhancing, hierarchical order,
based, as it would be, on the will to power and the urge to create a
higher, stronger being. The philosopher had foreseen a social system
founded on the relation between leaders and led, with an aristocracy of
blood and merit. With "a sure historic-political instinct," Specht
added, Nietzsche "knew the future and consciously prepared the way
for it."[36] The place of race, Volk and state were unclear in Nietzsche's
system, Specht admitted, but it was evident that he opposed the
dissolution of these values.

In Kurt Kassler's *Nietzsche and the Law*, even these uncertainties
were expunged. Nietzsche, he wrote, recognized "the strong, un-
breakable tie of the law to the power-political necessity of every *Volk*."
Law for Nietzsche was not an abstract codification of immutable
reason. It was a dynamic instrument in the life of a Volk and an
integral part of its biological and anthropological development which
served its political needs and its will to power (*Machtwillens*). Proper
law flowed from a healthy, völkisch life: "universal" human law was
both "life-estranged and an unhistorical, utopian conception."

---

34. Alfred Rosenthal, "Nietzsche und die Reform das Strafrechts," *Deutsche Juristen
Zeitung* 11, no. 19 (1906), 1069–1072; Josef Kohler, "Nietzsche und die Rechtsphilo-
sophie," *Archiv für Rechts und Sozialphilosophie* 1, no. 3 (1908), 355–360; Dietrich
Heinrich Kerler, *Nietzsche und die Vergeltungsidee: Zur Strafrechtsreform* (Ulm: Kerler,
1910).
35. H. Specht, "Friedrich Nietzsches Anthropologie und das Strafrecht," *Monatschrift für Kriminalbiologie: Organ der kriminalbiologische Gesellschaft* 30, no. 8 (1939).
36. Ibid., 358.

Nietzsche's rejection of equal rights—had he not written, "We feel all rights to be conquests"?—was closely linked to his hierarchical alternative.[37]

The struggle for self-assertion and heightening of power was the source of mutable law. There was no reason of law or natural law. Nietzschean law followed life, not vice versa; it was not transcendental but immanent, dynamic, anthropological, and biological.[38]

Nietzsche, Kassler continued, was the first thinker to perceive the centrality of race and racial hygiene and to consciously apply its imperatives to social life. Was he not determinedly against the procreation of the unworthy? The promulgation of National Socialist laws concerning racial hygiene and its protective measures against hereditary dispositions and illness ("*zur Verhuetung erbkranken Nachwuchs und zum Schutze der Erbgesundheit des deutschen Volkes*") in effect constituted the implementation of Nietzsche's vision.[39]

Kassler was by no means alone in using Nietzsche as the explicit justification for Nazi measures aimed at the incurably ill and sexual offenders.[40] And there was no shortage of appropriate Nietzschean recommendations advocating what he called "holy cruelty":[41]

> The biblical prohibition "thou shalt not kill" is a piece of naivete compared with the seriousness of the prohibition of life to decadents: "thou shalt not procreate!"—Life itself recognizes no solidarity, no "equal rights," between the healthy and the degenerate parts of an organism: one must excise the latter—or the whole will perish.—Sympathy for decadents, equal rights for the ill-constituted—that would be the profoundest immorality, that would be antinature itself as morality![42]

We have already seen how Nietzsche influenced advocates of euthanasia and was integrated into earlier eugenic thought. In the new legal order of the Third Reich medical practitioners of child euthanasia—such as Dr. Werner Catel—rested on Nietzsche as justification for their work. The force of this influence is not reduced by the ironic fact that,

37. Kurt Kassler, *Nietzsche und das Recht* (Munich: Ernst Reinhardt, 1941), 12–15, 22. The Nietzsche quote is from *Will to Power*, 74.

38. Kassler, *Nietzsche und das Recht*, 31–34.

39. Ibid., 50, 66–69.

40. Öhler, *Nietzsche und die deutsche Zukunft*, 45–46.

41. Nietzsche, *Gay Science*, 129.

42. Nietzsche, *Will to Power*, 389. This was by no means an isolated sentiment in his corpus. See too *Will to Power*, 141–142, 391–393; *Zarathustra*, 183–186; *Twilight of the Idols*, 536–538; *Genealogy of Morals*, 120–125.

as Ernst Klee has pointed out, Nietzsche's insanity would have rendered him an eminently suitable victim.[43]

The envisaged Nietzschean social order also entailed a positive eugenic programme to create the suitable masterly type. Breeding and selection in the service of higher development, Kassler reminded his readers, permeated all of Nietzsche's writings, and was linked to his deep concern with decadence, degeneration, and decline. To be sure, Nietzsche was wrong to believe that there were no original pure races— only races that had become pure.[44] Yet he still led the struggle against the deterioration of European blood.[45]

Kassler did not deny the difficulties but argued that Nietzsche was nevertheless useful in articulating the outlines of a race society. For those interested in the fusion of Nietzsche and a right-wing politics of racial hygiene, the differences were overwhelmed by the commonalities.[46] If Nietzsche had no closed racial system in the current sense, wrote another Nazi commentator, he was still a powerful pioneer of race culture. It was he who had rediscovered biology for philosophy. The biological viewpoint did not necessarily have a racial starting point but it did push open "a row of mighty doors that led to a racial view of life."[47]

His promoters highlighted Nietzsche's reassertion of instinct, his discovery of the body, and above all his naturalistic transvaluation in which the biological ethic replaced the moral one. Nietzsche's comments on the Jews were particularly relevant. The philosopher was hailed for performing a service to the history of the world with his insight into the history of Israel as "the denaturalization of natural values" (der Entnaturlichung der Naturwerte).[48] Nazism was clearly the countermovement leading the drive to renaturalization.

Nietzsche, such commentators stressed, had dismissed the "race swindle" because he dissociated himself from those who then represented race theory. But, in his own way, he "was the most acute anti-

43. Werner Catel, *Leben im Widerstreit: Bekenntnisse eines Arztes* (Nuremberg: Glock und Lutz, 1974), 179ff. Cited in Ernst Klee, *"Euthanasie" im NS-Staat: Die "Vernichtung lebensunwerten Lebens"* (Frankfurt am Main: S. Fischer, 1983), 16. On Nietzsche as a potential victim, see ibid., 17.

44. Nietzsche, *Daybreak*, 274.

45. Kassler, *Nietzsche und das Recht*, 70–79.

46. E. Kirchner, "Nietzsches Lehren im Lichte der Rassenhygiene," *Archiv für Rassen und Gesellschaftsbiologie* 17 (1926).

47. Heinrich Römer, "Nietzsche und das Rasseproblem," *Rasse: Monatschrift für den Nordischen Gedanken* 7 (1940), 59.

48. Ibid., 61.

Semite that ever was: he was the most radical discoverer of the unholy role that Judaism played in the spiritual history of Europe." His demonstration that Christianity was the ultimate Jewish consequence and that it engendered the spread of Jewish blood poisoning made the Jews the most fateful people of world history. Through this road Nietzsche was brought to the race problem, opening the door to racial hygiene in an attempt to break the degeneration of a thousand years.[49]

Nazified Nietzscheanism performed multiple functions and was diffused along the broad spectra of Nazi society. After appropriate editing, the philosopher's works were published and distributed at a dizzy pace.[50] They were integrated into the general school system[51] and served the particular needs of a variety of special-interest organizations.[52]

Nietzschean themes permeated everyday life. They informed the defining ideological contours of elite SS journals such as *Das Schwarze Korps:* "The soldier of the front," read one such article, "was the unity of Nietzsche, worker, peasant, and those bourgeois youth who were driven by race to a new configuration."[53] They formed the subject of rarefied university seminars; were broadcast on the airwaves in popular radio lectures advocating, for instance, Nietzschean conceptions of the role of labor in the new social order; and presented in lionizing talks to miners' and workers' organizations.[54]

49. Ibid., 63.
50. See for instance *Nietzsches Werken,* ed. Walther Linden, 4 vols. (Berlin and Leipzig: Deutsches Verlagshaus Bong, 1933). Part of the *Goldene Klassiker Bibliothek,* it was advertised as essential to understanding this "visionary of the future," his critique of Deutschtum and analysis of "the natural stratification of our Volk." See too the volumes of the collected works brought out by the Beck Verlag in cooperation with the Nietzsche Archives. Selected collections include Paul Bergenhahn, ed., *Judentum/Christentum/Deutschtum* (Berlin: Paul Stegemann, 1936); Hans Endres, *Rasse, Ehe, Zucht und Züchtung bei Nietzsche und heute* (Heidelberg: Carl Winter, 1938).
51. Walter Kaufmann has reminded us that while it was necessary to expurgate Nietzsche before integrating him into the schools the same was not necessary for Wagner (*Nietzsche,* 41).
52. A good example was the neopagan, anti-Christian *Deutsche Glaubensbewegung* of Jacob Hauer.
53. "Soldat und Bürger," *Das schwartze Korps* (4 April 1935), 9.
54. The Aryan seminar at the University of Tübingen included lectures such as "Nietzsche als Zeuge arischer Weltanschauung" (Nietzsche as Creator of an Aryan Worldview"). See Werner Wirth's summary of his lecture, "Nietzsche und das Christentum," *Deutscher Glaube* 6 (1939). In Berlin, Bäumler taught "Nietzsches Philosophie (Ethik und Philosophie der Geschichte)" in summer 1934, and in 1941, "Nietzsche-Grundprobleme der Geschichtsphilosophie" (Sinn und Form [January 1988] 186). For the radio lectures see Friedrich Wurzbach, *Arbeit und Arbeiter in der neuen Gesellschaftsordnung: Nach Aphorismen von Nietzsche* (Berlin and Leipzig: Deutsches Verlagshaus Bong, 1933); Wurzbach, *Nietzsche und das deutsche Schicksal* (Berlin and Leipzig: Deutsches Verlagshaus Bong, 1933). Ernst Horneffer's *Nietzsche als Vorbote der*

Nietzsche's inspiration was invoked not only as the warp and woof of national socialism's soldierly weltanschauung[55] and its injunction to "live dangerously"[56] but as a personal mobilizing myth in the conduct of battle itself. If Nietzsche figured centrally as an inspirational force in World War I, by World War II he was officially enshrined in the state's war-exalting ideology.[57] Under national socialism German youth, as one writer put it, was putting the Nietzschean conception of war as healthy liberator into practice. Both Nietzsche's thought and deed had living mythical import for the destiny of the German present: "Arm in arm he marches with every victim."[58]

As the tide went against Germany (especially on the Eastern Front) Nietzsche was increasingly called upon in the apocalyptic struggle against the pernicious forces of bolshevism and world Jewry. With defeat looming, his injunction to "Love your destiny" (*Liebe dein Shicksal*)—to be prepared for sacrifice—became a leitmotif. "Nietzsche is the herald of the Either-Or. He hates compromise and affirms the unavoidable authentic decision. He is called to give us strength in this total war."[59] The official October 1944 Nietzsche centenary ceremonies were conspicuously less joyful and Dionysian than the archive festivals of the past and centered around fate, loneliness, and Nietzsche's dictum that whatever did not destroy one made one stronger.[60] Alfred Rosenberg's paean to Nietzsche on that occasion was clearly informed by the desperate situation of the German war machine. National socialism, Rosenberg proclaimed, stood before the rest of the world in exactly the way Nietzsche had confronted the forces of his own time. What distinguished Nietzsche from other thinkers was his ability to think in radical extremes, to philosophize in warlike and soldierly terms, and to con-

---

Gegenwart was based upon lectures he had given to miners which were originally published in the *Deutschen Bergwerkszeitung*.

55. "'Gegen krämerseelen, wie Engländer und andere Demokraten!': Nietzsche, der Philosoph des Soldatentums," *Der deutsche Erzieher* no. 3 (1940), 68–70.

56. J. Hauer, "Gefährlich Leben: Zu Neujahr 1943," *Deutscher Glaube* 10 (January 1943).

57. Nietzsche's warrior side was emphasized even when other areas of disagreement were mentioned (August Faust, *Philosophie des Krieges: Schriftenreihe zur weltanschaulichen Schulungsarbeit der NSDAP* no. 17 [Munich: Zentralverlag der NSDAP, 1942], 39–43).

58. Richard Gröper, "Nietzsches Stellung zum Kriege," *Nationalsozialistisches Bildungswesen* 7, no. 4 (April 1942), 104. (Gröper had been in the forefront of those who enlisted Nietzsche in the World War I effort.)

59. Wilhelm Löbsack, "Nietzsche und der Totale Krieg," *Der Deutsche im Osten* 6, no. 5 (August 1943), 213.

60. Hubert A. Cancik, "Der Nietzsche-Kult in Weimar (II)," in *Die Religion von Oberschichten*, 105–106.

ceive of ultimate scenarios like the present war. Two principles—the destructive Bolshevik Jewish and the rejuvenative National Socialist European—were locked in mortal combat, the stakes a massive experiment around nature and life.[61]

Nietzsche fulfilled other important functions. His elevated stature and his cultured writings enabled certain members of the German intelligentsia to make the turn to nazism and to employ him as inspiration and rationalization. For the most famous amongst them, Gottfried Benn, Nietzsche had always been a central pillar, whom he naturally called upon in his polemics against the German intellectual exiles. In response to Klaus Mann's imprecations against Nazi "barbarism," for instance, Benn handily invoked Nietzsche who had posed the problem: "Where are the barbarians of the twentieth century?" and preceded it with the dictum: "A dominating race can grow up only out of terrible and violent beginnings."[62] After Nietzsche only one criterion for the historically authentic existed: "the appearance . . . of the new type, and he, one must say, is here. . . . An authentic, new, historical movement is at hand . . . typologically neither good nor evil, it is now embarking on its being. . . . History does not proceed democratically but elementarily and its turning points become ever more elemental."[63]

The Nietzschean factor was probably even more marked for the self-consciousness of many of the intellectual foreign collaborators and for those French and Belgian volunteers who joined the Charlemagne Brigade and the Waffen SS. Their nazism was rationalized in terms of the vision of an aesthetic new European order led by a sleek elite of authentic and hard new men, Übermenschen capable of the most radical acts. Christian de La Maziere describes his induction into the Waffen SS, for instance, in caricaturistic Nietzschean terms: ". . . these men fascinated me and I wanted to incorporate myself there. I perceived them as strong, generous and pitiless: beings without weakness who would never putrefy."[64] As a propagandist in the SS, Marc Augier reflected:

61. Rosenberg, *Nietzsche*, 16, 21–24.
62. Nietzsche, *Will to Power*, 464–465. Benn quotes this on p. 52 in his 1933 "Answer to the Literary Emigrants" (Benn, *Primal Vision*, ed. E. B. Ashton [New York: New Directions, 1971], 46–53).
63. First presented as a radio-lecture see his "Der Neue Staat und die Intellektuellen," *Gesammelte Werke*, 433–444.
64. Christian de La Maziere, *The Captive Dreamer*, trans. Francis Stuart (New York: Saturday Review Press. / E. P. Dutton, 1974). Quoted in Saul Friedländer, *Reflections of Nazism: An Essay on Kitsch and Death*, trans. Thomas Weyr (New York: Avon, 1986), 8.

These people thought the world anew. One felt as if one had arrived at the outermost periphery of the Nietzschean thought world and its creative passion. . . . A victory of the SS (which did not necessarily signify a victory for Germany) would have given birth to a world that, though certainly considerably shocking, would have been totally novel and probably truly great. . . . In this Hildesheimer cloister . . . Nietzsche's transvaluation of all values was being prepared. It is the only example in history of a philosopher who had such a following of armies, armored vehicles, airplanes, doctors, knights, bureaucrats, and hangmen. The SS brought about the hatred of the world because it posed a real danger to the present order.[65]

This theme appears constantly in the conceptions of non-German sympathizers. As Marcel Deat put it: "Nietzsche's idea of the selection of 'good Europeans' is now being realized on the battlefield, by the LFV and the Waffen SS. An aristocracy, a knighthood is being created by the war which will be the hard, pure nucleus of the Europe of the future."[66]

The Nazis were able to capitalize on Nietzsche's European dimension as part of its own conception of a continental order. Nietzsche's European thinking—on the surface a deficiency for a nationalist movement—became a distinct advantage: indeed, there was no other authority from whom the Nazis could draw sustenance for their imperial vision. Even when the differences between the Nietzschean and the Nazi idea of a united Europe were carefully spelled out—for instance by Kurt Hildebrandt—the thematic similarities remained: German leadership of a regenerated European culture and politics and the breeding of an aristocratic caste organized on the basis of vitalistic antidemocratic and anti-Marxist principles.[67]

Nietzsche turned from Germany to Europe, Hildebrandt wrote later, because he knew it was only the Germans who possessed the greatness to implement its rebirth. After *The Birth of Tragedy* Nietzsche became far more realistic and political. His goal became ever more clear—not pacifism and world citizenship, but "great war" and, above all, the war

65. Marc Augier, *Götter Dämmerung: Wende und Ende einer grossen Zeit* (Buenos Aires: Editorial Prometheus, 1950), 79–80. I thank George Mosse for this reference.

66. Marcel Deat, *Pensee allemande et pensee francaise*, 97–98. Quoted in Ze'ev Sternhell, "Fascist Ideology," in *Fascism: A Reader's Guide*, ed. Walter Laqueur (Harmondsworth: Penguin, 1979), 363. Bertrand de Jouvenel argued similarly that the Nietzschean conception of man as something to be overcome was a "heroic remedy" used by "all the statesmen who had been restorers of society: the Augustuses and the Napoleons had attempted to revive the manly virtues—the sense of initiative, responsibility, and command." He concluded: "The similarity of what Mussolini and Hitler are attempting today is striking" (*La Reveil de l'Europe* [Paris: Gallimard, 1938], 245–246). Quoted in Sternhell, *Neither Right nor Left*, 256.

67. For a nuanced yet affirmative picture see Kurt Hildebrandt, "Der 'gute Europäer,'" *Deutscher Almanach* (1930), 151–165.

for the leadership of Europe and the challenge to the German Volk to create it anew. For Nietzsche, therefore, modern nationalism was too provincial. His vision of a Great Politics was far grander than that.[68] Today's "good Europeans," proclaimed Rosenberg, were Germans because they were carrying out Nietzsche's vision of continental, revolutionary regeneration.[69]

Those most closely associated with the nazification of Nietzsche were fully aware of the casuistic need to selectively channel him into its collective and Germanic imperatives, to both unleash the Nietzschean dynamic and keep it under control. For a nationalist, anti-Semitic, and racist movement the exercise was unavoidable. The need for some kind of interpretation was openly acknowledged to be necessary because the "real" Nietzschean message had either been previously misunderstood or willfully distorted by Nietzsche's earlier, literary, and nihilist—usually Jewish—devotees.[70]

Collectivizing Nietzsche went on apace. Ernst Horneffer insisted that Nietzsche, far from preaching individualism, was interested in setting up a new society based on new bonds and new collective values. The Übermensch was "not a singular concept but a racial and species one [Art—und Gattungsbegriff] . . . the fruit of an immense, uninterrupted human breeding project."[71] The fact, wrote Hildebrandt, that Nietzsche had attacked the Hegelian deification of the state did not make him an antinationalist individualist. "He wanted to oppose the cold instrumental state and soulless organization not with the disconnected individual but with authentic Volksgemeinschaft."[72]

The move from the individual to the collective Nietzsche, Bäumler argued, was difficult but necessary. The propelling force of Great Politics, he declared, was the feeling of power "which, out of unvanquishable sources, burst forth from time to time not only in the soul of the individual but also in the humble classes (niederen Schichten) of the Volk."[73] After all, Nietzsche had written in The Will to Power: "We are more than the individuals: we are the whole chain as well, with the tasks of all the futures of that chain."[74] Whoever like Nietzsche

68. Kurt Hildebrandt, "Die Idee des Krieges bei Goethe, Hölderlin, Nietzsche," in Das Bild des Krieges im deutsches Denken, vol. 1, ed. August Faust (Stuttgart and Berlin: W. Kohlhammer, 1941), 406–407.
69. Rosenberg, Nietzsche, 22.
70. Weisser, "Der Erzieher Nietzsche," 125.
71. Horneffer, Nietzsche als Vorbote, 18, 12–14, 41.
72. Hildebrandt, "Die Idee des Krieges," 403.
73. Bäumler, Nietzsche als Philosoph, 171–172.
74. Nietzsche, Will to Power, 366.

took the body as guide, Bäumler proclaimed, could not be an individualist; nor could anyone who thought historically. One only had to consult the *Genealogy of Morals* to see that Nietzsche talked in historical categories such as species, races, nations, and classes. The collective from which the individual sprang and derived his strength was not generalized humanity but always a concrete entity: a race, a Volk, a class.[75]

In innumerable discussions, minor and major mediators of Nietzsche clarified the "real" nature of his relationship to Germany and the Germans.[76] Was not Nietzsche insistent upon the core distinction between what was *Deutsch* (i.e., the Roman and Christian influences upon Germany) and what was *Germanic* (i.e., its freedom-loving, warlike nature)? Was not Zarathustra a Germanic figure who had taken up the Germanic mission to protect the rights of the Volk?[77] Were not Nietzsche's radical criticisms and biting comments an index of his pain, commitment, and hopes for this people of becoming? These commentators loved to quote Nietzsche's words from 1885: "So far, the Germans are nothing, but they will become something. . . . We Germans desire something from ourselves that has not yet been desired from us—we desire something more!"[78] Only now was the realization dawning that Nietzsche and authentic German destiny were inextricably united. *Friedrich Nietzsche as German Prophet* and *Nietzsche and German Destiny* were typical of this genre.[79] The theme took on an incantatory quality. By 1942 few were startled to learn that Nietzsche's mission was essentially völkisch and racial: Zarathustra was a mystical vehicle designed to create a new myth for *Deutsch-Germanische Menschheit*.[80]

Nietzsche's pro-Jewish comments and biting contempt for anti-Semitism clearly needed special explanation. Anyone familiar with Nietzsche, wrote Bäumler, knew how opposed to the Jews he really was. His philo-Semitic comments were an attention-gaining device—playing the Jews against the Germans was part of his strategy to get the

75. Bäumler, *Nietzsche als Philosoph,* 172, 180–181.
76. Hans Eggert Schröder, "Nietzsche und die Germanen," *Germanien* 9, no. 5 (May 1937).
77. Bäumler, *Nietzsche als Philosoph,* 88–100.
78. Nietzsche, *Will to Power,* 68.
79. Wurzbach, *Nietzsche und das deutsche Schicksal;* W. Huhle, *Friedrich Nietzsche als deutscher Prophet* (Chemnitz: Werner Boehm, 1935).
80. Paul Schulze-Berghof, "Der Zarathustra-Dichter als Mystiker," *Die musische Erziehung* no. 9 (1942), 7–10.

Germans to listen to him![81] More important, as numerous commentators stressed, Nietzsche had only opposed nineteenth-century forms of conventional and Christian anti-Semitism because he stood for a newer and far more radical form. Nietzsche only dismissed that anti-Semitism which was limited to the confessional, economic, and social domains, overlooking the biological dimension. He really regarded Jews as nothing less than a "parasitic species" (*parasitäre Menschengattung*) endangering the very survival of the Nordic race.[82] And, of course, Nietzsche became a crucial source for that radicalized drive designated by Uriel Tal as "anti-Christian anti-Semitism."[83]

Perhaps the most extreme expression of this was Hans Eggert Schröder's 1937 *Nietzsche and Christianity*.[84] Like many völkisch characterizations of Nietzsche, it emphasized the centrality of *The Birth of Tragedy*. The role of the philosopher, wrote Schröder, had been to sense and interpret the still unconscious historical mission of his people. The advent of Socrates broke this trend when, as Nietzsche had shown, an antivölkisch principle penetrated Greek antiquity. This had prevented the Greeks from realizing their historical mission as carriers of a tragic culture in which martial values were dominant. Socrates the rationalist had destroyed the Dionysian essence of this culture. Nietzsche's first great transvaluation, his great challenge to Germany, was the revivification of such a tragic culture.

Socratism functioned like Christianity. As Nietzsche demonstrated in *On the Genealogy of Morals*, Christianity was a Jewish invention, a fiendishly clever way of infecting the hearts of other Völker with the world-endangering spirit of Judaism. Socratism was merely Christianity's prefiguration. Plato's moral fanaticism had, after all, destroyed paganism. What was Christianity if not "Platonism for the Volk"? For Nietzsche there was a common völkisch essence to both the Greek and German experience: tragic culture. The precondition for its re-creation lay, as Nietzsche had uncompromisingly made clear, in the overcoming of Christianity. Christianity represented the victory of the antivölkisch principle over nations. Judaized Christianity was racial decline and decadence: "the antiracial principle applied against the racial."[85]

81. Bäumler, *Nietzsche als Philosoph*, 157; Öhler, *Nietzsche und die deutsche Zukunft*, 87ff.

82. Kassler, *Nietzsche und das Recht*, 74ff.

83. Tal, *Christians and Jews in Germany*, chap. 5.

84. Hans Eggert Schröder, *Nietzsche und das Christentum* (Berlin-Lichterfelde: Widukind, 1937).

85. Ibid., 75.

The regeneration of tragic culture and the fighting community (*Wehrgemeinschaft*) was thus dependent on the simultaneous overcoming of Jewish Christianity and other forms of theoretical man. This and other Nietzschean völkisch schemes—positing, for instance, radical distinctions between Graeco-Jewish logocentric and Graeco-Germanic biocentric principles—abounded in the Third Reich.[86] The point of such naturalizing schemes was to create alternatives to humanism and transcendence, principles which undermined life.[87] Irrationalist, tragi-Dionysian Nietzschean culture counteracted traditional conceptions of Western morality and rationalist Enlightenment and Marxist notions of progress.

The demonstrable thickness and ubiquity of the Nietzschean presence should not blind us to the complexities of Nietzsche's image and functions within Nazi discourse. Besides unadulterated veneration, mindless blending, and ideological matchmaking, there were those who maintained distinctions, voiced qualifications, and demurred from claiming total identity.[88]

This was certainly so for Heinrich Härtle's official *Nietzsche and National Socialism* (a work published by the central Nazi publishing house). This much-quoted exercise explicitly defined and differentiated "the boundaries, relationships, and contrasts between Nietzsche's political thought and national socialism."[89] Given the multivalent nature of Nietzsche, Härtle argued, National Socialists had to engage in a self-conscious sifting out of "fruitful" Nietzschean ideas from less acceptable ones. Härtle enumerated the problems—the advocacy of racial mixture, the critique of the state, and individualism—but concluded nevertheless that Nietzsche's ideas were the building blocks of a future National Socialist philosophy.[90]

86. Werner Deubel, "Gräkogermanisch–Gräkojudaisch: Bemerkungen über die Herkunft des neuen Menschenbildes," *Völkische Kultur* 2 (1934), 440–443. Deubel protrayed the logocentric as inevitably declining. (Its villains ranged from Paul and Plato through Descartes, Kant, Marx, industrialism, positivism, Americanism, and bolshevism.) The Graeco-Germanic biocentric tendency instead resulted in the triumphant German cultural revolution. The heroes of this scheme included Heraclitus, Luther, Paracelsus, Herder, Goethe, Schiller and culminated with Nietzsche and Klages.
87. Günther Augustin, review of Hans Eggert Schröder's *Nietzsche und Christentum* in *Deutscher Glaube* 5 (1938), 212.
88. The group included Donndorf, Hildebrandt, Horneffer, Kassler, and Römer. All, however, no matter how consciously selective they were, remained very positive in their overall posture.
89. Heinrich Härtle, *Nietzsche und der Nationalsozialismus* (Munich: Zentralverlag der NSDAP, Frank Eher Nachf, 1937), 5.
90. Ibid., 164.

All those discussed so far proclaimed the integrity of the Nietzschean–
Nazi nexus. There were, however, numerous critics who voiced a
dogged opposition to his annexation and maintained an anti-
Nietzschean position throughout. Unimpressed by the casuistry and
ideological tailoring, they kept on arguing what many on the unper-
suaded right had been saying since the 1880s. Much like Nietzsche's
liberal defenders they insisted that a terrible mistake was being made.
As Ernst Krieck, professor of pedagogy at the University of Heidelberg
and a prominent Nazi ideologue, caustically remarked: apart from the
fact that Nietzsche was not a socialist, not a nationalist, and opposed to
racial thinking, he could have been a leading National Socialist
thinker![91] There was no way that Nietzsche could be considered a
National Socialist; Nietzsche, one Nazi commentator exclaimed, was
not the solution to but a manifestation of Europe's decay.[92]

Dietrich Eckart, the homespun Schwabing völkisch philosopher who
seminally influenced Hitler, dismissed Nietzsche early on as simply a
case of inherited mental disease.[93] Elements of the völkisch movement
remained unrepentant in their rejection. It was the height of absurdity,
they argued, to present Nietzsche's hatred of the Germans as a form of
"angry love"; he was an avowed antinationalist and the great maligner
of the German Reich and of Germanism itself. What could this advocate
of egoistic individualism possibly have in common with Nazi communitarianism or the goal of a völkisch organic racial totality? Nietzsche
had unequivocally condemned what he called the "race-swindle," had
only contempt for anti-Semitism, and was indeed something of a
Jew-lover.[94]

91. Georg Müller, *Nietzsche und die deutsche Katastrophe* (Gütersloh: C. Bartles-
mann, 1946), 15. On Krieck's anti-Nietzschean stance see Langreder, "Die Auseinandersetzung mit Nietzsche," 105ff. One should not exaggerate Krieck's opposition. It was,
after all, his journal, *Volk im Werden*, that published Falkenberg's "Nietzsche und die
politische Wissenschaft."
92. Christoph Steding, *Das Reich und die Krankheit der europaischen Kultur* (Hamburg: Hanseatische Verlagsanstalt, 1943).
93. Göbel, *Nietzsche Heute*, 72.
94. For a typical example of this ongoing Völkisch opposition to Nietzsche, see
Arthur Drews, "Nietzsche als philosoph des Nationalsozialismus?" *Nordische Stimmen* 4
(1934), 172–179. The phrase *angry love* is also Drews's, p. 177. He interestingly argues
that Heine's criticism of Germany, unlike Nietzsche's, did flow from love! The work that
most systematically paints Nietzsche as philo-Semitic is the Wagnerian Curt von Westernhagen's *Nietzsche, Juden, Antijuden* (Weimar: Alexander Duncker, [1936]). Kaufmann praises the work for differing "from other Nazi studies by being scholarly and
candid" (*Nietzsche*, 296–297, n. 11). In the context of Nazi Germany, Westernhagen's
implicit charge that Nietzsche was unacceptable because he was not anti-Semitic renders
the work more suspect than Kaufmann allows.

Nietzsche could be criticized and berated because he was not a living
functionary of the Reich but a dead philosopher. Thus Christian circles
and churches responding to attacks by Alfred Rosenberg and affiliated
neopagan groupings could freely polemicize against Nietzsche as a
means of opposing Nazi religious policy in general and Rosenberg's
ideas in particular.[95] The nationalist and racist tenor of the times were
deeply imprinted in these polemics—especially the Protestant ones. As
one neopagan commentator pointedly noted, these protests condemned
Nietzsche not for his anti-Christian ideas but for his lack of nationalist
fervor and his blaspheming of the German Volk![96] Ironically, in their
advocacy of a Christian Germany, these Christian polemicists railed
against Nietzsche's antinationalist, antiracist, and pro-Jewish positions
as unbecoming of the new society in which the churches too sought to
play a role.[97] Such religious polemics did not hesitate to invoke racist
arguments in their opposition to Nietzsche. A Catholic opponent railed
that Nietzsche's Polish origins rendered him not Nordic but Mon-
golian![98]

Certain secular critics argued in similar ways. In Alfred von Martin's
1941 essay on Nietzsche and Burckhardt, for instance, a work that
clearly favored the latter's conservative humanism over the revolutionary politics of the former, Nietzsche's philo-Semitism was defined as a
form of anti-Germanism.[99]

All this did not exhaust the functions of such discourse. Sophisticated

95. Karl Kindt, "Nietzsches Heidentum: Randglossen zu einem unausschöpferischen
Thema"; Carl Schweitzer, "Nietzsche und die reformatische Botschaft"; and Tim Klein,
"Erlebnisse um Nietzsche" in the Protestant journal *Zeitwende* 12, no. 1 (October 1935).
96. George Duwe, "Nietzsche der deutsche Denker: Eine Antwort an Prof. D. E.
Pfennigsdorf, Bonn," *Deutscher Glaube* 4 (1937). The other side of the irony was that
Duwe's article demonstrated the depth of Nietzsche's Germanism! Nietzsche was the
prophet of the German race-bound myths.
97. This was especially true for Protestant polemics. For an important example see
Göbel, *Nietzsche heute*. See too Karl Kindt, "Nietzsche und die Deutschen," *Zeitwende*
12, no. 1 (October 1935). A far more sophisticated balance sheet that upholds an essentially Christian vision and the unity of world and nature, life and death, and state and
Volk is Wilhelm Michel, *Nietzsche in unserem Jahrhundert* (Berlin-Steglitz: Eckart,
1939). For a Catholic example see *Amtsblatt des Bischöflichen Ordinariats Berlin* [Amt-
liche Beilage: Grundfragen der Lebensauffassung und Lebensgestaltung: Fünfter Teil der
"Studien zum mythus des XX Jahrhunderts"] (Bischöflichen Ordinariat, n.d.). I thank
Prof. Y. Arielli for the latter reference.
98. Karl Kynast, *Die Sonne* (1933), 19.
99. Alfred von Martin, *Nietzsche und Burckhardt* (Munich, 1941), 170. For Martin,
Burckhardt was a positive foil to the negative Nietzschean world that implicitly pointed
to national socialism. During the Third Reich this comparative topic enjoyed a particular
vogue for the allusive functions it evoked. See too the pro-Nietzsche work by Edgar Salin,
Jacob Burckhardt und Nietzsche (Basel, 1938) and Hans Joachim Schöps, *Gestalten an
der Zeitwende: Burckhardt, Nietzsche, Kafka* (Berlin: Vortrupp Verlag, 1936).

thinkers frequently used Nietzsche as the foil for what Jerry Muller has termed Aesopian criticism. By 1937, for instance, a disillusioned Hans Freyer[100] rediscovered Nietzsche's stress on the neglected role of culture and spirit and the need for critical and untimely meditations in the Third Reich.[101] Martin Heidegger similarly claimed (in 1966) that his mammoth lecture series on Nietzsche between 1936 and 1940 constituted an essential part of his confrontation (*Auseinandersetzung*) with national socialism.[102]

But all these scholarly presentations, the head-on criticisms, oppositional polemics, Aesopian deployments, indeed, the very employment of Nietzsche as a foil for coming to terms with national socialism *demonstrate the normative nature and the centrality of that thinker as definitive of the Nazi order.* This was as true for the more critical and nuanced approaches as it was for the crudely adulatory ones. Many perceived that the present revolutionary epoch had to be defined, grasped, and even opposed through such a confrontation with Nietzsche.

Philosophical surveys of the day routinely described Nietzsche as "belonging to the present."[103] Nietzsche was clearly transformed into a touchstone for critical reference. This is best illustrated in terms of what one recent scholar has called the "metadiscourse" of German philosophy under national socialism, the ways that various schools competed to interpret and justify nazism and the political moment in terms of their own philosophical agendae.[104] All the surviving philosophical streams indulged in this exercise. The neo-Kantians, for instance—a group that survived exceedingly well during the Third Reich—argued that the great idealist tradition and "the theory of objective values" was the appropriate philosophy of the German revolution.[105]

100. Freyer's earlier works, including *Antäus: Grundlegung einer Ethik des bewussten Lebens* (Jena: Eugen Diederichs, 1918) and *Prometheus: Ideen zur Philosophie der Kultur* (Jena: Eugen Diederichs, 1923), had been hailed as continuations of Nietzsche's project. His most famous work was *Revolution von rechts* (Jena: Eugen Diederichs, 1931).

101. Afterword in Friedrich Nietzsche, *Vom Nützen und Nachteil der Historie für das Leben* (Leipzig, 1937), 85–95; Muller, *The Other God*, 299–300.

102. See his interview in *Der Spiegel*, 30, no. 23 (1966), 204.

103. Gerhard Lehmann, *Die deutsche Philosophie der Gegenwart*, 184.

104. On the constellation of German philosophies during this period see Sluga, "Metadiscourse." Sluga demonstrates that, excepting Marxist and positivist philosophies, major philosophical streams had little trouble accommodating themselves to the regime. All sought in competing, metadiscursive manner to "generate the true philosophy of national socialism" and struggled over the question "which of them had properly identified the movement's inner truth and greatness" (p. 801).

105. Examples of better-known neo-Kantians who operated sympathetically with the regime include Nicolai Hartmann and Bruno Bauch, who founded the Deutsche philo-

Startling as the notion of a Kantian nazism may be, those advocating
such a position were impelled to do so vis-à-vis the perception that
Nietzsche constituted the prevalent standard of reference.[106] The leading
neo-Kantian, Bruno Bauch, had to argue that values were not Nietzschean in nature but objective, "that which gives our subjective lives their
content and determination." There was a difference between values and
purposes. Purposes existed only insofar as one posited them; possessed
of no fixed being, they were a becoming that "fitted into the totality of
the realm of value." This, Bauch argued, was the real meaning of
Nietzsche's transvaluation of all values. He had not preached relativism
but that every pursuit of values was a process of approximation to the
objective realm.[107] Nicolai Hartmann employed a similar tactic: he
criticized Nietzsche yet sought to integrate him into the objectivist vision,
to fuse him with Kant. Nietzsche was praised for his demonstration of
the plenitude of values and for demonstrating that morality and Christianity were not identical. The material ethics of the day required a
"synthesis of the Kantian apriority and timelessness of moral demands
with Nietzsche's recognition of the manifold of values."[108]

The neo-Kantians were arguing that only on the basis of a more
stable and objective scheme of values could national socialism be firmly
grounded. Nevertheless they, like so many others, were fully aware of
Nietzsche's axial role in the political and philosophical reality of the
Third Reich. The debate had to be conducted in his terms.

It was thus hardly fortuitous that the great minds of the time—
especially Jaspers, Jung, and Heidegger—all chose Nietzsche for sustained analyses. If little united their aims, approaches, and conclusions,
their use of Nietzsche as a relevant filter and their intense engagement
with him was in itself significant. All were complex works inevitably
stamped by, and revealing attitudes towards, the novel experience of
nazism.

This certainly applies to Karl Jaspers's patently non-Nazi *Nietzsche*
of 1936 with its impassioned plea for a nonideological Nietzsche who
demolished all finite positions.[109] The significance of this Nietzsche

---

sophische Gesellschaft designed to combat the intrusion of foreign ideas into German
philosophy (Sluga, "Metadiscourse," 798–799).

106. Ibid., 809.

107. See the *Blätter für deutsche Philosophie* 8 (1934) and the excellent summary by
Sluga, "Metadiscourse," 808ff.

108. Ibid., 810.

109. Karl Jaspers, *Nietzsche: Einführung in das Verständnis seines Philosophierens*
(Berlin and Leipzig: De Gruyter, 1936). Translated as *Nietzsche: An Introduction to the*

resided not in the positive content of his philosophy but in the courageous mode of his philosophizing. For Jaspers, Nietzsche's greatness
consisted of the ordered whirl of his thinking, an operation that incorporated contradiction in such a way that confusion gave way to a form
of thought that rendered the contradictions themselves meaningful.

Contemporary pro-Nazi critics within Germany such as Kurt Hildebrandt, exiled opponents without, and later commentators such as Walter Kaufmann criticized Jaspers for his purely epistemological Nietzsche
shorn of any positive vision or system.[110] Hildebrandt upbraided Jaspers for his distance from the regime, while Kaufmann reproached him
for a stress on ambiguity that precluded such an interpretation from
becoming a rallying point of any opposition.

In his extended 1936 critique, Hildebrandt sought to maintain
Nietzsche's timely and positive role. The existentialist Jaspers, he wrote,
had portrayed the most unexistential picture of Nietzsche possible.
While Nietzsche opposed transcendence, Jaspers wanted to return to a
softened version of it. Jaspers had left out the connection between
Nietzsche's life, work, passions, and values. He had moreover neglected
seminal texts such as *Zarathustra* and *The Genealogy of Morals:*
"Nietzsche is inspired by the passion for knowledge, but higher than
that knowledge stands creativity, the new valuation, the new legisla-
tion." Nietzsche had provided a philosophy in which meaning derived
from constant, creative struggle, as "norm and power of an emergent
world-epoch."[111] For Hildebrandt this was not "free-floating," as Jaspers had argued. Rather it was a dynamism that resolved itself into a
normative system and a positive community.

Even if Jaspers's Nietzsche carried with it no positive ideological
countercontent, in the context of the Third Reich the emphasis on
freedom of thought, "the systematically conscious domination of one's
own thinking,"[112] was both courageous and immediately meaningful.
As he later argued, one could plausibly ground a Nazi position "down

---

Understanding of His Philosophical Activity by Charles Wallraff and Frederic Schmitz
(Tuscon: University of Arizona Press, 1980).
    110. Kurt Hildebrandt, "Über Deuting und Einordnung von Nietzsche's 'System,'"
Kant-Studien 41, nos. 3/4 (1936), 221–293. For opponents, see the reviews by Karl
Löwith and Max Horkheimer in *Zeitschrift für Sozialforschung* 6 (1937), 405–414;
Kaufmann correctly locates and lauds Jaspers's explicitly anti-Nazi stance ("Jaspers's
Relation to Nietzsche," in Schilpp, ed., *Philosophy of Karl Jaspers*, 425ff) but faults him
for refusing to countenance any positive content within Nietzsche's philosophy
(pp. 431ff). See too in the same book Jaspers's "Reply to My Critics," 857–863.
    111. Hildebrandt, "Über Deutung und Einordnung," 229–230, 236ff.
    112. Jaspers, "Reply to My Critics," 857–863.

to every detail, upon Nietzsche; just as one can see the exactly opposite position represented by Nietzsche with equal vehemence." What was most important at the time was "demonstrating the factual movement of Nietzsche's thinking as a room-making, illuminating, dialectically daring, never fixating kind of thinking."[113]

The same shaping context, the looming background of nazism, helps to explain the marathon 1934–1939 Zurich seminar Jung held on *Zarathustra*. Jung's remarkable and sustained reflective project—with its deliciously detailed analysis of the inner workings and psychological structure of the Zarathustrian symbolic world—laid bare *Zarathustra* as an example of the creative and demonic gyrations of the collective unconscious. Moreover, it employed Nietzsche and *Zarathustra* as illustrations and affirmations of his own psychological system and sought to uncover some of the deeper, hidden connections between Nietzsche and national socialism.[114] After initial hesitations, he told his students,

> I myself agreed to risk the analysis of *Zarathustra*, chiefly because it is a very modern piece of work which has much to do with what is happening in our time; I thought it might be of great interest to look into the actual workings of the unconscious mind, which has anticipated all the great political and historical events of our days.[115]

Towards the end of the seminar Jung formulated its rationale in even blunter terms:

> Modern people follow Zarathustra. But he did not see that he was really anticipating the whole future development, that there would be a time when what he says here would come true. It is as if the whole world had heard of Nietzsche or read his books, and had consciously brought it about. Of course, they had not. He simply listened in to that underground process of the collective unconscious and he was able to realize it—he talked of it, but nobody else noticed it. Nevertheless, they all developed in that direction, and they would have developed in that direction even if there had been no Nietzsche. For they never understood it. Perhaps I am the only one who takes the trouble to go so much into the detail of Zarathustra—far too much, some people may think. So nobody actually realizes to what extent he was connected with the unconscious and therefore with the fate of Europe in general, for it is the same trouble all over the world.[116]

113. Ibid., 860, 859 respectively.
114. C. J. Jung, *Nietzsche's Zarathustra*. I first read these lectures in their original, unpublished form and would like to thank Gustav Dreyfuss for giving me access to them and Bernie Stein for alerting me to their existence.
115. Ibid., vol. 2, 893.
116. Ibid., vol. 2, 1518.

In its comparatively short history, Nietzsche commentary has spawned a few classics. Typically these creative works have told us as much about the author as their subject. Nietzsche the man and his protean works is splendidly made to light up Jung's own vision, a densely projective confirmation of his own psychological system. *Zarathustra*, proclaimed Jung at the opening session, had a great revelatory character. It poured out of Nietzsche as an almost autonomous production, an expression not of the personal but of the collective unconscious, "a condition of possession where he himself practically no longer existed."[117] Grasping it required a sophisticated psychological sense. But, Jung emphasized, it took "the experience of the war and of the postwar social and political phenomena to get an insight into the meaning of *Zarathustra*."[118] Nietzsche was, if anything, proof of the existence (and vitality) of the Jungian collective unconscious. He "tickled something in the unconscious; for he tried to formulate what is actually happening in the collective unconscious of modern man, to give words to that disturbance."[119]

Jung's *Zarathustra* seminar was a sprawling psychological investigation of virtually every aspect of the work; the implicit links to national socialism were brought to the fore only intermittently. Yet, when made explicit they illuminated both Jung's reading of Nietzsche and what he regarded as the ontology of nazism. His ambivalent views on nazism can be gleaned from the following:

> Well, we are not judges, we simply make statements. You know that there is nothing so evil that something good could not come out of it. . . . One cannot help admitting that Fascism has done any amount of good for Italy; it is a different country. And so there are plenty of people, foreigners (the Germans themselves are inclined to be prejudiced), who have seen and praised what has happened in Germany, and even in Russia, as a higher tendency. So it is exceedingly difficult to judge. From one aspect things are positive, and from another, quite negative.[120]

Over time he modified his view; nevertheless in a qualified—and changing—sense Jung consistently regarded nazism as a kind of

117. Ibid., vol. 1, 11. Jung argued that Nietzsche could take his material directly from the unconscious because he was completely severed from the mediating medieval tradition (vol. 2, 894). Much of the analysis involves ingenious interpretations of Zarathustrian symbols. When Nietzsche, for instance, says he "left the lake of his home" (vol. 1, 14), Jung takes this as confirmation of the transition to the collective unconscious. Lakes, he argues, are confined and locked into terra firma which always symbolize consciousness, whereas the sea, as symbol of the collective unconscious, has no real boundaries. The seminar discussions Jung conducted were remarkably open and receptive.
118. Ibid., vol. 1, 60.
119. Ibid., vol. 1, 104.
120. Ibid., vol. 1, 377–378.

Nietzschean project. Were not the SS schools at Ordensburgen (and the Communist party in Russia) projects in molding Nietzsche's new nobility? Nietzsche had foreseen exactly that, although, Jung hastened to point out, he meant "a real nobility—not one that is made but one that creates itself."[121]

Nietzsche's conception of life as *amor fati,* self-sacrifice, Jung argued,

> is the attitude now prevailing in Germany, it is the inner meaning of National Socialism. They live in order to live on—or to die. When you hear the really serious people talk, you realize that Nietzsche simply anticipated that style. They praise the attitude of being ready, and naturally any rationalist asks, for what? That is just the point—nobody knows for what. Therefore, they have no program; they have no mapped-out scheme which should be fulfilled. They live for the moment. They don't know where they are going. Very influential and competent people of that party acknowledge that they don't know, but one thing is certain: they are going, there is no return, they must risk it. Then the rationalist asks: Risk what? The answer is, Risk *it.* . . . This is of course pure madness from a rationalistic standpoint, and this is what Nietzsche means. One can say it is all pathological, or that it is a divine or a demoniacal madness, but that is exactly the madness Nietzsche means. So Nietzsche is in a way the great prophet of what is actually happening in Germany.[122]

For Jung, this purported psychological affinity between Nietzsche and the German people served also as an example and validation of his own theory. Nietzsche, he declared,

> anticipated, through his sensitivity, a great deal of the subsequent mental development; he was assailed by the collective unconscious to such an extent that quite involuntarily he became aware of the collective unconscious that was characteristic of his time and the time that followed. Therefore, he is called a prophet, and in a way he is a prophet. . . . [H]is life and fate, one could say, was a collective program; his life was a forecast of a certain fate for his own country.[123]

In Jung's system the conventional notion of the forerunner underwent metamorphosis, replaced by a theory of involuntary, anticipatory intuition:

> You see in how far Nietzsche is a forerunner. But the Germans of his generation and the next generation and all the following generations are not so gifted that they would learn it from Nietzsche; it just happens to them. And Nietzsche could foretell it because it happened to him; in a certain way he

121. Ibid., vol. 2, 1523–1524.
122. Ibid., vol. 1, 87–88.
123. Ibid., vol. 2, 1300.

anticipated in his own life and his own body what the future of his people would be.[124]

But Jung did not simply reduce Nietzsche to a prefiguration of nazism as an expression of the German collective unconscious. There were times when Jung was explicitly critical of nazism, portraying it as a misapplication of the Nietzschean world that to be properly comprehended entailed special preparation. It is worth quoting this in detail:

> Nietzsche himself would be highly astonished to hear such news. He surely never dreamt that he would be called the father of all this modern political evil. That really comes from the misunderstanding to which Nietzsche is exposed. For he made one considerable mistake which of course would not be generally considered a mistake. But *I* call it a mistake that he ever published *Zarathustra*. That is a book which ought not to be published; it should be reserved for people who have undergone a very careful training in the psychology of the unconscious. Only then, having given evidence of not being overthrown by what the unconscious occasionally says, should people have access to the book. . . . If a man reads *Zarathustra* unprepared, with all the naive presuppositions of our actual civilization, he must necessarily draw wrong conclusions as to the meaning of the "Superman," "the Blond Beast," "the Pale Criminal," and so on.[125]

Jung was quite aware that what Nietzsche had said in the chapter "The New Idol" could "be used in favor of a Fascist, National Socialist, or a Communist state, and it also can be used as the best argument against all these creations."[126]

For Jung, in effect, both nazism and Nietzsche were expressions of important, deep levels of the collective unconscious. As the seminar progressed, however, he indicated that he regarded the Nazi appropriation less salutary than the Nietzschean one. He illustrated this in his discussion of the passage where Nietzsche predicts: "Ye lonesome ones of today, ye seceding ones, ye shall one day be a people: out of you who have chosen yourselves, shall a chosen people arise: and out of it the Superman."[127] Jung interpreted the psychohermeneutic dynamics of this passage thus:

> You see, the Superman really is "a people," not one man; that can be understood very literally. For if these lonely or seceding ones integrate their unconscious, they are of course different from other people insofar as their consciousness is more extended, and then it is as if they were uniting the

124. Ibid., vol. 1, 495–496.
125. Ibid., vol. 1, 475–476.
126. Ibid., vol. 1, 582.
127. Nietzsche, *Zarathustra*, 189. Translated in ibid., vol. 2, 826.

statistics of a whole people in one psychology. . . . If one extends one's
consciousness so that one sees that one is many things besides one's ego, one
approaches a certain realization of the self. But it is also true in another way:
namely, if an attempt at an extension of consciousness appears somewhere
and is not realized, then it causes a sort of mental infection . . . or it causes
a mental epidemic such as one sees actually happening in Germany. That is
the Superman on the level of non-realization; the whole people is like one
man and one man is shown as an emblem or symbol of the whole nation.
That is the substitute for the integration of the consciousness of one individual. You see Germany *should* be one individual but with an integrated
consciousness; instead of that there is just no integration of the unconscious,
but the whole people is integrated into one sacred figure—which nobody
fully believes *could* be sacred. That is the unfortunate thing.[128]

Whichever way one reads it, Jung's *Zarathustra* of the 1930s left
little doubt of the relationship between that document and the apocalyptic politics of his own time and about the complex relations pertain-
ing between Nietzsche and national socialism. Martin Heidegger was
similarly concerned with this mutual complicity. We will not enter into
the current debate about Heidegger and national socialism nor the
purported links between his politics and his philosophy but shall limit
ourselves here to the Heidegger-Nietzsche relationship.[129]

Nietzsche and Nietzschean themes, especially the critique of values
and reason and the concomitant emphasis on an overcoming heroic
mythology, were among Heidegger's chief preoccupations from the
1930s. His *Nietzsche*—contained in the lectures (1936–1940) and ad-
joining treatises (1940–1946)—reflected his changing understanding,
expectations, and evaluations of both Nietzsche and national socialism.
Equally important, the "shattering" confrontation with Nietzsche generated what Heidegger considered to be a crucial shift in his own thinking, which provided, as he put it, the key to the mental road he had
traversed from 1930 to his 1947 "Letter on Humanism."[130]

In Heidegger's self-description Nietzsche assumed a core role in these
philosophical and political permutations. In an open letter to his friend
and fellow radical-right Nietzschean Ernst Jünger many years after the
war, he claimed that it was Nietzsche "in whose light and shadow all of
us today, with our 'pro-Nietzsche' or 'contra-Nietzsche' are thinking

128. Ibid., vol. 2, 827.
129. This—not so new—question has been revived by the publication and translation
of Victor Farias's *Heidegger und der Nationalsozialismus* (Frankfurt: Fischer, 1989). See
too Jürg Altwegg, *Die Heidegger Kontroverse* (Frankfurt: Athenaeum, 1988); Hugo Ott,
Martin Heidegger: Unterwegs zu einer Biographie (Frankfurt: Campus, 1988).
130. David Farrell Krell, foreword to Martin Heidegger, *Nietzsche: The Will to Power
as Art*, vol. 1, trans. David Farrell Krell (San Francisco: Harper and Row, 1979), xvi.

and writing."[131] Indeed, (at least in his self-presentation), Heidegger's affirmation and later negation of national socialism was causally connected with his initial adoption and subsequent rejection of Nietzsche.

Nietzsche is a relatively minor presence in *Being and Time* (1926), although the book deals with a Nietzschean problem, since it revolves around the anxiety attendant upon the recognition of nihilism and the sense that there can be no "objective" grounding for ethics.[132] Be that as it may, Heidegger's explicit turn to Nietzsche coincided with his attraction to the antidemocratic, radical-right thought of the Weimar Republic in 1929. Awareness of the contemporary crisis drew Heidegger ever closer to Nietzsche and it was then, if some major Heidegger scholars are to be believed, that these kinds of political and ideological motifs "entered into the heart of Heidegger's philosophy itself."[133]

The reasons for the shift to Nietzsche, however, are less important than the fact that, throughout the 1930s and 1940s, Heidegger's categories and thematics, his *Fragestellung* and metadiscourse, depended on the Nietzschean frame. Heidegger inherited Nietzsche's conviction that the history of philosophy had come to an end and that a new era was emerging. Nietzsche's formulation of the nihilist predicament remained the core issue from the 1930s. Moreover, Heidegger's initial solution for the overcoming of nihilism—through a heroic, existential, self-affirmative will—was unexceptionally Nietzschean. If later he chose to dissolve self-assertion and metaphysics in complete submission to the Voice of Being, his problematic nevertheless remained cast within

---

131. Martin Heidegger, "Zur Seinsfrage," *Wegmarken* (Frankfurt am Main: V. Klostermann, 1967), 252. Quoted in David Farrell Krell, "Analysis," in Heidegger, *Nietzsche*, vol. 4, 293.

132. Personal communication, Jerry Muller. See too Gerald Izenberg, *The Existentialist Critique of Freud: The Crisis of Autonomy* (Princeton, N.J.: Princeton University Press, 1976), 90ff.

133. Jürgen Habermas, "Work and Weltanschauung: The Heidegger Controversy from a German Perspective," *Critical Inquiry* 15, no. 2 (Winter 1989), 439, 441. Otto Pöggeler, Heidegger's student and critic, has argued that Nietzsche's function was already critical, evident in Heidegger's shift from Christian to neopagan themes, in his argument for a mythologizing recourse to the archaic, and in his plea for "a god who can save us." "Was there not . . . a road from Nietzsche to Hitler? Did not Heidegger attempt from 1929 on to find his path with Nietzsche through the creativity of the great creators, back to the tragic experience of life, and thus to an historical greatness, in order then to win back for the Germans the beginnings of Greek thought and a horizon transposed by myth?" (Pöggeler, "Den Führe führen? Heidegger und kein Ende," *Philosophische Rundschau* 32 [1985], 47). Quoted in Habermas, *Philosophical Discourse*, 440.

the radical Nietzschean critique of reason and the end of Western philosophy.[134]

The predicament of, and proposed solution to, European nihilism was the explicit basis of the Heideggerian meditations on the "inner truth and greatness of national socialism."[135] Heideggerian existentialism flowed from a particular radical analysis of this historical situation and the experience of nihilism. As Karl Löwith had already noted in 1939, the perception of decline and impending European catastrophe with its concomitant "will to rupture, revolution, and awakening" was not an idiosyncratic Heideggerian whim, but part and parcel of the post-1914 radical-right stock-in-trade, integral to the conservative revolutionary mentalité.[136] Löwith regarded Heidegger as an even more radical formulator of the German Revolution than its official ideologues (such as Ernst Krieck and Alfred Rosenberg). To be sure, Heidegger's metadiscourse of national socialism was quite different from its Kantian or Hegelian versions. What was essential was not the objective grounding, the national, social, or racial content of the movement, but the dynamics of the resolve as such—"existence reduced to itself and resting on itself alone in face of nothingness." Here only the radical will to the essence of being counted. It was this, argued Löwith, that had attracted Heidegger to the Nietzsche who "prefers to will nothingness than to will nothing at all."[137]

At that stage Heidegger could still approve of Nietzsche's conception

134. For a clear account of this change see J. L. Mehta, *The Philosophy of Martin Heidegger* (New York: Harper and Row, 1971), 81–122, especially 112–113; see too Jürgen Habermas, "The Undermining of Western Rationalism through the Critique of Metaphysics," in *Philosophical Discourse*. Habermas points out that from Schlegel to Nietzsche the critique of reason called for a new mythology. "But only Heidegger vaporized this concrete need by ontologizing it and foundationalizing it into a Being that is withdrawn from beings" (p. 139). See too George Lichtheim, "On the Rim of the Volcano: Heidegger, Bloch, Adorno," *Encounter* 22, no. 4 (April 1964).

135. For the troubled history of this phrase see Thomas Sheehan's excellent "Heidegger and the Nazis," *New York Review of Books* (16 June 1988); Martin Heidegger, *Introduction to Metaphysics*, trans. Ralph Manheim (New Haven: Yale University Press, 1959), 199.

136. [The article has appeared in English translation by Richard Wolin and Melissa J. Cox.] Karl Löwith, "The Political Implications of Heidegger's Existentialism," *New German Critique* no. 45 (Fall 1988). Although Heidegger's thought must obviously not be reduced to the conservative revolutionary mode of the interwar period, this did form part of its context (Jeffrey Herf, *Reactionary Modernism*, chap. 5; Pierre Bourdieu, *L'ontologie politique de Martin Heidegger* [Paris: Editions de Minuit, 1988]).

137. Heidegger's most accessible discussion of this Nietzschean theme in relation to nihilism can be found in his 1943 talk, "The Word of Nietzsche: 'God Is Dead'" (Heidegger, *The Question Concerning Technology and Other Essays*, trans. William Lovitt [New York: Harper and Row, 1977], 79). The passage in Nietzsche appears in *Genealogy of Morals*, 97. See too Löwith, "Heidegger's Existentialism," 133.

of will as "in itself simultaneously creative and destructive."[138] His Nietzsche posited nihilism not simply as a phenomenon of decay but as the intrinsic law of Western history. It contained a new unconditioned principle of revaluation that would no longer be based upon the lifeless, suprasensory world. Nihilism was here conceived as an intrinsic part of Nietzsche's ideal of superabundant life.[139]

These Nietzschean concerns, Heidegger made very clear, related directly to the German Revolution under way. In his famous 1933 rectorate speech "The Self-Assertion of the German University," the great transformation of German being (*Dasein*) was linked to the creative possibilities of the nihilistic moment—"if what the passionate seeker of God and the last German philosopher, Friedrich Nietzsche, said is true: 'God is dead.' "[140]

Apart from the defining predicament, Heidegger's linguistic tonalities and suggested resolution reverberated with (a suitably nationalized) Nietzsche. German science and the fate of the Volk were affirmed as a unity in their single essential will to power (*Wesenswillen zur Macht*.) German students and teachers were to establish a fighting community (*Kampfgemeinschaft*) whose combative will to service in knowledge would take them to the outpost of the most extreme danger of human existence. In the face of European decay nothing less than the most radical, self-affirming will was necessary:

> No one will even ask us whether we do or do not will, when the spiritual strength of the West fails and the joints of the world no longer hold, when this moribund semblance of a culture caves in and drags all that remains strong into confusion and lets it suffocate in madness.
>
> Whether this will happen or not depends alone on whether or not we, as a spiritual-historical people, still and once again will ourselves. Every individual *participates* in this decision, even he, and indeed especially he, who evades it.
>
> But we do will that our people fulfill its historical mission.
>
> We do will ourselves. For the young and the youngest strength of the people, which already reaches beyond us, *has* by now *decided* the matter.[141]

---

138. Heidegger, vol. 1, *Will to Power as Art*, 63. These lectures were given during Winter 1936–1937.

139. Heidegger, "Word of Nietzsche," 67–70.

140. *Die Selbstbehauptung der deutschen Universität* (Frankfurt: V. Klostermann, 1983). Translated as "The Self-Assertion of the German University" by Karsten Harries, in *Review of Metaphysics* 38 (1984/85), 470–480. This translation has not been entirely followed here.

141. "The Self-Assertion of the German University," 479–480.

Even if his activist solution was later replaced, Heidegger accepted
the redemptive possibilities inherent in the nihilist predicament. "We
experience precisely the most extreme nihilism not as a complete down-
fall but as the transition to new conditions of human existence," he
wrote in 1940.[142] Initially, Heidegger explicitly regarded both fascism
and nazism as potentially positive transitions to such new conditions.
They were essentially Nietzschean projects—the most radical attempts
to date to overcome Western nihilism: "The two men," Heidegger proclaimed in his 1936 lectures on Schelling, "who each in his own way,
have introduced a counter-movement to nihilism—Mussolini and Hitler—have learned from Nietzsche, each in an essentially different way.
But even with that, Nietzsche's authentic metaphysical domain has not
yet come into its own."[143]

Heidegger, to be sure, openly juxtaposed his conception of
Nietzsche's "authentic domain" with that of Bäumler who, he proclaimed, "does not grasp metaphysically but interprets politically."[144] It
was precisely the simplistic and politicized Nazi Nietzsche, one sympathetic commentator has argued, who provided "the context in which
Heidegger had to address the students attending his lectures. What they
heard from Heidegger was something different—it was in fact totally
out of context."[145]

---

142. Martin Heidegger, *Nietzsche*, vol. 4, *Nihilism*, trans. Frank A. Capuzzi (San
Francisco: Harper and Row, 1982), 50–51. Heidegger quoted Nietzsche:

> *Overall insight.* All major growth is in fact accompanied by a tremendous *disin-
> tegration* and *passing away:* suffering, the symptoms of decline, *belong* to the times
> of tremendous advance; every fertile and powerful movement of humanity has also
> *created at the same time* a nihilistic movement. It could turn out to be the sign of
> crucial and most essential growth, of transition to new conditions of existence, that
> the *most extreme* form of pessimism, *nihilism* proper, comes into the world. *This
> I have grasped.*

See Nietzsche, *Will to Power*, 69.

143. Quoted in Sheehan, "Heidegger and the Nazis," 43. In note 43 Sheehan observes
that these remarks were omitted from the published version of the Schelling lectures and
cites them from Carl Ulmer, *Der Spiegel* (2 May 1977), 10.

144. Heidegger, *Will to Power as Art*, 22. The main disagreement revolved around
Bäumler's sweeping rejection of the doctrine of eternal recurrence as a whim of Nietzsche.
Nietzsche, wrote Bäumler, was above all interested in the unlimited flux of becoming and
eternal recurrence was a denial of that doctrine. For Heidegger, eternal recurrence was a
central ingredient of Nietzsche's thought. Volume two of Heidegger's *Nietzsche* is entitled
The Eternal Recurrence of the Same (San Francisco: Harper and Row, 1984). "'Re-
currence' thinks the permanentizing of what becomes, thinks it to the point where the
becoming of what becomes is secured in the *duration of its becoming*" (Heidegger,
Nietzsche, vol. 3, *The Will to Power as Knowledge*, trans. Joan Stambaugh et al. [San
Francisco: Harper and Row 1987], 165).

145. Krell, "Analysis," in Heidegger, *Nietzsche*, vol. 4, 272.

"No Nazi hoodlum, to my knowledge," George Steiner correctly comments on *Being and Time,* "ever read or would have been capable of reading it."[146] In the same way Heidegger's *Nietzsche* was unquestionably written on a higher level than any Nazi rendering could muster. Certainly many of its insights into the critique of reason were enduring. But these lectures must have equally impressed and perplexed his bemused students. Nietzsche often became unrecognizable as he was ingested into the Heideggerian system of thought and framed within its heady vocabulary. The Übermensch, Heidegger told his students, "lives because the new mankind wills the Being of beings as will to power. It wills such Being because it is itself willed by that Being—the Being that is absolutely left to itself as mankind."[147]

These lectures were the putative crucible for Heidegger's switch. He grew doubtful, we are told, of the related redemptive powers of either Nietzsche or national socialism. This growing skepticism is usually represented as the major "context" and significance of these lectures. But within the contours of the Third Reich and Nietzsche's authorized role, the very use of Nietzschean categories and terminology formed part of an already-charged political context informing the audience's receptivity and predispositions. Students, like other Germans, had after all been repeatedly told that this was Nietzsche's time. It is unclear how they understood Heidegger's messages. While he obviously distanced himself from Bäumler-like interpretations, from simplistic equations of nihilism with bolshevism and from biologism, these were nevertheless dangerously connotive political categories that required greater critical analysis.[148] This aside, the radical tone of Heidegger's language and his choice of quotes appeared at times to render Nazi reality as somehow tame in terms of the Nietzschean vision that Heidegger seemed to commend to his audience:

> Man is *beast* and *Overbeast:* the higher man is Nonman and Overman: these belong together. With every growth of man in greatness and height, there is also growth in depth and terribleness: one should not will the one without the other—or rather: the more radically we will the one, the more radically we achieve precisely the other.[149]

146. George Steiner, "Heidegger, Again," *Salmagundi,* nos. 82–83 (Spring–Summer 1989), 45–46.
147. Heidegger, *Nietzsche,* vol. 3, 227.
148. Ibid., 231. "Just as Nietzsche's thought of will to power was ontological rather than biological, even more was his racial thought metaphysical rather than biological in meaning." Yet this clearly left room for "metaphysical racial thought"—whatever that meant.
149. Ibid., vol. 4, 51.

Whether or not the intention was critical, many passages could have been taken as validating the regime's self-conception and aims. Heidegger's analysis of the Übermensch as the new embodiment of the will to power expressed in "domination of the earth" was stated, after all, within a metadiscourse tailored to the prevailing political reality. The Übermensch, Heidegger emphasized, belonged to the "grand style" of human breeding and social organization in which the "sole meaning of the one who as legislator first posits the conditions of domination over the earth consists precisely in not being defined by such conditions."[150] Formulated within the actuality of the Third Reich in 1939–1940, Heidegger's acute description of the Nietzschean project must have had an immediate resonance that, given his purported critical intention, surely required further critical analysis.

He maintained his ambiguous language throughout: sifting the critical from the functionally necessary elements of the contemporary Übermensch and his domination over the earth became a delicate exercise indeed:

> We today are witness to a mysterious law of history which states that one day a people no longer measures up to the metaphysics that arose from its own history; that day arrives when such metaphysics has been transformed into the absolute. What Nietzsche already knew metaphysically now becomes clear: that in its absolute form the modern "machine economy" . . . demands a new kind of man who surpasses man as he has been hitherto. . . . [O]nly the Over-man is appropriate to an absolute "machine-economy": he needs it for absolute dominion over the earth.[151]

We must, however, return to the barometric role that Nietzsche played in the self-consciousness of the period. Heidegger's self-described reevaluation of both national socialism and his own thought was intimately bound up with his prolonged encounter with Nietzsche.[152] Heidegger initially greeted the Nietzschean transvaluation of values as the proper philosophical answer to the nihilist predicament and the activist will to power of the Nazi revolution as the appropriate political countermovement to nihilism, the proper (völkisch) human

---

150. Ibid., vol. 3, 232–233. See too Heidegger's revealing comments on the will to power, universal morality, and British and German standards in vol. 4, 144–145.

151. Ibid., vol. 4, 116–117.

152. Much of the contemporary literature argues that there never was a fundamental re-evaluation of national socialism and that to the end Heidegger remained wedded to the historical potential of national socialism, differentiating it from its debased historical actuality.

means to force Being to surrender its secret.[153] His rejection of crucial elements in national socialism, his work and Nietzsche's, and his abdication of will and self-assertion in the face of Being was brought home to him through

> the devastating, shattering realization that Nietzsche's philosophy of the Will-to-power was only the nihilistic culmination of something inherent in the very nature of the metaphysical tradition of the West as it had developed from Plato onwards. The realization that in his own philosophy, deliberately seeking to "overcome" metaphysics, this will, this nihilistic canker, was still a powerful driving force, standing between him and Being—the goal of his entire quest—seems to have led to the collapse of this will and to a complete surrender to the "Voice of Being."[154]

Since then, Nietzsche, despite his profound critique of philosophical humanism, came to represent not the overthrow but the last embodiment of the Western tradition of metaphysics. Nietzsche's will to power was based on an exaltation rather than a renunciation of the will. Henceforth, Nietzsche was not only unable to provide an antidote to nihilism, he even became an expression of it:

> Nietzsche understands his own philosophy as the countermovement to metaphysics, and that means for him a movement in opposition to Platonism.
> Nevertheless, as a mere countermovement it necessarily remains, as does everything "anti," held fast in the essence of that over against which it moves. Nietzsche's countermovement against metaphysics is, as the mere turning upside down of metaphysics, an inextricable entanglement in metaphysics, in such a way, indeed, that metaphysics is cut off from its essence and, as metaphysics, is never able to think its own essence.[155]

Heidegger substituted his original positive evaluation of the will to power as a lever to disclose Being for one that equated it with simple domination and the triumph of subject-centered technology, indeed, with the misguided self-asserting cultural project of modernity itself. Initially the Nietzschean frame of reference validated the Nazi enterprise—later the dismissal of the Nietzschean worldview formed the basis for the critique of nazism. As Richard Wolin succinctly puts it:

> National Socialism, which originally presented itself (in Heidegger's eyes) as a counter-movement to the nihilism of the Western "will to techne," and thus as a world-historical alternative to the "nihilism" so reviled by

153. For an excellent description of this dual structure and the parallel process of change see Richard Wolin, "The French Heidegger Debate," *New German Critique* no. 45 (Fall 1988), 154–156; Mehta, *Philosophy of Martin Heidegger,* 40.
154. Ibid., 112–113.
155. Heidegger, "Word of Nietzsche," 61.

Nietzsche, in the end proved to be only a different historical manifestation of that same nihilism, in the same way that Nietzsche's strident critique of metaphysics itself ultimately rested on metaphysical foundations. The equation according to which Heidegger proceeds, therefore, is: National Socialism = Nietzscheanism = metaphysics.[156]

Ultimately, both Heidegger's self-proclaimed acceptance and rejection of national socialism were based upon a Nietzschean frame of reference. In a memorandum composed at the time of his denazification proceedings, his distantiation was formulated wholly within this latterly formulated critique of the

> universal rule of the will to power within history, now understood to embrace the planet. Today everything stands in this historical reality, no matter whether it is called communism, or facism, or world democracy. This reality of the will to power can be expressed, with Nietzsche, in the proposition: "God is dead." . . . Had things been different, would the First World War have been possible? And even more, had things been different, would the Second World War have been possible?[157]

For Heidegger the original Nietzschean notion of the will to power became synonymous with subject-centered, dominating global technology and was employed as a means of obfuscating nazism's particular historical reality and reducing it to an undifferentiated indictment of modernity. His multipurpose, monolithic will to power encompassed everything and dully equated motorized agriculture with the gas chambers, the extermination of six million Jews with Allied treatment of East Germans.[158] Indeed, as George Steiner has suggested, Heidegger's refusal to come to terms with the Holocaust stemmed from his refusal to derive ethical principles from the "thinking of Being." Heideggerian thought in all its prodigal richness and diversity "neither contains nor

156. Wolin, "French Heidegger Debate," 156–157. The danger and absurdity of this kind of analysis in some of its contemporary guises is that national socialism now becomes indicted for its excess of humanism!

157. Martin Heidegger, "The Rectorate 1933/34: Facts and Thoughts," *Review of Metaphysics* 38 (1984/85), 484–485. His claim that already in 1932, under the influence of Ernst Jünger's works, he had formulated a conception of the will to power in order to counter it, as we have shown, disingenuously omitted his earlier, far more positive reading of its redemptive role.

158. For details and a fine analysis of these Heideggerian statements see Sheehan, "Heidegger and the Nazis," 41–42, 45. In this respect Heidegger was well ahead of the times, anticipating the arguments that were to be voiced during the recent so-called *Historikerstreit*, the debate amongst German historians concerning the uniqueness of the Nazi Holocaust. Heidegger's comparison of Russian treatment of East Germans with the mass murder of the European Jews is to be found in a letter of 20 January 1948 to Herbert Marcuse. See "Herbert Marcuse and Martin Heidegger: An Exchange of Letters," *New German Critique* (no. 53, Spring/Summer 1991), 28–32.

implies any ethics."[159] This too, perhaps, must be regarded as part of Heidegger's radicalization of the Nietzschean enterprise, a project whose stated task was, after all, to think in terms of categories beyond good and evil.

During the Third Reich, then, Nietzsche and Nietzschean categories were fundamental axes around which grasping, defining, and critiquing the era revolved. Even when the relationship was adversarial, there was a perceived need to confront its claims, to conduct arguments within its terms. A widespread sense prevailed that, in a profound if inchoate way, Nietzsche's "authentic metaphysical domain" was somehow bound up with the essence of the Nazi project. These hermeneutical questions and the nature of the Nietzsche–Nazi relationship have been the subject of heated and unresolved debate and reflection from the 1930s through our own time. They hold up a mirror to Nietzsche's ongoing role as a peculiarly sensitive symbol and seismometer of our own crucial existential and cultural concerns.

159. Steiner, "Heidegger, Again," 53–54.

CHAPTER IX

National Socialism and the Nietzsche Debate

Kulturkritik, Ideology, and History

Hitler ...: [that is] the mob that has read Nietzsche.
Alfred Kerr, *Die Diktatur des Hausknechts*

At tea spoke . . . about the decline of Europe, the
phenomenon of the debasement of once authentic spiritual
and historical phenomena, as illustrated by the relationship
of Spengler to Nietzsche and Schopenauer, or National
Socialism to the Reformation. It would seem that we no
longer have real history, but only mock semblances and
degenerate epilogues, counterfeit history.
Thomas Mann, *Diaries, 1918–1939*

What philosopher was hailed by Hitler and Mussolini as the
prophet of authoritarianism?
Friedrich Nietzsche.
Trivial Pursuit—American Parlor Game.

One commentator in Switzerland wrote in 1935:

Friedrich Nietzsche is held to be the pioneer, the ideological founder of the
Third Reich. With no other thinker does National Socialist ideology feel so
closely related, so internally linked as with Nietzsche. The leading spirits
of the Third Reich call upon him incessantly. Striking and most strange,
however, is the fact that the grimmest opponent of national socialism also
rests with such partiality on no other thinker as on Friedrich Nietzsche. How
is that possible and who is right? Are both camps perhaps correct, or
neither?[1]

1. D. Gawronsky, *Friedrich Nietzsche und das Dritte Reich* (Bern: Verlag Herbert
Lang, 1935), 5.

Diametrically opposed answers were already being provided at the very moment that both the Italian Fascists and the Nazis appropriated Nietzsche. The voluminous debate has been going on ever since. It is an argument that eludes resolution, entailing, as Jean Starobinski has pointed out, a "labyrinth of unverifiable hypotheses."[2] From our perspective this vast hermeneutic subliterature must be integrated into the contours and functions of changing Nietzsche discourse, linked to broader political and ideological questions, and regarded as part of a larger Kulturkritik in which Nietzsche became the prism through which to address the great issues surrounding secularity, modernity, and even the nature of humanity. Implicit in all this was the sense that Nietzsche and Nietzscheanism were bound up with the novel liberating and cataclysmic potential associated with the twentieth century. Although the debate over what Crane Brinton in 1941 dubbed the "gentle" versus "tough" Nietzsche went back, as we have seen, to the beginnings of Nietzsche reception itself, the Nazi experience added even more intensity to the question.[3]

The emergent authorized Marxist response was certainly tough. Extending, even radicalizing, the tradition of class analysis initiated by Franz Mehring, this Marxist approach regarded the official Nazi appropriation of Nietzsche as fitting. To be sure, a number of pre-1933 Marxist responses, drawing from the countertraditions described in chapter 6, were far removed from such orthodoxy. They heatedly denied the conjunction claimed by Italian fascism[4] and were appalled by its German version. "We request . . . forgiveness for placing together the names of Nietzsche and Hitler in the title of our essay," one author wrote in 1930. Nietzsche, this critic proclaimed, was like Marx. He aimed at human elevation beyond all caste and class antitheses. He would have been the greatest enemy of nazism, that fraudulent mass Jesuitism that aimed not at the uplifting of humanity but at its degrada-

2. Starobinski asks about both Rousseau and Nietzsche:

What would the thinker have thought, what might he have done, had he still been alive? Would he have agreed with those who thought he was on their side? If so, then he would be guilty of having supplied them with their weapons. But there is no way of knowing if he would have done so. On the other hand, if he had not been their precursor, at least in part, then how could they have appropriated him to such an extent? The argument goes on ad infinitum.

("Rousseau in the Revolution," *New York Review of Books* [12 April 1990], 47)
    3. Crane Brinton, *Nietzsche* (New York: Harper and Row, [1941] 1965), 184. The book was itself a participant in the discourse described in this chapter.
    4. Fritz Brügel, "Nietzsche und der Fascismus," *Der Kampf: Sozialdemokratische Monatsschrift* 21 (1928), 610–615.

tion. Its brutalized chauvinism, racism, and anti-Semitism would have been incomprehensible to the thinker whose favorite author was Heinrich Heine![5] Others on the left, like Ludwig Marcuse writing in *Das Tagebuch*, stressed that the problem was not Nietzsche but those on the right who systematically falsified his message.[6] Walter Benjamin's contemptuous 1932 attack on Förster-Nietzsche and the Archives relayed a similar message.[7]

Still, as the Nazi political takeover grew closer, for many of the most nondoctrinaire leftist thinkers Nietzsche had become a problem. Thus in 1929 Kurt Tucholsky, the free-wheeling political satirist of the radical *Weltbühne*, could still casually credit Nietzsche for having "given the Germans prose again."[8] In 1932 he still insisted upon clearly distinguishing the philosopher's works from the distorting machinations of the Archives.[9] He was aware too of the ease with which Nietzsche could be appropriated for virtually any cause:

> Some illiterate Nazis who want to be considered part of the Hitler intelligentsia because they once smashed the head of a political opponent with a telephone book, claim Nietzsche for their own. Who cannot claim him for their own? Tell me what you need and I will supply you with a Nietzsche citation . . . for Germany and against Germany; for peace and against peace; for literature and against literature—whatever you want.[10]

Nevertheless, Tucholsky caustically observed, the more one read Nietzsche the more strongly one felt that something was amiss. The only thing that one did not find in him was that for which he was endlessly cited: strength (*Kraft*). "What I possess to a high degree," Tucholsky wrote, "is a mistrust against false heros and I hold Nietzsche to be a secret weakling. He heroizes like one masturbates."[11]

Tucholsky voiced his suspicions satirically. He certainly would never have enunciated a systematic theory indicting Nietzsche as the most

5. Johannes Albert, "Nietzsche und Hitler: Zur Ideologie des Nationalsozialismus," *Sozialistische Bildung: Monatschrift des Reichsausschusses für Sozialistische Bildungsarbeit* no. 12 (December 1930), 353, 355–357.
6. Ludwig Marcuse, "Märchen von der unblefleckten Empfängnis," *Das Tagebuch* 12 (1931), 1331–1335; "Die Papas der Nietzscheaner," *Das Tagebuch* 13 (1932), vol. 1, 401–408.
7. Walter Benjamin, "Nietzsche und das Archiv seiner Schwester" in his *Gesammelte Schriften*, vol. 3, 323–326. ed. Hella Tiedemann-Bartels (Frankfurt: Suhrkamp, 1972), 323ff.
8. Kurt Tucholsky, *Gesammelte Werke* (Hamburg: Rowohlt, 1960), Volume 7: 1929 "Schwarz auf Weiss," p. 49.
9. Kurt Tucholsky, "Fräulein Nietzsche," *Gesammelte Werke,* vol. 10, 10–11.
10. Ibid., 14.
11. Ibid., 23, 14, 24.

crucial, shaping, ideological influence on the genesis and disposition of national socialism. That work was undertaken after the Nazi rise to power, by Hans Günther and far more extensively by Georg Lukacs. Both were actively involved in official Communist-party circles during the late 1920 and early 1930s, both contributed to *Linkskurve,* and both emigrated to the Soviet Union in 1932 where their ruminations on the Nietzsche–Nazi connection were published. These were animated by the official theory that fascism was a manifestation of monopoly capitalism under pressure and the guidelines for the anti-Fascist struggle established by the Seventh World Congress of the Communist International.[12] Working within this authorized framework they reinforced the Nietzsche–Marxist orthodoxy that was sustained in the Soviet Union until its demise.[13]

In contrast to Lukacs, Günther is only beginning to emerge from obscurity.[14] His important "The Case of Nietzsche" was published in 1935. Günther insisted that only the historical-materialist method would successfully unravel the Nietzsche mystery and decode the development of his thought. This consisted essentially in unmasking its ideological and class functions. Nietzsche, Günther argued, was not simply the ideologist of the ruling classes but specifically "the philosopher of Germany's ruling class."[15] Günther, like Lukacs, adopted a *Sonderweg* theory of German history. The German ruling class was essentially backward: Nietzsche's thought was an ideational expression of that condition. Nietzsche's brutal thought reflected Germany's economic and political retardation.

Nietzsche's critique of decadence, nihilism, and Kaissereich modernity, Günther argued, offered a merely symptomatic analysis of capitalism without ever penetrating to its social and economic foundations. Here was a romantic anticapitalism that, while posing as revolutionary,

12. I am indebted to an unpublished, untitled paper by Robert Holub on left-wing Nietzsche reception for these biographical details as well as his interpretive pointers to Günther's work.

13. Bernice Glatzer Rosenthal, "Current Soviet Thought on Nietzsche," in *Nietzsche heute: Die Rezeption seines Werkes nach 1968,* ed. Sigrid Bauschinger et al. (Bern and Stuttgart: Francke, 1988); Ernst Behler, "Nietzsche in der Marxistischen Kritik Ostereuropas," *Nietzsche-Studien* 10/11 (1981/1982). The overall changes in Eastern Europe and Russia will, no doubt, bring with them transformed, and more sympathetic, interpretations of Nietzsche. The case of East Germany is different, and will be discussed in the course of this chapter.

14. Günther's works, originally published in Moscow in 1935, appear in his *Der Herren eigner Geist: Ausgewählte Schriften* (Berlin and Weimar: Aufbau, 1981).

15. Hans Günther, "Der Fall Nietzsche," *Unter dem Banner des Marxismus* 11 (1935), 542.

defused real revolutionary activity and upheld the status quo.[16] Nietzsche's ambivalent longings—reaching backward into the past and forward into the future—encouraged the substitution of psychology and myth for philosophy and sociology.[17]

In Günther's view, however, what remained constant in Nietzsche's simultaneous affirmation and critique of capitalism was his demand for an oppressive class society. Here Günther established the Nazi connection. Nietzsche's panaceas of war and brutality, the reliance on primitive instinct, and the ideal of the Übermensch were all close to the spirit of national socialism and fodder for its propaganda machine. The Nazis admittedly interpreted their ideological forefather too narrowly— Nietzsche stood high above these pitiful Nazi phrasemongers—but his philosophy of paradoxes supplied the perfect model for Nazi ideology. The Nietzschean and the National Socialist spirit were one in the belief that power stood as the foundational principle of all social and historical life. Both, moreover, camouflaged "the most brutal *reaction* as the most *radical* revolution."[18]

Georg Lukacs, however, most systematically forged the Marxist Nietzsche–Nazi link in essays written during the 1930s and 1940s which culminated in his famous, controversial, postwar *The Destruction of Reason*.[19] Lukacs sought to analyze the forms of reactionary bourgeois irrationalism and to document "Germany's path to Hitler in the sphere of philosophy . . . how this concrete path is reflected in philosophy, and how philosophical formulations, as an intellectual mirroring of Germany's concrete development towards Hitler helped to speed up the process." Such a process, Lukacs insisted, occurred whether or not individual thinkers were aware of their sociohistorical functions. Ideas had their "historically necessary influence. In this sense,

---

16. Günther, *Der Herren eigner Geist*, 152, 264. See too the summary by Dennis M. Sweet, "Friedrich Nietzsche in the GDR: A Problematic Reception," *Studies in GDR Culture and Society* 4, 229.

17. Günther, "Der Fall Nietzsche," 556.

18. Günther, *Der Herren eigner Geist*, 29.

19. See Lukacs's Moscow essays, "Nietzsche als Vorläufer der faschistichen Aesthetik," *Internationale Literatur* (1934) reprinted in his *Werke*, vol. 10, *Probleme der Aesthetik* (Neuwied and Berlin: Luchterhand, 1969) and "Der deutsche Faschismus und Nietzsche," *Internationale Literatur* 12 (1943). Nietzsche is similarly brought into his 1934 "'Grösse und Verfall' des Expressionismus," reprinted in *Expressionismus: Der Kampf um Eine Literarische Bewegung*, ed. Paul Raabe (Zürich: Arche, 1987), especially p. 261. Although *The Destruction of Reason* was completed in 1952, his views were formed earlier during the wartime period.

every thinker is responsible to history for the objective substance of his philosophizing."[20]

Lukacs was in no doubt about the objective and ultimately progressive nature of the historical process. Much of his virulent opposition to Nietzsche was in reaction to the philosopher's negation of progressive historical development. Lukacs espoused a Marxist teleology that reduced the Nietzschean (and indeed the modernist) epistemological crisis of truth and reason to its symptomatic, self-sustaining, reactionary bourgeois class functions. Nietzsche's retreat into the sphere of myth, his substitution of interpretation for knowledge, and his denial of the existence of an objective external world, knowledge of which could point the way to human redemption, were nothing but reflections of a class situation and not inherently worthy philosophical truths.[21]

Lukacs attempted to put this into historical perspective. At its best, he wrote, bourgeois thought possessed a universal and progressive Hegelian thrust reflected in its systematic endeavor to comprehend the world's totality. This was observable when the ascending bourgeoisie opposed the reactionary aristocracy. After 1848, and especially after 1871, bourgeois thought increasingly lost these positive characteristics. In the face of the rising proletarian threat and its accompanying progressive Marxist philosophy, it gradually turned to an ever more radical, conserving, anti-objectivist, mythologizing irrationalism. Modern irrationalism was, indeed, the primary emergent counterrevolutionary ideology upholding monopoly capitalism, imperialism, and eventually fascism itself. As the alternative to the emerging socialist, proletarian worldview of dialectical and historical materialism, its denial of objectivity and rationality directly translated into opposition to social progress.

Lukacs insisted that the issue—systematically blurred by Nietzsche— had to be grasped within a starkly simple framework: "to side either with reason or against reason decides at the same time the character of a philosophy and its role in social developments." This did not mean, of course, that irrationalism had no coherent structure or deflective social functions. Its ideas amounted to a clearly reactionary political programme comprised of the "disparagement of understanding and reason, an uncritical glorification of intuition, an aristocratic epistemology, the rejection of socio-historical progress, the creating of myths."[22]

20. Lukacs, *Destruction of Reason*, 4.
21. Ibid., 322, also 87.
22. Ibid., 5, 10.

Antisocialist irrationalism for Lukacs was an international phenomenon of the imperialist period. Given the delayed development of German capitalism it was most developed there and exemplified by
"Nietzsche, who became the paradigm in content and methodology of
irrationalist philosophical reaction from the U.S.A. to Tsarist Russia,
and whose influence could not and cannot be rivalled by a single other
reactionary ideologist."[23]

Nietzsche's "most fundamental intellectual attainment"—the myth-
icization of history in nature and society—facilitated the self-annulment
of evolution and diverted attention from objective reality and the
socialist belief in progress beyond capitalist society. It resembled
Ernst Mach's later irrationalist subversion of scientific thinking.[24] By
means of the crassly self-contradictory doctrine of eternal recurrence,
Nietzsche reduced all becoming and historical events to manifestations
of eternal principles. This was "the philosophical expression of the fact
that, after subjective idealism and irrationalism had triumphed over
Hegel, bourgeois philosophy became incapable of any dialectical linking of becoming and being, freedom and necessity; it could express their
mutual relationship only as an insoluble antagonism or an eclectic
amalgam."[25]

Through a coarsening popularization,[26] Lukacs noted, Nietzschean
ideas percolated to thousands who had never heard of Nietzsche and
were quite unaware of the "immediate source of corruption." Regardless of the coarsening, for Lukacs the continuity was clear enough:
"Everything that had been said on irrational pessimism from Nietzsche
and [Wilhelm] Dilthey to Heidegger and Jaspers on lecture platforms

23. Ibid., 16–17.
24. Ibid., 368ff, 373–374.
25. Ibid., 378–379. This, Lukacs argued, was basically Hitler's epistemology except
that in place of eternal recurrence he incorporated Chamberlain's racial theory as the
new, complementary element (p. 380). Nietzsche's insistence on "immanence" and dismissal of "transcendence"—and with it the basis of all Christian or socialist morality
(p. 391)—was his epistemological strategy for deducing the everlastingness of capitalist
society (p. 385).
26. For Lukacs, popularization did involve coarsening. Nietzsche

possessed considerable philosophical gifts: for instance a high capacity for abstraction, and not in a formalistic sense, but a flair for conceptualizing living phenomena, for building a mental bridge between immediate life and the most abstract
idea and taking with philosophic seriousness phenomena of Being which only
existed in embryo. (ibid., 197)

Yet these gifts were willy nilly devoted to the cause of a "future sweeping power,"
bourgeois reaction, for whose advent, growth, and crucial symptoms he "had a decided
flair, the faculty of intellectual clairvoyance and anticipatory abstraction."

and in intellectual salons and cafes, Hitler and Rosenberg transferred to the streets."[27]

In order to make Nietzsche constitutive of this new, virulently antisocialist, proto-Nazi ideology, Lukacs had to resort to special explanations.[28] Thus he argued that although Nietzsche had never read a line of either Marx or Engels he nevertheless knew "instinctively" what he had to defend "and where the enemy lurks!" His "whole life's work was a continuous polemic against Marxism and socialism . . . for the reason that every philosophy's content and method are determined by the class struggle of its age."[29] The fact that he had stopped writing before the imperialist age began, far from being a hindrance,

> offered a favourable opportunity to conjecture and to solve in mythical form—on the reactionary bourgeoisie's terms—the main problems of the subsequent period. This mythical form furthered his influence not only because it was to become the increasingly dominant mode of philosophical expression in the imperialist age. It also enabled him to pose imperialism's cultural, ethical and other problems in such a general way that he could always remain the reactionary bourgeoisie's leading philosopher, whatever the variations in the situation and the reactionary tactics adopted to match them.[30]

Moreover, because he lacked all grasp of capitalist economics, Nietzsche's mythicizing always remained on the level of the "symptoms of superstructure." His uncommon gift was the

> ability to project, on the threshold of the imperialist period, a counter-myth that could exert such influence for decades. Viewed in this light, his aphoristic mode of expression appears the form adequate to the socio-historical situation. The inner rottenness, hollowness and mendacity of the whole system wrapped itself in this motley and formally disconnected ragbag of ideas.[31]

Moreover, it succeeded in maintaining a revolutionary tone and in replacing the merely external, social revolution with cosmic and biological notions that precluded the need for any real break.[32]

Lukacs viewed nazism as virtually indistinguishable from its Nietzschean philosophical reflection and expression. Nietzsche's call for

27. Ibid., p. 84, 85.
28. See the critical analysis by Georg Lichtheim in his *Lukacs,* chapter 7. See too Henning Ottmann, "Anti-Lukacs: Eine Kritik der Nietzsche-Kritik von Georg Lukacs."
29. Lukacs, *Destruction of Reason,* 313.
30. Ibid., 314–315.
31. Ibid., 319, 395.
32. Ibid., 317.

the transvaluation of all values, his cry to unleash the instincts, his belief in barbarity as a savior were all examples. Nietzsche "anticipated in theory the true course of developments. Most of his statements on ethics became a dreadful reality under the Hitler regime, and they also retain a validity as an account of ethics in the present 'American age.' "[33]

The Destruction of Reason also traced the other manifestations of post-Nietzschean German irrationalism. Yet Nietzsche remains its most paradigmatic figure:

> Hitler, in bringing irrationalism to practical fulfillment, was the executor of Nietzsche's spiritual testament and of the philosophical development coming after Nietzsche and from him. . . . Inevitable it was that the irrationalism in Nietzsche should turn against socialism. . . . For all the difference in level between Nietzsche the philosopher and Hitler the demagogue in intellect and culture—and, as we have stressed, this too expresses the inevitability of the historical development—, there was precious little difference in their knowledge and understanding of the adversary on precisely the cardinal issue. It was, one may safely say, as good as non-existent. And in Hitler's politics, we can see the translation of irrationalist philosophy into practice.[34]

If Lukacs's work enduringly defined the orthodox Marxist Nietzsche as the philosopher of fascism, many non-Marxist circles and critics of the time concurred with the Nietzsche–Nazi linkage, although they proceeded from different methodological assumptions and reached diametrically opposed political conclusions. Perhaps the most illustrious example was Thomas Mann who in 1943 described fascism as a kind of Nietzschean escape from "everything bourgeois, moderate, classical, [Apolline]." Mann's notes for the period describe fascism in directly Nietzschean categories:

> Intellectual-spiritual fascism, throwing off of humane principle, recourse to violence, blood-lust, irrationalism, cruelty, Dionysiac denial of truth and justice, self-abandonment to the instincts and unrestrained "*Life*" which in fact is death . . . Fascism as a Devil-given departure from bourgeois society which leads through adventures of drunkenly intense subjective feeling and

---

33. Ibid., 341. Lukacs realized that Nietzsche had no theory of Aryan supremacy and that his notions of master and slave races were couched only in general terms, that "took into account only socio-ethical considerations. Hence in this respect he was a direct forerunner of Spengler rather than Rosenberg." Still, Lukacs went on,

> stressing this difference is only a means of "denazifying" Nietzsche. Since . . . Nietzsche drew the same barbaric imperialist conclusions from a racial theory as did Rosenberg from Chamberlain's, the difference is—to borrow Lenin's phrase— merely that between a yellow devil and a blue one. (355–356; also 736)

34. Ibid., 752–753.

super-greatness to mental collapse and spiritual death, and soon to physical death.[35]

Both in America and Western Europe, similar sentiments were voiced by journalists, polemicists, politicians, religious critics, philosophers, and historians during the 1930s and 1940s. The popular press proposed the connections in sensationalist headlines. "Hitler War Urge Blamed on Insane Philosopher: Nietzsche Nazi Chief's Favorite Author, Catholic Women Told," proclaimed a Boston paper.[36] Before that, a sub-editor at the *Liverpool Evening Express* declared, "Nietzsche is the pre-Hitlerian man."[37]

Such attitudes were also expressed in more august assemblies. In 1935 Sir Herbert Samuel told the House of Commons that "among the things responsible for the difficulties in Europe are Germany and the Nietzschean philosophy."[38] In exile, the conservative former mayor of Danzig and ex-Nazi Hermann Rauschning wrote highly influential works presenting national socialism and Hitler himself in terms incomprehensible outside of Nietzsche's towering presence. The very title of his famous *The Revolution of Nihilism* was unmistakably Nietzschean.[39] In Rauschning's description Hitler's worldview was inconceivable without Nietzsche. Rauschning too was the source of Hitler's much-quoted neo-Nietzschean proclamation that "conscience is a Jewish invention."[40]

Historians and critics seeking to plumb the depths of this new German phenomenon also gave Nietzsche central prominence. The French historian Edmond Vermeil, for instance, posited that, although on a higher plane, Nietzsche—elitist, "true racialist," and advocate of planning that would transform European labor into a giant automation—was "the exact prefiguration of the Germany of the Third Reich."[41] Similarly, Maurice Samuel's perceptive 1940 study of anti-Semitism—

---

35. Quoted in T. J. Reed, *Thomas Mann,* 364–365.

36. *Boston Evening Transcript* (24 April 1940). Quoted in Rudolf E. Künzli, "Political Uses and Abuses of Nietzsche," *Nietzsche-Studien* 12 (1983), 429.

37. Conrad Quest in *Liverpool Evening Express,* 9 December 1935. Quoted in M. P. Nicolas, *From Nietzsche Down to Hitler* (London: William Hodge, 1938), 5.

38. Ibid., 5. Quote from speech of 20 March 1935.

39. Hermann Rauschning, *The Revolution of Nihilism* (New York: Alliance Book, 1939).

40. Rauschning, *Hitler Speaks,* 220. These seemingly credible works from a former intimate were extremely influential, although their reliability has been severely questioned.

41. Edmond Vermeil, 1939. *Germany's Three Reichs,* trans. E. W. Dickes (New York: Howard Fertig, 1969), 239. See too pp. 38–39, 232ff. For more positive comments see pp. 405–407.

the "core and centre of Nazism-Fascism as a revolutionary ideal"—
identified the anti-Christian nature of revolutionary Nazi anti-Semitism
and insisted upon Nietzsche's central shaping role.[42] Without supporting sources, Samuel indicted Nietzsche for the far more coarsened version of his ideas which crude anti-Semites, including Hitler, had been
sprouting for years:

> The school of Nietzsche would have it that the Jews themselves never en-
> tertained a non-force philosophy, but invented it for the undoing of the rest
> of the world, while they themselves clung steadfastly to the belief in their
> own destiny as the ruthless master people. The cells which they projected
> into the Roman empire were groups of fifth column operators entrusted with
> the mission of paralysing the will-power of the enemies of the Jewish people
> by preaching a Christian doctrine which the Jews themselves despised.[43]

Analyses of Nietzsche often comprised an integral part of a larger
history of German ideas, a *Sonderweg* that pointed towards a teleolog-
ically inevitable Nazi culmination. These studies typically constructed a
hypostatized German Mind. During the 1930s and 1940s works with
titles such as *From Luther to Hitler* and *Germany the Aggressor
Throughout the Ages* appeared.[44] In varying degrees of intensity and
sophistication they portrayed Nietzsche as somehow both archetypal
and maniacal, a man whose "poisonous fallacies" were fed to the German people, "whose extreme credulity, mental docility and moral ser-
vility has made them the victims of countless false prophets, among
whom in recent times Nietzsche, Treitschke, Bernhardi, Houston Stewart Chamberlain, Ewald Banse, and Adolf Hitler stand eminent."[45]
    Those diagnoses posited an unbroken German continuity and did
not overly concern themselves with historical context. These works
emphasized Nietzsche's typicality rather than his originality, viewing
him less as cause than as reflection, an expression and symptom of the
wider German culture that had produced him. Nietzsche's inner ten-

---

42. Maurice Samuel, *The Great Hatred* (New York: Alfred A. Knopf, 1940), 53.
Unlike many other observers, Samuel regarded the extermination of the Jews as essential
to the Nazi scheme of things (p. 137).
    43. Ibid., 125.
    44. William Montgomery McGovern, *From Luther to Hitler: The History of Fascist-
Nazi Political Philosophy* (Boston: Houghton Mifflin, 1941), 408–415, 627ff. "It is only
when we bear Nietzsche's philosophy in mind that we can understand the true meaning
of the official statement of the Nazis that '*right is whatever profits the National Socialist
movement and therewith Germany*' and that wrong is whatever hinders or handicaps this
movement" (p. 630).
    45. F. J. C. Hearnshaw, *Germany the Aggressor Throughout the Ages* (New York:
E. P. Dutton, 1941), 235, 272.

sions and contradictions were a precise replication of German mental structure.[46]

Rohan Butler's *The Roots of National Socialism, 1783–1933* (1941) exemplified this approach:

> For when the theory of national-socialism is viewed in relation to German political thought of the last century and a half it is seen to be stale stuff, stale and adulterated. . . . The exaltation of the heroic leader goes back through Möller van den Bruck, Spengler, Lamprecht, Chamberlain, Nietzsche, Lasalle, Rodbertus, and Hegel, back to Fichte's *Zwingherr zur Deutschheit*. . . . The Nazis say that might is right; Spengler said it; Bernhardi said it; Nietzsche said it; Treitschke had said as much; so had Haller before him; so had Novalis.[47]

Yet even here Nietzsche was often accorded a special place. As Butler concluded, the "real design" of the Nazis "was nothing less than the Nietzschean transvaluation of values, the education of Germans in Germanity, the nihilistic revolution which would not stop at smashing countries, but would wreck the very hearts of men and utterly destroy the civilization of the west."[48]

The perception of the Nietzsche–Nazi relationship, of course, went well beyond apparently disinterested historical diagnostics. Conservative and religious critics such as the Catholic personalist Nicolas Berdyaev and Walter Schubart integrated the connection into their respective brands of moralistic Christian *Kulturkritik*.[49] In their reflections on the secular evils of the contemporary age, for instance, Marx and Nietzsche were common sources of problems inherent in a modernity that led to either bolshevism or fascism. Like Marx, Nietzsche was indicted as a modern godless thinker whose influence actively moved towards the dehumanization of culture and society.[50] The movement, wrote Berdyaev, "toward super-humanity and the superman, toward super-human powers, all too often means nothing other than a bestialization of man. Modern anti-humanism takes the form of bestialism. It uses the tragic and unfortunate Nietzsche as a superior sort of justifi-

46. Gawronsky, *Nietzsche und das dritte Reich*, 52, 63.
47. Rohan D. Butler, *The Roots of National Socialism, 1783–1933* (New York: Howard Fertig, 1968), 276–277.
48. Ibid., 295, 154–167.
49. Nicolas Berdyaev, *The Fate of Man in the Modern World*, trans. Donald A. Lowrie (Ann Arbor: University of Michigan Press, 1961); Walter Schubart, *Dostojewski und Nietzsche: Symbolik ihres Lebens* (Luzern: Vita Nova, 1939). The Nietzschean-Dostoyevskean worlds were often compared and contrasted, with Dostoyevsky acting as the positive counterfoil to the religious faith that Nietzsche had so brutally smashed.
50. Berdyaev, *The Fate of Man*, 31.

cation for dehumanization and bestialization." The world was witness-
ing a form of bestialism far removed "from the old, natural, healthy
barbarism"; it was now "conscious, deliberate, the product of reflection
and civilization, self-justified."[51] In such works the solution to modern
bestialization was linked to the renewal of a spiritualized and humanizing Christian piety.

There were numerous representations that painted the obverse picture and denied any possible relationship whatsoever. Peter Viereck's
1941 study, *Metapolitics: The Roots of the Nazi Mind,* for instance,
rendered nazism as a Wagnerian affair. Nietzsche was the radical antithesis of both Wagner and nazism. The "soul," Viereck wrote, "which
most of the greatest Germans ended by choosing, from Goethe through
Nietzsche to Mann, is not the one Hitler claims to incarnate."[52]

Viereck enunciated a recurrent theme. Nietzsche was not the early
reflection of nazism but rather its most uncanny, highly critical
predictor.[53] Nietzsche's brilliant grasp of nazism's cultural roots was
the animating spirit behind Viereck's own book.[54] The French study by
M. P. Nicolas, *From Nietzsche Down to Hitler,* similarly insisted upon
the radically insulting nature of the comparison and the abyss separating Nietzsche from nazism.[55]

There was also unclassifiable Nietzscheana, esoteric literature produced by exiles. This is perhaps best illustrated by the Hamburg jurist
Alfred Rosenthal, a long-standing Nietzschean.[56] His pamphlet,
Nietzsche and Europe, and his book, *Nietzsche's "European Race-
problem": ("The Struggle for World Domination"),* written in Holland
during the 1930s, presented a Spenglerian Nietzscheanism advocating a

51. Ibid., 26–27, 28–29.
52. Peter Viereck, *Metapolitics: The Roots of the Nazi Mind* (New York: Capricorn
Books, [1941] 1965), 187.
53. Viereck would have done well to quote from Nietzsche's "The great man of the
masses" as an example of his prescience:

The masses must receive the impression that a mighty, indeed invincible force of
will is present; at the least it must seem to be present. Everyone admires strength
of will because no one has it and everyone tells himself that if he did have it he and
his egoism would no longer know any limitations. . . . [T]he great man possesses
all the qualities of the masses: they are thus all the less embarrassed in his presence,
thus he is all the more popular. He is violent, envious, exploitative, scheming,
fawning, cringing, arrogant, all according to circumstances. (*Human, All Too
Human,* 168)
54. "It is Nietzsche, then, who was the sole begetter of the present volume; it is he
whose quotations and over-looked chapter-epigraphs were its subterranean leitmotif"
(Viereck, *Metapolitics,* xix).
55. Nicolas, *From Nietzsche Down to Hitler.*
56. Alfred Rosenthal, "Nietzsche und die Reform das Strafrechts."

simultaneously anti–National Socialist yet martial and racist vision of Europe.[57] Through his Nietzschean–Spenglerian prism, and the categories of race and racial hygiene, Rosenthal deflected Nazi anti-Semitism onto the conflict between white Europe and its non-European colored enemies. Europe's future could be guaranteed only through the breeding of a new European caste created on Nietzsche's aristocratic principle. Needless to say, such ruminations remained wholly marginal and isolated from any identifiable political framework.

Despite the simplistic treatments of Nietzsche, a considerable amount of the mainstream literature written during the war did paint relatively complex portraits of him, whether negative or positive.[58] Crane Brinton's 1940 study, sensitive to the dynamics of ideas mediated by political culture, was not alone in its consciousness of the complexity. As he put it: "Nietzsche wrote much the Nazis find delightful; he also wrote much they cannot bear to hear, and certainly cannot bear to have repeated."[59] Heinrich Mann, whose passionate relationship to Nietzsche constantly changed, was aware of Nietzsche's complex contrariness, the brutal dangers as well as the lasting value in the mature re-evalution he wrote for *Mass und Wert*.[60] And in 1941 Karl Löwith subtly enunciated the vexed complexities of the question of Nietzsche as forerunner:

> To see the abyss which separates Nietzsche from his latter-day prophets, it suffices to read his writings against Wagner and his remarks on the Jewish

57. Alfred Rosenthal, *Nietzsche und Europa: Eine Übersicht für Weltleute* (n.p., [1937]). *Nietzsches "Europäisches Rasse-Problem": "Der Kampf Um die Erdherrschaft"* (Leiden: A. W. Sijthoff, 1935). On p. 9 Rosenthal defends the concepts of racial purity, racial cultivation, and decadence which he considered were central for Nietzsche.

58. For an example see Richard Maximilian Lonsbach, *Friedrich Nietzsche und die Juden* (Bonn: Bouvier, 1985). Lonsbach was the pseudonym of Richard Maximilian Cahen who published this in exile in Stockholm in 1939.

59. Brinton, *Nietzsche*, 222. In his 1964 preface he wrote:

> I did not then, and do not now maintain that Nietzsche was a "proto-Nazi," that he was directly responsible for Nazi "ideology," let alone that he helped the Nazis to power. How he would have hated the whole lot. But the use the Nazis made of much that Nietzsche wrote is an interesting and to some, one may hope, instructive case history of what can happen to the words of a subtle intellectual once they are common property. Nietzsche wrote in his final madness in *Ecce Homo*, "I am not a man: I am dynamite." But dynamite explodes somewhat unselectively. (p. vii)

Brinton added: "I find Nietzsche as a human being unpleasant and his influence on the whole regrettable" (p. ix).

60. Heinrich Mann, "Nietzsche," *Mass und Wert* 2 (1930), 277–304. In Mann's "Zum Verständnis Nietzsches," *Das Zwanzigste Jahrhundert* 6 (1896), 247, he denied that Nietzsche was the "philosopher of capitalism" and described the notion of Übermenschen as "nothing but a social and race-symbol" (pp. 246–251). Later he rejected what he regarded as the antidemocratic aspects of Nietzsche's thought.

question, and the converse question of what is German, without editing or excerpting. But this does not contradict the obvious fact that Nietzsche became a catalyst of the "movement," and determined its ideology in a decisive way. The attempt to unburden Nietzsche of this intellectual "guilt," or even to claim his support *against* what he brought about is just as unfounded as the reverse effort to make him the advocate of a matter over which he sits in judgment. Both crumble before the historical insight that "forerunners" have ever prepared roads for others which they themselves did not travel. More important than the question whether Nietzsche's historical effects speaks for him or against him is the discrimination of spirits according to their relationship to the period in general. However much Nietzsche sought to make time eternal, he was nevertheless . . . more of his own time than he desired to be, precisely because his stance towards it was polemical, untimely. As antagonist to Bismarck and Wagner, he moved within the circumference of *their* "will to power," and even his timeliness in the Third Reich rested upon the fact that it was the heir of the Second.[61]

Most bourgeois treatments of the 1930s and 1940s, even if they were nuanced, nevertheless presented static, balance-sheet analyses. To varying degrees Nietzsche was either indicted for or absolved from Nazi complicity. These studies were usually static because they lacked any explicit theoretical and critical political framework into which both a creative analysis of fascism and nazism and a complex reassessment of the Nietzschean impulse within these constellations could be made.[62]

The most innovative efforts were undertaken neither by bourgeois critics nor orthodox Marxists but by dissidents from both worlds: the Western Marxists. In 1939, Ernst Bloch complained that anti-Fascists could talk of Nietzsche and Wagner only in terms of the Nazi connection. Yet Bloch himself exemplified the creative spurts, the boundlessly renewable forms Nietzsche discourse could assume even under—perhaps because of—these circumstances. This process of radical and unorthodox rethinking, as Jürgen Habermas has reminded us, was clearly a product of the times:

> The victory of the Fascist movement in Italy and the National Socialist takeover of power in the German Reich were—long before Auschwitz—phenomena from which issued waves not only of irritation but also of fas-

61. Karl Löwith, *From Hegel to Nietzsche,* 200.
62. The religious conservative critics we have already mentioned constitute an exception. Notions of national character and the German mind as well as psychologizations of Nietzsche do not amount to broader frameworks. What follows are examples that locate Nietzsche affirmatively. It is also true, however, for Lukacs's dismissal of Nietzsche. No matter how much one may disagree with his interpretation, his negation was embedded within a clearly delineated theoretical and political framework.

cinated excitement. There was no theory of contemporaneity not affected to its core by the penetrating force of fascism.[63]

Few such radical theories could be undertaken without reference to nazism and to Nietzsche. Within this process of rethinking, often a positive side of Nietzsche emerged, one from whom selected materials for an anti-Fascist position could be mined.

If Nietzsche had been crucial in defining the age for the right, he performed a similar function for neo-Marxists like Bloch, Adorno, Horkheimer, and most idiosyncratically Georges Bataille.[64] These thinkers adopted an approach that differed drastically from that of Lukacs. Lukacs's *Destruction of Reason*, Adorno declared,

> revealed most clearly the destruction of Lukacs's own. In a highly undialec-
> tical manner, the officially licensed dialectician sweeps all these irrationalist
> strands of modern philosophy into the camp of reaction and Fascism. He
> blithely ignores the fact that, unlike academic idealism, these schools were
> struggling against the very same reification in both thought and life of which
> Lukacs too was a dedicated opponent. Nietzsche and Freud are simply la-
> belled Fascists and he could even bring himself to refer to Nietzsche, in the
> condescending tones of a Wilhelmian school inspector, as a man "of above-
> average abilities." Under the mantle of an ostensibly radical critique of
> society he surreptitiously reintroduced the most threadbare cliches of the
> very conformism which that social criticism had once attacked.[65]

These thinkers were certainly aware that any simplified notion of irrationalism overlooked the rationality often present in irrational pro-test, and that irrationalism was often to be found in reason.[66] They were all critical of reason itself or, at least, of what they termed "instrumental reason." In addition, they were wary of a simplistic progressive teleol-ogy that assumed an untroubled eventual union of subject and object. They also acknowledged a potentially creative role for the irrational. Such predispositions contained a bias favorable to Nietzsche; they were grist for the Nietzschean mill. These ruminations on both national so-cialism and Nietzsche constituted a broad cultural criticism that re-volved around the more generalized problems of capitalism, secularity, and modernity. Indeed, they often equated the specific historical expe-rience of nazism with these phenomena.

63. "Between Eroticism and General Economics: Georges Bataille" in Jürgen Hab-ermas, *Philosophical Discourse*, 216.
64. For Bloch, Adorno, and Horkheimer, Nietzsche, important as he was, was only one element in their reconsiderations. For Bataille he was absolutely central.
65. Theodor Adorno, "Reconciliation under Duress," in *Aesthetics and Politics* (Lon-don: NLB, 1977), 152.
66. Ottmann, "Anti-Lukacs," 574.

If for Lukacs irrationalism, and Nietzschean irrationalism in particular, was simply the ideational equivalent of fascism, the maverick Ernst
Bloch adopted far more complex attitudes towards these questions.[67] His
irrationalism possessed negative and positive as well as reactionary and
progressive components that had to be carefully sifted, its creative possibilities and redemptive future-oriented impulses identified. "It is necessary," he wrote, "everywhere to occupy the dream areas of the imagination instead of neglecting them altogether and thereby abandoning
them to those who are bent on deception and the destruction of reason."
Indeed, he proclaimed: "There won't be a muffled, or indeed even a real,
revolution in this Germany which is not anointed with a drop of the oil
of irrationalism."[68]

Bloch's philosophical confrontation with nazism and fascism, *Erbschaft dieser Zeit* (Heritage of Our Times), was published in his Zürich
exile in 1935.[69] It posited the central notion of *Ungleichzeitigkeit* (dis-
simultaneity): the present contains social and cultural structures of the
past together with those "pregnant with the future." The work, composed in an appropriately expressionistic montage, sought to salvage
from the contradictory inheritances of the past a usable cultural heritage for the capitalist and Fascist present. He castigated Marxists for
rejecting irrationalism, thus allowing the Nazis to monopolize it. This
enabled the Nazis to annex the positive, authentic elements of noncon-
temporaneity as well as the more destructive ones. The task was to
harness such forces for progressive rather than reactionary purposes.[70]

In this context Bloch reexamined Nietzsche's still-untapped positive
potential. If Nietzsche enunciated reactionary themes—which Bloch
recognized—he nevertheless also stood for dynamic forward movement, for utopia.[71] Although notions such as the Übermensch had dehumanizing, brutalizing effects, Nietzsche had intended something different. He had painted the portrait of future, unconditioned man, a
vision of liberating Dionysian *Ungleichzeitig* potential:

    67. While the Nietzschean moment in Bloch undoubtedly occurred, it should not be
overexaggerated (Tony Phelan, "Ernst Bloch's 'Golden Twenties': *Erbschaft dieser Zeit*
and the Problem of Cultural History," in *Culture and Society in the Weimar Republic*, ed.
Keith Bullivant [Manchester: Manchester University Press, 1977], 113ff). Bloch was
considered so heretical that the orthodox position on Nietzsche expressed in the GDR never
even referred to the Bloch interpretation (Sweet, "Friedrich Nietzsche in the GDR," 228).
    68. Oskar Negt, "Ernst Bloch: The German Philosopher of the October Revolution,"
New German Critique no. 4 (Winter 1975), 12, 14.
    69. Ernst Bloch, *Erbschaft Dieser Zeit* (Zürich: Verlag Oprecht and Helbling, 1935).
    70. Neville and Stephen Plaice, introduction to Bloch, *Heritage of Our Times*, xii–
xiii.
    71. Ibid., 52.

At the zero-point of mechanical existence there are not only the various *übermenschlichen* beasts, there is also a recollection of *Dionysus*. The predator in tropical, not cold terms, the Thracian forest against the cold reified bourgeois citizen. Dionysus as a symbol of abstractly fantastic escape into anarchy; only here do we grasp Nietzsche's *serious* impact on the age. Only here did Nietzsche express his age in watchwords, in watchwords of an indistinct countermovement of the "subject." . . . Dionysus ran amok against all "domestications," however, remote. . . . Thus Dionysus is also not merely the unrestrained reflex of the capital which causes discipline, moderation, justice, and bourgeois virtue to be dismantled in good time, but he is a formal dissipation into an indeterminate being beside oneself, being-outside-time per se.[72]

This Dionysus was the man who had still not yet become himself; one who smashed false forms, not at any closed point of advanced capitalism, but always within the unexpected eruptions, the turning points of history. Bloch Marxified Nietzsche by projecting onto him visionary language more Blochian than Nietzschean. His Nietzsche sought a worldliness forged in utopian fire, and preached the end of the static, closed worldview far removed from eternal recurrence. Bloch's Dionysus was, in fact, Nietzsche's mythological name for the historically repressed Subject, who had still not realized its historical role. This undetermined Dionysian side of Nietzsche, Bloch argued, Fascist interpreters like Bäumler wanted to replace with an emphasis on the role of force (*herrschender* Gewalt). For redemptive traces of the Nietzschean vision were apparent even in the ruins of the present. Dionysus was not the night into which reaction fled but rather the fiery serpent placed on the flags of revolution, the utopian flash of lightning.[73]

Adorno and Horkheimer's classic 1944 *Dialectic of Enlightenment* was similarly a confrontation with national socialism and fascism and the roots of contemporary barbarism that refused to be contained within those self-defined historical boundaries. As Marxists they also indicted the bourgeoisie, but in quite un-Marxist fashion equated enlightenment with the entire imperial project of Western thought. Considered thus as a project of totalizing, "instrumental reason" aimed at making "man master"—enlightenment could be traced as far back as Genesis. Elsewhere, Horkheimer even rendered Marx himself, with his reduction of man to an *animal laborans* and his reification of nature as

72. Ibid., 325–326.
73. Ibid., 328, 330, 331.

a field for human exploitation, complicitous.[74] From this perspective Adorno and Horkheimer could regard nazism not as a revolt against enlightenment but as an integral part of its own intolerant, totalizing dialectic.

This entailed not only the analysis of fascism but also what Jürgen Habermas has described as the desire "to enlighten the Enlightenment about itself in a radical way." In this context Nietzsche emerged as "the great model for the critique of ideology's totalizing self-overcoming." In all probability, the Nietzschean strain also predisposed them to dismiss the rational content of modernity and to insist upon the pervasive links between reason and domination, power and validity.[75]

Adorno and Horkheimer turned to black writers of the bourgeoisie, the Marquis de Sade and Nietzsche, in order "to conceptualize the Enlightenment's process of self-destruction."[76] They stressed that Nietzsche stood virtually alone in his time in grasping the dialectic of the Enlightenment: both as a demystifying expression of antipathy to domination and as a tool for such domination. At the same time they identified the ironic proto-Fascist consequences of this critique in the hands of Nietzsche's reactionary followers:

> Nietzsche was one of the few after Hegel who recognized the dialectic of enlightenment. And it was Nietzsche who expressed its antipathy to domination: "The Enlightenment" should be "taken into the people, so that the priests all become priests with a bad conscience—and the same must be done with regard to the State. That is the task of the Enlightenment: to make princes and statesmen unmistakably aware that everything they do is sheer falsehood. . . ." On the other hand, Enlightenment had always been a tool for the "great manipulators of government (Confucius in China, the *Imperium Romanum,* Napoleon, the Papacy when it had turned to power and not only to the world). . . . The way in which the masses are fooled in this respect, for instance in all democracies, is very useful: the reduction and malleability of men are worked for as "progress"!
>
> The revelation of these two aspects of the Enlightenment as an historic principle made it possible to trace the notion of enlightenment as progressive thought back to the beginning of traditional history. Nevertheless, Nietzsche's relation to the Enlightenment, and therefore to Homer, was still discordant. Though he discerned both the universal movement of sovereign Spirit (whose executor he felt himself to be) and a "nihilistic" anti-life force in the enlightenment, his pre-Fascist followers retained only the second as-

74. See the excellent summary by Jay, *Dialectical Imagination,* 258–259. On the Dialectic of Enlightenment see Jay, 253–280.

75. Jürgen Habermas, "The Entwinement of Myth and Enlightenment: Max Horkheimer and Theodor Adorno," in *Philosophical Discourse* 107, 121.

76. Ibid., 106.

pect and perverted it into an ideology. This ideology becomes blind praise of a blind life subject to the same nexus of action by which everything living is suppressed.[77]

For Adorno and Horkheimer, Nietzsche's critique of enlightenment was not simply a creative insight. If it contained the seeds of its own misappropriation, it was also—and this was reminiscent of Bloch—the site of potential liberation in the darkest of times:

> Not to have glossed over or suppressed but to have trumpeted far and wide the impossibility of deriving from reason any fundamental argument against murder fired the hatred which the progressives (and they precisely) still direct against Sade and Nietzsche. They were significantly unlike the logical positivists in taking science at its word. The fact that Sade and Nietzsche insist on the *ratio* more decisively even than logical positivism, implicitly liberates from its hiding-place the utopia contained in the Kantian notion of reason as in every great philosophy: the utopia of a humanity which, itself no longer distorted, has no further need to distort. Inasmuch as the merciless doctrines proclaim the identity of domination and reason, they are more merciful than those of the moralistic lackeys of the bourgeoisie. "Where do your greatest dangers lie?" was the question Nietzsche once posed himself, and answered thus: "In compassion." With his denial he redeemed the unshakable confidence in man that is constantly betrayed by every form of assurance that seeks only to console.[78]

Horkheimer and Adorno did add some critical reservations. If Nietzsche had perceived the dialectic of enlightenment, the same pitfalls were detectable in his own work. At the same time that Nietzsche formulated his incisive critique of enlightenment—like de Sade and even Kant before him—he contributed to its calculating, instrumental logic, that formal rationality which had led to the horrors of twentieth-century barbarism. Nietzsche's will to power like Kant's categorical imperative sought independence from the constraints of external forces, and in its desire to control nature and to make humans the measure of all things was an integral part of the catastrophe.[79] The German Nietzsche, they wrote

> makes beauty dependent on extent; despite all the twilight of the idols, he cannot abandon the idealistic convention which would accept the hanging of a petty thief and elevate imperialistic raids to the level of world-historical missions. By raising the cult of strength to a world-historical doctrine, Ger-

77. Theodor Adorno and Max Horkheimer, *Dialektik der Aufklärung* (Amsterdam: Querido, 1947). Translated as *Dialectic of Enlightenment* by John Cumming (New York: Seabury, 1972), 44.
78. Ibid., 118–119. The passage referred to appears in *Gay Science,* 220.
79. Jay, *Dialectical Imagination,* 265.

man Fascism also took it to an absurd extreme. As a protest against civilization, the master's morality conversely represents the oppressed. Hatred of atrophied instincts actually denounces the true nature of the task-masters—which comes to light only in their victims. But as a Great Power, or state religion, the master's morality wholly subscribes to the civilizing powers that be, the compact majority, resentment, and everything that it formerly opposed. The realization of Nietzsche's assertions both refutes them and at the same time reveals their truth, which—despite all his affirmation of life—was inimical to the spirit of reality.[80]

Paradoxically this theme of human hubris and critical theory's deemphasis of man's total autonomy resembled the religious conservative critique of Nietzsche that we have confronted throughout this work.[81] Both after all were forms of *Kulturkritik* and not really concerned with differentiated historical analyses of national socialism and fascism. Critical theory finally subsumed or integrated nazism into its broader ongoing concerns: the general Western tendency to domination and instrumental rationality and a capitalism that leads towards the total administration of things.

In the final analysis, *Dialectic of Enlightenment* never resolved its overall ambivalence towards Nietzsche who combined the roles of culprit, symptom, critical diagnostician, and liberating visionary. At all times, however, his salience and symbolic centrality was quite unmistakable.

Except for an early critical comment around 1930 (dubbing Nietzschean morality "reactionary and romantic"),[82] Georges Bataille (1897–1962) was not plagued by any such ambivalence. Of all the post-Marxist thinkers under consideration, Bataille was the most radically and idiosyncratically Nietzschean. His life reads like the incarnation of that ultimate and unattainable Nietzschean project where, un-

---

80. Adorno and Horkheimer, *Dialectic of Enlightenment*, 100–101. For further criticism of Nietzsche and his effects on mass culture see pp. 233–234.

81. Jay, *Dialectical Imagination*, 266, has made a similar point in a different context. Deemphasizing the total autonomy of man was part of the consistent refusal of critical theory to construct a positive anthropology of man; such centrality denigrated the natural world.

Critical Theory, for all its insistence on a standard against which the irrationalities of the world might be measured, was not really a radical humanism at heart. Horkheimer's interest in religion, which surfaced in later years, was thus not as fundamental a departure from the premises of his earlier work as might appear at first glance. (*Dialectical Imagination,* 266)

82. Georges Bataille, "The 'Old Mole' and the Prefix *Sur* in the Words *Surhomme* [Superman] and *Surrealist*" in George Bataille, *Visions of Excess,* 38.

like most German applications, the dynamic was neither tamed nor channeled but unleashed for its own unbounded sake. As Bataille's friend Michael Leiris put it:

> After he had been the impossible one, fascinated by everything he could discover about what was really unacceptable . . . he expanded his field of vision . . . and, in the consciousness that a human being is only really a human being when, in this state of being without measure or standard, he seeks his own standard, he made himself into the man of the impossible, desirous of reaching the point where above and below become blurry in a Dionysian vertigo and where the distance between totality and nothing is eliminated.[83]

Bataille, in Jürgen Habermas's phrase, "tried to take up the impossible heritage of Nietzsche as critic of ideology."[84] He envisaged a variety of Nietzschean forms (in constantly changing, small political groupings) which by definition were meant to sunder rather than stabilize organized frameworks. Here was a Communist intent not on creating but breaking limits, obsessed with the Nietzschean rebellion against system itself, and aspiring to what he termed the realm of heterogeneity: all those elements that resisted assimilation into everyday bourgeois life and eluded science but were revealed in moments of fascinated shock while shattering confident perceptions of the subject and his world.

Bataille's penchant for radical critique, his desire to shock and transgress the respectable bourgeois world made him not all that distinct from the heterogenous fascism he analyzed and purportedly sought to critique. During the 1930s, for instance, Bataille's political group of intellectuals, Contre-Attaque, was labeled as *"sur-fasciste,"* and Bataille later admitted that he and his friends had shared a certain "paradoxical fascist tendency."[85]

For all that, Bataille's Nietzsche was presented as the quintessential counterfoil to fascism and national socialism. What distinguished Bataille from bourgeois commentators, who similarly rejected the Nietzsche–Nazi identity, was the determinedly radical and irrationalist Nietzschean basis upon which he did it. For Bataille, after all, fascism and nazism were ultimately forms of taming control that constricted human possibility. Nietzsche was instead "the fiercest of solvents," the unique apostle of the most radical, even violent, will to autonomy, and

83. Quoted in Jürgen Habermas, "Between Eroticism and General Economics," 211.
84. Ibid., 211.
85. Allan Stökl, introduction in Bataille, *Visions of Excess,* xviii.

the visionary of a previously unimagined limitlessness. "This total liberation, as he defined it," Bataille wrote later, "of human possibility, of all possibility, is surely the only one not yet attempted."[86] (Bataille parenthetically qualified this by adding "Except by myself"!)

The pathos-laden nature of Nietzsche's experience and his labrynthine thought—"without any hope of appeal"—could not possibly be integrated into any political system, and so had to be suppressed by it.[87] To make Nietzsche "the collaborator in causes devalorized by his thought," Bataille insisted, "is to trample upon it, to prove one's ignorance even as one pretends to care for that thought."[88]

> Fascism and Nietzscheanism are mutually exclusive, and are even violently mutually exclusive, as soon as each of them is considered in its totality: on one side life is tied down and stabilized in an endless servitude, on the other there is not only a circulation of free air, but the wind of a tempest; on one side the charm of human culture is broken in order to make room for vulgar force, on the other force and violence are tragically dedicated to this charm. . . . There is a corrosive derision in imagining a possible agreement between Nietzschean demands and a political organization which impoverishes existence at its summit, which imprisons, exiles, or kills everything that could constitute an aristocracy of "free spirits."[89]

Bataille's anti-Fascist Nietzsche was not sterilized or endowed with liberal respectability: his central categories were violence, sexuality and evil. And, like the Fascist politics he attacked, the revolt against the domination of rationality remained constitutive. In order to escape that domination the self had to be "fully lost in immanence to establish the whole man as a completely unsubordinated realm."[90]

Bataille's Nietzsche was thus not the philosopher of the will to power but "the philosopher of evil" conceived as "concrete freedom, the troubling break with taboo."[91] Here was the extreme edge of Nietzscheanism, purposely cut off from all bounded frames, pursuing the unconditional and unconditioned Nietzschean dynamic for its own sake. This obviously contradicted the harnessed Nietzsche reception within German political culture. It was a free-floating radicalism that would later

86. See Georges Bataille's 1949 "On Nietzsche: The Will to Chance, Preface" in the special issue on him in *October* 36 (Spring 1986), 48.

87. See Bataille's 1937 essay, "Nietzsche and the Fascists," in *Visions of Excess*, 187, 191 (his italics).

88. Bataille, "On Nietzsche," 50.

89. Bataille, "Nietzsche and the Fascists," 185–186.

90. Allen S. Weiss, "Impossible Sovereignty: Between *The Will to Power* and *The Will to Chance*," October 36 (Spring 1986), 137.

91. Bataille, "On Nietzsche," 50–51.

characterize the potent postwar French appropriation of Nietzsche in all its radical, if politically indeterminate, poststructural variations. Bataille's Nietzsche is de-instrumentalized and de-ideologized. Far from aiming at constructive political constitution this was a vision that desired "signal dissolution in totality." At the same time Bataille attempted to sketch the outlines of his essentially Nietzschean anti-Fascist community: "The only society full of life and force, the only free society is the *bi-* or *polycephalic* society that gives the fundamental antagonisms of life a constant explosive outlet, but one limited to the richest forms."[92] Bataille argued that the very essence of what he desired, universal community, lay in its unlimited and dynamic Nietzschean nature: only fear of these characteristics had prevented its realization thus far. Lack of courage had produced the more familiar, particularistic ones. The very possibility of (a properly conceived) universal community emanated from the Nietzschean predicament and would be the outcome of an authentically Nietzschean engagement:

> The search for God, for the absence of movement, for *tranquility*, is the fear that has scuttled all attempts at a universal community. . . . For universal existence is unlimited and thus restless: it does not close life on itself, but instead opens it and throws it back into the uneasiness of the infinite. Universal existence, eternally unfinished and acephalic, a world like a bleeding wound, endlessly creating and destroying particular finite beings: it is in this sense that true universality is the death of God.[93]

It was not merely the radical nature of this vision that rendered it politically untranslatable. There was also an internal irony here. The universal Bataille–Nietzschean community was heterogeneous. Yet, as Allen Weiss has pointed out, heterogeneity is naturally incommunicable. Bataille's authentic Nietzschean community is thus ultimately condemned to self-contradictory silence or betrayal.[94] In political terms, at least, there could be no such thing as "pure" Nietzscheanism.

We must therefore return from these dissident intellectuals to the mainstream, and from France to Germany. As the war ended, Nietzsche's role within the politics and culture of Germany underwent thorough revision. If under national socialism he represented the normative core, those now at the defining center regarded him as an altogether suspect figure. No longer prophet and incarnation of the national destiny, he was typically metamorphized into an antithesis of what was

92. Bataille, "Propositions," in *Visions of Excess*, 199.
93. Ibid., 201.
94. Weiss, "Impossible Sovereignty," 142.

required for the reconstruction of a "democratic," anti-Fascist German identity.

This new Nietzsche mirrored larger transformations of political, cultural, and intellectual life wrought under occupation between 1945 and 1949. Scholars have variously described this process, designed to create a more "rational" political culture, as one of "de-ideologization" and "de-radicalization."[95] The Nietzsche legacy was exceedingly adaptable, but it could hardly thrive in a culture in which deradicalization was at a premium.

As in the past, Nietzschean themes retained their centrality, located still within the frame of larger questions of national history, identity, and collective moral purpose. But now, as with his early detractors, the philosopher and his world were incorporated as an essentially negative, dangerous part of the German inheritance. In the immediate postwar climate Nietzsche could not again assume the mantle of inspirational national authority.

The philosopher appeared everywhere in the flood of self-reflective *Schuldfrage* writings—discussing national guilt—fulfilling a variety of functions. In the shadow of the immediate past he was overwhelmingly portrayed as somehow complicit and "responsible," a cause or at least a major contributor to the catastrophe. It was simple to make him part of a general German self-indictment or to externalize and deflect national guilt onto him. If Nietzscheanism had created the catastrophe, the solution was to be found by emphasizing opposing values. Thus, many of the suggested remedies for the German Problem were formulated within explicitly anti-Nietzschean frames; antidotes were found in Enlightenment, rationalist, liberal, and Christian themes suppressed during the Nazi period.

The reassessment began quickly. Already in 1945 in public lectures, Otto Flake, the well-known critic and political commentator, presented a balance sheet, analyzing the relationship between German history, nazism, and Nietzsche.[96] Confrontation with guilt, Flake argued, made it imperative to confront Nietzsche. Had he lived, Flake proclaimed, he

---

95. See for instance Karl Dietrich Bracher, *The Age of Ideologies: A History of Political Thought in the Twentieth Century*, trans. Ewald Osers (London: Weidenfeld, 1984); Jerry Z. Muller, *The Other God that Failed*, chaps. 9, 10.

96. Otto Flake, *Nietzsche: Rückblick auf Eine Philosophie* (Baden-Baden, 1946); see too the afterword to the 1947 2d ed. of the book reprinted in *Die Deutschen: Aufsätze zur Literatur und Zeitgeschichte* (Hamburg: Rütten und Löning, 1963). The work argued that Nietzsche had penetrated the German nation more deeply than Goethe and almost as deeply as Luther.

would presumably have found himself on the list of war criminals headed for Nuremburg.[97] Nietzsche was, no doubt, a phenomenon of the highest rank, a master of the German language. His gentle nature did not fit with the spirit of the Third Reich. Paradoxically, however, nazism did base itself upon his merciless teachings of human conduct. Nietzsche had summoned up the whole ideality of will in order to deliver the demon of the deed.

In Flake's view, Nietzsche was not an accidental meteor; he was the most extreme expression of an inherent, postreformationist German tendency, the last consequence of Luther's "open" spirituality (*eroffnete Seelenlage*). Both shared the same boundlessness, the renunciation of bonds, the hubris of self-creation, and the undervaluation of reason.[98]

These discussions inevitably reflected on the vexed question of mediation and the nature of the writer's responsibility for his ideas.[99] All thinkers, Flake wrote, began with something that was given rather than chosen. Still, in practice one had to accept the notion of responsibility in order "to have a norm, a measure of judgment." Nietzsche, therefore, had to be held accountable for his choice of ideas, the most dangerous being power. Having lived through the wars that Nietzsche had believed were so healthy, one knew now where his renunciation of moderation and ethics led: "Atrocity, bestialization, the desecration of man was the end result of the teaching of the beautiful beast of prey."[100]

To be sure, Flake admitted, there was a yawning gulf between the writing table and the real world. Praxis inevitably required translation to the masses in whose sphere even the most elevated notions had to operate within organizational structures. Praxis transformed everything into a matter of order, control, and obedience. Anyone who offered a teaching for humanity had to take this into account. The responsibility was grave indeed, for in such contexts ideas became the most dangerous, explosive dynamite in existence. Nietzsche lacked precisely this awareness of responsibility, a fact that distinguished him from those intellects capable of keeping their ideas under control. Flake was not persuaded by Nietzsche's reflections on the subject: "The thought

97. Otto Flake, "Friedrich Nietzsche," *Die Deutschen*, 56–70, 56.
98. Flake, "Afterword," 70–72.
99. See Alfred Weber's critical yet sympathetic "Nietzsche und die Katastrophe," in his *Abschied der bisherigen Geschichte: Überwindung des Nihilismus* (Hamburg: Claasen and Göverts, 1946).
100. Flake, "Friedrich Nietzsche," 57, 69.

frightens me that many people who are unauthorized and wrong-headed will cite me as an authority for their actions."[101]

Flake ironically argued that it was not good enough to categorize Nietzsche as endlessly ambiguous (*unfassbar vieldeutig*). Nietzsche's predisposition towards ambiguity had simply reinforced a fateful German tendency to be imprecise and indecisive. This ideological tendency was a component of the German problem. For four centuries the whole nation had increasingly lacked concrete thinking—Nietzsche was the culmination.

Flake, like most *Schuldfrage* writers, had no sophisticated dialectic of enlightenment. He posited for the new Germany the resurrection of a simple, able reason, "enduring, objective, capable of crystallizing values serving the general populace."[102] In this postwar German frame Nietzsche was the incarnation of a brutalized radical counter-Enlightenment and the enemy of liberal, humane values essential to the re-creation of a civilized society.

Works such as Alfred von Martin's *Intellectual Precursors of the German Collapse* typified this kind of literature with its search for culprits, its idealist assumptions concerning the role of ideas in the historical process, and its prescriptions for overcoming these deficiencies. Nietzsche was centrally indicted. Even if he had intended everything "aesthetically" and had only provided his readers with pictures and images, wrote von Martin, they had had a gruesome and dangerous effect.[103] Nietzsche's radicalized doctrine of the will to power and his atheism had destroyed not only God but the idea of humanness. While other radical critics of religion like Feuerbach and David Friedrich Strauss had left altruism intact, nothing was forbidden to Nietzsche's Übermensch.

Von Martin was amongst the first to recognize the implications of Lebensphilosophie applied to politics. This politics of "heroic realism" associated with Nietzsche, Sorel, and Jünger, he argued, was tied to the breakdown of the old order and was a key ingredient in the emergence of notions in which "all clear political contours: 'right' and 'left' merge indistinguishably into an iridescent . . . iconoclastic effect. With it political thought assumed an ambiguous and double-edged character."[104]

---

101. Quoted in Peters, *Zarathustra's Sister,* viii.
102. Ibid., 71–72.
103. Alfred von Martin, *Geistige Wegbereiter des deutschen Zusammenbruchs* (Recklinghausen: Bitter, 1948), 30.
104. Ibid., 25.

Nietzsche, concluded von Martin, believed that nihilism could be overcome and that rebarbarization was curative. Yet what had begun as the great Yes, the dream of an elevated life, had ended up in complete demonism.[105] Friedrich Meinecke's 1946 overview of *Die deutsche Katastrophe* was similarly informed by a conception of the demonic in his analysis of Nietzsche and his image of nazism:

> In Nietzsche's realm of ideas, which now began to exert a powerful influence over all yearning and restless spirits, there were gathered together almost all the noble and ignoble desires and self-longings which filled this period—a demonic phenomenon in the disruptiveness of its character and influence. Nietzsche's superman, destroying the old tables of morality, guided like a mysteriously seductive beacon an unfortunately not small part of the German youth, guided it forward into a wholly dark future which must be conquered.[106]

The most famous and creative example portraying both nazism and Nietzsche in devil-like terms is Thomas Mann's 1947 epic, *Doctor Faustus*. In that monumental effort to encompass national socialism and the German catastrophe, Nietzsche is omnipresent.[107] The life of the central character, Adrian Leverkühn, is patterned on Nietzsche's, and the Nietzsche motif, as T. J. Reed has pointed out,

> works out the parallel between pathological and political collapse which is an implied judgement on German politics. It also links the Devil to politics in another way; not only has Germany "sold her soul to the Devil," but the

105. Ibid., 35–45.
106. Friedrich Meinecke, *The German Catastrophe: Reflections and Recollections,* trans. Sidney B. Fay (Boston: Beacon, 1963), 24. The conservative historian Gerhard Ritter similarly located the Nietzschean danger as it interacted with flaws in the German character. Nietzsche's central metaphysical categories were "certainly not intended by him as a glorification of a politics of brutal force in the trivial sense given them by later writers." Nevertheless, his limitless individualism and his aphoristic style fostered such misunderstandings and reinforced "the fatal effects of the German tendency toward 'political metaphysics' and the radicalism of pure thought" (Ritter, *Europe and the German Question,* 1948; rev. ed., *The German Problem* [Columbus: Ohio State University Press, 1965], 117–118).
107. Thomas Mann, *Doktor Faustus* (Stockholm: Bermann-Fischer, 1947); translated as *Doctor Faustus* by H. T. Lowe-Porter (New York: Alfred A. Knopf, 1948). See Gunilla Bergsten's *Thomas Mann's 'Doktor Faustus': The Sources and Structure of the Novel,* trans. Krishna Winston (Chicago and London: University of Chicago Press, 1969), 57ff. Mann wrote:

> *Doctor Faustus* has been called a Nietzsche-novel, and, indeed, the book, which for good reasons avoids mention of Nietzsche's name, contains many references to his intellectual tragedy, even direct quotations from the history of his illness. It has also been said that I had bisected myself in the novel, and that the narrator and the hero each embraced a part of me. That, also, contains an element of truth—although I, too, do not suffer from paralysis. ("Thomas Mann's Answer," *Saturday Review of Literature* 32 [1 January 1949], 23)

individual Faust (Adrian) also "is" the thinker whose ideas set the fateful movement going.[108]

Critics in the German Democratic Republic were later quick to point out the problematic nature of the demonic category, labeling it as bourgeois mystification.[109] Even though analysts like von Martin regarded Nietzsche as pernicious, East German Marxists took von Martin to task for appealing to this suprahistorical category that disembodied Nietzsche's ideas from their concrete social context. As one commentator put it, von Martin transformed Nietzsche's philosophy into a mere point of contact with a demonic sphere that had always been part of an eternal German national character severed from all specific economic and historical roots.[110]

Whatever the merits and demerits of this analysis, most of these bourgeois writers believed that the antidote to such demonism was clear: renewed and healthy social bonds could be established only on the basis of a return to universal history and some combination of the bourgeois Enlightenment legacy and the Christian tradition.

Organized Christian religions and Christian critics contributed heavily to the post-Nazi onslaught on Nietzsche. "After the German catastrophe in which he was so involved, a thorough reconsideration of Nietzsche is a requirement that we cannot quarrel with, else we would be coresponsible for the confusions that an unexamined Nietzsche would always bring forth."[111] Nietzsche and his unsupervised followers were coresponsible for both the anti-Christianity that raged during the Hitler years and the accompanying decline of the German spirit.[112] The recurring notion of Nietzsche's peculiar magical potency again surfaced. In his dark medicine cabinet, the same writer went on, there were prescriptions that were bound to lead to the most atrocious crimes against humanity. National socialism had applied these teachings and

108. Reed, *Thomas Mann*, 369.
109. The East German Marxist critic Stanislaw Lem wrote of Mann's *Doctor Faustus* that fascism was an impersonal mechanism not a mythical devil, and its meaning could not be disclosed by reference to some traditional, higher cultural order ("Über das Modellieren der Wirklichkeit im Werk vom Thomas Mann," *Sinn und Form*, cited in Reed [*Thomas Mann* 393ff]). Reed argues that not the devil-Faust myth but the Dionysiac one stands at the center of the novel. Unlike other mythological themes, he argues, it serves as a means to analyze forces observable in man and society.
110. Bernhard Kaufhold, "Zur Nietzsche-Rezeption in der westdeutschen Philosophie der Nachkriegszeit" in *Beiträge zur Kritik der gegenwärtigen bürgerlichen Geschichtsphilosophie*, ed. Robert Schulz (Berlin: Deutscher Verlag der Wissenschaften, 1958), 279–409, see especially p. 326; Sweet, "Friedrich Nietzsche in the GDR," 232.
111. Heinrich Scholz, *Begegnung mit Nietzsche* (Tübingen: Furche-Verlag, 1948), 36.
112. Ibid., 3.

had ended up bestializing almost every sphere of life. Anti-Nietzschean (and pro-Kierkegaardian) lessons had to be taught to a disoriented youth who were bereft of notions of good and evil and who, faced with the ideological competition of the four-zone occupation system, were devoid of spiritual bearings.

The title and content of Ernst Barthel's *Nietzsche as Seducer* typified these sentiments. Nietzsche's influence, Barthel wrote, was immense. Whether he was misunderstood was irrelevant; "he was literally the pied piper of Hamlin who seduced us into Europe's deepest catastrophe around the year 1940." Barthel's solution to such sorcery was the conventional fusion of humanity with the teachings of Christ. But he unconventionally endowed Nietzschean sorcery with a divine function. Nietzsche as Antichrist had been "sent into the world so that the ensuing ruthless experiment would provide fruitful soil for Christian teachings in the future."[113]

For many Christian writers such as Walther Künneth, Hitler was simply designated "the executor of Nietzsche's *Ideenwelt*,"[114] rendered possible by Nietzsche's radicalism of subjective disconnectedness. Such critics naturally opposed Otto Flake's indictment of Protestantism. Nietzsche was not the last consequence of the Protestant Reformation but precisely the departure from it, the descent from its *Evangelium*, "the play thing of an antidivine satanic spirit, [who] became the embodiment of the purely demonic man." In this vision Nietzsche and Hitler were no longer simply linked but fused into an indissoluble entity: "The demonic human type Nietzsche–Hitler—opposite them stands the evangelical, reformational man with his knowledge of the forlornness of our existence."[115]

Not all Christian analyses were entirely dismissive. Konrad Algermissen in his *Nietzsche and the Third Reich* stressed the power and continuity of the Christian thematic within Nietzsche and speculated on how the Protestant element in his thought would have ended up had he not gone insane.[116] Some, like Theodor Steinbüchel in his "Christian

---

113. Ernst Barthel, *Nietzsche als Verführer* (Baden-Baden: Hans Bühler Junior, 1947), 7–8, 173.
114. Walter Künneth, "Friedrich Nietzsche, ein Künder der deutschen Katastrophe," *Zeitwende* 19, no. 11 (May 1948), 694.
115. Ibid., 705.
116. Konrad Algermissen, *Nietzsche und das dritte Reich* (Celle: Verlag Joseph Giesel, 1946). Algermissen waited for the end of the Third Reich before he penned his anti-Nazi attacks. During the Nazi years he bitterly attacked the Bolsheviks (*Die Gottlosenbewegung der Gegenwart und Ihre Überwindung* [Celle: Verlag Joseph Giesel, 1933]).

meditation" on Nietzsche, went even further and edged towards the kind of deepened Nietzscheanized forms of Christianity discussed in chapter 7. Nietzsche had recognized the great crisis of godlessness and immanence that confronted the nineteenth century. He had gone to the root: the question of giving meaning to human existence in the world. He had realized that people alone were responsible for their condition. The apparent loss of transcendence endowed them with their own god-like and demonic potential. Nietzsche's critique of Christianity went far deeper than the flat eighteenth-century materialist critique. The problem was that he had misunderstood that "real Christianity is not without the demonic that Nietzsche so strongly stressed; it too was not without the devil."[117]

But such reflections were more the exception than the rule. Under watchful Allied eyes Nietzschean dangers were stressed in the education of teachers who were to guide the newly reconstructed liberal democracy. Nietzsche did not belong to those who could help in "the spiritual reconstruction of our people, for he fought on the other side of the barricades." Although he was a great poet and penetrating psychologist, it was better to have a small talent serving a good cause than a great talent harnessed to an evil one.[118] Many of these treatments did allude that not all Nazis had been Nietzscheans and that there was much in the Nietzsche corpus that was incompatible with national socialism. Nevertheless, they stressed the affinities and, already in 1946, were fearfully anticipating a Nietzschean revival that would oppose his indictment as a Nazi and offer him as a basis for the cultural reconstruction of Germany.[119]

Numerous voices opposed this dismissal of Nietzsche; their provenance and credibility varied considerably. In 1947, the former head of the Nietzsche Archives, C. A. Emge—who had been appointed to that position because he was "a Nazi professor of legal philosophy at Jena and a prospective Nazi Minister in the Thuringian Government"— could portray the whole anti-Nietzsche mood as scapegoating.[120] Nietzsche, Emge proclaimed, was the convenient whipping boy of the

117. Theodor Steinbüchel, *Friedrich Nietzsche: Eine christliche Besinnung* (Stuttgart: Deutsche Verlags-Anstalt, 1946), 23.

118. Alfred Meusel, "Zur charakteristik der soziologischen und politischen anschauungen Friedrich Nietzsches," *Pädagogik: beiträge zur erziehungswissenschaft* 3, no. 2 (1948), 56.

119. Georg Müller, *Nietzsche und die deutsche Katastrophe* (Gütersloh: C. Bartelsmann, 1946), 17.

120. Kessler, *Diaries,* 426.

day. Neither Hitler, Mussolini, nor Rosenberg had the right to call on Nietzsche. Indeed, under his tenure not one of these men had ever posed questions to the Archives! Emge not only sought to exculpate Nietzsche from the Nazi connection but also to draw a message that differed considerably from other contemporary reassessments. After Nietzsche there should no longer be any "light-headed rationalism" (*leichtsinnigen Rationalismus*).[121]

For old members of the Weimar radical right—like Heidegger and the Jünger brothers—the Nietzschean predicament of nihilism and the will to power were again deployed but in such nebulous ways that they served to deflect any particular confrontation with the German Schuldfrage. They explicitly unlocked these categories from the German and Nazi context and universalized them, portraying them as part of the still-unresolved condition of modernity. In 1949 Friedrich Georg Jünger—the first of this circle to write a full-length postwar study of Nietzsche—made it quite clear that the defeat of national socialism had not really resolved any of the basic questions unleashed by the undifferentiated will to power: "The era of world wars, the struggle for domination of the earth (*Erdherrschaft*) has begun—we are still in the middle of it."[122] The manifestations were easily identified:

> Western nihilism is as a whole no phenomenon of exhaustion (*Ermüdungserscheinung*), but—as the thoroughly nihilistic consequences of its science and technology demonstrate—the most active and energetic form of the will to power, the most destructive that as yet has been at work, for we have not left nihilism behind us, we are still in the middle of it. But we are at the same time working to overcome it. We find remedies against it. We heal ourselves in the middle of destruction. And we still shall catapult forward through the catastrophes.[123]

The Heideggerian ring was evident. Like Heidegger, Jünger made no attempt to come to grips with the specificities of the Nazi atrocities or with genocide. Instead, all evil was collapsed into the notion of a destructive will to power equated with Western technology. Moreover, the very same circles that had done everything to harness Nietzsche in new and radically nationalist form now represented him anew as a

121. C. A. Emge, "Nietzsche als Sundenbock," *Berliner Hefte* no. 1 (1947), 47.
122. Friedrich Georg Jünger, *Nietzsche* (Frankfurt am Main: Vittorio Klostermann, 1949), 47.
123. Ibid., 49.

"bulwark of independent mind" unaffiliated with any state or party framework.[124]

There were, however, other early defenders of Nietzsche not associated with the radical right. Pondering on the prospects for Nietzsche's denazification, the Nietzsche scholar Karl Schlechta was quick to suggest an updated role for the philosopher. It was probably true that Nietzsche was the most dangerous of all the philosophers who had been blamed for the total state. Yet paradoxically that same quality made him indispensable to the postwar present. For, Schlechta insisted, the problem of nihilism which Nietzsche had both diagnosed and confronted had still not yet been overcome. Schlechta provided a novel explanation for the prevalent fear of Nietzsche, conveniently bypassing its recent, obvious cause: "We are afraid of Nietzsche precisely because of his honesty, and the truth is that we are still afraid of truth and prefer authority at any price." There was no difference between the intoxication of the National Socialist yesterday and the postwar hangover (*Katzenjammer*). Both atmospheres were grossly removed from the pure air of Nietzsche's intellectual integrity. The time would come when a discussion of the real Nietzsche would begin again.[125]

Within the German Federal Republic there was no institutional framework for outlawing Nietzsche; the possibility of more sympathetic interpretations always existed. Despite the present negative climate, Schlechta could hold out the hope for a future possible revival. The same could not be said for the German Democratic Republic. In line with long-standing Marxist orthodoxy on the philosopher, Nietzsche was officially proscribed within East Germany and tabooed as the primary philosopher of a brutalized German fascism.[126] The Archives had already been placed under lock and key by the Soviets in their Occupied Zone.[127] They were only reopened to the public in 1991 post-unification Germany.[128]

Nevertheless, already in the East Germany of 1986—well before the Berlin wall came crashing down and when unification was regarded as

---

124. See, for instance, Friedrich Georg Jünger, *Aufmarsch des Nationalismus* (Leipzig, 1926), 171.
125. Karl Schlechta, "Entnazifierung Nietzsches? Wandel im Urteil und Wertung," *Göttinger Universitäts Zeitung* 2, no. 16 (18 July 1947), 3–4.
126. Sweet, "Friedrich Nietzsche in the GDR."
127. See "A philosopher who was a non-person in the worker and peasant State," *The German Tribune*, no. 1436 (23 September 1990), 10. I thank Jerrold Kessel for this reference.
128. See "Nietzsche in Weimar: Gedenkstaette wiederöffnet," *Frankfurter Allgemeine Zeitung* (21 May 1991). I thank Jerrold Kessel for this reference.

little more than a utopian fantasy—a far-reaching and sympathetic reconsideration of Nietzsche was under way.[129] This willingness to open up debate and to view Nietzsche in a more complex and positive fashion perhaps signaled a rapidly changing political and intellectual climate.[130] Still, this receptiveness should not be overexaggerated. There were moves to publish carefully selected works—*Untimely Meditations* and *The Gay Science*—for the East Germans, but the potential publisher and commentator, Friedrich Tomberg and Renate Reschke, found that the opposition spearheaded by Wolfgang Harich and Manfred Buhr was strong enough to prevent their publication until the unforeseen end of the German Democratic Republic.[131] Little wonder, then, that Nietzsche sympathizers tended to view the postwar Nietzsche less as a pioneer than a victim of national socialism.[132]

Notwithstanding all the changes, the dominant perception of Nietzsche in German popular culture remains to this day closely and uncomfortably bound to the National Socialist experience (illus. 17). Most of the major intellectuals have typically tempered their admiration with a historically conditioned and Enlightenment-oriented wariness.[133] Clearly, the resuscitation of Nietzsche into a European vogue figure required that he emigrate. France and the nascent, politically ambiguous, poststructuralist revolution of the 1970s was tailor-made for him. There Nietzsche has assumed virtually canonic status, but it is no ac-

129. The challenge to the orthodox position came from Heinz Pepperle, "Revision des Marxistischen Nietzsche-Bildes," *Sinn und Form* 38, no. 5 (1986) and the orthodox counterattack from Wolfgang Harich, "Revision des Marxistischen Nietzschbildes," *Sinn und Form* 39, no. 5 (1987). Harich insisted that his orthodoxy be personally enforced by Erich Honecker. Nevertheless, in the *Sinn und Form* symposium featuring Stephan Hermlin, the overwhelming opinion tended to be sympathetic ("Meinungen zu einem Streit," *Sinn und Form* 40, no. 1 [1988], pp. 179–220).

130. See the perceptive comments in Charles S. Maier, *The Unmasterable Past: History, Holocaust and German National Identity* (Cambridge: Harvard University Press, 1988), 148, 212, n. 60. The articles by Dennis M. Sweet are also useful ("Friedrich Nietzsche in the GDR"; "Nietzsche Criticized: The GDR Takes a Second Look," *Studies in GDR Culture and Society* 7), especially the comments on Renate Reschke's earlier attempt to broaden the approach. I thank Prof. Klaus Berghahn for the latter references.

131. See "A philosopher who was a non-person," 10, for a summary. The only breakthrough was a facsimile edition of *Ecce Homo* published by Mazzino Montinari and Karl-Heinz Hahn, director of the Goethe–Schiller Archives in Weimar.

132. See the Westdeutschen Rundfunk talk by Richard Maximilian Lonsbach, "War Nietzsche Ein Wegbereiter des Dritten Reiches?" in his *Friedrich Nietzsche und die Juden*.

133. In Germany the charged Nazi past endows terms that elsewhere appear academic and abstract—emancipation, reason, enlightenment—with immediate resonance and rich political connotations. See the interesting comments by Joachim Whaley, "Enlightenment and History in Germany," *The Historical Journal* 31 (1 March 1988), 195–199.

cident that the most vociferous and sophisticated critic of these manifold French Nietzscheanisms is the German Jürgen Habermas.[134]

If progressive circles continue to be wary of the philosopher, the
materials and potential for a reactivation of a radical-right German
Nietzsche may not be entirely exhausted. There does exist a contemporary German intellectual New Right that incorporates its Nietzsche
into obscure magazines like *Wir selbst, Aufbruch, Criticon,* and *Mut:* it
is propagated by men like Armin Mohler (formerly Ernst Jünger's sec-
retary), Caspar von Schrenk-Notzing, and Henning Eichberg and is
supported by wealthy foundations.

This New Right has incorporated Jünger and Heidegger themselves
into the prophetic pantheon and seeks to integrate older Nietzschean
themes into the changed historical and intellectual circumstances of
what it regards as a hopelessly Westernized post-Nazi Germany. Perhaps the most articulate spokesmen of this romantic anti-capitalist
trend, which characteristically merges many themes of the extreme left
and extreme right, is Gerd Bergfleth whose writings contain a venomous
hatred for the "palavering" and "cynical" Enlightenment.[135] Bergfleth
is animated by a seething resentment of Americanization, liberalism,
Marxism, and democracy brought to Germany in the wake of World
War II. These values, he argues, were reimported by returned Jewish
refugees such as Theodor Adorno and Ernst Bloch, representatives of an
enlightened cosmopolitan Judaism who had no sense of "German
uniqueness, or romantic yearning, the link with nature or the still not
extinguished memory of a pagan-German past."[136] Because the Nazi
experience had made such völkisch ideals taboo,[137] this rootless
"Jewish left-wing intelligentsia" had been able "to remodel Germany
according to their own cosmopolitan standards. In this they have succeeded so well that for two decades there has been no independent
German spirit at all."[138]

---

134. This may indeed be the proper context in which to view Habermas's main work,
The Philosophical Discourse of Minority.
135. Gerd Bergfleth has an essay entitled "Die zynische Aufklärung" in his collection
characteristically entitled *Zur Kritik der Palavernden Aufklärung* (Munich: Matthes and
Seitz, 1984). The motto on the back cover reads: "*Eher wird ein Kamel durch ein
Nadelöhr gehen, als eine Ahnung durch einen aufgeklärten Kopf, wenn schon das Hohle
darin viel grösser ist.*" I thank Professor Leo Lowenthal who, when he was in Jerusalem,
drew my attention to this reference.
136. Bergfleth, "Die zynische Aufklärung," 181.
137. See Ian Buruma's perceptive article, "There's no Place Like Heimat," *New York
Review of Books* (20 December 1990), 34–43.
138. *Konkret,* 10 October 1990. Quoted in Buruma, "Heimat," 37. For Bergfleth
Nazi racism was the extreme particularist mirror-image of the extreme, unmediated

In Bergfleth's eclectic vision, Nietzsche appears as a central figure underlying his tragic Dionysian programmatic prophecy of necessary destruction and decline followed by a postrationalist renewal rendered possible through madness,[139] eros, and especially Death.[140] Bergfleth distinguishes between two different halves of Nietzsche. There is the dubious, nihilistic, great progenitor of "leftist irony" from whom the exhausted post–World War II left has derived its resigned and self-deluding inspiration. But there is also Nietzsche the tragedian, the philosopher who ultimately stands above nihilism. Here he figures as part of Bergfleth's revived neoromantic Spenglerian gloss on the *Untergang* of the Western world and its primal possibilities of post-technological renewal, one characterized by the last possible Zarathustrian recognition of authenticity: "O Zarathustra, everything about me is a lie; but that I am breaking—this my breaking is *genuine*."[141]

The new intellectual right remains a fringe phenomenon that, as Peter Glotz, the former Secretary-General of the SPD, perceptively notes, to date fortunately has not teamed up with its more populist right-wing counterparts.[142] Nevertheless, given the multiple revisionist tendencies at work in contemporary Germany, it would be as grave an error to totally dismiss this phenomenon as it would be to exaggerate its importance. The story of the Nietzsche legacy has not yet run its full course.

---

cosmopolitanism of the Enlightenment. Moreover, he suggests, the very universality of the Enlightenment contained a trap for its Jewish proponents resulting in the Holocaust:

> "All men will become brothers" implies the destruction of those who do not want to be brothers. One cannot exclude the conclusion, paradoxical though it may be: the destruction of European Jewry has *one* of its roots in the Enlightenment, exactly in that "transition to humanity" on which liberal Judaism rested. ("Die zynische Aufklärung," 184)

139. It is no accident that in *Palavernden Aufklärung* Bergfleth includes a translation of Bataille on Nietzsche's madness. Such left–right borrowings are palpable. In a private correspondence Jerry Muller pointed out to me that the German New Right owes a debt not only to French leftist Nietzscheans like Bataille but also to the French New Right and Alain de Benoist (Alain de Benoist, *Nietzsche: morale et grande politique* [Paris, 1973]).

140. Bergfleth, "Zehn Thesen zur Vernunftkritik," nos. 6–8 in *Palavernden Aufklärung*, 10–11.

141. Bergfleth's "Über linke Ironie," in *Palavernden Aufklärung*, 179. See too the quote from *Zarathustra*, 369.

142. Peter Glotz, "The New Right in the New Order," *Liber* no. 1 (February 1990), 20.

CHAPTER X

Nietzscheanism, Germany, and Beyond

I am a *Doppelgänger*, I have a "second" face in addition to
the first. And perhaps also a third.

Nietzsche, *Ecce Homo*

This study has set out to establish the nature, extent, and dynamics of
Friedrich Nietzsche's impact upon German politics and culture. That
impact was always historically conditioned. The history of the Nietzsche legacy, we have argued, must be regarded as the open-ended,
dynamic history of its manifold appropriations, the product of an ongoing dialogue between the Nietzschean oeuvre and its various interested mediators acting within diverse institutional frameworks and
changing cultural and political contexts. Nietzscheanism in Germany
acted as a force upon, while being re-created by, the charged circumstances out of which that country's turbulent history has been made
since the 1890s.

We have sought to assess the philosopher's imprint on some of the
dramatic milestones of late nineteenth- and twentieth-century German
history and to analyze the reciprocal ways in which those events themselves helped to shape his changing image and functions. Together with
this chronological dimension, we have also examined the role that
Nietzschean impulses played within the increasingly fractured, crisis-
ridden worlds of German religion and socialism and their multifunc-
tional infusion into a host of currents, marginal as well as central. These
included the artistic avant-garde, the Stefan George circle, vegetarians,
sexual liberationists, the Youth movements, feminism, Zionism, expressionism, völkisch groups, conservative revolutionaries, and, of course,
national socialism.

Most previous studies have sought to press this rich complexity into a narrow essentialist framework, classifying the various deployments either as deviations from or faithful representations of the "real" Nietzsche. Whether such a single, grand metanarrative does or does not best account for Nietzsche's thought—a methodological problem which itself must be considered part of Nietzsche's ongoing legacy!—it does not make for good cultural history. No prior, singular (and, in any case, disputed) master interpretation has been able to do justice to the astonishing range of that influence and its pervasive penetration into contradictory areas of political and cultural life. Whether one approves of the fact, a variety of movements and ideologies did annex (or actively resist) Nietzsche. The goal of this work has been to analyze and understand rather than judge and grade the history of these mediated affirmations and negations, their casuistic strategies and transmutive applications. It has sought to enrich our understanding of the manifold ways in which a complex of ideas, catchwords, and images—quite apart from their validity—permeated the cultural and political sensibilities of German society.

The workings of diverse pro- and anti-Nietzschean impulses within Germany were particularly dense, marked, and fateful. What specifically rendered the encounter so fateful in that country? What accounts for the manifold forms of Nietzscheanism and their special resonance there?

The answer, at one level, is obvious enough. Regardless of how passionately he was received elsewhere, Germany was the philosopher's home. The density of responses, the depths of reverence and antagonism he evoked, and the fact that an encounter with him became almost mandatory was related to this elementary biographical circumstance. Nietzsche was born and died in Germany and articulated a peculiarly German predicament. At any rate, this is how many of his compatriots increasingly viewed the matter. Despite his innumerable anti-Germanic statements, a variously interpreted conception of his "Germanness" became itself an enabling appropriative factor.[1] Deutschtum was thus

---

1. Throughout this work we have considered some of the textual bases for such exercises. Consider the range of interpretive and casuistic possibilities which follow Nietzsche's motto quoted at the beginning of this chapter:

Even by my descent, I am granted an eye beyond all merely local, merely nationally conditioned perspectives; it is not difficult for me to be a "good European." On the other hand, I am perhaps more German than present-day Germans, mere citizens of the German Reich, could possibly be—I the last anti-political German. And yet my ancestors were Polish noblemen: I have many racial instincts in my body from that source. (Ecce Homo, 225)

integrated into the diverse renderings of Nietzsche's thought, facilitating his incorporation into any number of German movements, ideologies, and institutions.[2]

Still, prior to the 1890s the Nietzschean explosion within German political and cultural life was anything but self-evident. As late as 1888 Nietzsche noted that he had been discovered everywhere—except Germany.[3] Why, then, did Nietzscheanism thrive during the last decade of the nineteenth century and thereafter?

Nietzsche and the Nietzscheans, we have argued, were both makers and beneficiaries of a European-wide antipositivist and modernist shift in sensibility that manifested itself during that decade. But beyond that, and tied in with ideologies of Nietzsche's putative "Germanness," there emerged an especially favorable conjunction between Nietzsche's iconoclastic corpus and central events and developments on the German historical landscape. Nietzschean impulses were especially well equipped and sufficiently flexible to influence and render meaningful some of the "extraordinary" moods and events that characterized German history after 1890: the critical discontent and prophetic intimations pervading fin-de-siècle Wilhelmine society; the modes in which World War I was heralded and perceived; the polarized, increasingly brutalized disposition of the Weimar Republic; the self-representation and policies of national socialism; and finally the need for a negative foil to a "normalized" and "respectable" national identity in the post–World War II era.

Any generalization concerning Nietzscheanism in Germany must remain tentative. One can say, however, that it did tend to thrive in extreme circumstances and in situations characterized by an acute consciousness of political, personal, and institutional crisis. To be sure, there were Nietzscheans of many kinds. But what almost all had in common was a general desire to challenge and go beyond accepted assumptions and conventions. Thus, to take one conspicuous instance, Nietzsche's subliminal as well as explicit presence pervaded the diverse, probing "masterworks" of the Weimar Republic, ranging

---

Needless to say, all three faces became part of the discussion as did the various possible meanings attached to the notion of "anti-political" so effectively politicized by Thomas Mann in his *Reflections of a Nonpolitical Man.*

2. Here the comparison with Darwin may be instructive. Darwinism was also a major fin-de-siècle frame of reference that was pressed into protean political and cultural service. But Darwin's assimilability into German culture, as Alfred Kelly has pointed out, was inhibited by the fact that he was not a German and thus unamenable to attempts to link him to the German spirit (Kelly, *The Descent of Darwin,* 7).

3. Nietzsche, *Ecce Homo,* 262.

from Ernst Bloch's *Spirit of Utopia* to Martin Heidegger's *Being and Time,* Franz Rosenzweig's *The Star of Redemption,* and Oswald Spengler's *The Decline of the West.* Despite their obvious differences, all were characterized by an acute sense of rupture and nihilistic breakdown; all explored novel and radical ways in which to conceptualize, and respond to, an unprecedented political, moral, religious, and cultural predicament. Regardless of the institutions to which they belonged and the particular ideologies they professed, Nietzscheans typically championed postorthodox approaches and solutions.

This even applied, at least in one important case, to the unlikely world of German liberalism. Nietzsche was crucial not only to Max Weber's grasp of modern culture and its dilemmas but also to what can only be described as his postliberalism.[4] This "liberal in despair"[5] turned to Nietzsche as a central pillar in his attempt to save liberalism by going beyond—some would say unrecognizably beyond—the classical assumptions of the creed.[6] The Nietzschean element in his thinking went beyond the conviction that the most important characteristic of the political leader consisted of the "will to power."[7] More fundamentally, his advocacy of plebiscitary democracy was linked to his convic-

---

4. The cardinal role of Nietzsche in Weber's thought has been increasingly recognized. He is reported to have said:

> The honesty of a scholar in our day, and even more of a philosopher of our day, can be judged on the grounds of how he defines his relationship to Nietzsche and Marx. He who denies that he would have been unable to achieve the work of both of them, belies himself just as much as the others. The world in which we live in as intellectual beings bears largely the imprint of Marx and Nietzsche. (Eduard Baumgarten, *Max Weber: Werk und Person* [Tübingen, 1964], 544ff., n. 1).

See Wolfgang Mommsen's pioneering work *Max Weber und die deutsche Politik, 1890–1920* (Tübingen: J. C. P. Mohr, 1959) trans. Michael S. Steinberg, *Max Weber and German Politics, 1890–1920* (Chicago and London: University of Chicago Press, 1984). See too Robert Eden, "Weber and Nietzsche: Questioning the Liberation of Social Science from Historicism," in Mommsen and Osterhammel, eds., *Max Weber and His Contemporaries,* 405–421; Eugene Fleischmann, "De Weber à Nietzsche," *Archives Européennes de Sociologie* 5 (1964), 190ff.; Lawrence A. Scaff, *Fleeing the Iron Cage: Culture, Politics and Modernity in the Thought of Max Weber* (Berkeley and Los Angeles: University of California Press, 1989).

5. This is the title of the last chapter of Wolfgang Mommsen's excellent *The Age of Bureaucracy: Perspectives on the Political Sociology of Max Weber* (Oxford: Basil Blackwell, 1974).

6. J. G. Merquior, "Georges Sorel and Max Weber," in *Max Weber and His Contemporaries,* 165. Mommsen also stresses the peculiarities of Weber's liberalism. One clear example of Weber's departure from a (Kantian) liberal position was his denial of universal and objective values and his Nietzschean insistence that these were purely spontaneous individual creations (*The Age of Bureaucracy,* 7).

7. "Parlement und Regierung im neugeordenetem Deutschland," in Weber's *Gesammelte politische Schriften,* ed. Johannes Winckelmann (Tübingen, 1958), 329, 338.

tion that only extraordinary, value-setting personalities would be able
to provide a modicum of salvation within the iron cage of routinization
and rationalization and be able to act as a brake on the conformities of
the bureaucratic age. Creative Nietzschean individualism had somehow
to be integrated into mass politics.[8]

In its various guises, then, Nietzscheanism did tend to nudge political
and cultural life into more radical or, at least, nonconformist directions.
In fluid tandem with the master's guidelines, it both undermined and
superseded orthodox left–right, progressive–reactionary, and rational–
irrational categories and distinctions. It could effect this above all because it was a mediated phenomenon. It acted more as an infiltrating
sensibility than a constituting presence. In that sense there was never a
pure Nietzscheanism. If it tended to radicalize institutions, it was also
harnessed by them. Institutionalization inevitably entailed structuring,
a process in which the putative Nietzschean dynamic underwent some
form of domestication. Many such annexations did indeed tame, triv-
ialize, or deflect the dynamic, but not always. In the case of the Nazis
its lethal potential was unleashed, selectively deployed for murderous
uses.

After 1914, mirroring larger developments and tendencies within
Germany, the Nietzsche legacy became increasingly identified with its
nationalist, radical right, and Nazi versions. But this was always a
highly disputed—and for many a quite scandalous—custodianship.
There were always Nietzscheans from across the political spectrum who
continued to construct competing interpretations of a legacy that was
notoriously unamenable to monopoly and homogenization.

If only because of its mediated nature, Nietzscheanism possessed no
inherent political personality. It functioned as a historically dynamic
phenomenon simultaneously influencing, reflecting, and being reshaped
by the fluid political and cultural circumstances of which it was a part.
This continues to be the case, and it will be interesting to observe the
ways in which German unification will affect the nature and tone of
Nietzsche representations.

Whatever these may turn out to be, Nietzsche's contemporary rever-
berations go well beyond Germany. Although Nietzsche's influence in
Germany was indubitably profound, it was never limited to that country. The historically mediated renderings of his messages and the rich

8. See Mommsen, *Max Weber and German Politics*, on the Nietzsche connection and
the difficulty of assigning Weber any precise political position. See too Mommsen, *The
Age of Bureaucracy*, 96, 105ff.

symbolic meanings and expressive uses of his legacy have always transcended national boundaries.

What has enabled the untimely Nietzsche to be perennially timely? What accounts for the insistently international fascination? In the final analysis, the answer must be sought in his almost uncanny ability to define—and embody—the furthest reaches of the general post-Enlightenment predicament; to encapsulate many of its enduring spiritual and intellectual tensions, contradictions, hopes, and possibilities. If there is one constant in the history of Nietzsche reception it is the continuously reinterpreted perception that Nietzsche was paradigmatic. From the 1890s through to the present, his life and thought have provided an acutely relevant prism through which to express and confront the changing meanings and problems of a generalized and ultimate modernity most radically conceived, in the words of Leszek Kolakowski, as the belief "in the unlimited possibility of mankind's self-creation."[9] Precisely because this promise, as well as its interconnected destructive potential, lies at the center of our ongoing concerns, Nietzsche has not been exhausted by any particular political system or cultural time frame.

While his paradigmatic status has not varied, perceptions as to the nature and content of the paradigm have changed in response to shifting intellectual, political, and generational circumstances. Today, for instance, he is regarded as the quintessential prophet of fashionable postmodernity. The notoriously vague and shifting meanings of terms like *modern, modernism,* and *postmodern* need not detain us here.[10] For our purposes, these designations may themselves be regarded as landmarks of changing modes of historical self-understanding, and that Nietzsche—the man of multiple faces—has consistently been regarded as the very embodiment of these changing conditions and self-representations.

Nietzsche is perhaps the most crucial shaping force upon the leading poststructuralist and deconstructionist currents of the day. He stands at the center of a French-inspired conception of culture characterized by a radically skeptical perspectivism, a sense of heterogeneity and playfulness, and an emphasis on difference.[11] As pure metaphilosopher,

9. Kolakowski, "On the So-Called Crisis of Christianity" in his *Modernity on Endless Trial,* 90–91. See too his fascinating reflections on the complexity of Nietzsche's modernity in the opening essay (from which the book takes its title), 8–9.

10. See the rather uneven collection of essays, *Nietzsche as Postmodernist.*

11. As a good example of this, see David B. Allison ed., *The New Nietzsche: Contemporary Styles of Interpretation* (Cambridge, Mass.: MIT Press, 1985).

314 Nietzscheanism, Germany, and Beyond

prophet of fragmentation and discontinuity, of power discourse, and of the illusory, metaphorical nature of truth itself, he has keenly influenced and been reconstructed to fit what his present-day champions take to be our own age of radical ideological and epistemological indeterminacy. The traces of a more positive, substantial, and programmatic Nietzsche, once so crucial to the history of his reception, have, for the moment, been virtually erased.[12]

Whatever disputed political functions this ironic Nietzsche may serve, his postmodern guise may not be the last word. It too must be considered part of the ongoing history of interested and selective paradigmatic representations. While we cannot predict its future contours, the Nietzsche legacy will in all probability live on as a dynamic force and assume new forms, responding to the dilemmas and needs of changing times and integrated into our own tentative self-definitions and cultural representations. Because Nietzsche remains the most potent symbol of the variegated, continuously experimental, post-Enlightenment project, his legacy and its seemingly boundless capacity for renewal will persist (as will the opposition to it). Our relationship to him will, surely, continue to confirm Ernst Bertram's dictum that "great men are inevitably our creation, just as we are their's."[13]

---

12. See the interesting critical comments by Robert C. Solomon, "Nietzsche, Postmodernism, and Resentment: A Genealogical Hypothesis," in *Nietzsche as Postmodernist,* 291–293.
13. Ernst Bertram, *Nietzsche,* 5.

Nietzsche and Nazism: Some Methodological and Historical Reflections

Unfortunately, man is no longer evil enough. Rousseau's opponents who say "man is a beast" are unfortunately wrong. Not the corruption of man but the extent to which he has become moralized is his curse.

Nietzsche, *The Will to Power*

The *sick* are man's greatest danger; *not* the evil, *not* the "beasts of prey."

Nietzsche, *On the Genealogy of Morals*

The hermeneutical question concerning "the real Nietzsche" since 1945 has been indissolubly linked to his relationship with nazism. The issue is still with us. The dominant postwar images—embodied in the opposed representations of Georg Lukacs and Walter Kaufmann—have either condemned Nietzsche as centrally complicit in the Nazi evil or lauded him for being unblemished and opposed to all nazism's intentions and actions. Both these approaches were less interested in tracing actual historical paths than pursuing their own value-laden interpretations. This may or may not have constituted good philosophy; it certainly did not facilitate good cultural history. Essentially dismissive of the complex mediation of ideas, they produced portraits written in either the condemnatory or apologetic mode. We have already examined Lukacs on this point. At the other end of the spectrum, Walter Kaufmann's highly influential 1950 *Nietzsche* portrayed the nazified Nietzsche as a pure distortion, a radical inversion of everything that the prophet of creativity, cultured and critical individualist, and good European had actually stood for.[1] Kaufmann's "gentle," sterilized delineation so ignored or denatured the power-political dimensions of Nietzsche, as Walter Sokel has suggested, that readers must have felt baffled that anyone could possibly have attempted to make the Nietzsche–Nazi connection in the first place.[2]

To opt for one of these interpretations would be beside the historical point. For the historian interested in the role, dynamics, and effects of ideas within a political culture, the question of valid or invalid interpretation and applications must be set aside. To argue for the centrality of interested, mediated appropriations does not, of course, render irrelevant the role of the Nietzschean text in this process. Even if, for a moment, we retain the language of "distortion" or "misinterpretation," approaches such as Kaufmann's leave us oblivious to the possibility that, as Martin Jay has put it,

> the potential for the specific distortions that do occur can be understood as latent in the original text. Thus, while it may be questionable to saddle Marx with responsibility for the Gulag Archipelago or blame Nietzsche for Auschwitz, it is nevertheless true that their writings could be misread as justifications for these horrors in a way that, say, those of John Stuart Mill or Alexis de Toqueville could not.[3]

Jacques Derrida has similarly pointedly asked with reference to Nietzschean politics, especially its National Socialist variant: "One may wonder how and why what is so naively called a falsification was possible (one can't falsify just anything)."[4]

Derrida's insistence on a degree of complicity derives from a sense of the complex rather than simple nature of the text and flows from an analysis that highlights rather than blurs the distinctions between the master and his National Socialist appropriators:

1. Over the past few years Kaufmann's interpretation of Nietzsche has been coming increasingly under attack. See Michael Tanner's comments on Kaufmann's "perniciousness" as a Nietzsche commentator, his "hegemony," and his "intellectual dependants" in "Organizing the Self and the World," *Times Literary Supplement* (16 May 1986), 519.

2. See Walter Sokel's perceptive remarks in "Political Uses and Abuses of Nietzsche in Walter Kaufmann's Image of Nietzsche," *Nietzsche-Studien* 12 (1983). Kaufmann, writes Tanner, "peddled a view of Nietzsche which certainly eliminated any possibility of offence being given to anyone of a liberal humanist outlook" ("Organizing the Self," 519).

3. Martin Jay, "Should Intellectual History Take a Linguistic Turn? Reflections on the Habermas–Gadamer Debate," in his *Fin-de-Siècle Socialism* (New York: Routledge, Chapman, and Hall, 1988), 33.

4. Jacques Derrida, *The Ear of the Other*, 23–24.

Nietzsche's utterances are not the same as those of the Nazi ideologists and not only because the latter grossly caricature the former to the point of apishness. If one does more than extract certain short sequences, if one reconstitutes the entire syntax of the system with the subtle refinement of its articulations and its paradoxical reversals, et cetera, then one will clearly see that what passes elsewhere for the "same" utterance says exactly the opposite and corresponds instead to the inverse, to the reactive inversion of the very thing it mimes. Yet it would still be necessary to account for the possibility of this mimetic inversion and perversion. If one refuses the distinction between unconscious and deliberate programs as an absolute criterion, if one no longer considers only intent—whether conscious or not—when reading a text, then the law that makes the perverting simplification possible must lie in the structure of the text "remaining" (by which we will no longer understand the persisting substance of books, as in the expression *scripta manent*). Even if the intention of one of the signatories or shareholders in the huge "Nietzschean Corporation" had nothing to do with it, it cannot be entirely fortuitous that the discourse bearing his name in society, in accordance with civil laws and editorial norms, has served as a legitimating reference for ideologues. There is nothing absolutely contingent about the fact that the only political regimen to have *effectively* brandished his name as a major and official banner was Nazi.

I do not say this in order to suggest that this kind of "Nietzschean" politics is the only one conceivable for all eternity, nor that it corresponds to the best reading of the legacy, nor even that those who have not picked up this reference have produced a better reading of it. No. The future of the Nietzsche text is not closed. But if, within the still-open contours of an era, the only politics calling itself—proclaiming itself—Nietzschean will have been a Nazi one, then it is necessarily significant and must be questioned in all of its consequences.

I am also not suggesting that we ought to reread "Nietzsche" and his great politics on the basis of what we know or think we know Nazism to be. I do not believe that we as yet know how to think what Nazism is. The task remains before us, and the political reading of the Nietzschean body or corpus is part of it.[5]

The implications of the Nietzsche text then are far more complex than the kind of unidirectional original sin Lukacs imputed to it, and more muddied than Kaufmann allowed.[6] The explosive and experimen-

5. Ibid., 30–31.
6. Eric Vögelin early on stressed this point:

What deserves some attention, however, is the fact that Nietzsche's work lends itself easily to such misinterpretations. This fact should not be denied. There is no sense in pretending that the horror passages which are quoted with equal delight by the critics and the National Socialist admirers are not to be found in the work. Their existence should not be an incentive either to whitewash or to condemn Nietzsche, but rather to explore the structure of thought which produced them.

tal Nietzsche corpus contained myriad possibilities that profoundly affected almost every vital area of twentieth-century postliberal consciousness and political culture including, quite patently, nazism.

The methodological and substantive difficulties of this question are legion; witness the various and highly contradictory ways in which historians, philosophers and critics have tried to comprehend the relationship. This may relate to Derrida's assertion that we do not "as yet know how to think what Nazism is." Moreover, the preparedness to grant a connection in the first place is often a function of a particular a priori attitude to Nietzsche or a particular methodological approach to nazism. Those inclined to structuralist and social history, for instance, are suspicious of any ideational or ideological account (let alone the particular Nietzschean strand), and are very much disinclined to regard nazism as "a particular frame of mind."[7] Even for those sympathetically disposed to such analysis, the problem of assessing the role and influence, the "causal" force, of ideas in history remains highly controversial. There can be no question here of attempting to resolve the matter. But it would be worthwhile to examine some of the major ways in which historians and critics have subsequently categorized the Nietzsche–Nazi relationship, demonstrated or denied the transmission belts of influence, posited its causal relations, and assessed its overall historical significance.

The problem of assuming this relationship has long been recognized. Already in 1939, Ernst Bloch argued that the Nietzsche (and Wagner) Nazi connection was built upon a method of empty analogy, torn out of its proper historical and ideological context.[8] More recently, Thomas Nipperdey has pointed out the ahistorical nature of analyses that indict Luther, Frederick the Great, Bismarck, Nietzsche, and Hitler in one straight line. "It is a rather petty endeavour to stretch Wagner or Nietzsche or Max Weber on the Procrustean bed of our concept of democracy and to examine them for 'pre-Fascist' tendencies or results. This is the tyranny of suspicion."[9]

("Nietzsche, The Crisis and the War," *Journal of Politics* 6, no. 1 [February 1944], 201)

7. Geoff Eley, "The German Right, 1860–1945: How It Changed," in his *From Unification to Nazism: Reinterpreting the German Past* (Boston: Allen and Unwin, 1986), 234. See too his remarks on intellectual history that "makes its connections by lifting ideas from their sensible context" (ibid.).

8. Bloch, "Über Wurzeln des Nazismus," 319–320.

9. Thomas Nipperdey, "1933 and the Continuity of German History" in H. W. Koch, ed., *Aspects of the Third Reich* (New York: St. Martin's, 1985), 493, 504.

Opposition to what has been described as teleological "Nazi pedigree hunting in the realm of ideas" has if anything become more widespread, reinforced by such persistent examples. E. Sandvoss's 1969 *Hitler and Nietzsche* posited the relationship as a comparative parallelism
that blurred all distinctions between symmetry and causal influence,
and that left unexamined the empirical transmission belts through
which it must have operated.[10]

In his agonized 1947 reevaluation of Nietzsche, Thomas Mann even
managed to reverse the conventional direction of this cause-effect relationship! He unhappily described Nietzsche as "a pacemaker, partici-
pating creator and prompter of ideas to European—to world fascism."
In terms remarkably reminiscent of Lukacs's materialist theory of pre-
figurative reflection, Mann added:

> I am inclined here to reverse cause and effect and not to believe that
> Nietzsche created fascism, but rather that fascism created him—that is to
> say: basically remote from politics and innocently spiritual, he functioned as
> an infinitely sensitive instrument of expression and registration, with his
> philosopheme of power he presaged the dawning imperialism and as a quiv-
> ering floatstick indicated the fascist era of the West.[11]

10. David Blackbourn and Geoff Eley, *The Peculiarities of German History: Bourgeois Society and Politics in Nineteenth-Century Germany* (Oxford: Oxford University
Press, 1984), 6. E. Sandvoss, *Hitler und Nietzsche* (Göttingen: Musterschmidt, 1969). We
still do not know enough about these transmission belts. The scholarly consensus is that
Hitler had either not read Nietzsche or read very little. His youthful companion August
Kubizek in his memoir *The Young Hitler I Knew* (trans. E. V. Anderson [Boston: Houghton Mifflin, 1955]) claims that young Hitler did read Nietzsche. No work by Nietzsche,
however, was found in Hitler's library, although it did include a slim volume dedicated to
him by Himmler entitled *Von Tacitus bis Nietzsche: die Gedanken und Meinungen aus
zwei Jarhtausenden* (Robert L. Waite, *Hitler: The Psychopathic God*, 62). Hitler nevertheless espoused a popularized Nietzscheanism as it had filtered down to him and which
he selectively applied to his own peculiar mode of thinking. Even if one disregards the
many Hitler quotations from the now-questionable Rauschning, this is patently obvious
in *Hitler's Table Talk* 1941–1944 (trans. Norman Cameron and R. H. Stevens [London:
Weidenfeld and Nicolson, 1953]), 720–722.

11. Ibid., 93–94. This was a far cry from what Mann had written in his diary as late
as 1936:

> A revolting article from the Berliner Tageblatt . . . maintains that the "Nietzschean
> Manes" are by no means in exile today, but have remained in Germany. It goes on
> to say that there are only surface differences between Nietzsche and National
> Socialism—the latter can lay rightful claim to him.—This should rather be said
> about Sorel. But Nietzsche, who stood for utmost "intellectual rectitude," for the
> Dionysian will to know, who smiled at *Faust* for being a "tragedy of knowledge"
> because he knew better, who was ready to endure every suffering caused by the
> truth and for the sake of truth—this man then they want to claim in connection with
> myths of action of a mass appeal roughly of the level of the most degenerate
> popular dirty songs. What filth.—Bergson, Sorel, Peguy are the real spiritual fore-
> runners of fascism. It was they who distorted socialism into nationalism. What,
> then, is "German" about it? (*Diaries*, 254–255)

Criticisms of the Nietzsche–Nazi link have by no means been made only by scholars wary of intellectual explanations. Recently, for instance, Berel Lang, while insisting upon the importance of ideas in grasping nazism, especially its genocidal side, has argued that Nietzsche is specifically exempt from such accusations of affiliation. For Lang it is not to Nietzsche but to the intolerant universalizing aspects of the Enlightenment that one must look. In his view, the links between Nietzsche and nazism are based on unadulterated "misappropriation":

> To be sure, misappropriation has causal consequences no less certainly than does affiliation, and again there is no certain line between the two. But for Nietzsche's historical aftermath, what is at issue is an instance of misappropriation, not of deduction and not even . . . of affiliation. Far from being entailed by the premises underlying Nietzsche's position, the conclusions drawn are inconsistent with them. To reconstruct in the imagination the events leading up to the Nazi genocide against the Jews without the name or presence of Nietzsche is to be compelled to change almost nothing in that pattern. This contrasts sharply with the results of the same experiment as it might be applied to a number of other ideas and thinkers whose absence would entail significant revisions in the process of Enlightenment affiliation—even, perhaps in its eventual outcome.[12]

For many still in the perplexing process of thinking through what nazism is, Lang's position is entirely unpersuasive. An exceptionally wide range of contemporary critics, philosophers, and historians continue to sense a profound affinity, positing in various ways and at different levels of complexity the complicity of Nietzschean impulses within nazism. Continuing through the present time no other philosophical figure has been more repeatedly invoked in historical explanation, none has served as a more fruitful springboard for speculative metahistorical notions of nazism and its central murderous drives. Moreover, these exercises at least attempt to confront what much of recent historiography has attempted to duck: the vexed question of Nazi motivation and intent. This view implies that in some meaningful way nazism was, at least in part, a frame of mind and that ideas (in their most general sense) were both central to its disposition as a historical project and to its subsequent comprehension.[13]

---

12. Berel Lang, *Act and Idea in the Nazi Genocide* (Chicago and London: University of Chicago Press, 1990), 197–198.
13. I have tried to argue for the indispensability of a more sophisticated cultural and intellectual history in "Nazism, Normalcy and the German *Sonderweg*," in *Studies in Contemporary Jewry* 4 (1988). Such a history would establish precisely the nature of reciprocal influences within their proper contexts by tracing mediating links, their diverse effects, and mapping out relevant discourses. See too Berel Lang, *Act and Idea*, 167–168.

What specific Nietzschean sources and causes have been invoked within this general constellation? A few examples will have to suffice. There is firstly an ongoing analysis that argues from a position of historical and ideational affiliation (conscious or otherwise). While affiliation is synonymous neither with identity nor with causation, it does imply a certain common sensibility. J. P. Stern's *Hitler* is one example. Stern carefully spells out the differences and qualifications, yet in the final analysis his Hitler is best comprehended as a man animated by a concentrated and politicized ideology of the will derived from and in (parodistic) symmetry with Nietzsche.[14] Karl Dietrich Bracher's view of nazism as a revolutionary and perverted reversal of ordinary moral values designed to serve an ideological system of terror and extermination is conceived in similarly affiliative Nietzschean terms: "Hitler himself, with his ideological fixation and his sense of mission as saviour of a world doomed by racist decline, was the prototype of such a transvaluation, taking literally Nietzsche's vision of *Umwertung aller Werte* and transcending *bürgerliche Moral.*"[15]

It should come as no surprise that many of the metahistorical musings on nazism focus on the Nietzschean element. As in the past, many of these transmit their own ideological and religious messages. Most recently, for example, the conservative Christian critic Roger Scruton has argued that the fundamental precondition for the death camps of the twentieth century was contained in the Godless naturalizing language and assumptions of thinkers like Nietzsche and Marx:

While many intellectual historians are likely to dissent from Lang's position on the Nietzsche–Nazi relationship, they will probably approve of his comments on the role of ideas in history.

14. Stern emphasizes that Nietzsche was "the most critical of modern philosophers" and that he was "not taken in by his own abstractions" (*Hitler*, 72, 74). Nevertheless he does state: "It seems, then, that 'the Will' is for Hitler what, in German popular mythology, it was for Schopenhauer and Nietzsche: the agent of a law of nature and of history, an all-encompassing metaphysical principle: in short, creator of the world and all that is in it" (p. 70). On Nietzsche's preoccupation with the *Will to Power* he writes:

Every book Nietzsche published and every posthumously edited collection of notes has something to say on the topic, so much so that an account of his entire work could be written *sub specie voluntatis*. And it is certainly true that there are many occasions when Nietzsche argues as though "the Will" were just such a disembodied, independent metaphysical principle as Hitler seems to have in mind, an unmoved mover that lies behind the empirical world and explains men's activities in the world, something like Hegel's "Spirit" whose realization is the universal history of mankind (p. 71).

15. See Karl Dietrich Bracher, "The Role of Hitler: Perspectives of Interpretation" in Laqueur, ed., *Fascism*, 208.

Those very philosophies which enjoin us to place man upon the throne from which God was taken away for burial, have been the most influential in creating the new image of man as an accident of nature, to whom nothing is forbidden or permitted by any power beyond himself. God is an illusion; so too is the divine spark in man . . . the machine which is established for the efficient production of Utopia has total license to kill. Nothing is sacred. . . . Such is the liturgical language of the religion of the Antichrist.[16]

The danger of such secular philosophies, the distinguished philosopher Leszek Kolakowski has argued, consists of their Promethean hopes which undermined Christian assumptions "of our weakness and misery":

Two great ideas of the nineteenth century which, despite all that separates them, perfectly embodied this Promethean expectation—those of Marx and of Nietzsche—were anti-Christian in their roots, and not as a result of accidental historical circumstances. . . . Nietzsche knew that Christianity is the awareness of our weakness, and he was right. Marx knew this too, and from the young Hegelians, he took over and transformed the philosophy (more Fichtean than Hegelian) of self-creation and futuristic orientation. . . .

The vitality of the Christian idea has certainly weakened in proportion to the universalization of the Promethean hope and in proportion to the growth of people's belief that their ability to perfect themselves and society knows no limit. . . . We have witnessed the gradual growth of this hope, and the two versions of it mentioned—Nietzsche's and Marx's—produced the ideological cover that served to justify the two most malignant tyrannies that our century has seen.[17]

Nietzsche here serves as a kind of vital, long-term precondition of nazism. It is linked to an argument that holds—without always satisfactorily establishing the empirical connections—that it was the radically experimental, tradition-shattering Nietzschean mode that rendered nazism thinkable. (Such an analysis, of course, implies a certain view of nazism itself.) Proponents of such a reading have little difficulty in locating supporting passages from the master. Because of a newly found courage for experimentation, Nietzsche noted in *Daybreak*, "Individuals and generations can now fix their eyes on tasks of a vastness that would to earlier ages have seemed madness and a trifling with Heaven and Hell. We may experiment with ourselves! Yes, mankind

16. Roger Scruton, "The Philosopher on Dover Beach," *Times Literary Supplement* (23 May 1986). Berdyaev's 1935 *The Fate of Man in the Modern World*, as we have seen, followed a similar line, linking Marx and Nietzsche as similar dehumanizing, naturalizing forces.
17. Leszek Kolakowski, "On the So-Called Crisis of Christianity," in his *Modernity on Endless Trial* (Chicago and London: University of Chicago Press, 1990), 90–91.

now has a right to do that."[18] In drafts for a sequel to *Zarathustra* and on the basis of his definition of the new Enlightenment's credo that "nothing is true, everything is permitted," Nietzsche went even further: "The *consequences* of your doctrine must wreak fearful havoc: but *countless are destined to perish from them. We are submitting truth to an experiment!* Maybe mankind will perish in the process! So be it!"[19]

Viewed in this way nazism, with its radicalism and vast transformative scale, becomes a consciously applied Nietzschean project. Nietzsche "prepared a consciousness that excluded nothing that anyone might think, feel, or do, including unimaginable atrocities carried out on a gigantic order."[20]

It is, above all, through this emphasis on a boundless *novum* that the sense of Nietzsche's connection to nazism's most revolutionary and destructive sides persists. Different historians and critics have identified varying aspects of that impulse as complicit in genocide and atrocity. While all assume Nietzsche's centrality, the explanations for his presence differ decidedly.

For orthodox Marxists the Nietzsche–Nazi fusion reflects the capitalist economy in crisis. It was the ideological expression of an aggressive imperialist bourgeoisie and its barbarizing tendencies and the logical result of a class-sustaining irrationalism bent upon defeating its socialist and other enemies.

Yet for the non-Marxist Ernst Nolte, in his 1963 *Der Faschismus in seiner Epoche,* nazism represented the ultimate revolt *against* the bourgeoisie[21] and what he termed its project of transcendence. At that stage of his career, Nolte insisted upon the radical uniqueness of Nazi anti-Semitism and its extermination practices, and maintained that there was an essential *unity* between the bourgeois and Marxist projects

---

18. Nietzsche, *Daybreak,* 204. See also 190–191:

> To construct anew the laws of life and action—for this task our sciences of physiology, medicine, sociology and solitude are not yet sufficiently sure of themselves: and it is from them that the foundation-stones of new ideals (if not the new ideals themselves) must come. So it is that, according to our taste and talent, we live an existence which is either a *prelude* or a *postlude,* and the best we can do in this *interregnum* is to be as far as possible our own *reges* and found little *experimental states.* We are experiments: let us also want to be them!" (190–191)

19. Nietzsche, *Gesammelte Werke* (Leipzig: Kröner), vol. 12, 410. Quoted in Lukacs, *Destruction of Reason,* 346–347. The emphasis on radical experimentality and great health is spelled out in *Human, All Too Human,* 8.

20. Kurt Rudolf Fischer, "Nazism as a Nietzschean Experiment," *Nietzsche-Studien* 6 (1977), 121.

21. Ernst Nolte, *Der Faschismus in seiner Epoche* (Munich: Piper, 1963). Tr. Leila Vennewitz, *Three Faces of Fascism* (New York: New American Library, 1969), 537–567.

of transcendence.[22] In Nolte's rendering, Nietzsche is portrayed as the most crucial figure of this ongoing impulse against bourgeois and Marxist realization. He above all incarnates the impetus to the sensuous renaturalization of the world and points to the creation of a new, wholly nondecadent man. The Nietzschean and Nazi projects thus become virtually identical. Hitler, wrote Nolte, "was possessed by 'something' which was not trivial." As the "termination of an age" he was the most radical manifestation of an impulse best articulated by Nietzsche.[23] In this view, the notion of destruction or extermination—*Vernichtungsgedanke* as Nolte puts it—was bound to become central to Nietzsche's late philosophy.[24] It is worth quoting him at length:

> Nietzsche's real enemy is obviously the concept of realization; it is at this that he aims such terms as *ressentiment, decadence,* and *"total degeneration."* From a philosophical standpoint there is only one unassailable counterconcept: that of the wholly non-decadent man, the "beast of prey, the magnificent, roaming blond beast lusting for booty and victory," the magnificent animality of "the pack of blond beasts of prey." . . .
>
> It cannot be doubted that Nietzsche's whole thought represents a more radical . . . more persistent countermovement to the Marxist conception and that the idea of extermination (*Vernichtungsgedanke*) represents the negative aspect of its innermost core. For if history is not an *Attentat* thousands of years old, then only the extermination of the perpetrator of this crime can restore things to their true balance. Nietzsche is not in a banal sense the spiritual father of fascism; but he was the first to give voice to that spiritual focal point towards which all fascism must gravitate; the assault on practical and theoretical transcendence, for the sake of a "more beautiful" form of "life."[25]

22. On the centrality of anti-Semitism and the uniqueness of the exterminations see Nolte, *Three Faces,* 502. For his argument that Hitler's anti-Marxism was a function of his desire to annihilate the Jews and not the other way around, as he later claimed, see p. 458. On Nolte's evolution and his place in the *Historikerstreit* see Steven Aschheim, "History, Politics and National Memory: The German *Historikerstreit,"* *Survey of Jewish Affairs* (1988). For the most thoroughgoing discussion see Charles S. Maier, *The Unmasterable Past.*

23. Nolte, *Three Faces,* 534. While Nolte noted that there were many objections to Lukacs, he agreed that at the end of the nineteenth century a major change in the spiritual climate of Europe took place. Nietzsche's role was clear:

> With no immediate relevance to the political events of the day, the Nietzschean doctrine, which alone permitted the equation of socialism, liberalism, and traditional conservatism, was adopted and developed by a circle of fascistoid authors: the doctrine of the revolt of the slaves and of the impoverishment of life through Judeo-Christian resentment. (p. 22)

24. Ibid., 555. For the phrase *Vernichtungsgedanke* see the German edition *Der Faschismus in seiner epoche* (Munich: R. Piper, 1963), 533. The choice of phrase in the post-Holocaust era is telling; far more than "destruction" (usually rendered as *Zerstörung*), *Vernichtung* has become associated with "extermination."

25. Nolte, *Der Faschismus,* 533–534.

The Nazi exterminations were thus best understood as the most desperate (and essentially Nietzschean) "assault ever made upon the human being and the transcendence within him."[26] Although Nolte himself did not demonstrate the connections, we have already seen that this closely resembled how various Nietzschean Nazi sources defined their own project as the creation of an immanent, renaturalized and antitranscendental society.[27]

In a much later work, Nolte spelled out the specifically Jewish turn nazism gave to this Nietzschean framework. What Hitler meant by the word *Jew*, Nolte wrote in his controversial *The European Civil War, 1917–1945*, was that complex of phenomena related to progress, industrialization, and the control of—and estrangement from—nature, emancipation, and individualism

> that first Nietzsche and then other life philosophers such as Ludwig Klages and Theodor Lessing declared as a threat to life. Hitler therefore had the same world-historical process in mind that for Marx was simultaneously progress and decline, which can be called the intellectualization of the world. But . . . Marx, and Nietzsche, Lessing, and Klages were always far from maintaining that this process was attributable to a concrete, human cause. Hitler then made the step, which was a radical overturning of all previous ideologies . . . whereby he attributed to a human group the power to bring about a transcendental process.[28]

In Nolte's new book, *Nietzsche and Nietzscheanism* (1990), Nietzsche remains the inspirational center of the Nazi exterminatory drive.[29] Nolte focuses on the nature of exterminatory thought and language within the Nietzschean corpus. Once again, Nietzsche's positive quest for life affirmation is linked to his call for the brutal destruction of those life-denying, emancipatory forms responsible for the prevailing

---

26. Nolte, *Three Faces*, p. 534. In his *In Bluebeard's Castle: Some Notes towards the Re-definition of Culture* (London: Faber and Faber, 1971), George Steiner presents a similar thesis. Although he does not name Nietzsche, Steiner's view of the Holocaust is presented as an event motivated by the rage against debilitating morality and conscience and the belief that the latter was "a Jewish invention" (pp. 35ff). But Steiner does not limit his respectful treatment of Nietzsche to this implicit dimension. Indeed, he is explicitly invoked not as the inspirer but rather as presager and superb diagnostician of the Holocaust (pp. 38, 42), very much aware (together with Kierkegaard) of the barbarizing qualities that can inhere in culture (pp. 63–64).

27. Alfred Bäumler, *Nietzsche der Philosoph*, 30; Heinrich Römer, "Nietzsche und das Rasseproblem," *Rasse: Monatschrift für den Nordischen Gedanken* 7 (1940), 61; Richard Öhler, *Nietzsche und die deutsche Zukunft*.

28. Ernst Nolte, *Der europäische Bürgerkrieg, 1917–1945: Nationalsozialismus und Bolschewismus* (Frankfurt and Berlin, 1987), 514–515.

29. Nolte, *Nietzsche und der Nietzscheanismus*.

decadence and decline of vitality.[30] Nolte emphasizes a (somewhat neglected) passage in *Ecce Homo* as a salient example of such intentions:

> Let us look ahead a century and assume the case that my attempt to assassinate two millenia of antinature and human disfiguration has succeeded. That new party of life which would take the greatest of all tasks into its hands, the higher breeding (*Höherzuchtung*) of humanity, including the merciless extermination (*schonungslose Vernichtung*) of everything degenerating and parasitic, would make possible again that excess of life on earth from which the Dionysian state will grow again.[31]

The list of Nietzsche's antilife opponents–Christian priests, vulgar Enlighteners, democrats, socialists, the degenerate masses—is so great, Nolte now argues, that it *dwarfs* the Nazi "implementation."[32] "If [Nietzsche's] 'extermination' is understood literally the result must be a mass murder, in comparison with which the later real 'Final Solution' of the National Socialists assumes almost microscopic proportions. The 'purity' of the conception was far more gigantic than the 'impurity' (*Unreine*) of the reality."[33]

Both the tone and grammar of this passage indicate that Nolte's Nietzsche has become neatly embedded within his post-*Historikerstreit* ideological framework. The philosopher appears as a central protago-

30. Ibid., 192–193.
31. Ibid., 193–194. Nolte also included this quote in his *Der Faschimus*, 533. The Kaufmann translation again renders Nietzsche more genteel and less biological than my more literal translation above indicates. For instance, he translates *schonungslose Vernichtung* as "relentless destruction," a far more impersonal, almost agentless description. *Schonungslose Vernichtung* so resembles Nazi vocabulary and action that it should more properly be read as "merciless or brutal extermination." Kaufmann moreover translates *Hoherzüchtung der Menschheit* as the attempt "to raise humanity higher" thereby omitting its breeding, biological connotation (*Nietzsche, Genealogy of Morals*, 274).
32. In an obscure passage in *Three Faces of Fascism*, Nolte had already hinted at this theme. The positive aspect of both Hitler's and Nietzsche's ideas, he wrote, "was completely outweighed by the concrete aspect of their negative will. Many decades in advance Nietzsche provided the political, radical anti-Marxism of fascism with its original spiritual image, an image of which even Hitler never quite showed himself the equal" (p. 557).
33. Nolte, *Nietzsche*, 195. In Nolte's view this was true for both the Bolshevik and National Socialist implementations. In characteristically evasive language (what constitutes "pure" or "impure" extermination?) Nolte explains these processes: Marx's revolution assumed an impure character when the bourgeoisie refused their historically determined role and when the Bolsheviks were confronted with an obdurate majority peasantry. What history could not naturally finish would have to be done through human exterminatory agency. Nolte describes the Nietzsche case in the following vague terms: Nietzsche's conception had to take an impure form when it became clear that it would not be a matter of the strong few destroying the many weak but rather a case where the anxiety and perception of threat "set a biological, indeed, a metabiological, extermination into motion, in which humanity and, above all, the Master and Super-Race would be secured against the most dangerous of all assassinations" (p. 269).

nist and prophet of Nolte's all-embracing vision of the twentieth-century world-historical Bürgerkrieg, the war between the dialectically linked forces of bolshevism and national socialism. Nolte's Nietzsche functions as the "presager (*Vorhersage*) of the great civil-war and the concept of the indispensable extermination."[34] He weaves this extermination concept into his substantive chronology of the relationship between these two historic forces and their destructive drives. The cultured Nietzsche, almost despite himself, is driven to "foresee the great world civil-war and create the extermination concept (*Vernichtungskonzept*) which was the counterconcept to another and more original (*ursprünglicheren*) exterminatory conception."[35] Nietzsche is thus ensconced in Nolte's dubious reduction of nazism and its atrocities to a reaction to an earlier Marxist version of the same thinking, and in which the Holocaust is an anticipatory act of German self-defense against the perception of Jewish genocidal intentions.[36]

In Britain and the United States the perception of Nietzsche as the major force behind the creation of a radicalized, novel, and uniquely murderous form of anti-Semitism has had to contend with Walter Kaufmann's interpretive hegemony and thus only recently has found its historians. We have already referred to Uriel Tal's pioneering effort to sift an "anti-Christian, anti-Semitic" strand from other forms. But it has been George Lichtheim and Conor Cruise O'Brien who have linked the philosopher directly to nazism's atrocities and its ultimate concrete expression: Auschwitz. The fashionable notion that Nietzsche was not anti-Jewish but anti-Christian, they argue, ignores the fact that what Nietzsche most bitterly detested in Christianity was its Jewish origins. As Nietzsche wrote in *The Antichrist*, the Jews, with their desire to survive at any price, were "the *most catastrophic* people of world history." They radically falsified

all nature, all naturalness, all reality, of the whole inner world as well as the outer . . . out of themselves they created a counter-concept to *natural* conditions: they turned religion, cult, morality, history, psychology, one after

34. Ibid., 88, 192.

35. Ibid., 89. Nolte writes that while Marx and Nietzsche developed juxtaposed conceptions bound up with the conditions of the time, neither desired to create *Bürgerkriegskonzeptionen*. Once decisive steps to realize their visions were taken, however, the end was inevitable (p. 276).

36. Nolte gets caught up in the kind of dubious ideological history of reception discussed in chapter 1. Given his conception of how it ought to have proceeded he can only express surprise that "the concept of the 'party of life' does not appear anywhere and the not infrequent discussions on 'Marx and Nietzsche' revolve mainly around the juxtaposition of 'collectivists' and 'individualists'" (ibid., 268).

the other, into an *incurable contradiction to their natural values* . . . by their aftereffect they have made mankind so thoroughly false that even today the Christian can feel anti-Jewish without realizing that he himself is *the ultimate Jewish consequence.*[37]

These writers stress that Nietzsche is the decisive force in the fateful switch from a "limited" Christian anti-Semitism to an unlimited, secular anti-Christian brand, which concretely paved the way towards nazism and the Holocaust. Hitler, O'Brien writes, learned from Nietzsche "that the traditional Christian *limit* on anti-Semitism was itself part of a Jewish trick. When the values that the Jews had reversed were restored, there would be no limits and no Jews."[38]

George Lichtheim has argued in a similar vein. The slow percolation of Nietzschean ideas antithetical to the Judeo-Christian inheritance and its humanist offshoots were absolutely essential, he argues, to the genesis and disposition of nazism. Only when such notions successfully gripped certain German minds did Auschwitz become possible.[39] Lichtheim's Nietzsche is the proto-Fascist who had already written in 1884:

A doctrine is needed powerful enough to work as a breeding agent: strengthening the strong, paralyzing and destructive for the world-weary. The annihilation of the decaying races. Decay of Europe. . . . Dominion over the earth as a means of producing a higher type.—The annihilation of the tartuffery called "morality." . . . The annihilation of *suffrage universel.*[40]

37. Nietzsche, *The Antichrist*, 593. These quotes can be amplified from elsewhere. In *On the Genealogy of Morals*, after paradoxically portraying Jesus as the realization of Judaism, Nietzsche wrote, "What is certain, at least, is that *sub hoc signo*, Israel, with its vengefulness and revaluation of all values, has hitherto triumphed again and again over all other ideals, over all *nobler* ideals" (p. 35). The Jews, he added, had

a world-historic mission. The "masters" have been disposed of; the morality of the common man has won. One may conceive of this victory as at the same time a blood poisoning (it has mixed the races together)—I shan't contradict; but this intoxication has undoubtedly been *successful*. The "redemption" of the human race (from the "masters," that is) is going forward; everything is becoming visibly Judaized, Christianized, mob-ized (what do the words matter!) (p. 36)

Careful readers will note that Nietzsche referred in the main to the priestly period: "Originally, especially at the time of kings, Israel stood in the right, that is, the natural relationship to all things" *The Antichrist*, 594, 594–598. Interested appropriators (and later historians) seldom bothered with such qualifications. For a perspective of how this fitted into a broader stream of thought see Steven Aschheim, "'The Jew Within': The Myth of 'Judaization' in Germany."

38. Conor Cruise O'Brien, *The Siege* (London: Weidenfeld and Nicolson, 1986), 59, 57–59, 85. O'Brien cites the last pages of Hitler's *Table Talk* as evidence without naming the specific passage. Presumably he refers to the last entry where Hitler describes Paul's Christianity as a Jewish maneuver creating "a rallying point for slaves of all kinds against the elite, the masters and those in dominant authority" (*Hitler's Table Talk*, 721–722).

39. George Lichtheim, *Europe in the Twentieth Century*, 185.

40. Nietzsche, *Will to Power*, 458–459.

This Nietzsche, Lichtheim argued, provided a section of the intellectual elite with the necessary Weltanschauung—including its most radical form of anti-Christian anti-Semitism culminating in the Holocaust. For Lichtheim, Nietzsche's radical atheism had nothing to do with the Feuerbachian tradition that sought to replace theism with humanism. This antihumanist atheism, moreover, "did away with the old naive and self-contradictory Christian anti-Semitism by indicting the Jews collectively as the original inspirers of that poisonous infection known as belief in Christ." All this was wholly consistent with Hitler's long-term aims: "It is not too much to say," Lichtheim argued, "that but for Nietzsche the SS—Hitler's shock troops and the core of the whole movement—would have lacked the inspiration which enabled them to carry out their programme of mass murder in Eastern Europe."[41]

These kinds of explanations, no doubt, also have their shortcomings.[42] Recent functionalist scholarship, for instance, has provided a structural-bureaucratic account of mass murders in which the whole question of psychological motivation and ideological inspiration is virtually bypassed. Clearly, for events as complex and thick as these, there can be no question of a theoretical or methodological monopoly. Nevertheless, explanations that entirely dismiss nazism's frame of mind and render ideational motivations as mere background leave an essential dimension untapped. In this respect the more conventional modes of historical analysis soon reach their limits and leave one with a sense of frustrating incompleteness. Because such functionalist approaches miss an important core, cultural and intellectual explanations will continue to be attempted despite all the difficulties. Nietzsche will retain a central

41. Ibid., 186.

42. This applies to both the antibourgeois and anti-Christian accounts. George L. Mosse, for instance, has recently gone so far as to suggest that the Nazi project represented the defense of bourgeois morality, not the attack against it: far removed from Rauschning's portrait of Nazi nihilists breaking all limits in a kind of Nietzschean ecstasy, according to Mosse, nazism was actually the attempt to preserve a middle-class world of respectability against all those outsider and deviant groups that threatened it. Yet bourgeois morality while often illiberal had never before assumed genocidal dimensions and what requires explanation is the galvanizing motor that, translated into the bureaucratic, murderous impulse, enabled nazism to transcend middle-class morality while embodying it (*Nationalism and Sexuality,* 133–152). Bernard Wasserstein has argued that the notion of a Christian limit is problematic indeed and adduces numerous examples of Christian violence upon Jews in which tens of thousands were murdered. Still, a theological, historical, and moral gulf separates these pogroms from the bureaucratized, ideological, and total mass murder of the Holocaust ("Change in Israel," *Times Literary Supplement* [10 October 1986], 1123–1124). Others have argued that for the functionaries of genocide, theory and ideology played virtually no role at all. Whether as cause or post facto rationalization, however, some ideational justification had to enter.

place in such accounts. There are many reasons for this, but above all he will remain relevant as a key to explaining national socialism's attraction to the outmost limits, its arrival at a grotesque *novum* of human experience. Naggingly, the thematic resemblances represent themselves.[43]

Nazism was undoubtedly a multifarious historical phenomenon. Its revolutionary thrust sat side by side with petit-bourgeois and provincial concerns. The perception nevertheless persists that its historical significance resided in its unprecedented transvaluations and boundary-breaking extremities and its emphases on destruction and violent regeneration, health and disease. Nazism in this sense continues to be regarded by many as a politics—however debased and selectively mediated—wrought in the "Great" Nietzschean mode.

43. Robert Lifton's *The Nazi Doctors: Medical Killing and the Psychology of Genocide* (London: Papermac, 1987) represents a recent expression of this perception. From Nietzsche the Nazis received the notion of "violent cure" and the notion that "We have to be destroyers!" (*Will to Power*, 224).

The Nazis found that tradition in Nietzsche whom they interpreted as advocating war as therapy for weakness and the cultivation of "that deep impersonal hatred, that cold-blooded murderousness coupled with a good conscience, that communal, organizing zest in the destruction of the enemy" as a path to collective health. Above all, Nietzsche's vision was one of all-consuming illness and cure. The condition, he declared, was "not . . . sickness but *sickliness*," by which he meant perpetual weakness and concern with morality. Nietzsche went on to declare that "one is healthy when . . . one feels that the 'bite' of conscience is like a dog biting on a stone—when one is ashamed of one's remorse," and one can attribute "more *health of soul*" to a criminal who "does not slander his deed after it is done" than to the sinner who "abases himself before the cross" (Lifton, *Nazi Docters*, 486).

The respective (and always selective) quotes appear in *Human, All too Human*, 176, and *Will to Power*, 29–30, 134–135.

Index

Designer: U.C. Press Staff
Compositor: Braun-Brumfield,Inc.
Text: 10 / 13 Sabon
Display: Sabon
Printer: Maple-Vail Book Mfg. Group
Binder: Maple-Vail Book Mfg. Group

Kaplanma@mail1.bc.edu

552-0563